The Social World of the Babylonian Priest

Culture and History of the Ancient Near East

Founding Editor

M.H.E. Weippert

Editor-in-Chief

Jonathan Stökl

Editors

VOLUME 103

The titles published in this series are listed at *brill.com/chan*

The Social World of the Babylonian Priest

By

Bastian Still

BRILL

LEIDEN | BOSTON

The Library of Congress Cataloging-in-Publication Data is available online at http://catalog.loc.gov
LC record available at https://lccn.loc.gov/2019007934

Typeface for the Latin, Greek, and Cyrillic scripts: "Brill". See and download: brill.com/brill-typeface.

ISSN 1566-2055
ISBN 978-90-04-39995-2 (hardback)
ISBN 978-90-04-39996-9 (e-book)

This book is printed on acid-free paper and produced in a sustainable manner.

Contents

Acknowledgments

This book has its foundations in my doctoral dissertation that I carried out in the framework of the European Research Council (ERC) Starting Grant Project, 'By the Rivers of Babylon: New Perspectives on Second Temple Judaism from Cuneiform Texts', between 2010 and 2014 under the supervision of Caroline Waerzeggers. I completed my dissertation during fellowships at Leiden University in 2014–2015, the Ludwig Maximilian University of Munich (LMU) in 2015–2016, and the Free University of Amsterdam (VU) in 2016–2017. I am honored to have earned the 'Best PhD Dissertation in the Field of Assyriology and Mesopotamian Archaeology' in 2017 by the International Association of Assyriology, which provided a grant that helped finance this publication. A HUSS-Lab postdoctoral fellowship at the American University in Cairo (2018–2019) that was sponsored by the Andrew W. Mellon Foundation enabled me to focus on revising and finalising this book. I thank all these institutions for their support.

It is a pleasure to take this opportunity to express my gratitude to the many people who contributed to the making of this book. My foremost gratitude and warmest appreciation belong to Caroline Waerzeggers, my teacher and mentor from the first day I entered university. I am indebted to her for her invaluable advice, wisdom, generosity, and moral support over the years. She has left a deep impression on me as a scholar and as a person. I am also grateful to my first co-supervisor Karen Radner who welcomed me with her infectious spirit and enthusiasm at the University College of London (UCL) and later again in Munich. My UCL colleagues and roommates Jonathan Stökl, Silvie Zamazalová, and Mikko Luukko deserve my thanks for all their advice, feedback, and encouragement. I am obliged to the Trustees of the British Museum for giving me permission to access the Students' Room and study cuneiform tablets in their care during my stay in London and on various visits thereafter. I am indebted, in particular, to Christopher Walker and Jonathan Taylor for their incredible generosity and assistance.

A special token of appreciation is due to my project colleagues at Leiden University for creating the stimulating, constructive, and heartening environment in which I was able to finish the first draft of my dissertation: Tero Alstola, Jason Silverman, and Rieneke Sonnevelt. My graduate school experience would have been considerably less rewarding without them. I thank all the colleagues I worked with at LMU, especially Claudia Horst, Petra Oppermann, and Robert Schiestl. As members of the new Lehrstuhl für die Alte Geschichte des Nahen und Mittleren Ostens led by Karen Radner, they provided me with a warm environment in which I could teach, write, and prepare for my dissertation defense. I want to express my gratitude to Kristin Kleber who gave me the opportunity to join her team at the VU and discuss various aspects of my work with Mark Tamerus, Pieter Alkemade, and Michèle Meijer. Special thanks is extended to Bert van der Spek who remains part and parcel of the VU with his across-the-board knowledge, light-heartedness, and fun version of Assyriology.

It was both an honour and a pleasure to discuss my dissertation and exchange views with the members of my doctoral defense committee, Jan Gerrit Dercksen, Michael Jursa, Olaf Kaper, Kristin Kleber, Marten Stol, Bert van der Spek, Karel van der Toorn, and Willemijn Waal, in addition to my two promotors, Wilfred van Soldt and Caroline Waerzeggers. Their poignant questions and observations have helped me transform my project from a dissertation into this book. The anonymous reviewers, whose meticulous readings and clever suggestions made the manuscript stronger, also warrant my deep appreciation as do Katelyn Chin and Christina Sargent, whose guidance helped me navigate the publishing process at Brill without complications.

Over the years I was fortunate to experience stimulating conversations, invaluable support, useful feedback, and generous access to unpublished research material from many other friends, colleagues, and scholars: Kathleen Abraham, Sander Amelink, Eric Bosse, Jaap Geraerts, Andrea Giolai, Melanie Gross, Bram Jagersma, Barbora Jancikova, Pyhai Jin, Theo Krispijn, Julia Krul, Amélie Kuhrt, Tracy Lemos, Juval Levavi, Joris Leverink, Guido van Meersbergen, John Nielsen, Daniel Soliman, Joyce de Thouars, Cornelia Wunsch, and Ran Zadok. Mark Heerink, too, is especially appreciated for his advice in all matters PhD and whiff-whaff.

And, finally, I want to thank my family: Georg, Mady, Julian, Eva, Kristina, the boys, and especially Hanan for the love, patience, encouragement, and close reading of the entire manuscript.

Figures and Tables

Figures

Tables

Abbreviations

A	Tablets in the Bodleian Library Collection, Oxford
AB	Tablets in the Bodleian Library Collection, Oxford
ABC	A.K. Grayson, *Assyrian and Babylonian Chronicles*, Locust Valley 1975
ABL	R.F. Harper, *Assyrian and Babylonian Letters Belonging to the Kouyounjik Collection of the British Museum*, 14 vols, London – Chicago 1892–1914
ADFU	Ausgrabungen der Deutschen Forschungsgemeinschaft in Uruk-Warka
AfO	Archiv für Orientforschung
AH XV	C. Waerzeggers, *The Ezida Temple of Borsippa: Priesthood, Cult, Archives* (Achaemenid History 15), Leiden 2010
Amherst	Tablets from the former collection of Lord Amherst
AmM	Reign of Amēl-Marduk (562–560 BCE)
AnOr	Analecta Orientalia
AnOr 8	A. Pohl, *Neubabylonische Rechtsurkunden aus den Berliner Staatischen Museen 1. Teil* (AnOr 8), Rome 1933
AnOr 9	A. Pohl, *Neubabylonische Rechtsurkunden aus den Berliner Staatischen Museen 2. Teil* (AnOr 9), Rome 1934
AOAT	Alter Orient und Altes Testament
AoF	Altorientalische Forschungen
ArOr	*Archiv Orientální*
AUWE	Ausgrabungen in Uruk-Warka: Endberichte
AUWE 8	K. Kessler, *Uruk: Urkunden aus Privathäusern: die Wohnhäuser westlich des Eanna-Tempelbereichs*, vol. 1 (AUWE 8), Mainz 1991
AUWE 12	E. von Weiher, *Spätbabylonische Texte aus dem Planquadrat U 18* (Spätbabylonische Texte aus Uruk 4 = AUWE 12), Mainz a.Rh. 1993
BaF	Baghdader Forschungen
BBSt	L.W. King, *Babylonian Boundary Stones and Memorial Tablets*, London 1912
BE 8	A.T. Clay, *Legal and Commercial Transactions dated in the Assyrian, Neo-Babylonian and Persian Periods, Chiefly from Nippur* (The Babylonian Expedition of the University of Pennsylvania Series A: Cuneiform Texts 8/1), Philadelphia 1908
BIN	Babylonian Inscriptions in the Collection of James B. Nies
BIN 1	C.E. Keiser, *Letters and Contracts from Erech Written in the Neo-Babylonian Period*, by Babylonian Inscriptions in the Collection of James B. Nies, vol. 1 (BIN 1), New Haven 1917
BiOr	Bibliotheca Orientalis
Berens	T.G. Pinches, *The Babylonian Tablets of the Berens Collection* (Asiatic Society Monographs 16), London 1915
BM	Tablets in the British Museum, London

BR 8/7	M. San Nicolò, Babylonische Rechtsurkunden des ausgehenden 8. und des 7. Jahrhunderts v. Chr., 1. Hälfte, München 1951
BRM 1	A.T. Clay, *Babylonian Business Transactions of the First Millennium BC* (BRM 1), New York 1912
BRM 2	A.T. Clay, *Legal documents from Erech, dated in the Seleucid Era* (BRM 2), New York 1913
BRM 4	A.T. Clay, *Epics, hymns, omens and other texts* (BRM 4), New Haven 1923
BSA	Bulletin on Sumerian Agriculture
BZAW	Beihefte zur Zeitschrift für die alttestamentliche Wissenschaft
C	Tablets in the Bodleian Library Collection, Oxford
CAD	*The Assyrian Dictionary of the Oriental Institute of Chicago*, Chicago 1956–2010
Cam	Reign of Cambyses (530–522 BCE)
Camb	J.N. Strassmaier, *Inschriften von Cambyses, König von Babylon (529–521 v. Chr.)* (Babylonische Hefte 8–9), Leipzig 1890
CHANE	*Culture and History of the Ancient Near East*, Leiden 2000–
CM	Cuneiform Monographs
CT	*Cuneiform Texts from Babylonian Tablets in the British Museum*, London 1896–
CUSAS	Cornell University Studies in Assyriology and Sumerology
Cyr	Reign of Cyrus II (539–530 BCE)
Dar	Reign of Darius I (521–486 BCE)
Dar	J.N. Strassmaier, *Inschriften von Darius, König von Babylon (521–485 v. Chr.)* (Babylonische Hefte 10–12), Leipzig 1890
EAH	Tablets in the E.A. Hoffman collection, Yale University, New Haven
Esh	Reign of Esarhaddon (680–669 BCE)
F	Tablets in the Bodleian Library Collection, Oxford
FLP	Tablets in the Free Library of Philadelphia
FN	Family name
GMTR	Guides to the Mesopotamian Textual Record
HdO	*Handbuch der Orientalistik*, Leiden 1952–
IOS	Israel Oriental Series
Iraq 59	M. Jursa, Neu- und spätbabylonische Texte aus den Sammlungen der Birmingham Museums und Art Gallery, *Iraq* 59 (1997), 97–174
JCS	Journal of Cuneiform Studies
JCS 39	T.G. Lee, A Receipt from the Reign of Cambyses, *JCS* 39 (1987), 49–53
JEOL	Jaarberichten Ex Oriente Lux
JHS	Journal of Hellenistic Studies
JNES	Journal of Near Eastern Studies
Kan	Reign of Kandalānu (647–627 BCE)
KVM	Tablets in the Kalamazoo Valley Museum, Kalamazoo
L	Tablets in the Museum of the Ancient Orient, Istanbul

LB	Tablets in the collection of de Liagre Böhl, Leiden
l., ll.	Line, lines
m	Mina (1/2 kg)
MDOG	Mitteilungen der Deutschen Orient-Gesellschaft zu Berlin
Mich	E.W. Moore, *Neo-Babylonian Documents in the University of Michigan Collection*, Ann Arbor 1939
MLC	Tablets in the Morgan Library Collection, Yale Babylonian Collection, New Haven
MOSS	*Midden-Oosten Stimuleringsfonds Symposia*, Leiden 1999–2004
NABU	Nouvelles Assyriologiques Brèves et Utilitaires
NBC	Tablets in the Nies Babylonian Collection (Yale Babylonian Collection, New Haven)
Nbk	Reign of king Nebuchadnezzar II (605–562 BC)
Nbk	J.N. Strassmaier, *Inschriften von Nabochodonosor, König von Babylon (604–561 v. Chr.)* (Babylonische Hefte 5–6), Leipzig 1889
Npl	Reign of king Nabopolassar (626–605 BCE)
Nbn	Reign of king Nabonidus (556–539 BCE)
Nbn	J.N. Strassmaier, Inschriften von Nabonidus, König von Babylon (555–538 v. Chr.) (Babylonische Hefte 1–4), Leipzig 1889
Ner	Reign of king Neriglissar (560–556 BCE)
Ner	B.T.A. Evetts, *Inscriptions of the Reigns of Evil-Merodach (BC 562–559), Neriglissar (BC 559–555), and Laborosoarchod (BC 555)*, Leipzig 1892
OBO	Orbis Biblicus et Orientalis
OECT	Oxford Editions of Cuneiform Texts
OECT 10	G.J.P. McEwan, *Late Babylonian Texts in the Ashmolean Museum* (OECT 10), Oxford 1984
OECT 12	F. Joannès, *Les tablettes néo-babyloniennes de la Bodleian Library conservées à l'Ashmolean Museum* (OECT 12), Oxford 1990
OLZ	Orientalistische Literaturzeitung
Or	Orientalia (n.s.)
PIHANS	Publications de l'Institut historique-archéologique néerlandais de Stamboul
PN	Personal name
PTS	Tablets in the collection of the Princeton Theological Seminary
RA	Revue d'assyriologie et d'archéologie orientale
RA 10	L. Legrain, Collection Louis Cugnin: Catalogue, Transcription et Traduction, RA 10 (1913), 41–68
RBC	Rosen Babylonian Collection
rev.	Reverse
RGTC	Répertoire géographique des textes cuneiformes
RLA	Reallexikon der Assyriologie

SAA	State archive of Assyria, Helsinki 1988–
SAA 10	S. Parpola, *Letters from Assyrian and Babylonian Scholars* (SAA 10), Helsinki 2003
SAA 17	M. Dietrich, The Babylonian Correspondence of Sargon and Sennacherib (SAA 17), Helsinki 2003
SAA 18	F.S. Reynolds, *The Babylonian Correspondence of Esarhaddon and Letters to Assurbanipal and Sin-šarru-iškun from Northern and Central Babylonia* (SAA 18), Helsinki 2003
SAAB	State Archives of Assyria Bulletin
Smith Coll.	C.H. Gordon, *Smith College Tablets. 110 Cuneiform Texts Selected from the College Collection*, Northampton 1952
SpTU 2	E. von Weiher, *Spätbabylonische Texte aus Uruk, Vol.* 2 (ADFU 10), Berlin 1983
SpTU 3	E. von Weiher, *Spätbabylonische Texte aus Uruk, Vol. 3* (ADFU 12), Berlin 1988
SpTU 4	E. von Weiher, *Uruk: Spätbabylonische Texte aus dem Planquadrat U 18, Vol.* 4 (AUWE 12), Mainz 1993
š	Sheqel (8.3 g)
Ššu	Reign of Šamaš-šumu-ukīn (667–648 BCE).
TCL	Textes cunéiformes du Musée du Louvre, Paris 1910–
TCL 9	G. Contenau, *Contrats et lettres d'Assyrie et de Babylonie* (TCL 9), Paris 1926
TCL 12	G. Contenau, *Contrats néo-babyloniens*, vol. 1: *De Téglath-Pileser III à Nabonide* (TCL 12), Paris 1927
TCL 13	G. Contenau, *Contrats néo-babyloniens*, vol. 2: *Achéménides et Séleucides* (TCL 13), Paris 1929
TEBR	F. Joannès, *Textes économiques de la Babylonie récente*, Paris 1982
TuM 2/3	O. Krückman, *Texte und Materialien der Frau Professor Hilprecht Collection of Babylonian Antiquities im Eigentum der Universität Jena*, vols. 2–3: *Neubabylonische Rechts- und Verwaltungs-Texte*, Leipzig 1933
UET 4	H.H. Figulla, *Business documents of the New-Babylonian period* (Ur Excavations, Texts 4), London 1949
VAB	Vorderasiatische Bibliothek
VS 1	J.C. Hinrichs, *Vorderasiatische Schriftdenkmäler der königlichen Museen zu Berlin*, vol. 1, Leipzig 1907
VS 3–6	A. Ungnad, *Vorderasiatische Schriftdenkmäler der königlichen Museen zu Berlin*, vols. 3–6, Leipzig 1907–1908
VS 15	O. Schroeder, *Vorderasiatische Schriftdenkmäler der königlichen Museen zu Berlin*, vol. 15, Leipzig 1916
WdO	Welt des Orients
WZKM	Wiener Zeitschrift für die Kunde des Morgenlandes

Xer	Reign of Xerxes (486–465 BCE)
YBC	Tablets in the Yale Babylonian Collection, New Haven
YOS	Yale Oriental Series, New Haven – London – Oxford 1915–
YOS 1	A.T. Clay, Miscellaneous Inscriptions in the Yale Babylonian Collection (YOS 1), New Haven 1915
YOS 3	A.T. Clay, *Neo-Babylonian letters from Erech* (YOS 3), New Haven – London – Oxford 1919
YOS 6	R.P. Dougherty, *Records from Erech, Time of Nabonidus (555–538 BC)* (YOS 6), New Haven 1920
YOS 7	A. Tremayne, *Records from Erech. Time of Cyrus and Cambyses (538–521 BC)* (YOS 7), New Haven – London – Oxford 1925
YOS 17	D.B. Weisberg, *Texts from the Time of Nebuchadnezzar* (YOS 17), New Haven 1980
ZA	Zeitschrift für Assyriologie und Vorderasiatische Archäologie
ZAR	*Zeitschrift für Altorientalische und Biblische Rechtsgeschichte*

Introduction

This book presents an investigation into Babylonian society, focusing on the priestly community of the city of Borsippa during Neo-Babylonian (ca. 620–539 BCE) and early Persian rule (ca. 538–484 BCE), together commonly referred to in the literature as the Neo-Babylonian period. The political changes affecting Babylonia, the area of present-day central and southern Iraq, during that time provide the backdrop for this study in which I investigate a complex of social interactions that took place among the priestly families of Borsippa in this period and attempt to reveal and dissect the underlying dynamics. I draw on sociological theories and studies of anthropology, especially those concerned with historical and present-day Hindu society, which exhibit parallels with ancient Babylonia. In addition, a range of procedures taken from social network analysis is applied in order to examine and interpret the mechanics of these social events. The aim of this study is to contribute towards a better understanding of the Babylonian priesthood as a distinct social group and investigate how its members interacted among themselves and within society at large. At the same time, while my focus is primarily on the priest, this study strives for a more sophisticated appreciation of the organisation of ancient Babylonian society as a whole. In order to fully unravel past societies, a social perspective is indispensable, yet, such an approach is still largely missing in Neo-Babylonian studies and related fields.

1 State of the Art

With an estimated 50,000 archival documents surviving from the Neo-Babylonian period, conditions for studying Babylonian society at that time seem auspicious.[1] However, this potential has not yet been realised to its full extent. Existing studies on Neo-Babylonian society can be divided into three (not mutually exclusive) types, each with its own limitations.[2]

First, there are the archival studies like those of the Ea-ilūtu-bani archive by F. Joannès or of the Egibi archive by C. Wunsch and K. Abraham.[3] These

1 For the estimated size of the Neo-Babylonian corpus, see Streck 2010: 48 and Jursa 2005: 1.

2 This overview does not include the large numbers of medico-ritual, religious, literary, and royal texts that can be added to the corpus and on which much research is being conducted. The following survey only pertains to studies of the legal administrative texts.

3 Joannès 1989, Wunsch 1993, Wunsch 2003, and Abraham 2004. Other examples include Kessler 1991, Jursa 1999, Baker 2004, Frame 2013, Waerzeggers 2014, and Abraham [*forthcoming*].

 | DOI:10.1163/9789004399969_002

publications present close analyses of individual family archives and their protagonists. Their focus commonly lies on providing transliterations, translations and commentaries of the archival texts and on studying the genealogies, property portfolios, investment strategies, inheritance practices, and legal procedures documented in these texts. The resulting micro-narratives of individual Babylonians and their families are indispensable for writing a social history of first millennium Babylonia from the bottom up. Yet, few authors have attempted to transcend the boundaries of the individual archive and situate its protagonists within their larger social fields.[4]

Second, there are the prosopographical studies that assemble data on the human resources of particular Babylonian institutions during the Neo-Babylonian period such as the Ebabbar temple of Sippar and the Eanna temple of Uruk.[5] These studies provide an invaluable pool of data on collective career trajectories, professional associations and social networks, yet their potential for structural analysis has remained untapped so far.[6]

Third, there are the studies that approach Neo-Babylonian society from a functional-economic perspective.[7] Tracing the development of the fiscal, monetary, and agricultural systems during the Neo-Babylonian period, these works are generally interested in larger economic trends. Another major concern is with the operation and development of Babylonia's major institutions,

---

A number of articles can be added to this list including Beaulieu 1991, Beaulieu 1993, and Beaulieu 2000 on archives from Larsa; Jursa 2005b for a text group from Nippur; and Joannès 1980 and Wunsch 2005 for material from Babylon.

4 Waerzeggers 2014, for example, studies the archive of Marduk-rēmanni in the conventional way, while linking this man's biography into the Achaemenid imperial politics of that time. An early example is Jursa 1999: 111–125, where the credit partners of Bēl-rēmanni, a priest from Sippar, have been examined in light of their institutional affiliations to the temple and their professional contact with the protagonist. Cf. Abraham [*forthcoming*] for a study of the Atkuppu archive from Borsippa, which makes an effort to examine the social background of the family's contacts.

5 Kümmel 1979, Jursa 1995, Bongenaar 1997, Da Riva 2002, Janković 2004, Zawadzki 2006, Kleber 2008, Waerzeggers 2010, Zawadzki 2013, and Kozuh 2014 some of which put particular effort in reconstructing the cultic organisation.

6 The study by J.P. Nielsen 2011 presents an exception, although the focus is not on a particular institution but on the formation and distribution of kin-groups in the early Neo-Babylonian period in general. Taking a look at the available sources from various cities, this study provides much information on the professional affiliations and careers of individual Babylonians and the social standing of their families. While he uses a much larger, and geographically diverse, section of the available data, and presents a much more structural analysis compared to other publications of this type, it is still predominantly descriptive.

7 Jursa 1995, Da Riva 2002, van Driel 2002, Kleber 2008, and Jursa *et al.* 2010 among others.

the palace and the temple,[8] and their economic and juridical impact on society. Making use of a much larger and more diverse set of primary sources compared to the archival studies, these works have developed useful typologies and arrived at significant generalisations.[9] These typologies, however, are often too static as they focus on the object or content of social interactions and disregard the identities of those brought together by these encounters. In recent years, interest in these matters has risen, but these efforts remain on a small scale.[10]

Apart from the limitations of each of these approaches to Babylonian society, current scholarship suffers from insufficient awareness of the emic value of the labels used to describe historical actors and social groups. Individuals, families and entire segments of society are described as lower class, upper class, bourgeoisie, nobility, urban elite, nouveaux riches, citizens, burghers, aristocrats, patricians, rentiers or entrepreneurs.[11] While these labels can help readers to get to grips with the wide social range and substantial economic inequality that existed within Babylonia's heterogeneous population, many of the aforementioned classifications derive from scholarship on pre-modern and modern Europe. It remains far from clear what they imply in the specific context of the Neo-Babylonian period or whether they can be applied at all. Moreover, in Neo-Babylonian studies these classifications have so far been primarily based on economic and/or legal criteria. Failing to offer a more socially informed underpinning is to ignore the complexity of this ancient society. Did

---

8 The publications listed in footnote 5 should be mentioned again as they have provided much of the groundwork.

9 The works by van Driel 2002 and Jursa *et al.* 2010, in particular, deserve mention. Among their multiple insights one could note the reconstruction of the fiscal apparatus by van Driel 2002, Part III, or the typologies of private archives and the generalising remarks on the business profiles of their owners found in Jursa *et al.* 2010, Chapter 3. Of particular importance here has been the application of two contrasting socioeconomic ideal types known as 'rentier' and 'entrepreneur' to our sources (Jursa *et al.* 2010: 282–195; for these typologies and their implications, see Chapter 5.3). Important generalisations have also been formulated for Babylonia's agriculture and economy, in terms of regional and diachronic agricultural trends (Jursa *et al.* 2010, Chapter 4), the development and monetisation of the Neo-Babylonian economy (Jursa *et al.* 2010, Chapter 5) and the role of the 'market' therein (van Driel 2002).

10 See footnotes 4 and 6 above.

11 See, for example, van Driel 2002, Abraham 2004, Kleber 2008, Zadok 2009, Jursa *et al.* 2010, Waerzeggers 2010, and Nielsen 2011. While the use of terms like 'urban elites', 'citizen' or 'upper class' is widespread in Neo-Babylonian studies, more objectionable labels such as 'burgher' (Jursa 2005: 8) or 'patrician' (Beaulieu 2006: 193) are found rarely and usually placed within inverted commas.

Babylonians also identify themselves as aristocrats or entrepreneurs and, as a result, did they organise in distinct groups? If so, then this raises the questions of where exactly different social groups or segments should be located within Babylonian society, to which extent they overlapped and were considered distinct from each other, and whether or not they can be distinguished and reconstructed on the basis of more than their economic profile and/or legal status.

The aim of this study is to begin to answer these questions by taking a particularly well-documented segment of Babylonian society as a case study.

2 Research Questions

It would be far too ambitious to attempt a study of the entire Neo-Babylonian society. In this book I focus on one particular group: the 'priests'. This does not mean that my investigation is not concerned with society as a whole. A better understanding of the internal dynamics of the priestly stratum and the interactions it maintained with the out-group provides a perspective on the layout of Babylonian society at large and the social mechanics that were in operation at the time. Moreover, the priests are by far the best-represented group in our documentation and their occupational association to the temple forms a further frame of reference for understanding their motivations, relationships and activities.

Much has been written about the Neo-Babylonian temple and its personnel.[12] This scholarship serves as point of departure for the present investigation. Priests were responsible for the execution of the time-honoured worship of the gods inside the temple. As explained in more detail below, the Babylonian priesthood was a thoroughly hierarchical institution, divided into multiple professional groups including brewers, butchers, oxherds, and reed-workers each with its own concerns over time, area, and tasks.[13] Unexplored so far is the question of how these priests interacted outside of the temple with the larger Babylonian society.

Thus, this book seeks to reconstruct the social world of the Babylonian priest through a close analysis of their social interactions. In doing so, this study seeks to realise two principal research aims. First, it attempts to assess the influence of the temple fabric on the behaviour of priests within society

12 See, for example, Kümmel 1979, MacGinnis 1995, Bongenaar 1997, Da Riva 2002, Beaulieu 2003, Kozuh 2014, Zawadzki 2006, Kleber 2008, Zadok 2009, Waerzeggers 2010, and Zawadzki 2013.

13 See, for example, Kümmel 1979, Bongenaar 1997, and Waerzeggers 2010.

or, in other words, to examine to what extent the temple-based hierarchy and the professional organisation of the priests influenced or shaped their lives outside of their cultic activities. Second, it seeks to firmly locate the priests in Babylonian society or, in other words, to investigate, by closely analysing the patterns of their interactions, whether priests can be identified as a distinctive social segment in society and how they related to, or interacted with, other social groups. Ultimately, the book argues, firstly, that temple-based hierarchies informed the social interactions of the priesthood in daily life to a significant extent, and secondly, that the priesthood should be seen as a distinct group in a larger elite segment of society that shared a particular social identity.

3 Methodology

My investigation is built around four domains of social relationships:

- Marriage
- Landholding
- Silver lending
- Friendship

The choice to investigate these spheres of interaction is based on the fact that they cover a good part of the priest's daily life, representing key and recurring events in which individuals, families, and groups came into formal contact with each other. Moreover, while there are various domains that are left undocumented, these four types of interaction can be captured adequately in the available documentation.

I analyse these four types of interaction in a two-pronged approach. The first step is to examine the personal relationship and social background of the actors involved in the documented social interactions by analysing how people involved in a transaction were connected and with whom people interacted in their own social group and from other social groups. In doing so, I generate comprehensive profiles of the individuals interacting in particular social events that detail in descriptive and quantitative terms the type of society encountered in the Neo-Babylonian period. Was it for example an open society, in which different people interacted freely, or was it a closed one, made up of self-segregating groups and thus stratified?

These statistics form the point of departure for the next phase of the investigation. On the basis of the quantitative results, I attempt to uncover more fundamental dynamics, norms or social customs that regulated these social events and thus patterned Babylonian society. I also examine whether interaction was driven by more than just economic motivations, but was inspired by, for example, ideological or religious considerations. It is in this phase that complementary concepts of the social sciences are introduced, concerned with, among others, kinship, tie strength, social boundaries, and identity. Studies of anthropology provide a useful frame of reference and offer examples of how dynamics of interaction may have worked. Special attention is given to ethnographies of Hindu society on the Indian subcontinent, which show parallels with the material from ancient Babylonia. Finally, by adopting a network approach and carrying out a range of procedures from the field of social network analysis, I explore how some of these social mechanisms operated in practice, while reinforcing my interpretation with a methodologically sound foundation. The present investigation is among the first to apply social network analysis to ancient Babylonian society.[14]

4 Case Study: the Priestly Community of Borsippa

I take the priestly community of Borsippa as the principal level of analysis. While my investigation may therefore be classified as a meso-level analysis located between the archival and functional-economic studies reviewed above, it still is informed by individual micro-level archives. Moreover, as my analysis becomes more abstract towards the end, I am able to link my findings to larger macro-level trends in Babylonian society.

The sources used in this book are the private archives of the priestly families that lived in the city of Borsippa during the Neo-Babylonian period.[15] Located on the side-branch of the Euphrates river, not twenty kilometres southeast of the capital, Borsippa was the political and religious sister-city of Babylon at the time.[16] Its tutelary deity was Nabû, the Babylonian god of writing and patron of scribes.[17] He had taken up residence in the Ezida, the city's main temple, towards the end of the second millennium BCE when he was called 'King of Borsippa' for the first time.[18] By then Nabû was commonly identified as the son of Marduk,[19] the patron god of Babylon, who had been elevated as head

14 Other studies that have applied network analysis to cuneiform texts are Waerzeggers 2014b and Wagner *et al.* 2013.

15 Zadok 1998, Jursa 2005: 76–94, Waerzeggers 2005, Zadok 2009, and Waerzeggers 2010.

16 See, for the history of Borsippa during the second and first millennia BCE, Unger 1932 and, more recently, Waerzeggers 2010: 4–10.

17 See, for the history of the god Nabû in Babylonia, Pomponio 1978 and Pomponio 2001.

18 Pomponio 1978: 61.

19 In the early second millennium BCE Nabû was classified as minister and scribe of Marduk, and only venerated in the Esagil temple in Babylon. Cf. Pomponio 2001.

of the Babylonian pantheon at around the same time. Together, father and son became the primary gods in Babylonia during the first millennium BCE; their temples, the Esagil and Ezida in Babylon and Borsippa, respectively, became the most important cultic centres in southern Mesopotamia. Throughout this period both native and foreign rulers made sure to show proper reverence towards these temples and acknowledge their privileged positions.[20]

Nearly 3,500 cuneiform tablets were discovered in the late nineteenth century at Birs-Nimrud, the ancient site of Borsippa, unfortunately under unofficial circumstances and without documentation.[21] The tablets gradually appeared on the antiquities market from where they were bought by museums and private collectors all over the world; the lion's share can nowadays be found in the British Museum in London, the Vorderasiatisches Museum in Berlin, and the Musée du Louvre in Paris.[22] Although the archaeological context of these tablets is lost, their original interconnections can be reconstructed on the basis of museum registers. Together with prosopographical considerations, scholars like G. van Driel, C. Waerzeggers, and R. Zadok were able to reconstruct more than twenty individual family archives.[23] This corpus has remained largely unpublished.

Most of these archives belonged to the families who owned priestly titles in the Ezida temple or one of Borsippa's secondary sanctuaries dedicated to Nabû's consort Nanāya and minor gods of the local pantheon.[24] They include the archives of the following families: Ahiya'ūtu (16), Atkuppu (133), Bēliya'u (375), Ea-ilūtu-bani (325), Ibnāya A (41), Ibnāya B (22), Ibnāya C (4), Ibnāya D (3), Iddin-Papsukkal B (6), Ilia A (269), Ilia D (57), Ilšu-abūšu A (25) (+ the slave Balāṭu (18)), Ilšu-abūšu B (15), Kudurrānu A (38), Lā-kuppuru (30), Mannu-gērûšu (30), and Rē'i-alpi (400+).[25] Large parts of these archives are concerned with the management of cultic duties in Ezida and other local temples. These affairs have been the subject of an extensive study by C. Waerzeggers (2010). But the archives also contain ample information on everyday affairs outside of the temple. An important preoccupation of these families was the management of urban and landed real estate, such as the acquisition of new property (including slaves), harvest estimates, and house rent collections. Liquid capital

20 Waerzeggers 2011.

21 See, for example, Waerzeggers 2010: 15–16.

22 Waerzeggers 2005.

23 Van Driel 1989, van Driel 1992, Waerzeggers 2005, Jursa 2005: 76–94, Zadok 2009, and Waerzeggers 2010: 15–16.

24 See Waerzeggers 2010: 20–32 for the local pantheon of Borsippa.

25 This list is taken from Waerzeggers 2010: 16. The numbers in brackets refer to the number of texts attributed to the archive. See, for an overview of these archives, Jursa 2005: 77–94.

was often used in silver lending or invested in small-scale business enterprises such as, for example, beer brewing. Besides letters, memoranda, and lists of various sorts, these archives also contain information on more momentous and exceptional (family) affairs such as marriage, adoption or legal disputes. The archives from Borsippa can, in these respects, be compared with other priestly archives from Babylonia.[26]

Yet the corpus also has its drawbacks. Particularly frustrating is the fact that it sheds light almost exclusively on the group of priests. Babylonian priests were an integral part of a larger segment of urban society, yet the study of this larger segment is problematic, as families with different professional profiles have remained largely outside of the documentation. There are thus far only three archives from Borsippa that lack a priestly or temple background: Banê-ša-ilia (11), Gallābu (59), and Iddin-Papsukkal A (22).[27] Even if the protagonists of the latter two archives belonged to families that performed cultic functions in the Ezida temple, the evidence suggests that these particular members engaged in different lines of work and were, unlike their relatives, not enrolled in the local priesthood.[28] Still, we should be aware that they belonged to a similar, if not the same, social circle as the priestly families under investigation. Moreover, the fact that texts from these archives entered museum collections together with other priestly archives, with which they also share prosopographical connections, further suggests that these individuals belonged to the same milieu and perhaps lived in the same neighbourhoods, as did the priests.[29] It remains unclear, therefore, how far the protagonists of these three archives were actually removed from the priestly group. Various methods and abstractions have to be made in order to delineate the priestly core in the larger urban elite population more comprehensively (see Introduction 5).

The priestly families documented in this corpus occupied the highest echelons of local society during Neo-Babylonian and early Persian rule.[30] Not only did these men occupy lower/mid-ranking positions, such as judge, notary

26 For example, the archive of Bēl-rēmanni (Jursa 1999), the archive of Marduk-rēmanni (Waerzeggers 2014), and the Nappāhu archive (Baker 2004).

27 Waerzeggers 2010: 16. However, one has to maintain the possibility that their temple affiliations are lacking due to accidents of recovery rather than due to a historical absence, seeing that the archives in question are relatively small.

28 Jursa 2005: 82–85 and Waerzeggers 2010: 79. The Gallābu family in Borsippa is known to have performed the homonymous barber's service (*gallābūtu*) in the Ezida temple. The Iddin-Papsukkal is a well-known temple-enterer's family in Borsippa. The Banê-ša-ilia family can so far not be connected to the local temple institution at all.

29 Waerzeggers 2005.

30 In the new order that came into existence after the failed revolts of 484 BCE, these priestly families had lost their privileged standing in society to a group of people whose loyalty to

scribe or tax collector,[31] but the two most senior posts in Borsippa, those of chief temple administrator or 'bishop'[32] (*šatammu*), and city governor (*šākin-ṭēmi*), were customarily drawn from among the members of the city's most prominent priestly families too.[33] The latter often managed to maintain their positions in religious as well as civic institutions over multiple generations and clearly played a leading role in the government of their town.[34]

Recent study has demonstrated that the average income range of these families was between three and thirty times the minimum household subsistence requirement.[35] Even if the majority of the local families must have fallen between five to nine times minimum subsistence level, and only few might actually have generated a thirty times subsistence income, it is important to realise that in this book we are dealing with well-to-do families. With their middling to high income these families generally belonged to the urban upper stratum. Moreover, affiliation to this stratum was expressed through the use of three-tier genealogies ('PN, son of PN, descendant of FN'), i.e. the use of family or clan names.[36] These functioned as indisputable markers of descent and qualified their bearers as the traditional and native Babylonians par excellence. It should be realised that individuals lacking this nominal affiliation presumably constituted the greater part of the Babylonian population.

Persian rule was warranted. See, for example, Waerzeggers 2003/2004, Kessler 2004, and Pirngruber [*forthcoming*].

31 See, for example, Wunsch 2000, Baker and Wunsch 2001, and Jursa and Waerzeggers 2009.

32 Based on the *šatammu*'s religious authority as head of the priesthood or his administrative and judicial powers, scholars have proposed the translation 'bishop' or 'chief temple administrator', respectively. Cf. Bongenaar 1997: 12^{+25} and Waerzeggers 2010: 43^{+222} for references.

33 See Waerzeggers 2010: 65–73 for a prosopography of the *šatammu* of Ezida and *šākin-ṭēmi* of Borsippa. For their role in the temple and civic administration, see Waerzeggers 2010: 42–45. Note that the office of *šākin-ṭēmi* was being curtailed in the reign of Xerxes, and presumably abolished later, cf. Joannès 1990a: 180, Waerzeggers 2004: 161–162, Jursa 2005: 50^{+296}, and Kessler 2006: 40.

34 Note, however, that this local authority was checked to some extent by the appointment of royal officials inside the temple administration. The most common titles are the 'royal resident' (*qīpu*) and the 'royal commissioner' (*ša rēš šarri bēl piqitti*), which were brought in from outside the community. See, on these royal officials, Jursa 2005: 49–51. Cf. Kleber 2008 (Uruk) and Bongenaar 1997 (Sippar). For a fresh and very intimate account of the interactions between various temple and royal officials as based on the early Neo-Babylonian letter corpus from Uruk, see Levavi 2018.

35 Jursa *et al.* 2010: 296–305.

36 Nielsen 2011. Note that throughout this book the terms 'family' and 'clan' are used interchangeably to refer to kin groups that were defined by actual or perceived familial ties and claimed descent from a common ancestor (or ancestral occupation), i.e. shared a family name.

The Borsippa corpus covers the entire so-called 'long sixth century',[37] between the rise of the Neo-Babylonian dynasty under Nabopolassar in circa 620 BCE and the failed revolts against the Persian king Xerxes in 484 BCE, when the majority of archives from northern Babylonia, including Borsippa, abruptly break off.[38] It offers the largest collection of private archives from Babylonia during the first millennium BCE. While direct contact between the individual archive holders is documented rarely, there are clear prosopographical links between the archives, as protagonists share a fair amount of direct and indirect contacts. With approximately 7,000 individuals mentioned in the course of the Neo-Babylonian period in the above-listed private archives alone, this corpus offers a unique insight into the functioning of a community in first millennium BCE Babylonia.[39] Moreover, this corpus further differs from corpora of other cities in that it pertains to a much wider section of temple personnel. In Borsippa, like in other cities, the temple's middle stratum, made up of brewers, bakers, and butchers, is best represented, but a number of archives pertain to families of the very highest and lower priesthoods (see below). This corpus thus presents an opportunity to investigate the social interactions of a local community of priests in relatively complete terms.

5 The Babylonian Priest

In this book, I use the term 'priest' to denote a person who actively participated in temple worship. However, I often use the term 'priestly' more broadly to include inactive members of a priest's paternal family or clan. This usage is warranted by the particular workings of the prebendary system that underpinned the division of cultic labour in Babylonian temples.

37 This term was coined by M. Jursa in Jursa *et al.* 2010: 5.

38 Waerzeggers 2004.

39 This number is based on an on-going project to assign each individual in the Borsippa corpus a unique number. This is a crucial step towards the creation of a prosopographical database and facilitate the application of modern research methods such as social network analysis. Thus far the Gallābu, Ea-ilūtu-bani, Ilia A, Ilia C, Ilia D, and the Rē'i-alpi archive have been submitted to this ID processing. These six archives amount to some 1,175 texts in which approximately 4,642 unique individuals are mentioned. This gives an average of 3,95 unique individuals per text. The archives listed above on pp. 7–8 amount to some 1,899 texts and thus give an estimation of approximately 7,501 unique individuals. If the various temple files, the smaller archives and dossiers, and the large number of unassigned texts are included in this analysis, the number of individuals mentioned in the Neo-Babylonian corpus of Borsippa can be raised to well over 11,000.

Assyriologists have defined the term 'priest' in two different ways. On the one hand, there are scholars who apply it to ritual specialists functioning as mediators between human and divine realms.[40] This definition is based on a modern, western perception of the priest as a privileged interlocutor of the divine. According to this definition, the Mesopotamian priesthood includes ritualists such as diviners, exorcists, and prophets, while it excludes more mundane cultic workers such as temple brewers or gate-keepers. On the other hand, a more inclusive use of the term priest has been advocated by C. Waerzeggers (2010: 34ff.) who defines a priest as 'a person who enjoyed the right to partake in the temple worship on account of his possession of the required legal title and on account of his ritual qualifications'. This definition, which I employ in this book, emphasises two dimensions, a legal and a practical one. The legal dimension refers to the ownership of a so-called *isqu* ('share' or 'lot'), a term customarily translated in the literature as 'prebend'.[41] A prebend gave its owner the rights to enjoy an income from the temple, usually in the form of sacrificial remainders and other raw materials, in exchange for the performance of a cultic service specific to a time, task, and area, such as baking bread, gate-keeping, basket-weaving, fishing, and cultic singing.[42] Passed down from father to son, prebendary titles forged long-lasting connections between families and certain priestly tasks. However, possession of a legal title did not automatically mean that a person was able to participate in temple worship. In order to be initiated to the active priesthood, strict rules of purity had to be observed relating to all aspects of the person including descent, mind, and body.[43] As a result of these regulations, prebend-ownership and active priesthood could be dissociated in practice, as ritually unfit prebend-owners were allowed to hire suitable substitutes to perform the temple service attached to their prebend. However, the heritability of prebends, the recruitment of substitutes within the circle of prebend-owners, and the general reluctance to sell prebends outside of the paternal clan were all factors that worked together to ensure a far-reaching association between the prebend-owning family and the actual performance of the priestly task.

---

40 Sallaberger and Huber Vulliet 2005 and Löhnert 2007.

41 See, Cocquerillat 1955: 39, van Driel 2002: 33, and Waerzeggers 2010: 34^{+190} for the background of the term in Ancient Near Eastern studies.

42 Recent studies on the Babylonian prebendary system include MacGinnis 1991, Bongenaar 1997, MacGinnis 1999, Jursa 1999 van Driel 2002, van Driel 2005, Corò 2005, and Waerzeggers 2010.

43 See Chapter 6.1.2. On the requirements and procedures to enter the Mesopotamian priesthood see, Sallaberger and Hubert Vulliet 2005, Waerzeggers and Jursa 2008, Löhnert 2007, and Löhnert 2010.

This mechanism allows for a delicate but crucial simplification of the data, which involves taking families as the principal objects of analysis, rather than individual persons, and using clan names as indicators of certain priestly identities. In particular, this procedure is based on the following two observations.

Firstly, it is a valid simplification to connect families with specific priestly professions (for example, to consider the Ilia family as a clan of brewers or the Ibnāya family as a clan of butchers). The recent prosopographical study of Borsippa's main temple by C. Waerzeggers has shown that most priestly families in this city specialised in one particular profession.[44] This stands in sharp contrast to smaller Babylonian temples such as the Ebabbar temple in Sippar, where priests were often engaged in more than one trade.[45] While in Borsippa the traditional relationship between priestly offices and families is thus generally well established, there are some families for which this relationship is more ambiguous or poorly expressed, if not lacking altogether.[46] In these cases, I make artificial simplifications. The evidence for each 'ambiguous' family (or family branch) is considered individually in the following analysis whenever possible, but there are only two possible outcomes: either the family is classified as temple-based and attributed to a specific priestly group or it is perceived as non-members of the priesthood and, hence, as outsiders.[47]

Secondly, it is an acceptable simplification to attribute an individual's documented priestly profession and the correlating (priestly) status to all members of his family, even if for these members no positive evidence of their involvement in temple worship or in the prebendary system is present. Because the prebend system of the sixth century BCE was established in the early part of the first millennium, and given the reluctance to alienate prebends outside of the paternal family, it follows that most prebends existed within a community of heirs.[48]

6 The Temple Hierarchy

The various priesthoods of a Babylonian temple were ordered in a rigid hierarchy along an all-embracing axis of relative purity and physical proximity to

44 Waerzeggers 2010: 78–80.

45 Bongenaar 1997.

46 See Waerzeggers 2010: 16 for a list of archives from Borsippa with the professional affiliation of their protagonists.

47 See, for example, page 167 of this book concerning the protagonists of the Gallābu archive.

48 Van Driel 2002: 67–75, Waerzeggers 2010: 8, Jursa 2010: 162, and Nielsen 2011: *passim*.

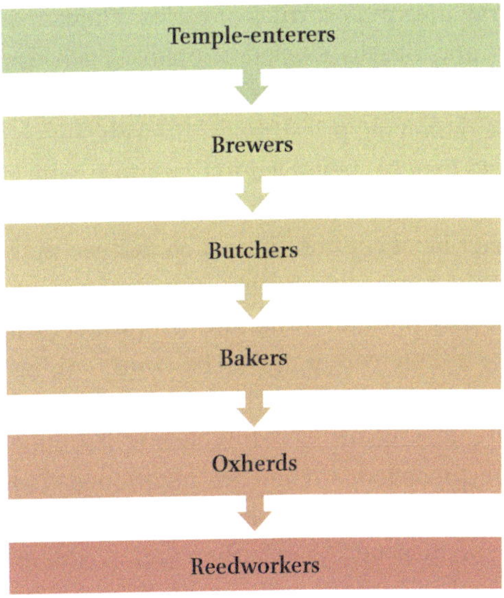

FIGURE 1 Abstract representation of temple hierarchy

the gods.[49] This meant that priests who worked in close contact with divine statues had to comply with more stringent purity rules than those working in more peripheral areas of the temple. In the abstract sense we could imagine the hierarchy in the temple assuming the form of a ladder (figure 1).

Located at the very top of the temple hierarchy was the group of so-called temple-enterers (*ērib-bīti*s). Both the chief temple administrator (*šatammu*) and the city governor (*šākin-ṭēmi*), the foremost positions in the local religious and civic institutions, were traditionally recruited from this group.[50] The temple-enterers enjoyed a particularly privileged position in the temple and were allowed access to the most sacred areas, especially the cellae of the gods.[51]

The temple-enterers embodied the gods' most intimate servants who took care of their primary needs. Their individual tasks could vary considerably, as singers, exorcists, and artisans such as goldsmiths or jewellers could all have *ērib-bīti* status.[52] It stands beyond dispute that these men, due to their intense

49 Sallaberger and Hubert Vulliet 2005: 620–621, Waerzeggers and Jursa 2008, and Waerzeggers 2010: 42–49.

50 Waerzeggers 2010: 46.

51 See, for example, Kümmel 1979: 163, Bongenaar 1997: 147–148, van Driel 2002: 88, Waerzeggers and Jursa 2008: 14–15, and Waerzeggers 2010: 46.

52 Van Driel 2002: 89, 123–124. See also Lambert 1957 for an edition of VS 1 15, a text from Hellenistic Uruk that informs us about the traditionally perceived composition of the *ērib-bīti*s.

contact with the divine, had to observe the strictest rules of purity. They were therefore submitted to consecration and ritually shaved, probably each day when on duty.

Below the temple-enterers are the purveying priesthoods. Brewers, butchers, bakers, oil-pressers, fishermen, and oxherds belonged to this group, which had a dual role in the temple service.[53] They were in the first place responsible for the production of specific sacrificial commodities such as beer, milk or bread, which usually happened in the temple workshops. But they also assumed a more ceremonial role when they presented the finished products in the temple courtyard (*kisallu*) during a daily ceremony.[54] The courtyard has been identified as an area of restricted access and only the consecrated, ritually shaved priesthoods could participate in this ritual.[55] It is clear that among the food purveyors the brewers took precedence. They are mentioned first in lists of cultic personnel before the butchers and the bakers.[56] After these three professions no strict hierarchy can be established, although the oxherds seem to have ranked below the brewers, bakers, and butchers. While purveying priests thus belonged to the consecrated priesthoods, they were denied access beyond the inner courtyard into the living quarters of the gods, which was the prerogative of the temple-enterers alone.[57]

The next group is made up of service personnel. This group consisted of prebendaries that had a supportive role in the daily management of the liturgy, like measurers, doorkeepers, scribes, and barbers. As C. Waerzeggers argues, this group was not so much ranked above or below the food purveyors but rather in a parallel hierarchy.[58] It is not clear whether all the priests in this group were consecrated and shaved. However, it stands to reason that this depended on the specific duty determined by their prebend. A doorkeeper on duty at the entrance of the divine cella must have been obliged to meet high standards of purity and was presumably submitted to shaving whereas a measurer active in the temple storerooms did not have to fulfil these criteria.

The final group is made up of 'minor' craftsmen, including potters, builders, and reed-workers.[59] In contrast to the previous groups, these priests were not engaged in the sacrificial system. Instead they were responsible for its

53 Van Driel 2002: 117–123.
54 Waerzeggers and Jursa 2008: 14–17, Waerzeggers 2010: 113–118.
55 Waerzeggers and Jursa 2008: 15–17.
56 See Waerzeggers 2010: 48+252 for various examples. It should be noted that the relative status between bakers and butchers is not always clear.
57 Waerzeggers and Jursa 2008: 14–17.
58 Waerzeggers 2010: 49.
59 Ibid.

maintenance and protection by, for instance, baking earthenware containers, repairing brick walls, and fixing reed structures. There is no evidence that these craftsmen were consecrated or had to comply with any rules of purity beyond a minimum degree of hygiene. As we have seen, however, artisans belonging to the more important crafts like the goldsmiths were consecrated and had to meet standards of purity, especially when their tasks brought them in close contact to the gods in which case they belonged to the ranks of the temple-enterers.[60]

7 Main Protagonists of this Study

In the following pages I introduce the most important priests who feature in this study. Starting with the top-ranking prebendaries of Ezida, the temple-enterers, I subsequently address their lower-ranking colleagues, viz. the brewers, the bakers, the oxherds, and the reed-workers, thereby following the Babylonian temple hierarchy as outlined above. The same order of discussion is adopted in the analyses in ensuing chapters. After listing the local families known to have been enrolled in the individual priesthoods, I give a brief overview of the most relevant archives and pay special attention to the business activities, family position, and major life events of the principal protagonists. While many more archives and texts are used, the following individuals and families form the foundation of this book.

7.1 *Temple-Enterers*

In Borsippa temple-enterers (*ērib-bīti*) came from the following families: Ahiya'ūtu, Aqar-Nabû, Arad-Ea, Arkāt-ilāni-damqā, Ēdu-ēṭir, Iddin-Papsukkal, Ilī-bāni, (Ea-)ilūtu-bani, Kidin-Nanāya, Naggāru, Nappāhu, and Nūr-Papsukkal.[61] Our main source is the cluster of archives of the Ea-ilūtu-bani family, which was the subject of a 1989 study by F. Joannès. I refer to it as a cluster because this text group, consisting of some 325 documents, is made up of the independent archives of three families: Ea-ilūtu-bani, Ilī-bāni, and Nannāhu. Their archives merged as a consequence of intermarriage and they were eventually deposited together.[62] Covering an unusually long period of time (ca. 687–486 BCE), this archive cluster informs us on six successive generations. The texts are distributed evenly and often report on the activities of siblings and in-laws.

60 Van Driel 2002: 123.

61 See Waerzeggers 2010: 79, 73–76 for a prosopography of temple-enterers in Borsippa.

62 See Joannès 1989: 122 for a schematic representation of transmission.

While it thus provides us with a relatively broad account of the families, it lacks the density of information found in some of the other archives discussed below. Here, I only introduce the main representatives of the three families in the briefest of terms. For a more detailed account, the reader is referred to the 1989 study of Joannès.

With forty-six and sixty-five attestations, Zēru-Bābili (fourth generation, ca. 580–545 BCE) and his son Mušēzib-Bēl (ca. 561–509 BCE) are the best-attested individuals of the Ea-ilūtu-bani family branch. Of particular importance for the formation of this text group was the marriage between Mušēzib-Bēl and ᶠHubbuṣītu//Ilī-bāni,[63] the sister of the two protagonists of the Ilī-bāni archive: Nādin (aka. Dadia, attested thirty-seven times between ca. 555 and 539 BCE) and Širiktu (attested thirty-five times between ca. 555 and 521 BCE). Besides being intermarried, the Ea-ilūtu-bani and the Ilī-bāni families were further connected through shared contacts and overlapping business interests. The Nannāhu family branch is almost exclusively represented by a man called Ahušunu (attested thirty-two times between ca. 522 and 492 BCE). His texts entered the archive cluster as a result of his marriage with ᶠLurindu (sixth generation, ca. 494 and 492 BCE), the daughter of Mušēzib-Bēl//Ea-ilūtu-bani and his wife of the Ilī-bāni family.

There is only circumstantial evidence that the main family branches of this archive cluster were involved in the cult. Firstly, both Mušēzib-Bēl and his father are attested as temple craftsmen, more specifically as goldsmiths.[64] Secondly, the archive contains various texts belonging to a certain Zēru-Bābili/Šumā/Ea-ilūtu-bani (ca. 587–550 BCE), who is commonly identified as temple-enterer of Nabû in the sources. Even though F. Joannès (1989: 37–38[65]) has shown that, despite the onomastic similarities, he should not be equated with Mušēzib-Bēl's father, this Zēru-Bābili was obviously closely related to the archive-holding branch of the family. Finally, while the Ea-ilūtu-banis and the Ilī-bānis are well-known temple-enterer clans in Borsippa, the Nannāhu clan is thus far only attested as cultic 'entertainers' (*kurgarrû*), a prebendary

63 She was previously married to Mušēzib-Bēl's older brother. After ᶠHubbuṣītu's death, Mušēzib-Bēl preserved the alliance between the two families by marrying his late wife's niece, ᶠAmat-Sutīti//Ilī-bāni. See Waerzeggers 2002 for other examples of affinal endogamy in the Neo-Babylonian period.

64 See Waerzeggers 2010: 39 for the temple goldsmiths in Ezida. Cf. Bongenaar 1997: 363ff. for the same profession in the Ebabbar temple of Sippar. While there is so far no evidence that the service of the goldsmith was integrated into the prebendary organisation, it is very likely that these craftsmen working in close proximity of the statues of the gods enjoyed temple-enterer status.

65 Following an earlier observation by San Nicolò 1947: 155. Cf. van Driel 1992: 34.

profession whose status in the temple hierarchy is not entirely clear.[66] Yet, the fact that this task was performed in close proximity to the gods and the additional fact that the Nannāhu family received a temple-enterer's daughter in marriage, suggest that this family was of comparable priestly status. Hence, in the following study I subsume the information of the Nannāhus under the category of temple-enterers.

One has to realise that our knowledge about temple-enterer families from Borsippa is restricted, even if references to individual temple-enterers, many of whom served as chief temple administrator (*šatammu*) or city governor (*šākin-ṭēmi*), can be found throughout the documentation.[67] While they provide a unique insight into the upper reaches of the temple administration and the circle of leading families, they do not assist us in reconstructing (and contextualising) the functioning of these priestly families in their community. Besides the archive cluster discussed above, there is only one more archive in the corpus belonging to a temple-enterer, the Iddin-Papsukkal (B) archive.[68] Unfortunately, this 'archive' consists of less than ten texts and does very little to alleviate the gap in our documentation.

7.2 *Brewers*

Families identified by C. Waerzeggers as belonging to the ranks of the brewers (*sirāšu*) include Ahiya'ūtu, Ardūtu, Huṣābu, Ilia, Ilšu-abūšu, Kudurrānu, Lākuppuru, Mannu-gērûšu, and Šikkûa.[69]

With up to ten private archives the brewers are the best-represented priesthood in Borsippa.[70] Totalling nearly 300 texts, the Ilia (A) archive is our foremost source on this prebendary group.[71] Not only does it provide a unique glimpse into the organisation of the prebendary brewers, it also informs us in great detail about the family's marriage alliances and genealogy, indeed resulting in one of the largest and most complex family trees reconstructed for the Neo-Babylonian period so far.[72]

66 For the *kurgarrû*, see Maul 1992, George 2000: 270–271, Rollinger 2000: 73, Linssen 2004: 17, 120, and Peled 2014.

67 See footnote 50, above.

68 Jursa 2005: 85 and Waerzeggers 2005: 361.

69 Waerzeggers 2010: 79. There are several more families that might have been affiliated to this priesthood, but the evidence remains weak so far: Aqar-Nabû, Allānu, Kinia, Naggāru, Ninurta-ušallim, Šēpê-ilia, and Zērūtu. See Waerzeggers 2010: 188–195 for a full prosopography of the brewers.

70 Jursa 2005: 76–94.

71 The following information on the Ilia (A) archive can be found in Jursa 2005: 85–87 and Waerzeggers 2010: 372ff.

72 Waerzeggers 2010: 735–737.

The archive spans 119 years (ca. 520–489 BCE) and covers five successive generations. However, the vast majority of the texts relate to Marduk-šumu-ibni (aka. Ardia)/Šulā, who was active for no less than fifty-four years. As he was the first son of Šulā's second marriage, Marduk-šumu-ibni, together with his two younger siblings, saw the paternal estate divided in favour of his older half-brother, who received a share of two-thirds in accordance with the Neo-Babylonian law of inheritance.[73]

To some extent, this disadvantageous position determined the course of Marduk-šumu-ibni's professional life. Much of his energy went into the service of the gods. Besides the prebends inherited from his father, Marduk-šumu-ibni often helped other relatives discharging their prebendary obligations, which occasionally allowed him to assume ownership over additional service days. Marduk-šumu-ibni also owned various plots of land, but his shares were often fragmentary and much of the property was managed on a communal basis with his younger brothers. Rather than buy additional land, Marduk-šumu-ibni usually resorted to property exchange in order to improve his inherited estates. That this might have been a result of a shortage of liquid assets is suggested by the fact that silver lending plays only a very minor role in his business affairs (see Chapter 3.2).

While his family maintained close marriage ties with the fellow brewer clan of the Ilšu-abūšu, Marduk-šumu-ibni himself was married to [f]Inṣabtu//Ša-nāšišu, a clan that would rise to considerable power in Babylon and Sippar in the course of the reign of Darius I.[74] The couple had three daughters and a son. Even if Marduk-šumu-ibni could not be counted among the richest individuals of Borsippa, he nevertheless enjoyed considerable prestige in the community. One of his daughters was married to the chief temple administrator (*šatammu*) of Ezida, while the other was wed to the son of Šaddinnu//Bēliya'u, an overseer (*šāpiru*) of the temple bakers (see below). Marduk-šumu-ibni was also closely associated to Nabû-zēru-ušebši//Ilia (D), the city governor (*šākin-ṭēmi*) of Borsippa, with whom he held a prebend in joint ownership. Finally, towards the end of his career Marduk-šumu-ibni was also active as a notary scribe, a responsibility that can only have further promoted his standing in the community.

7.3 *Bakers*

Not far below the temple brewers ranked the priesthood of the bakers (*nuhatimmu*). According to C. Waerzeggers' estimation, up to one hundred

73 Roth 1995: 148.

74 See, for example, Waerzeggers 2014 and Waerzeggers [*forthcoming*].

individual bakers might have been employed by the Ezida temple at any given moment. They were recruited from the following families: Bēliya'u, Esagil-mansum, Kidin-Sîn, Nabû-mukīn-apli, Šēpê-ilia.[75]

The oldest and most prominent among these families were the Kidin-Sîns and the Šēpê-ilias. Not only did their involvement in this trade date back to at least the eighth century, but also they still accounted for fifty-five percent and twenty-nine percent of all known bakers by the end of the long sixth century. In contrast, the Nabû-mukīn-apli clan did not sustain such stability. While this family still owned a considerable share of the baker's service in the seventh century, their patrimony was almost completely lost to the Bēliya'us in the course of the sixth century BCE. This last family is not attested until the reign of Nebuchadnezzar II and might only have settled in Borsippa around the 550s BCE. It has been argued that the Bēliya'us, perhaps together with the Esagil-mansum family,[76] were part of a larger group of families that moved from the capital of Babylon to the burgeoning provincial towns during the reign of Nebuchadnezzar II.[77] The old and native Kidin-Sîn and Šēpê-ilia families did not associate much with the immigrant families of the Bēliya'u and the Esagil-mansum, practically dividing the ranks of bakers in two contrasting camps (see Chapter 3.3 and Chapter 4.2.3).

Today most of our attention goes to the Bēliya'u family, which has left the only baker's archive from Borsippa recovered so far.[78] It consists of some 375 documents belonging to Šaddinnu//Bēliya'u, second son of Balassu and ᶠQunabātu//Esagil-mansum, who can be followed for over fifty years (between ca. 536–484 BCE). Šaddinnu was married to ᶠNanāya-damqā//Ṣillāya, whose family had no obvious ties to the temple. The couple had at least one son, who married the daughter of the local brewer Marduk-šumu-ibni//Ilia (see above).

Even if his family lacked roots in the locale and could therefore not call on a particular family tradition as bakers of Nabû, Šaddinnu was nonetheless able to make a career in this line of business. Besides inheriting a number of service days from his father, he acquired additional prebends from various colleagues early on in his career. Moreover, from 518 BCE onwards, Šaddinnu assumed greater responsibility within the ranks of the bakers as supervisor of specific service units (*bēl-šapatti*), and more importantly, by occupying the position

75 See for the following Waerzeggers 2010: 207–208.

76 Zadok 2005b.

77 See for more on this trend of immigrating families Waerzeggers 2014.

78 The following information can be found in Jursa 2005: 81–82, Waerzeggers 2010: 475ff. The edition of this archive is in preparation by J. Wojciechowska.

of overseer (*šāpiru*) of all the bakers of Nabû, a post traditionally held by the Kidin-Sîn family.[79]

Besides the substantial part that concerns Šaddinnu's activities as temple baker, the archive reflects the usual interest of first millennium priests in real estate, slave ownership, and silver lending. Yet, in many ways Šaddinnu differed from his fellow priests as he more successfully engaged in entrepreneurial activities alongside his priestly functions. One of his particular enterprises involved the acquisition of vacant or dilapidated houses and urban plots, with the aim of subsequently renting them.[80] He invested a considerable amount of silver in this niche, as the archive contains evidence for over a dozen of such acquisitions, some from insolvent debtors. Even if other priestly families made money with similar activities too, their involvement was usually modest compared to Šaddinnu's. That his entrepreneurial aspirations could at least in part be understood against his immigrant background and lack of historical roots in Borsippa is suggested by the business profile of other migrant families in first millennium Babylonia, like the Ṣāhit-ginês from Sippar, who were also able to gain a foothold and thrive both inside and outside of the temple institution on an even larger scale than Šaddinnu.[81]

7.4 *Oxherds*

The prebendary oxherds (*rē'i-alpi*) stood on a lower echelon of the large and diverse subdivision of the purveying priesthoods.[82] While these priests were in the first place cattle breeders who looked after the bulls destined for the offerings, they were also responsible for dairy production. In Borsippa, over the course of the long sixth century, the homonymous Oxherd or, Rē'i-alpi family exercised a near-monopoly on this trade.

This at least can be drawn from the Rē'i-alpi family archive.[83] With over 400 documents, this is the largest archive from Borsippa and the third largest private archive from first millennium Babylonia.[84] While it attests to five consecutive generations (ca. 620–484 BCE), the majority of the documents concern Nabû-mukīn-zēri/Aplā (ca. 560–500 BCE) and his son Rēmūt-Nabû (ca. 525–492

79 Waerzeggers 2010: 209–212.

80 Jursa *et al.* 2010: 170f.

81 Waerzeggers 2014.

82 Information on this prebend in Ezida can be found in Waerzeggers 2010, Chapter 7.

83 Jursa 2005: 93f. For a discussion of the prebend-related dossiers, see Waerzeggers 2010: 553ff. An edition of this archive is in preparation by R. Zadok.

84 After the Egibi archive (approximately 1,700 texts) and the Murašû archive (approximately 730 texts), see Jursa 2005: 65–67 and 113–114, respectively.

BCE) of the third and fourth generation, respectively. Nabû-mukīn-zēri (aka. Murašû) was married to fNanāya-bulliṭiš//Mubannû, with whom he had two children: a daughter named fInbā who married into the Šarrahu family and a son named Rēmūt-Nabû, the second protagonist of the archive. Rēmūt-Nabû was married twice: first to a woman of the Ardūtu family, a minor brewer clan, and later to fAhattu//Arad-Ea. The latter wife assumes an active role in the archive, especially after her husband's death when she temporarily took over the family's affairs.

Besides a large number of title deeds, loans and some slave texts, the archive informs us in great detail about the management of the temple service and provides us with a unique insight into the organisation of the Oxherd clan at large. The clan managed its prebendary patrimony with great fluidity and ease, reflecting a general attitude of co-operation and solidarity that transpires equally in business affairs outside of the temple. It has been suggested that it was exactly this principle of solidarity that allowed Nabû-mukīn-zēri and Rēmūt-Nabû to expand their prebendary portfolio massively and acquire a highly influential position among the oxherds of Ezida.[85] Moreover, the family was very rich, as can be seen from the fact that the value of Rēmūt-Nabû's property portfolio amounted to well over a talent of silver by 502 BCE.[86]

Even if the Rē'i-alpi family qualifies as a genuine priestly family, we see throughout this study that the oxherds often did things their own way. They distort the overall picture and complicate attempts to generalise larger sets of data on more than one occasion. While, according to the *communis opinio*, the oxherds are to be situated on a medium-low rung of the temple hierarchy, the family manifests itself as a major player in the priestly community of Borsippa. Is this due to the efficient family organisation or to their wealth? Or was their status in the temple simply more significant than previously thought? The oxherds had (ab)used their influence in the past, as can be seen in SAA 10 353.[87] In his letter to the Assyrian king Esarhaddon (680–669 BCE), royal agent Mār-issār reported that the oxherds[88] of Borsippa had refused to draw up accounts of their live-stock, withheld various offerings, and bribed the city governor (*šākin-ṭēmi*) and chief temple administrator (*šatammu*), who were said to do the oxherds' bidding. Moreover, around the same time the oxherds

85 Waerzeggers 2010: 287.

86 Although he might have been forced to sell much of his property by the end of that year, see Waerzeggers 2010: 646–649.

87 Parpola 1993: 289–291.

88 While the letter mostly refers to *rē'û* (lúsipa), lit. 'shepherd', it uses at least once the full term *rē'i-alpē* (lúsipa-gud.níta.meš, see l. 24). Moreover, that both terms were interchangeable has been shown by C. Waerzeggers 2010: 274+943.

seem to have forged a marriage alliance with the chieftain of the Gambūlu tribe according to the reports in SAA 18 56,[89] which should further underline their prominent social standing in the community.

7.5 *Reed-Workers*

Located at the lowest fringes of the temple hierarchy were the minor craftsmen, among which we find the reed-workers (*atkuppu*). Usually mentioned after the prebendary food preparers and the temple's support staff, the reed-workers were responsible for making cultic baskets and presumably keeping up the reed structures in and around the temple precinct. As noted earlier, there is no evidence that reed-workers belonged to the consecrated priesthood, participated in the daily ceremony on the temple courtyard or had to comply with any rules of purity beyond a minimum degree of hygiene. As was the case with the oxherds, the service of the reed-workers in Ezida was in the hands of the homonymous Reed-worker, or Atkuppu, family.

The Borsippa corpus is unique in that it offers us the possibility to study a family of minor temple craftsmen through the Atkuppu family archive.[90] It spans some 120 years and attests to five successive generations between circa 608 and 485 BCE. Consisting of only 110 documents, however, it is limited in size compared to the archives discussed above, and its textual coverage is rather shallow. To some extent, this is mitigated by the fact that the majority of the texts pertain to the third and fourth generations. The third generation is represented by Marduk-šumu-ibni (aka. Sūqāya)/Nabû-ēṭir. He married ᶠKāribtu//Adad-nāṣir, whose family held no cultic function according to the extant documentation. The fourth and best-attested generation is represented by their four sons: Nabû-šumu-uṣur (aka. Nabû-uṣuršu), Nabû-iddin, Murānu and Iqīša. The four brothers worked in close co-operation and seem to have managed the archive in close succession between circa 534 and 494 BCE.

While property and family documents are largely missing, the available evidence indicates that the family had modest financial means compared to, for example, the Bēliya'u or Rē'i-alpi families. Besides a small share in the reed-worker's prebend, the Atkuppus owned not more than two small date gardens. Moreover, their business ventures were of relatively humble proportions, and while occasionally engaging in moneylending, they were usually indebted for

---

89 Reynolds 2003: 42–43. Note, however, that the father of the groom is referred to as 'chief shepherd of Nabû' (ˡᵘ́gal-sipa.meš *ša Nabû*) and not as 'oxherd', but that this is meant seems likely in the light of the previous letter.

90 Jursa 2005: 80. An edition of this archive is currently in preparation by K. Abraham, who kindly allowed me to use a preliminary edition of these texts.

higher sums than they themselves extended – all of which points to limited cash reserves.

Even if there is no doubt that the Atkuppus were part of the priestly community of Borsippa, it is demonstrated that the family represents the edge group in our data sample, located at the fringes of the social unit under investigation not only in terms of temple status, but also in social standing, social behaviour, and interaction.

8 Book Structure

This book is divided into two parts. In Part 1 (Chapters 1–4) I investigate specific social events and interactions of the priesthood of the Ezida temple in Borsippa. Chapter 1 is devoted to the marriage practices of the priests. With the help of social network analysis, I reconstruct the marriage alliances of the Borsippean priesthood and reveal that this community observed a complex marriage system known as hypergamy. Functioning as a building block in society, marriage deeply affected the social organisation of participating families as well as the execution of their cultic duties. Chapter 2 explores various aspects of landownership. I first look into the history and origins of *hanšû* land, which had been granted to Borsippean families by early first millennium kings. Based on the naming patterns of these landed estates, I reconstruct the range of original beneficiaries. I then assess which value this land held for the descendants of the original beneficiaries during the long sixth century. The second part concerns the sales of property, which is examined in the light of existing marriage ties and professional affiliations. An examination of the patterns of tenancy and agricultural collaboration concludes this chapter. By taking a closer look at the background of tenants, it is possible to determine on whom the priests relied for the management of their landed property. Chapter 3 investigates credit operations. By looking into the various prebendary groups individually, it can be shown that the patterns of silver lending, while depending on personal circumstances, were equally influenced by professional affiliation and faintly follow the temple-based hierarchy. Chapter 4 reconstructs circles of trust and intimacy. In the first part I subject the various archives to a quantitative examination. A comparison between the numbers of individuals mentioned only once in the archives and those attested more often inform us about the structure of the personal networks of trust and intimacy on a general level. At the same time, it is examined whether or not different social and economic attitudes of the protagonists are reflected in purely quantitative terms. In the second part I draw on the concept of tie strength developed in the social sciences to complement this quantification with a more qualitative analysis. Focusing on the most frequently attested individuals, I take a closer look at the personal networks of the priests, the kinds of individuals that may be classified as 'friends', and their roles in the lives of the protagonists.

In Part 2 (Chapters 5–6) I take a step back and examine the interactional pattern of the Borsippean priests as a whole. It is approached from a more theoretical perspective and linked with broader social phenomena of Neo-Babylonian society. Chapter 5 starts by evaluating possible causations behind the pattern of interaction reconstructed in Part 1. Drawing on the concept of homophily, I propose an interpretation that allows for a reasonable degree of agency and choice on the part of the priests, while leaving room for limiting factors of interaction, such as geographic space and demography. Moreover, by further developing the concept of homophily, it is shown that the interaction of the priests is in line with the economic motivations nurtured by this social group as rentiers. At the same time it is argued that classifications like rentiers and entrepreneurs are characterised by more than economic criteria. Chapter 6 is concerned with reconstructing the collective social identity of the Babylonian priest. The outlines of the interactional pattern points to the existence of a social boundary that separated the social group of the priests from the rest of society. I try to reconstruct the symbolic and material resources on which Babylonian priests drew to create and maintain their social in-group by investigating a series of identity markers, including professional affiliation, property ownership, historical consciousness, literacy, and language.

The study's principal findings are summarised in the conclusions.

PART 1

Social Interactions among Priests in Borsippa

CHAPTER 1

The Hypergamous Marriage System

Since the emergence of Assyriology in the nineteenth century scholars have shown only a limited interest in Babylonian marriage practices of the first millennium BCE. Investigations tended to approach the subject from a rather asocial and ahistorical perspective. Most studies are products of an academic tradition that strongly focused on philological aspects and legal implications on the matter. Many scholars were in the first place *Rechtshistoriker* who analysed Babylonian marriage for its legal implications, the particular contract types, and specific formulae and clauses used in these agreements.[1] Other scholars were concerned with the material aspects of the dowry, mostly from a philological perspective in trying to identify the semantic meaning of the various components of the marriage settlement.[2] As previously mentioned, Neo-Babylonian studies suffer from a general negligence of social approaches and this is most apparent in the study of marriage practice.[3]

The following investigation sets out to remedy this by investigating the social implications of marriage in Babylonian society. More precisely, this chapter attempts to reconstruct the patterns of marriage in the priestly community of Borsippa. This is the first effort to map a Babylonian marriage network on any scale. At the basis of this endeavour lies a quantification of the data, which tells us what kind of marital unions the prebendary families arranged for their male and female members in practice. This 'descriptive-quantitative analysis' can be found in Appendix 1. It serves as a data set that can be analysed with regard to the social implications of marriage among the local priesthood and help us to determine how, and to what extent, marriage alliances configured the social organisation of this community. I make use of social anthropological

1 See for example the entry 'Ehe' in *RLA* 2 by Korošec 1938 and the entry 'Inzest' by Petschow 1976/80, in *RLA* 5. More recent studies on marriage during the first millennium BCE include Roth 1989, Roth 1989b, Abraham 1992, Wunsch 2003 and, Oelsner, Wells and Wunsch 2003: 933–948. For the Old Babylonian marriage, see Westbrook 1988; for the Middle Babylonian evidence, cf. Slanski 2003: 501–505.

2 See, for example, Wunsch 1995/1996, Roth 1990 and Roth 1991.

3 Exceptions being the study by Roth 1987 on the household type in first millennium Babylonia, and an article on a particular case of consanguine endogamy in Sippar by Waerzeggers 2002.

 DOI:10.1163/9789004399969_003

studies and theories in order to further our understanding of the dynamics of these marriages. By converting marriage ties into a directed graph I reveal that the priestly families of Borsippa observed a complex marriage system known in anthropological literature as *hypergamy*. This system, which is observed in some parts of the Indian subcontinent (see Chapter 1.2), involves the marriage of a lower-status bride to a higher-status groom. Moreover, I show that the purity-based hierarchy of the temple served as the central guiding principle in the arrangement of alliances in Borsippa. In this study, marriage is thus appreciated as a fundamental building block of Babylonian society, which allowed individuals and families to consciously shape their social environments by organising elements within their in-group and keeping the out-group effectively at bay.[4]

1 Marriage in Borsippa: Sacerdotal Endogamy

A most remarkable marriage in the history of Borsippa took place on April 14, 559 BCE, the first day of the first month of the first year of King Neriglissar.[5] On this symbolic day, the king gave his daughter, ᶠGigītu, in marriage to the temple-enterer and recently appointed chief temple administrator (*šatammu*) of Ezida, Nabû-šumu-ukīn of the Arkāt-ilāni-damqā clan.[6] While the marriage contract is damaged and most of the details are now lost, we are left with little doubt that this alliance had strong political motivations. Neriglissar was a usurper king who had seized the Babylonian throne after murdering his predecessor.[7] He was also of Aramean origin, which meant that he came from a distinctively different background than the old-stock Babylonian families that dominated the urban centres in the alluvium.[8] By publically allying with

4 Similar strategies were and are still used to great effect by (religious) communities across the globe. See, for example, Broekman 2010 (Egypt, priesthood of Amun), Hebrew Bible, Leviticus 21:10 and Ezekiel 44:22 (Judaism), Dumont 1970: 125–129 (classical India), and Fuller 1984: 26 (modern India).

5 Julian dates in this study have been reconstructed on the basis of Parker and Dubberstein 1956.

6 This union is recorded in *Ner* 13 (Roth 1989: 49–50), a text written in the capital of Babylon, and found either there or in the Ezida temple of Borsippa, which owned this copy according to the postscript. Cf. Waerzeggers 2005: 345. For the person of Nabû-šumu-ukīn/Širikti-Marduk/Arkāt-ilāni-damqā, see Zadok 2005a: 642 and Waerzeggers 2010: 72.

7 According to Berossos, Neriglissar was married to the daughter of Nebuchadnezzar and before seizing the throne had killed his king and brother-in-law, Amēl-Marduk, cf. Verbrugghe and Wickersham 1996: 60.

8 Jursa 2014b: 127–130.

Nabû-šumu-ukīn, who was not only the chief temple administrator (*šatammu*) but also the son of the former city governor (*šākin-ṭēmi*) of Borsippa and a descendant of an old and illustrious local clan, Neriglissar was clearly making an effort to conciliate or, indeed, reward an influential faction of the local Borsippean elite.[9]

While this alliance is an indisputable testimony to the influence, authority, and prestige enjoyed by the priesthood of Nabû in Borsippa, evidence for such political marriages are all but absent from the extant documentation, which might suggest that they occurred only rarely in first millennium Babylonia.[10] This follows, too, from the marriage alliances found in the Borsippa corpus, which indicates that the priestly families pursued an alliance policy that was not only geared near-exclusively towards the local community but involved a well-defined and highly restricted social group. It will become clear in the course of this chapter that outside political elements, let alone the royal family itself, are hard to accommodate in this priestly marriage system, which was ideologically informed, exceptionally complex, and subject to strict conventions.

A total of eighty-one marriages from the long sixth century has been incorporated in the descriptive-quantitative analysis (Appendix 1).[11] While it seems that the prebendary groups in Borsippa kept different marriage agendas if taken in isolation,[12] considering the information as a single data pool and quantifying the entire set, the general conjugal preferences become immediately clear (see figure 2). The preferential marriage among the priestly families of Borsippa is the one within the prebendary group. Almost half (43%) of all marriages were arranged among prebendary families of the same professional affiliation. This type is closely followed by marriage with prebendaries from other priesthoods (37%). Finally, marriage with non-prebendaries families accounted for only twenty percent of all unions.[13]

---

9 Waerzeggers 2010: 72.

10 The Neo-Assyrian royal letter SAA 18 5, for example, reports on the alliance between the daughter of the chieftain of the Gambūlu tribe and a local temple-enterer of Nabû sometime during the mid-seventh century BCE. See Reynolds 2003: 42–43. For Bēl-iqīša/Bunanu, the chieftain in question, see Radner 1999: 315f. s.v. *Bēl-iqīša* 7; Frame 1992: 81, 111, 199ff.

11 Note that there are more attestations of marital unions in the Borsippa corpus. However, in this analysis only the unions for which both the family name of the bride and groom are available are used. See Appendix 1.

12 For example, whereas some groups, like the brewers, engaged predominantly in intra-prebendary unions (Appendix 1.2), the oxherds did not at all (Appendix 1.5).

13 This concerns families whose involvement in the prebendary system of the Ezida temple is not specified in the extant documentation.

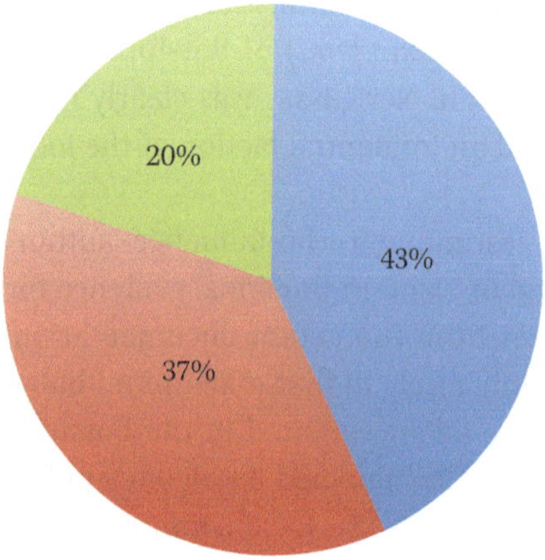

FIGURE 2
Marriage type in Borsippa

The conclusion that the priesthood of Borsippa constituted a highly endogamous group is inevitable. Priests most often engaged in occupational endogamy, i.e. marriage within their own prebendary group.[14] The evidence becomes even more telling if we combine the data of the first two marriage types (i.e. intra- and inter-prebendary unions): eighty percent of all the marriages were arranged with fellow priestly families, and this is only the minimum. The remaining twenty percent consists of unions with families from different social backgrounds: families with prebendary ties in neighbouring cities[15] or clans who may have had links to the Ezida temple but are not covered by the available sources, for example.[16] They are all classified as 'non-prebendary' here, not so much out of conviction but due to the lack of concrete information. It is not unlikely that additional information on the Ezida temple and its community would show that many families were in one way or another related to the religious establishment of Borsippa. Evidence for unions between priestly families and individuals from the lower strata of society, identified by the non-usage of three-tier genealogies, i.e. family names, is as yet entirely missing.

In summary, marriage within the own prebendary group seems to have been the preferred form according to the quotient generated by the evidence from the descriptive-quantitative analysis. The fact that almost as many marriages

14 Other scholars speak of 'group-specific endogamy'. See, for example, Jursa *et al.* 2010: 29.
15 See, for example, Bēl-eṭēru (Appendix 1.1c) and Rišāya (Appendix 1.2c).
16 See, for example, Rēʾi-sisê (Appendix 1.1c) and Ṣāhit-ginê (Appendix 1.4c).

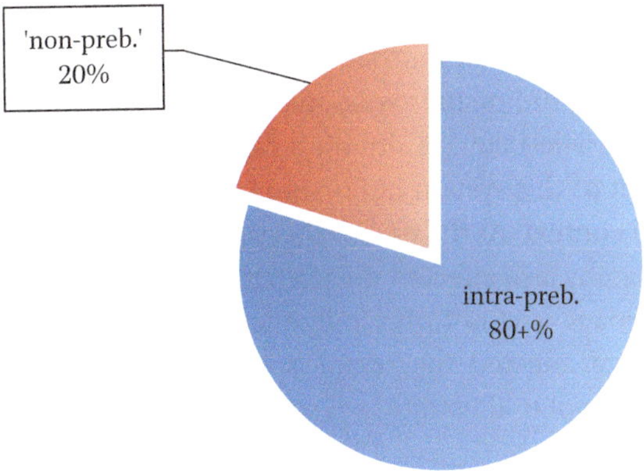

FIGURE 3
Sacerdotal endogamy

were arranged across the prebendary pool as within particular groups undermines the idea that marriage among the Borsippean priesthood was rigidly governed by concerns of temple ranking.[17] Clearly, the purity-based hierarchy did not *compel* priests to look for marriage partners within their own prebendary group. Still, it would be wrong to dismiss the importance of the temple hierarchy altogether as I show that it influenced the dynamics of marriage in a particular way. At this point, I propose that the marriage pattern of the Borsippean priesthood can best be designated as *sacerdotal endogamy*, given that more than eighty percent of all unions were arranged within the wider prebendary circle (see figure 3).

Having said this, portraying the priesthood merely as endogamous would oversimplify the matter. Endogamy, or rather the endogamous unit, is not a static entity of equal participants but quite the opposite. It has proven to be very dynamic and susceptible to hierarchical chains in many societies.[18] Moreover, it has been suggested that endogamy is not an independent principle that imposes hierarchy as much as a corollary and an expression of an existing hierarchy.[19] What then was the hierarchical principle that governed sacerdotal endogamy in Borsippa?

In the following pages I draw on sociological theories and ethnographic studies to argue that the marriage pattern in Borsippa can best be understood by using the concepts of *wife-giver* and *wife-taker*. According to this principle,

17 See Introduction 6.
18 Dumont 1970: 112–124, Black 1972, Dumont 1983: 41–52, Parkin 1990, and Goody 1990, Chapter 4.
19 Dumont 1970: 125.

marriage alliances give rise to asymmetric relations between the two parties, which have consequences for their choice of marriage partners in succeeding generations. It seems that in the case of Borsippa wife-givers were usually inferior in status with respect to their wife-takers, a situation called *hypergamy* in anthropology. The specific layout of this system in Borsippa can be explained once it is placed in its historical context. At the end of this section I show that the wife-givers/wife-takers hierarchy also affected the execution of the temple service, thus showing that marriage was not only influenced by the temple fabric, but that in turn marriage affected the temple's internal dynamics. I use social network analysis as a tool to illustrate and substantiate the above argumentation.

2 The Concept of Wife-Giver and Wife-Taker

The first study that needs to be mentioned in this section is *Les Structures Élémentaires de la Parenté* (1949) by Claude Lévi-Strauss.[20] This monograph has been a major influence in the study of family, kinship, and marriage and brought about a shift in anthropological thinking about society. Lévi-Strauss proposed an overarching theory of kinship using various ethnographic records of societies in Asia, Australia, and elsewhere.[21] This theory, which became known as the 'alliance theory' and polarised the field of kinship studies in mid-twentieth-century anthropology,[22] was based on the taboo of incest and the fundamental notion of reciprocity. For Lévi-Strauss, the prohibition of incest was in fact a fundamental rule of reciprocity since it forced men to exchange their women and thus form the basic structures of society. Although the taboo of incest is clearly a negative rule, he emphasised that it was accompanied by positive ones, namely in the form of exogamous rules (defining a group outside which marriage was arranged) and endogamous rules (defining the group within which marriage was arranged). Reciprocity lay at the basis of Lévi-Strauss' theory of kinship organisation and he consequently proceeded to study the elementary structures of various forms of marital exchange.

20 First translated into English by James Harle Bell in 1969 under the title *The Elementary Structures of Kinship*.

21 Cf. Dumont 1971 and Uberoi 1994 for a general overview of this theory and its broader implications for the studies of kinship as well as marriage in rural India.

22 Lévi-Strauss' alliance theory became opposed to the so-called 'descent theory' developed mainly by British anthropologists, most notably Radcliffe-Brown and Evans-Pritchard, among others, working in African societies. Cf. Barth 2005: 1–57.

An important case study in *Les Structures Élémentaires* revolves around the common type of marriage known as unilateral cross-cousin marriage in which the man preferably marries his mother's brother's daughter.[23] This form of marital exchange represents, in Lévi-Strauss' theory, the 'generalised exchange' and needs a minimum of three and a maximum of *n* involving parties: group X gives a wife to group Y, who gives a wife to group Z, etc. This form is 'indirectly reciprocal' since group X, which initiated the chain of transaction will have to wait until it receives a bride, in this case from group Z. It is thus ideally perceived as a cycle and presupposes a concept of speculation or credit: in the end group X can only hope that the chain of transaction will be closed by receiving a wife from Z. This interpretation has received much criticism from later scholars.[24] First, Lévi-Strauss' concept of kinship is purely structural. Second, his types of exchange were ideal types that arguably overemphasised and idealised the principles of reciprocity at the expense of actual details in the field.[25]

Lévi-Strauss, however, was duly aware of these issues. He observed that in 'generalised exchange' all involved parties adopt two functions vis-à-vis each other, that of *wife-givers* and *wife-takers*. In the case above, group Y is the wife-taker of X and the wife-giver of group Z, while group Z is a wife-taker of Y and wife-giver of X. Without delving deeper into this matter, Lévi-Strauss already suggested that these unilateral and continuous relations might give rise to a hierarchy between wife-givers and wife-takers. While this type of intermarriage 'presupposes equality', it also is 'a source for inequality'.[26]

A champion of the alliance theory was Louis Dumont who refined it and applied it to Indian society. He argued that 'affinal alliance' was a fundamental principle of Indian society and demonstrated with various ethnographic examples a tendency for 'hierarchisation' within the endogamous group.[27] In his comprehensive and seminal monograph on the caste system, *Homo Hierarchicus: The Caste System and Its Implications*,[28] Dumont described various forms

23 See Bourdieu 1977: 30–71, for a comprehensive critique of earlier anthropological approaches to this idealised form of marriage.

24 The main critics of Lévi-Strauss' theory can be found in Leach 1961 and Needham 1962. See also Dumont 1971 for a general overview.

25 Cf. Coelho de Souza 2009, Parkin 2005: 208–228.

26 Lévi-Strauss 1969: 266. See more recently Parkin 1990: 473ff.

27 Dumont 1983: 48.

28 Dumont 1970, translated from the original 1966 French edition, *Homo Hierarchicus: Le Système des Castes et ses Implications*. Note, however, that this work has been rightly criticised for giving an overtly static, idealised, and in a certain sense very Brahmanical

of marriage, in particular the so-called hypergamous marriage. It is the norm in this marriage practice that the man's family takes a wife from a lower status family, i.e. women marry up in the hierarchy.[29] This form, observed Dumont, is congruent with the classical Brahmanical ideal of marriage as being a 'gift of a maiden': a lower status family gives a daughter in marriage to a Brahmin family in exchange for spiritual goods.[30] For the gift to be meritorious it is paramount that that the family receives no payment for the girl.[31] Brahmins occupied the highest rung in traditional Hindu society, above the so-called *varṇas* of warriors (*kṣatriya*), farmers (*vaiśya*), serfs (*śūdra*), and 'untouchables'.[32] The Brahmin caste was privileged, enjoyed legal immunity, and, thanks to its high state of purity, was invested with religious authority. Brahmins are the Hindu priests par excellence.[33] In a non-Brahmanical hypergamous marriage the motives are the same other than the fact that the lower family does not give up a daughter for spiritual benefits, but for a similar reason, namely the prestige of being affiliated with the higher status family of the groom. The hierarchical relations established (or indeed reaffirmed) by marriages were maintained over time and often accompanied by additional obligations in gift-giving and ceremonial matters that were transmitted to succeeding generations, ideally perpetuating this one-way traffic.[34] Communities were very cautious never to inverse and never to breach a certain direction of intermarriage.

It has been demonstrated that communities practicing hypergamy display more fundamental traits than simply the acknowledgement of the wife-takers' superior status over their wife-givers. As a rule, the hypergamous system exists in communities that do not proclaim preferential marriages with specific relatives, which in Indian society is frequently the cross-cousin. Additional characteristics of this system are a transitive hierarchy and a non-reciprocal structure (see Chapter 1.4).[35] More contemporary examples of communities

---

account of India's caste system, cf. Heesterman 1985, Inden 1990, and Dirks 2001. See Quigley 1993: 21–53 for a concise overview of Dumont's reconstruction of the caste system and its critique.

29 As opposed to *hypogamy* where the wife's family is generally of superior status vis-à-vis the husband's (see below).

30 Dumont 1970: 117.

31 Ibid.

32 Dumont 1970: 66–75, Flood 1996: 58–61.

33 Fuller 1984.

34 Dumont 1970: 122–123.

35 Parkin 1990: 473–475.

that practice hypergamy can be found in various parts of India like Kashmir, Gujarat, and Kerala.[36]

It should be noted that hypergamy is only one of several hierarchical marriage systems. Another model, found for example in the Gilyak society in eastern Russia[37] or the Kachin people in highland Burma,[38] is known as 'reversed hypergamy' or *hypogamy*. In this system it is the wife-giver who is perceived as superior to the wife-taker.[39] This system too involves a distinct set of underlying implications. Hence, the hypogamous model occurs with preferential marriage ideologies, an intransitive hierarchy, and a marriage alliance that is at least indirectly reciprocal.[40] A marriage system that is non-hierarchical is usually called *isogamous*. Communities that adhere to this model require that marriage alliances be arranged between parties of equal status and rank.[41]

One has to bear in mind that the characteristics associated with these systems are of course idealised and prone to a higher degree of variability and complexity in practice. An extreme example is found in Mamboru, in eastern Indonesia, where both marriage systems, hypogamy and hypergamy, co-exist in the same society.[42] Nonetheless, these ideal types function as frames of reference, which can help us to detect the presence of such marriage systems in a community like the one under investigation in this book.

3 Visualising the Marriage Network

The eighty-one marriage alliances from Borsippa form a relatively modest sample. Yet they are already too many to be analysed from a simple list or table. In order to lay bare more fundamental dynamics of marriage in Borsippa and examine how these fit in with the insights gained from the anthropological literature, it is necessary to find a way to structure the data more efficiently. Social network analysis is a helpful tool to plot the alliances conjointly and reassemble them into an interlocking marriage system. Before I convert the

36 Pocock 1954, Gough 1961, Pocock 1972, Madan 1975, Fuller 1976, Parry 1979. Cf. Goody 1990: 214–219, and Quigley 1993: 87–101 for a brief overview of hypergamy in India.

37 Black 1972.

38 Leach 1954.

39 See also Sprenger 2010 for a study on the ritual superiority of wife-givers among the Rmeet (Lamet) up-landers in northern Laos.

40 Parkin 1990: 475–477.

41 Dumont 1970: 116 and Quigley 1993: 101–111.

42 Needham 1987 and Parkin 1990: 478.

data into a graph, however, a short introduction of social network analysis is in order.

Social network analysis (SNA) uses, in broad terms, a combination of mathematics and social sciences to examine relations and structures in a quantifying manner. Launched in the 1960s, it has proven to be one of the most rapidly growing academic sub-disciplines, equipped with its own terminology, handbooks, and technical toolbox.[43] SNA has been applied in numerous studies covering subjects from occupational mobility, diffusion and adoption of innovations, exchange and power, belief systems, spreading patterns of contagious diseases, computer viruses, trade, happiness, friendship, emotional contagion, and telecommunications to ancient societies.[44]

SNA was initially used to examine contemporary social phenomena. From there it slowly made its way into historical investigations. A pioneering study in this respect is Padgett and Ansell 1993, in which the authors successfully apply SNA to examine political mobilisation in fifteenth-century Florence.[45] In her study of the personal network of Theophylact, an influential archbishop in Byzantine Bulgaria, Mullett 1997 showed that it could equally be used for ancient societies. Another, more exhaustive application of SNA on the ancient world, in this case Byzantine Egypt, can be found in Ruffinni 2008. Finally, the introduction of SNA in cuneiform studies is owed to Waerzeggers 2014b.[46] In her article she describes how it could be applied to the first millennium cuneiform data and outlines its potentials for improving our understanding of Babylonian society.[47]

SNA attempts to study the relations between actors in a given context. The web that connects all these actors via their interrelationship forms the network. One of the basic aims of SNA, which is also one of its greatest assets, is to depict social networks comprehensibly as a matrix, sociogram or graph. The simplified structure can then be investigated as to how it governed and influenced the actors that make up the network. The illustrative power of SNA proves to be adequate enough for our purpose, and besides plotting the marriage network as a 2D representation, only a limited number of theoretical concepts from SNA is applied in this study.[48]

---

43 Scott 1991: 7–37.

44 For a selection of studies that approached the subject from an SNA perspective, see Wasserman and Faust 1994: 5f.

45 Other earlier examples are Rosenthal *et al.* 1985 and Carpenter 1994.

46 Note that Schloen 2001 uses the concept of networks (without applying actual network analysis) throughout his study.

47 See also Wagner *et al.* 2013 in which a quantitative network analysis is used to reconstruct the chronology and textual clusters in cuneiform archives.

48 See Scott 1991, Wasserman and Faust 1994, Newman 2010, and Prell 2012 for comprehensive handbooks of SNA. The application of SNA in social-anthropology can be found in

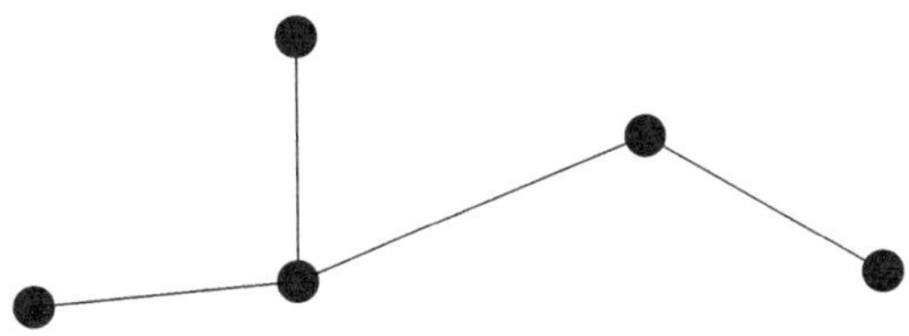

FIGURE 4 Simple graph

The principles used in the visualisation of networks, i.e. graphs, are straightforward. Networks are made up of actors represented by *nodes* (also called vertices), and their interrelationships are represented by *lines* (or edges). This results in simple 2D representations like figure 4 (above). When considering the data from Borsippa, rather than take the individual brides and grooms as actors, which would result in a densely populated but little connected web, I follow the methodology applied by Padgett and Ansell 1993 and take the various Borsippean families as actors. The individual families or clans thus serve as principle objects of analysis. The marriage alliances represent the interconnecting lines between the clan of the husband and the clan of the wife. This results in the graph depicted in figure 5 (next page).

It is important to realise that this alliance network depicts the accumulation of the eighty-one marriages of the priestly families from Borsippa. Since these were arranged over a period of more than 100 years, the network does not capture one particular moment in time.[49] Instead, in this network the assemblage of all the marriages during the long sixth century has been collapsed so that it depicts the culmination of the alliance system until 484 BCE when the documentation breaks off. It does not, therefore, present any historical development and the network can be characterised as diachronically 'flat'.

While this is an obvious downside, it should be noted that a diachronic examination is fruitless in our case. The available evidence on marriage alliances grows in conjunction with the Borsippa corpus, which, like the Neo-Babylonian corpus in general, is 'top-heavy', i.e. it accumulates towards the end of the period.[50] Hence, while the evidence from before the reign of Nabonidus (until 555 BCE) accounts for less than a dozen marriages, more than half appears during the reign of Darius I (521–486 BCE). I was unable to find any evidence

Hage and Harary 1983. The following remarks can be found in these works. The following networks have been visualised using the freeware program Gephi (https://gephi.org).

49 The earliest securely datable union was arranged before 590 BCE (EAH 203, Nbk 14). The latest marriage may have been arranged as late as 485 BCE (BM 29021, Xer 01).

50 Jursa 2005: 1ff.

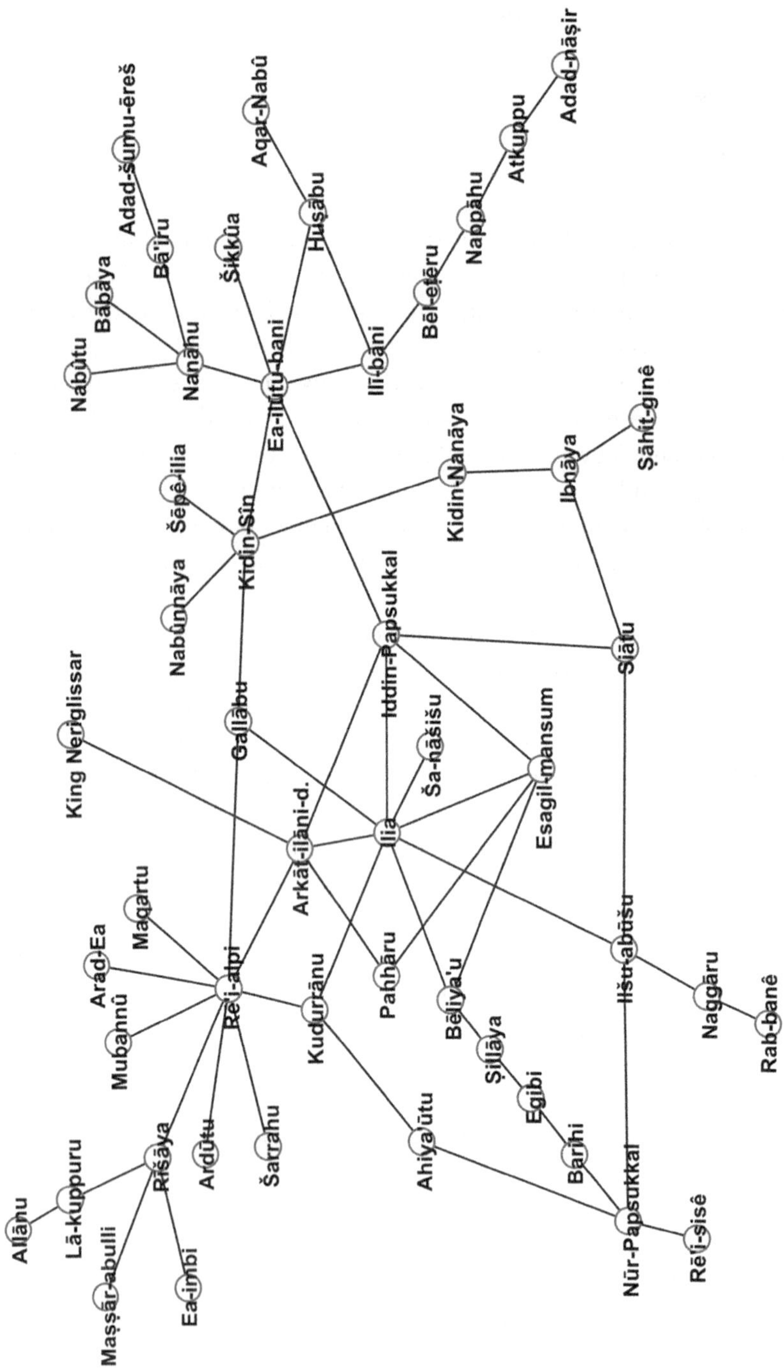

FIGURE 5 Borsippa marriage network (undirected)

indicating that the marriage system in Borsippa was profoundly affected by any historical event of the time. Quite the contrary, it seems to have been robust and altogether static.[51]

Returning to the network proper, it may appear rather messy at first glance. Yet, upon closer scrutiny several patterns can be observed. One can see, for example, that the Ilia family is well embedded and takes up a central position in this network.[52] On the other hand, the Rē'i-alpi and Ea-ilūtu-bani families, which both occupy edge positions in the temple hierarchy, form a kind of bridge, connecting a range of clans to the rest of the network. Moreover, the graph shows that by the early fifth century all the participating families were indirectly related by marriage. This highlights the great cohesion between the priestly families and demonstrates that the degree of endogamy was extremely high.[53]

So far, I have depicted the network as an undirected dichotomous graph. This means that a certain tie between two actors is binary: either it is present or not. However, many social relations are directional, i.e. directed from one actor to another but not necessarily the other way around. The classical example concerns friendship.[54] When asked to name three friends one might name X, Y, and Z. However, when in turn they are asked the same question the affection is not necessarily reciprocated. In networks representing friendship patterns, ties are therefore usually directional and a graph consisting of these directional ties is called a *directed graph*, or short *digraph*. It is the convention in such networks to use arrows to indicate the orientation from the sender to the receiver of a given relation. I show that in Borsippa the relationship between the family of the wife and the family of the husband, which in accordance with the aforementioned theories are labelled 'wife-giver' and 'wife-taker' respectively, was also a directional one. In figure 6 (next page), I have converted the

51 While the marriage of Neriglissar's daughter with the chief temple administrator (*šatammu*) of Ezida may have temporarily upset the alliance system and its internal hierarchy, the consequences seem to have affected only the family of the groom and not the marriage circuit in general (see pp. 62–63).

52 Note, however, that this is a direct result of the generous amount of data on the marriage alliances of the Ilia clan, found especially in the Ilia (A) archive. It remains to be seen whether this family would assume a similar position in case we had the complete marriage system.

53 Note that a couple of families (Asû ∞ Eppēš-ilī, Basia ∞ Basia, and Banê-ša-ilia ∞ Banê-ša-ilia) remain isolated from the reconstructed marriage network and have been removed from the graph.

54 See, for example, Wasserman and Faust 1994: 121ff., Prell 2012: 10–11.

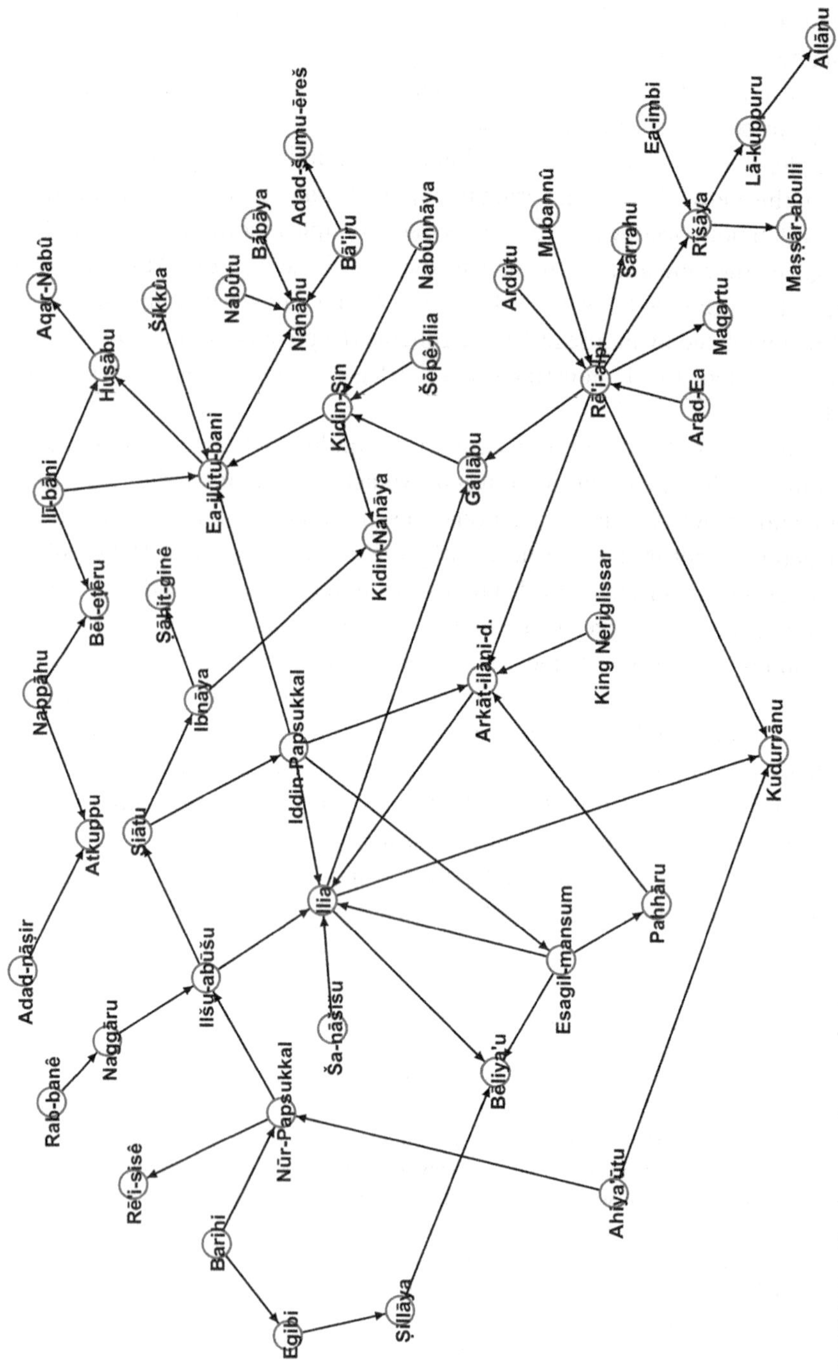

FIGURE 6 Borsippa marriage network (directed)

undirected graph of figure 5 into a digraph. The arrows indicate the movement of the bride in a given marriage.

4 Wife-Givers and Wife-Takers in Borsippa

Having defined the components of the network and applied the necessary concepts, this section presents a close analysis of the digraph in figure 6. In particular, I explore what the abstract features of this network can tell us about the nature of the marriage system in the priestly community of Borsippa.

Let us start with relative hierarchy. The most striking feature of this network is that in the eighty-one marriage alliances found over a period of 140 years, or roughly five generations, the direction of intermarriage was never reversed. In other words, once family A received a wife from family B, family A never returned a wife to B. Their roles as wife-giver and wife-taker vis-à-vis each other were never violated once established. Marriage alliance in Borsippa was thus strictly *asymmetrical* or *unilateral*. It has been suggested that in societies in which brides move in one direction only, there is a possibility that a relative status difference arises between the two alliance partners.[55] There are two possibilities: either the wife-giver is inferior in status to his wife-taker or vice versa. The following evidence suggests that in the case of Borsippa it was the wife-taker who assumed the superior position.

The first argument can be inferred from the asymmetrical character of Neo-Babylonian marriage agreements. It was the custom in Babylonia that the bride was transferred to the household of the groom upon marriage.[56] Marriage was therefore patrilocal, i.e. located at the husband's residence. In addition to a bride, the household of the husband also received a dowry (*nudunnû*). It was the absolute rule that the bride's family made some kind of wealth available, however modest. Bridewealth, a compensatory payment made by the groom to the family of the bride and a custom well-known from the earlier Old-Babylonian period and still common in some parts of the globe,[57] is only very

---

55 Parkin 1990: 347ff. See also Chapter 1.2.

56 Or his father, depending on whether or not the husband had been emancipated from his father's *potestas*, Oelsner, Wells and Wunsch 2003: 938–944. Cf. Wunsch 2003.

57 The use of bridewealth, previously known also as bride-price, has been studied most extensively for the African continent, cf. classical studies such as Evans-Pritchard 1951, Goody and Tambiah 1973, and Kuper 1982. The custom, however, is not restricted to this part of the world. See Goody 1990 for a study that addresses this and other marriage phenomena across time and space. For bridewealth in the Old-Babylonian marriage, see Westbrook 1988: 101f. For possible Middle-Babylonian evidence, see Slanski 2003: 501f. An

rarely attested in the Neo-Babylonian period, if at all.[58] Among the more than fifty marriage agreements from first millennium Babylonia one can only find very few references to payments or gifts made by a groom to the family of his bride.[59] These cases, however, confirm rather than contradict the rule. The first three instances of such payments refer to it as '(marriage) gift'. This term (*biblu*) is found in a dowry receipt from the Ṣāhit-ginê family from Sippar, dated to the early reign of Darius I,[60] and then resurfaces in two rather exceptional marriage agreements from fourth century Susa, the Persian royal court in Elam, involving Egyptians couples.[61] These *biblu*s consisted of silver and/or jewellery, and were transferred to the agent of the bride. Yet, at least two of these texts[62] clarify that this payment did not remain with the family of the bride but was transferred to her (and her husband) upon marriage, together with the dowry. The *biblu*, therefore, does not qualify as bridewealth. Rather, it should be seen as a personal endowment to the bride and her new household. It represents a marriage gift that is referred to as an 'indirect dowry' in anthropology.[63] It is not impossible that the presentation of the *biblu*, perhaps as a betrothal gift, was part of a marriage celebration, in which case these endowments could have had a distinct symbolic character. This may also have been the case in the marriage contract of ᶠNanāya-kānat, written in the Judean settlement of Āl-Yahūdu, and published by K. Abraham 2005/2006. The text states that her husband covers his mother-in-law with a garment worth of five shekels of silver (ll. 19–22). While this gesture is found in only one other marriage agreement – the lack of family names and the absence of a dowry allows us to situate this alliance among the lower stratum of Sippar's community – it is occasionally found in other legal transactions such as adoptions and house sales.[64]

extensive study of marriage practices, and in particular the use of marriage gifts in ancient Palestine can be found in Lemos 2010.

58 Waerzeggers 2001.

59 See Roth 1989 for a study of Babylonian marriage agreements.

60 BM 64195+ has been published in Waerzeggers 2001. For a full edition and study of the Ṣāhit-ginê family archive, see Waerzeggers 2014.

61 TEBR 93/94 and TEBR 78a edited by Joannès 1984: 71ff., and re-edited by Roth 1989 no. 34 and no. 35 respectively. Cf. the discussion of these contracts by Abraham 1992, Waerzeggers 2001, and Abraham 2005/2006: 204. See Joannès 1990c for two further texts concerning the Egyptian community of Susa.

62 Unfortunately, the critical passage in TEBR 78a is broken.

63 The term was first coined by J. Goody in Goody and Tambiah 1973: 2, and refers to a marriage gift presented by the (family of the) groom to the bride, or her agent who subsequently returns it to her as part of, or, as supplement to her dowry. See also Lemos 2010 for a survey of this practice in Ancient Near Eastern marriage.

64 The marriage agreement BM 59584 has been published by Wunsch 2003: no. 1. For the act of presenting a garment in other legal contexts see, for example, Wunsch 2003: 9f., Abraham 2005/2006: 204.

Abraham offers two interpretations. Based on the endowment of garments in other legal contexts, she suggests that the provision in ᶠNanāya-kānat's marriage contract may signify 'a symbolic act whose purpose was to motivate the bride's mother to relinquish the rights over her daughter'.[65] Alternatively, the garment might have functioned as indirect dowry (similar to the *biblu*), which was only presented to the bride upon marriage. This interpretation may be supported by the fact that the garment is referred to as the 'ZI-IN-DI' of ᶠNanāya-kānat (l. 21). While its exact meaning escapes us, Abraham's different interpretations of the term all imply that the gift was ultimately destined for the bride.[66]

A final text that should be mentioned here is *Nbk* 101, the marriage contract of Dāgil-ilī and ᶠLā-tubāšinni.[67] It is said that the latter's mother who came from established Babylonian descent received a slave, worth 30 shekels of silver, and an additional 30 shekels as compensation (*kūm*) for her daughter. This time there are no allusions that the gift was destined for the bride upon marriage. While it therefore appears that Dāgil-ilī offered bridewealth to his mother-in-law, C. Wunsch has come up with a different interpretation (2003/2004: 189). Placing this contract in its archival context, she showed that we are not dealing with a genuine marriage agreement as much as a 'Quasi-Verkauf zur Sklavin'.[68] ᶠLā-tubāšinni was an adoptive daughter who was supposed to take care of her mother in old age. By offering a slave and silver (worth a total of 60 shekels of silver), Dāgil-ilī not only bought out ᶠLā-tubāšinni,[69] but also provisioned his 'mother-in-law' with sufficient funds and manpower to see to her maintenance in future years. Moreover, the fact that some thirty years later ᶠLā-tubāšinni went to court to contest the (unfree) status of her children suggests that by the time of her marriage she was considered unfree herself.[70]

In summary, even though marriage gifts presented by the groom to the family of the bride, and perhaps even genuine bridewealth, were not unknown among Babylonia's lower strata and foreign minorities, it seems to have played no part at all in Babylonian priestly or elite marriages. In these social circles marriage was fully asymmetric and only knew a one-directional transfer of a bride and property in the form of a dowry to the household of the groom.[71]

65 Abraham 2005/2006: 204.
66 Abraham 2005/2006: 205.
67 Edited both by Roth 1989: no. 4 and Wunsch 1997/1998: no. 1.
68 Wunsch 2003/2004: 189.
69 Note that according to BM 61737, 1 mina of silver is exactly the amount an adoptive daughter needs to pay when leaving her mother, see Wunsch 2003/2004: no. 8.
70 For a discussion and edition of ᶠLā-tubāšinni's court case, see Wunsch 1997/1998: 62–67, 75–77.
71 Note that the use of dowry has been associated with societies that knew a high level of stratification, while bridewealth is often found in societies with minimal social

However, more evidence can be gathered on the dyadic level, that is, between any two nodes in the network. The second and more important argument concerns the (temple) status of marriage partners. If one compares the status of intermarrying families with the religious hierarchy of the temple, an interesting pattern emerges. From the eighty-one marriages incorporated in this study, it transpires that priestly families of lower rank often provided brides to families affiliated to more senior priesthoods. Hence, daughters of the Oxherd family married sons from barber and temple-enterer families,[72] while prebendary bakers and butchers provided wives to families belonging to the ranks of brewers and temple-enterers.[73] The same pattern prevails in marriages with families outside of the prebendary circle. Non-priestly clans usually acted as wife-givers of priestly ones. For example, the Nūr-Papsukkals (temple-enterer) married a daughter from the Barihi clan, the Bēliya'u (baker) family received a bride from the Ṣillāyas, and a man from the Atkuppu (reed-worker) family married a woman from the Adad-nāṣir clan.[74] All this points to a tendency among the well-born women of Borsippean families to marry men of higher (temple) status. However, I showed at the beginning of this chapter that there are many alliances between families with the same professional affiliation (43%). This happened, for example, within the ranks of bakers (e.g. Bēliya'u ∞ Esagil-mansum), brewers (e.g. Ilia ∞ Ilšu-abūšu), and temple-enterers (e.g. Arkāt-ilāni-damqā ∞ Iddin-Papsukkal). While this is at odds with what has been observed so far, taking a closer look at the families concerned and examining their role in the temple (and civic) institution(s) reveals that this distinct marriage pattern was usually maintained in one way or another. Hence, the Bēliya'u family held the prestigious position of overseer (*šāpiru*) of the bakers, while the Esagil-mansums remained of subsidiary importance in this line of work.[75] Whereas no less than four city governors (*šākin-ṭēmi*) and four chief temple administrators (*šatammu*) had risen from the ranks of the Ilia clan, the Ilšu-abūšu family had only occupied the post of royal commissioner (*qīpu*) once.[76] A similar story holds true for the last

stratifications, according to the ethnographic record, cf. Goody and Tambiah 1973, Goody 1990, Lemos 2010.

72 For example, the Rē'i-alpi family provided wives to the Gallābu (barber), Kudurrānu (brewer), and Arkāt-ilāni-damqā (temple-enterer) families. See Appendix 1.5b.

73 For example, both the Ibnāya (butcher) and Kidin-Sîn (baker) families gave daughters in marriage to Kidin-Nanāya (temple-enterer). See Appendix 1.1b. The Ilias (brewers) received a wife from the Esagil-mansum family (baker). See Appendix 1.2b.

74 Nūr-Papsukkal ∞ Barihi (Appendix 1.1c), Bēliya'u ∞ Ṣillāya (Appendix 1.3c), and Atkuppu ∞ Adad-nāṣir (Appendix 1.6).

75 See Introduction 7.3.

76 Waerzeggers 2010: 65ff. The *qīpu* from the Ilšu-abūšu family is mentioned in two texts: VS 6 155 (Dar 29), and TEBR 80 (Dar x). It should be noted that, while the *qīpu* did enjoy a

marriage partners: with no less than seven city governors, including an alliance with the royal family of Neriglissar, and five temple-enterers, the Arkāt-ilāni-damqā family can be identified as the ranking marriage partner compared to the Iddin-Papsukkals, who could only boast one city governor and one chief temple administrator during the long sixth century.[77] It is thus possible to conclude that in the marriage system of Borsippa lower status brides married higher status grooms. In other words, wife-givers were of lower status vis-à-vis their wife-takers. The status difference between marriage partners conforms to the purity-based hierarchy of the temple, which served as guiding principle in this local alliance system. While these assertions apply to most parts of the network, there are some notable exceptions to the rule. Hence, one can find various marriages between lower status men and higher status women, as well as alliances between families of seemingly identical (temple) status. These apparent inconsistencies in the local marriage system of Borsippa are addressed below (Chapter 1.5).

The third argument pointing to a status difference between wife-giver and wife-taker involves what might be called the reiteration of hierarchy. We have just seen that once a certain hierarchy was established between a wife-giver and wife-taker family this was never violated. However, there is evidence that some families repeated the marriage alliances in succeeding generations, thus reaffirming the status difference over a longer period of time.[78]

Finally, there is also evidence from outside the realm of marriage proper that testifies to the wife-givers' subordinate status in Borsippa. Following several well-documented cases, it appears that the family of the wife-giver took up a supporting, perhaps even subservient, role in the temple service of the clan to which it had given a bride.[79] This dynamic also affected the patterns of

---

great authority in the temple as royal representative, he stood outside of the priesthood and did not enjoy religious authority, see Bongenaar 1997: 34ff. and Kleber 2008: 26–27. For the interaction of the *qīpu* with his colleagues in the temple, see Levavi 2018.

77 Waerzeggers 2010: 65ff.

78 Ea-ilūtu-bani ∞ Ilī-bāni 3x (Appendix 1.1a) and Ilia ∞ Ilšu-abūšu 4x (Appendix 1.2a).

79 The effects of the wife-givers and wife-takers relation on the cultic organisation of the temple is examined in detail in Chapter 1.6. The phenomenon of rendering services in exchange for a bride is called 'brideservice' by anthropologists, see Goody 1990: 347ff. The concept of labour in return for marriage is not unknown in the Ancient Near East, though usually involves an obligation from the side of the husband, i.e. the wife-taker. Examples of this can be found in Genesis 29: 15–30 where Jacob has to work seven years for each of his two wives, Leah and Rachel. Similarly, I Samuel 18:25 tells us that Saul promised to give his daughter in marriage to David on the condition that he fights in his army and collect one hundred Philistinian foreskins. It should be noted, however, that brideservice was not a common marriage gift in ancient Palestine, see Lemos 2010: 45.

tenancy and the sales of property among some prebendary groups (Chapter 2.2 and Chapter 2.3).

The features of the network observed so far would suggest that we are dealing with a hypergamous marriage system. In its ideal form, however, this system dictates that individuals, families or groups giving brides are inferior to those receiving them. In other words, women have to marry up. Since this is not always the case in our data we cannot speak of a strict form of hypergamy in Borsippa. We shall return to this matter later in this section (Chapter 1.5).

Let us now turn to the transitivity of this network. While reciprocity was the key to Lévi-Strauss' alliance theory, scholars have noted that some communities adhere to marriage systems of a fundamentally non-reciprocal nature[80] as did the Borsippean priesthood. I have already shown that the marriage settlement itself was asymmetric, and that there were no cases of direct reciprocity on the dyadic level between two intermarried families, i.e. wife-exchange. The network, however, carries a more fundamental quality. If we take a closer look at the network, pick a random family as a starting point, and follow the chains of alliances as indicated by the arrows, we soon realise that not one single chain goes back to its starting point. Hence, cycles, also referred to as close loops or walks, are completely absent. In keeping with social network analysis, we can describe this network as acyclic.[81] This implies that the marriage system of our priests was strictly and entirely non-reciprocal. This, I argue, results from the transitive nature of the hierarchy established between wife-givers and wife-takers upon marriage.

According to the Oxford English Dictionary, a (logical or mathematical) relation is described as transitive 'if [a relation] holds between a first and second item, and also between the second and a third, it necessarily holds between the first and the third'.[82] To give a basic example, if A is smaller (taller, smarter, faster, etc.) than B, and B is smaller than C, then A is automatically smaller than C too.[83] I show that the marriage system of the priests was regulated by this concept of transitivity and illustrate its impact on the choice of marriage partners by considering a specific alliance cluster on the *triadic* level of the network, that is between any three nodes; in this case involving the Ilī-bāni ('A'), Ea-ilūtu-bani ('B'), and Huṣābu ('C') families.

---

80 See, for example, Parkin 1990, Hage and Harary 1996.

81 See, for example, Hage and Harary 1983: 80ff., Wasserman and Faust 1994: 119, 234–248, and Newman 2010: 6.4.2.

82 Oxford English Dictionary 1989, volume XVIII, p. 407, s.v. 'transitive'.

83 See for the application of this form of transitivity in human society, Hage and Harary 1983: 71ff. and Hage and Harary 1996. It should not be confused with the concept of transitivity usually found in SNA literature where it refers to the measure of the completeness of relational triads, cf. Wasserman and Faust 1994: 243ff. and Newman 2010: 7.9.

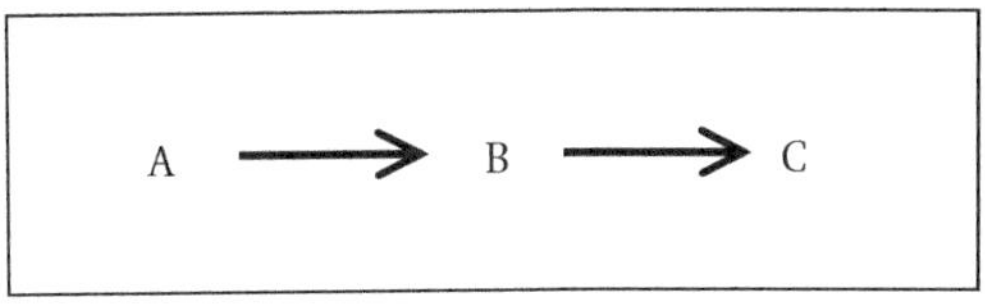

FIGURE 7 Relative marriage hierarchy

The first marriage in this cluster was arranged between the Huṣābu and Ea-ilūtu-bani families.[84] Since the Huṣābu clan received the bride it became the wife-taker and the superior party. In subsequent years the Ea-ilūtu-bani family widened its horizon and started to ally with the Ilī-bānis.[85] The Ea-ilūtu-bani family secured altogether three wives from this clan and their alliance became one of the strongest in our network. As a result, Ilī-bāni was the wife-giver of Ea-ilūtu-bani, and Ea-ilūtu-bani was the wife-giver of Huṣābu, which resulted in the following relative ranking from bottom to top (see figure 7 above).

In the final marriage of this cluster, which happened some years later, the Huṣābus received a bride from the Ilī-bāni family.[86] The latter had thereby 'jumped' over the Ea-ilūtu-banis while abiding by the correct marriage direction up the established hierarchy. This example shows that in Borsippa the sense of inferiority was imputed not only to direct wife-givers, but also to a family's wife-giver's wife-givers. In other words, the marriage hierarchy was of a transitive nature.

The transitive hierarchy made it impossible or presumably inappropriate for the Huṣābu family to present a bride to the Ilī-bānis, a family of lower marital status, but it was possible to receive one, since this did not violate the established hierarchy (see figure 8). The marriage cluster I just discussed is only one example in a network that is in fact made up of a number of overlapping acyclic sub-structures; families could be and often were involved in several of these chains simultaneously. Note for example the series of marriages between:

Esagil-mansum → Paḫḫāru → Arkāt-ilāni-damqā → Ilia

From the latter's perspective this entire chain of families was excluded as potential wife-takers, but not as wife-givers. Hence, the Esagil-mansum family could and eventually did ally with the Ilia by giving them a daughter in

84 BM 82640 = AH XV no. 45 (534 BCE), see Appendix 1.1b.
85 TCL 13 174 (524 BCE), see Appendix 1.1a.
86 NBC 8404 (518 BCE). See Appendix 1.1b.

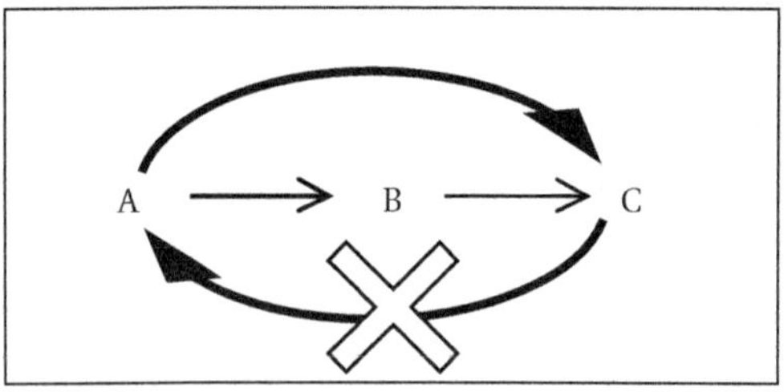

FIGURE 8 Transitive hierarchy

marriage.[87] The Ilia and the Esagil-mansum families were also involved as wife-givers in an acyclic marriage chain with Bēliya'u.

In conclusion, we can remark that from the viewpoint of the wife-taker it was undesirable to give brides to any direct or indirect wife-giver, i.e. to marry against the hierarchy. While this is clearly a negative rule, transitivity also had a positive side: families were in general free to arrange marriages with any party as long as it was oriented up the established hierarchy. A marriage system of this kind unavoidably assumes the form of a ladder, yet a ladder in which it was possible to jump over the next step as long as it was a higher one. It should be noted that the concept of transitivity is, again, one that is usually associated with hypergamous marriage systems in the anthropological literature.[88]

5 Hypergamy in Historical Context

In the previous paragraphs I demonstrated that the marriage system of wife-givers and wife-takers involved status differences and relative hierarchies. Wife-takers took precedence over wife-givers but were themselves outranked by their own wife-takers. We came across various features that encourage an interpretation of this system as a hypergamous marriage system: the superior position of the wife-taker, the asymmetric matrimonial flow, a non-reciprocal alliance system and a transitive hierarchy. However, while the status difference between wife-givers and wife-takers often conformed to the purity-based hierarchy of the temple, not all priestly marriages seem to have followed this example. Is there a way to explain these exceptions?

87 Appendix 1.2b.
88 Parkin 1990.

One of the best-known examples of a hypergamous marriage system is found in the Kangra District in northwest India.[89] Research has shown that communities in this region were (and often still are) strongly divided along caste lines and ranked according to a principle of relative purity (or impurity). An important stimulus in this alliance system is the desire to give an unsolicited gift, the most prestigious one being the 'gift of a maiden' (see Chapter 1.2), to a spiritual (caste) superior, in order to improve one's own status in the present and the following life as well as that of one's children. As in the marriage system of Borsippa's priestly community, the hierarchy in this Indian society assumes the form of an open-ended ladder. Scholars have, however, not failed to note that this ideal hypergamous system entails some serious (demographic) flaws that can only be neutralised by a violation of the preferential rules of marriage and its hierarchy.[90]

It is unavoidable that in a system of obligatory and pervasive hypergamy, in which women are obliged to marry up, an excess of 'unmarriageable' men forms at the foot of the hierarchical ladder and of women at its summit: whom do daughters of the highest group marry and where do the sons of the lowest group find their brides? Hypergamy gives rise to so-called bottlenecks. In order to countervail these congestions, communities must and have been known to resort to various compromising strategies. Several ethnographies show that a breaking down of the endogamous unit by marrying inferior women from outside the caste system is often detected among the lower fringes, whereas superior groups at the top of the ladder preferred polygamy or resorted to more drastic measures like female infanticide.[91] Other examples from the ethnographic record include prolonged celibacy and marriage among equals. I argue that similar, but not the same, dynamics of adjustment can account for exceptions encountered in Borsippa's marriage network. In order to do this, we need to take into account the historical context of this community and its alliance system.

Among Ancient Near Eastern historians there is the general idea that the first quarter of the first millennium was a formative period for Babylonian society presented in the documentation from the long sixth century, the period subject to our study.[92] Not unlike various long-term economic and social processes – most notably, the widespread adoption of family names – also the religious, purity-based hierarchy of the temple originated in the centuries prior

89 Parry 1979. Cf. Quigley 1993: 87ff.

90 See, for example, Parkin 1990, Goody 1990: 216–127, and Quigley 1993: 87–101.

91 Dumont 1970: 118, Parry 1979: 214, 218, 244, Parkin 1990: 475, and Goody 1990: 214–219.

92 See, for example, van Driel 2002, Jursa *et al.* 2010, and Nielsen 2011.

to our documentation, presumably when families were presented with land rights and specific temple functions by various early kings.[93] That these rights could be renegotiated, reshuffled and reinstalled by royal involvement, is exemplified by the reinstallation of the priesthood of the oxherds in the seventh century, probably by the Assyrian King Esarhaddon.[94] However, evidence from Borsippa suggests that the Ezida temple already knew an elaborate administration and organisation, and thus a religious hierarchy during the eighth century BCE.[95] It seems only reasonable to develop this line of thought and argue that the marriage system reconstructed in this chapter was already in place for a considerable amount of time prior to our documentation. The network therefore represents a well-developed stage of the marriage system. If so, one might think that in the early days the priestly community of Borsippa practiced a 'clean' form of hypergamy, but before long, the priestly clans must have faced the inevitable bottlenecks inherent in the system.

The unions between temple-enterer women and men from brewer clans represent the first series of marriages that contradict the rules of a clean hypergamous marriage model in long sixth century.[96] Not unlike various high caste families in India, it seems that relatively early on the temple-enterers of Borsippa had troubles finding suitable partners for their daughters and had to make a concession. The temple-enterers' reaction was apparently to marry their daughters to the group that occupied the rung just below them in the temple hierarchy, i.e. the brewers. A seemingly natural consequence of this intermarriage was that the relative status of the brewers increased over time.[97] The positions of the chief temple administrator (*šatammu*) and city governor (*šākin-ṭēmi*) can be used as status indicators of the families concerned. While in the earlier periods these positions were manned solely by temple-enterers,[98] already during the early seventh century the position of city governor was occupied by a descendant of Ilia, a family of brewers *pur sang*, just like the

93 See, for example, van Driel 2002: 67–75, Paulus 2014: 79ff., and Nielsen and Waerzeggers 2016.

94 SAA 10 no. 353 and Waerzeggers 2010: 281–283. King Nebuchadnezzar also praises himself in his inscription for having appointed new fishermen for the regular offerings of the god Marduk in Babylon (Langdon 1912: Nbk no. 19, ll. 14–17).

95 VS 1 36, a mid-eighth century *kudurru*, is our primary source on the organisation of the Ezida temple and the composition of the priesthoods during that time. It mentions various temple-enterers, a temple administrator, a cultic singer, and the overseers of the brewers, bakers, and butchers. Cf. Thureau-Dangin 1919 and Paulus 2014: 683–688.

96 Appendix 1.1b.

97 Note again that Parry 1979: 204ff. observed a very similar dynamic among the highest Rajput castes in the Kangra region.

98 Waerzeggers 2010: 66–73.

position of the chief temple administrator in the late seventh century.[99] Not only did the (relative) position of the brewer increase over time, but, by marrying their daughters to lower status groups the temple-enterers were in a sense placing themselves on the same level – this resulted in a flattening of the top of the hierarchy. One might imagine that it changed from figure 1 (Introduction 6) into something like the 'status ladder' of figure 9 (below).

That this dynamic did not only affect the position of the brewers but also of the butchers and perhaps the bakers can be deduced from the fact that in the sixth century the position of city governor was temporarily in the hands of Ibnāya, a prominent family of butchers.[100] Needless to say, this marital counter-measure clearly had more profound ramifications in the community.

More extreme examples of inverse hierarchical marriages, like the union between the relatively low-ranking oxherds and temple-enterers or brewers, can be explained by considering the position of the families in question. Hence, while the latter were ideologically of superior status, the specific families who acted as wife-givers seem not to have had a very strong tradition in Borsippa or had lost their standing in the community and their influence in the temple organisation. For instance, by the time they allied with the Oxherds, the Arad-Ea

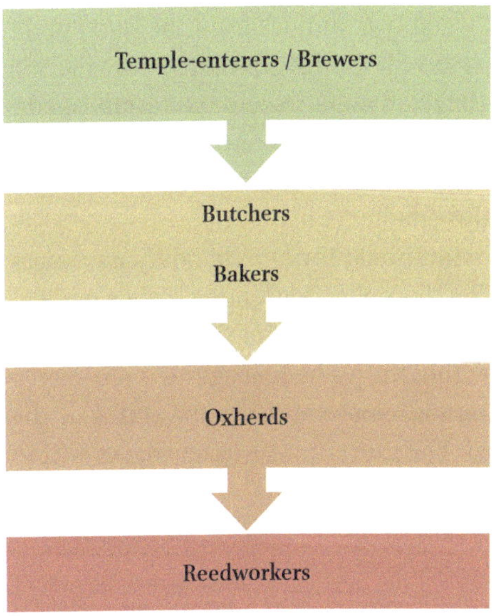

FIGURE 9 Flattening of relative social hierarchy

99 Frame 1984.
100 Zadok 2005a: 638 and Waerzeggers 2010: 68.

(temple-enterer) and the Ardūtu (brewer) families were no more than minor clans of peripheral status in Borsippa's priestly community.[101]

Another trend that might reflect an adjustment of the ideal hypergamous system involves intra-prebendary marriages. I have said at the beginning of this chapter that most marriages (43%) were arranged within the professional prebendary group. While these speak against a strict hypergamous model, I was able to show that a relative hierarchy was still maintained in marriage alliances, at least judging from a number of well-attested cases.[102] However, the status difference between wife-givers and wife-takers is certainly not always clear-cut. Again, the Indian caste system can help us come to grips with this state of affairs. Traditional Indian society was theoretically and on a scriptural level hierarchised according to four *varṇa*s, but reality has revealed that communities were (and often still are) hierarchised in castes (*jāti*), sub-castes, sub-sub-castes, etc. whose internal ranking was far from static but fragile, fluid, and constantly re-negotiated.[103] Perhaps one should envisage a similar reality for the Borsippean priestly community. While on an ideological level it was hierarchised according to professional groups and their relative status of purity in the temple, hierarchy permeated the individual priesthoods too, pinning every prebendary group, clan and if necessary even individual lineage on its place on the ladder. If the status difference between two families from the same prebendary group was not clear or yet unresolved, it might have been the marital union itself that triggered or resolved the relative status, and thus established a new, or delineate firmly a pre-existing, hierarchy between wife-giver and wife-taker. Evidence supporting this can be found in the organization of the temple cult, discussed in the final section of this chapter (Chapter 1.6).

An alternative explanation of the widespread intra-prebendary marriages could be that it constituted a sort of collective policy. Marrying a higher-ranking family did not only determine one's own status but also that of the professional group at large. While marriage within the prebendary group presumably increased the stratification of the internal hierarchy, it left the status of the group with regard to others untouched. The same applies to marriages within

101 Appendix 1.5b. Note that while a member of the Arad-Ea family occupied the post of royal commissioner (*qīpu*) of the Esagil temple in Babylon around Dar 29 (VS 6 155), and another member had been appointed as 'canal inspector' (*gugallu*) of Borsippa around the same time (VS 6 160), the family had married their daughter to the Rē'i-alpis at least three decades earlier. Moreover, this family is only very rarely attested in the Borsippa corpus.

102 See Chapter 1.4.

103 See, for example, Flood 1996: 58ff.

the clan, be it on an even lower level.[104] This strategy in a sense stabilised the overall hierarchy. It might not be a coincidence that we find a repetition of intra-prebendary marriage alliances precisely among temple-enterers and brewers, the two highest prebendary groups.

A final strategy that may have been introduced to alleviate the constraints of the hypergamous model was intermarriage with outsiders. While this can be observed throughout the prebendary group,[105] it is perhaps most distinguishable among the lower ranking priesthoods. Hence, the only family known to have given a wife to the Reed-workers is the Adad-nāṣir family, a clan with no priestly affiliation. At least three of the marriage partners of the Rē'i-alpi family can be designated as outsiders: whereas the Šarrahu and the ᶠMaqartu families lacked a temple background, the Rišāya family is so far only attested as priests in the neighbouring town of Dilbat. The latter may therefore also have been outsiders in a real geographical sense.[106] While the evidence is admittedly limited, it might indicate that there was a (greater) tendency among lower-fringe families to welcome outsiders into the alliance system. This is supported by the ethnographic record from India where a similar dynamic is found especially among lower-caste families.[107]

In the end, if we take into account the fact that status differences existed not only *between* prebendary groups but also *within*, then the overall ratio of hypergamous marriages to contra-hypergamous marriages is roughly seventy to thirty percent. Hence, the marriage pattern I have reconstructed for Neo-Babylonian Borsippa seems to have developed out of a traditional hypergamous alliance system, of which the basic outlines are still visible. One should also remember that the alliance system represents an organic entity that was maintained during the (oft-times turbulent) centuries of the first millennium BCE. The repeated wars, political alliances, and dynastic changes on the one hand and the later economic growth on the other hand must all have had their effects on the established social hierarchy more than once. Moreover, the prosperous times of the Neo-Babylonian Empire created ample possibilities for the entrepreneurial (middle) strata of society to rise in status,[108] while every change of leadership meant the potential end of a clan's leading position.[109]

104 Endogamous alliances within the kin-group are attested for the Banê-ša-ilia (VS 4 150), Basia (BM 21975), Ibnāya (VS 4 176), Ilia (BM 26544), Ilī-bāni (TuM 2/3 1), Kidin-Sin (BM 94697), Lā-kuppuru (BM 29385), and Nannāhu (VS 6 95) families.

105 Appendix 1.

106 For the Rišāya family from Dilbat, see Appendix 1.2c.

107 See Chapter 1.2, especially the literature found in footnote 36.

108 Beaulieu 2000.

109 See pp. 62–63. Cf. Jursa 2007.

Finally, adherence to the hypergamous ideal depended also on local demography. Not everyone could hope to marry off his or her daughter in this way, and it might at times have been difficult to find a suitable wife-taker or wife-giver in the immediate vicinity. No system could have persisted throughout the first millennium without adaptation. In this light, it is all the more remarkable that the hypergamous model is still very much intact in the Borsippean temple community of the long sixth century.

6 Wife-Givers and Wife-Takers in the Cult

While the temple hierarchy influenced the dynamics of marriage within the community, serving as an important guiding principle in the alliance system, I already hinted that the relative hierarchy between wife-givers and wife-takers also had consequences for the organisation and execution of the temple service.

The usual practice concerning the temple service was that the priest who had certain duties in the liturgy performed this himself. In the case of the purveying priesthoods, the temple service included a preparatory assignment like brewing or baking, as well as participation in the daily sacrificial ceremonies performed in more holy spaces near to the cellae of the gods.[110] A priest, however, could choose to relinquish the obligations resting on his prebend, and was required to do so in case of sickness and other physical or mental impairments that made him unsuitable to perform his temple service.[111] For this purpose priests could lease parts or the entirety of their prebend to deputies in exchange for a fixed rent.[112] This employment was regulated with a legal contract whose formulary could be easily adapted to specific circumstances and needs.[113] A recurring characteristic in these contracts is the use of the expression *ana ēpišānūtu*, literally 'for the performance of'. I therefore speak of 'performance contracts'.[114]

110 Waerzeggers 2010.

111 Waerzeggers 2010: 291f.

112 Jursa 1999: 44–52, van Driel 2002: 138–140, and Waerzeggers 2010: 173–185.

113 Jursa 2005: 34–35 and Waerzeggers 2010: 176f.

114 Note that the term *ēpišānūtu* is not found in all service contracts. Internal information in these contracts on for example the required duties and fixed terms reveal however their true nature as performance contracts, *ēpišānūtu* contracts. Cf. van Driel 2002: 135–140, and Waerzeggers 2010: 173–185 for examples of formulaic variations. Performance contracts among the oxherds of Ezida usually refer to 'to stand service' (*manzaltu izuzzu*). See Waerzeggers 2010: 191f.

Assyriologists have often approached these performance contracts from a purely economic perspective. Deputies are perceived as entrepreneurs who welcomed the opportunity to assist in the temple service in return for an additional source of income, while priests are characterised as prebend owners who had little interest in performing the cultic task themselves.[115] However, it has been argued recently by C. Waerzeggers that cultic collaboration was not governed by opportunistic economic behaviour (2010: 180–185). By taking a closer look at the social profile of those involved in the temple service of the brewers of the Ezida temple, she showed that deputies were predominantly recruited from within the group of prebendary brewers; participation of outsiders was restricted to peripheral and menial tasks.[116] Hence, collaboration was largely based on professional affiliation. However, in the following I show that the specific dynamics of cultic organisation were also influenced by existing marriage alliances. It is in the context of these performance contracts that we can detect the effects that marriage had on the organisation of the temple. In order to do this, I examine several pairs of families for which we are particularly well informed in terms of both their marriage alliances and their collaboration in the cult.

The first case concerns the arrangements between the Ilia and Kudurrānu families, both prominent members of the brewers of Ezida. Taking a look at their history as collaborators in the cult it seems that from the reign of Nebuchadnezzar II (604–562 BCE) until 509 BCE the Ilia family always called upon the Kudurrānus for support in the temple service.[117] This relationship, however, suddenly reversed in 507 BCE. From that moment until the end of the documentation, the Ilias always performed the temple service of members from the Kudurrānu family.[118] An explanation for this change can be found once the performance contracts and their marriage alliance are placed side by side (see figure 10).

This swapping of roles coincided with a marriage between the Ilia family (wife-giver) and Kudurrānu family (wife-taker), arranged in the reign of Darius

115 See, for example, San Nicolò and Ungnad 1929: 495, McEwan 1981: 106–109, MacGinnis 1991: 76–78, Jursa 1999: 45, van Driel 2002: 138, and Jursa 2011: 163–164.

116 For a similar observation, see Kessler 1991: 62 who writes that 'Die Berechtigung zur Durchführung der Dienstschichten scheint ... einen kleinen Kreis privilegierten Personen übertragen gewesen sein'.

117 Jakob-Rost 1985 (between 604 and 562 BCE), BM 94738 = AH XV no. 11 (540 BCE), BM 94791 = AH XV no. 12 (between 555 and 529 BCE) and BM 94984 (509 BCE).

118 BM 95187 = AH XV no. 32 (506 BCE), Berens 106 (after 506 BCE), BM 82804 (503 BCE), BM 17695 = AH XV no. 38 (500 BCE), BM 26758 = AH XV no. 39 (499 BCE) and BM 94699 = AH XV no. 43 (between 506 and 486 BCE).

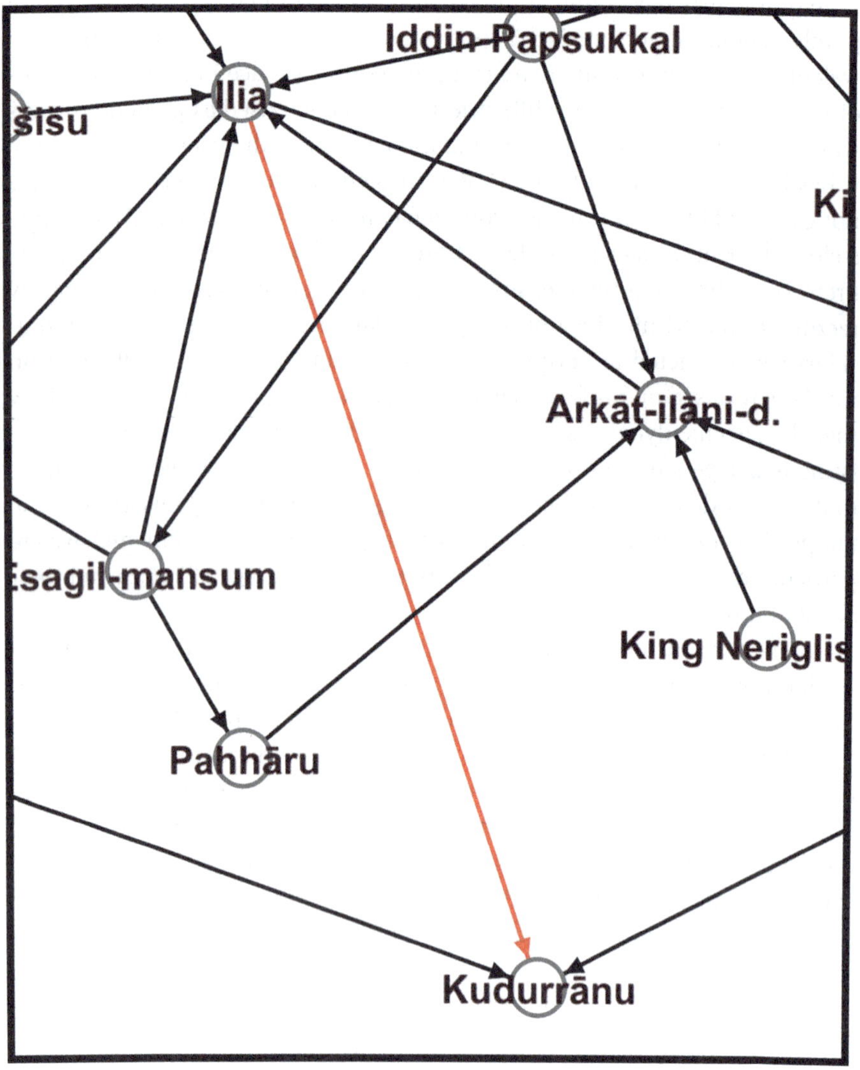

FIGURE 10 Marriage ties vs. temple service (1)

I (521–486 BCE).[119] While its precise date is unknown, a hint is provided by a contract dated 512 BCE that records the sale of two slaves between the father of the bride and his (future) son-in-law.[120] Slaves were common dowry components. It could, therefore, be argued that the marriage took place in that same year. The Ilia family would then have assumed the role of wife-giver in 512 BCE. Yet, the Kudurrānus only gave up their role as deputy in the temple

119 Appendix 1.2a.
120 BM 26543//BM 102293//EAH 220.

service after 509 BCE, suggesting that they performed the temple service of their (inferior) wife-giver for three years or so. At the same time, it should be noted that the sales contracts make no mention of the bride. This business affair might, for all we know, have been an early business encounter that eventually led to an alliance between these families. Moreover, performance contracts were legally binding contracts that bound the parties sometimes for a period of several years. One could not simply withdraw from this commitment. Some time could thus have elapsed before the role of wife-giver was mirrored in the performance contracts.

While one may question the causality between marriage and cultic support, and the significance of one marriage alliance as the sole factor in the matter, this is not the only case in which a marriage seemingly prompted a family of brewers to perform the temple service of its wife-taker (figure 11, below). It has been said earlier that the Ilia and Ilšu-abūšu clans engaged in repeated marriage alliances.[121] The first union was arranged in the early years of King Nabonidus (555–539 BCE). The daughter from the Ilšu-abūšu family is mentioned in the Ilia archive in 554 BCE, probably in relation to a field or house belonging to her dowry.[122] Although there is little documentation, it is significant that some ten years later the Ilšu-abūšu family performed the Ilias's temple service.[123] Another example involves the Kudurrānu and Ahiya'ūtu clans (figure 11). In 505 BCE the latter gave a daughter to the Kudurrānus in marriage.[124] Turning to their relationship in the context of the temple service one finds that it was always the Ahiya'ūtu, i.e. the wife-giver family, that lent a helping hand and never the other way around.[125]

While information on performance contracts for other priesthoods of Ezida is far less generous, the existing evidence points in the same direction. In 485 BCE, a member of the Esagil-mansum family received wages for having performed one full day of the baker prebend of the Bēliya'u clan.[126] Turning to their marriage records, it appears that the Bēliya'u family received a wife from the Esagil-mansums in the reign of Nabonidus, more than fifty years earlier (figure 11).[127] The Esagil-mansum family was thus not only the wife-giver but also the 'cultic-support-giver' of the Bēliya'u family.

The available evidence is relatively modest but suggestive nonetheless. There is no evidence that a wife-taker family ever performed its wife-giver

121 Appendix 1.2a.
122 BM 87267.
123 BM 24480 = AH XV no. 10.
124 Appendix 1.2a.
125 BM 94638 = AH XV no. 3, VS 6 115, and BM 82721.
126 BM 29234.
127 Appendix 1.3a.

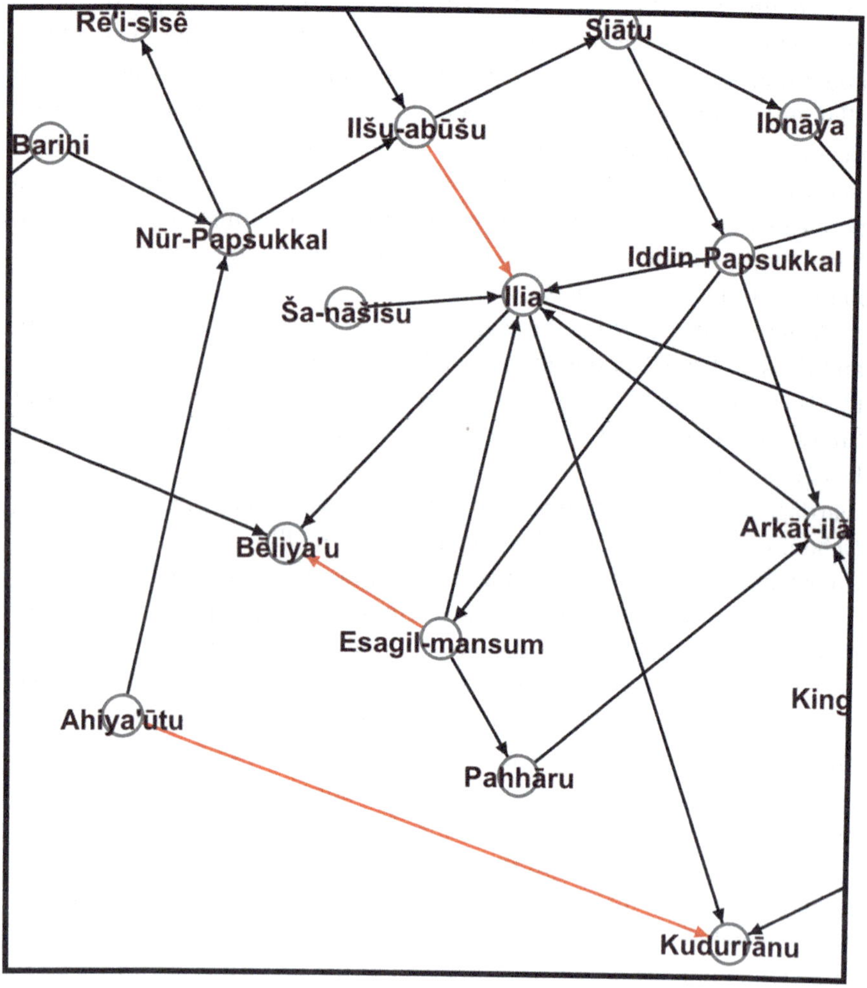

FIGURE 11 Marriage ties vs. temple service (2)

family's temple service after they arranged a marriage alliance. The opposite, however, is attested more than once. It seems that the unidirectional flow between wife-giver and wife-taker not only entailed a transfer of a bride and her dowry, but it could also result in a kind of service obligation. Once again one can turn to the ethnographic record of rural India for parallels. In Pandit society in northern India, the initiation of the relative status between wife-giver and wife-taker also gave the former specific ritual obligations regarding his wife-takers.[128]

128 Madan 1975: 304–305, Dumont 1983: 86–104, and Parkin 1990: 477.

A final aspect that should be mentioned here is the tentative confirmation of the transitivity of wife-giver/wife-takers hierarchy in the temple service. We have seen earlier that the entire marriage network was essentially made up of chains of wife-givers and wife-takers. A wife-taker took precedence over its direct and indirect wife-givers, which were all excluded as potential wife-takers. However, as these relations were transitive, it was possible to jump over one's direct wife-taker and ally with the wife-taker's wife-taker. This mechanism created the acyclic paths seen in our network. Let us take a final look at the relationship between the Ilšu-abūšu, the Ilia and the Huṣābu families as presented in the directed marriage graph of figure 6 (above). In light of the transitive wife-giver/wife-taker hierarchy, the two former families were inferior to the latter. The Ilia family was an indirect wife-giver of Huṣābu via the chain:

Ilia → Gallābu → Kidin-Sîn → Ea-ilūtu-bani → Huṣābu

The Ilšu-abūšu family via the same chain as well as via:

Ilšu-abūšu → Siātu → Iddin-Papsukkal → Ea-ilūtu-bani → Huṣābu

Turning to the performance contracts, it can hardly be a coincidence that precisely Ilšu-abūšu and Ilia are found performing the temple service of Huṣābu, and not vice versa.[129] The second example concerns the Ahiya'ūtu family, which is found performing the service of both the Ilšu-abūšu and the Ilia clans.[130] As is shown in the alliance network, the Ahiya'ūtu was an indirect wife-giver to both families via the chain:

Ahiya'ūtu → Nūr-Papsukkal → Ilšu-abūšu → Ilia

Once again, the evidence is modest but indicative: not only the relation between direct wife-givers and wife-takers but also the wider transitive mechanism of the marriage network influenced the cultic organisation of the Ezida temple. This would also explain why the Naggārus, a family with no links to the profession of the brewer, are attested as taking on performance duties of the Ilia clan.[131] For if we check the marriage alliance network one last time, it appears that the Naggāru family was indeed an indirect wife-giver of Ilia:

Naggāru → Ilšu-abūšu → Ilia

129 OECT 12 A 109 (Ilšu-abūšu) and TuM 2/3 207 (Ilia).
130 BM 96179 = AH XV no. 54 (Ilšu-abūšu) and BM 94793 (Ilia).
131 VS 6 139.

Conclusion

In this chapter I have investigated marriage alliances, the first type of social interaction in the priestly community of Borsippa. It offers the very first attempt to map out a Babylonian marriage network on any scale. Existing studies on marriage in Assyriology focus primarily on its philological and legal implications. However, it is apparent from the approach in this chapter that there is much to discover once we appreciate the social dynamics that surround Babylonian marriage.

The evidence that can be gathered from the descriptive-quantitative analysis (see Appendix 1) portrays the priesthood of Borsippa as a highly endogamous community. With more than eighty percent of the attested marriages arranged within the prebendary circle, it is clear that the Borsippean priests actively used marriage alliances to keep their ranks closed. A very important observation for the following investigation and the eventual reconstruction of this community is the fact that marriages with families from the lower strata of society, which are identified by the lack of family names, are completely absent. This gives us a first and very clear indication of how these priestly families perceived of and maintained themselves as an exclusive social unit in wider society.

In this chapter I investigated the underlying social mechanisms of this sacerdotal endogamy. In order to handle the complexity of the marriage alliances, I used social network analysis and converted the 81 unions into a directed graph. This resulted in a network that illustrates properties of a marriage system that are overlooked when considering the unions in isolation. In the jargon of graph theory, the marriage network appears to be entirely acyclic and transitive, thus revealing an alliance system that was non-reciprocal and hierarchised. In order to understand how these dynamics functioned in practice I borrowed the concept of wife-givers and wife-takers from the anthropological literature on kinship. This concept supposes that at the event of marriage the parties adopt two functions vis-à-vis each other, i.e. that of wife-giver and wife-taker. Ethnographic studies have revealed that in communities adhering to a non-reciprocal marriage system there is a probability that a relative status difference arises between wife-giver and wife-taker, a dynamic that I was also able to detect in Borsippa's priestly community.

The evidence from Borsippa suggests that wife-takers assumed the superior role. In marriages that exhibit a clear status difference between the family of the husband and the family of the wife, it is the latter, the wife-giver, that was of lower status according to the temple hierarchy. Another important feature of the priestly marriage system is its transitive mechanism. Once a wife-taker family received a bride, it never returned one to the wife-giver family. Moreover, not only the direct wife-giver was ruled out as receiver of brides but also the indirect wife-givers. Contra-hierarchical marriages seem to have been avoided. On the other hand, a wife-giver could ally with a once or twice removed wife-taker, since this did not run counter to the established transitive pecking order.

All the properties of the priestly marriage system that I was able to reconstruct match a specific type of alliance model known as hypergamy that is practiced, for example, in contemporary communities in northern India. In this system, which is highly informed by the Vedic religious ideology, wives should be of lower status than their husbands, i.e. wife-givers are inferior and women marry upward; marriage alliances involve a unilateral flow and are non-reciprocal; and there exists a transitive hierarchy that can be conceived of as an open-ended ladder. In an ideal Vedic hypergamous system, marriage does not so much trigger a relative hierarchy in itself but rather follows an existing hierarchy independent of the alliance system. In Borsippa, the likely candidate for such an external pecking order is the purity-based temple hierarchy. That this is indeed the conceptual context for the observed marriage pattern seems to be confirmed by placing the marriage system in its historical context and considering the practical shortcomings inherent to a hypergamous marriage model. The marriage system of the Borsippean priesthood came into being sometime in the early first millennium BCE, when the priestly families received their cultic rights in the form of royal sponsorship. In the early phase of the alliance system, marriage would have neatly followed the established temple hierarchy: priests offered their daughters in marriage to more senior colleagues. Sooner or later, however, the community faced the flaws of any hypergamous system when the daughters of the highest prebendary group had problems finding suitable husbands of superior status. Evidence suggests that they were married to men from the second highest group, thereby violating the desired hierarchy but limiting the damage to a minimum. This compromising marriage strategy resulted in a flattening of the hierarchy as the second highest group moved to the highest status level. There is evidence that the same dynamics affected the third-highest group. It should be stressed that this did not affect the purity-based temple hierarchy itself. Rather, it meant that high administrative offices at the temple and in the city became available to lower-ranking groups when they had previously been open only to the highest group of temple-enterers. Other marriage strategies have been observed too. While some groups contracted marriages within their prebendary group, resulting in an increasing internal stratification while stabilising the overall hierarchy at the same time, there is some evidence that among the lower priesthood outsiders were welcomed in the alliance system. The marriage network reconstructed for Neo-Babylonian Borsippa thus presents a well-developed stage of the original marriage system. This makes it all the more remarkable that the outlines of this traditional praxis are still very much visible in spite of the turbulent history of first millennium Babylonia.

For now, I conclude that the marriage practice of the Borsippean priesthood was in the first place regulated by the purity-based temple hierarchy. The quantitative analysis shows that following this hierarchy was the preferred direction of marriage. This was not done consistently, however. In cases in which families did not contract a hypergamous marriage, it might have been that the marriage itself demarcated a relative status difference, if one did not already exist that has simply not been revealed in the documentation. Why then would a family decide to collectively assume an inferior position on account of a single marriage alliance? The reasons might have ranged from the simple lack of suitable marriage partners to the pursuit of a different alliance strategy all together. The potential financial and/or social opportunities afforded by the wife-taker family's economic standing or political influence might at times have been more important than ideological considerations. I would thus argue that there were essentially two different hierarchies in practice: the temple hierarchy, independent of marriage (but presenting the ideal blueprint), and the wife-giver/wife-taker's hierarchy, dependent on marriage. While ideally governed by the ideology of ritual purity, marriage also left its mark on the temple organisation itself. Marriage did not only entail a movement of brides and property in the form of the dowry, but also of labour in the form of cultic support. This was exclusively and without exception provided by the wife-giver.

It is in the light of the relative inferiority of wife-givers and the obligations assigned to them that the marriage mentioned at the very beginning of this chapter, the marriage between King Neriglissar's daughter and the chief temple administrator (*šatammu*) of the Ezida, becomes even more controversial. Not only was a marriage alliance between the royal house and the local urban population unheard of in the first millennium BCE, this royal favouritism, in this case towards the Arkāt-ilāni-damqā family, must surely have upset the social stratification of the local priestly community in unprecedented ways. More significantly, it might have raised some serious ideological questions. By offering his daughter in marriage to the chief administrator of the temple, King Neriglissar entered the local alliance system as a wife-giver. Did this not make the royal family inferior to the Arkāt-ilāni-damqā and all its wife-takers according to the customs and regulations of this hypergamous system? If so, then how was this expressed? It is unlikely that we will ever be able to solve these questions. The puzzling circumstances of Neriglissar's son-in-law soon after the wedding[132] and the high-profile case in which he was forced to give up property immediately following the fall of this royal dynasty[133] suggest that the new administration of King Nabonidus and perhaps the local community were eager to undo the arrangements of this controversial alliance.

---

132 Only several months later a certain Rēmūt-Bēl//Ilia had replaced him as chief temple administrator (*šatammu*) of Ezida. See Waerzeggers 2010: 72.

133 For the text in question, HSM 1895.1.1, see Zadok 2005a: 649–650. A committee of judges, a palace scribe, and an agent of the *sukallu*-official attended the transaction. Note that his brother, Mušēzib-Marduk, already sold a house to a royal merchant in BM 85364 (Ner 03).

CHAPTER 2

Landholding

This chapter deals with land ownership in the priestly community of Borsippa. In M. Jursa's words, land constituted the 'second pillar of the subsistence strategy of priests' after prebends.[1] As a result, it represented a major income-producing asset for this social group. In the following, I examine the complex relationship between the priestly families and their landholdings. Rather than examine its economic and monetary value, however, I explore the function of land ownership in the social organisation of this community.

How should we imagine the rural environment of Borsippa? Based on the information contained in the private archives, R. Zadok (2006) described the local countryside as a fertile and water-abundant region, featuring a belt of marshes surrounding the city, fed by several branches of the Euphrates river, such as the Arahtu, Pallukkatu, and Borsippa canals.[2] These conditions allowed for an intensive agricultural regime, geared largely toward date palm cultivation, while the marshland provided pasture for raising cattle.[3] Concentrated mainly in the north, around the Borsippa-Babylon axis, the city's hinterland was divided into various agricultural sub-sectors and irrigation districts, dotted with a large number of farms and villages, and crisscrossed by a network of watercourses and land roads.

Besides the occasional references to crown and temple estates,[4] the archives inform us, above all, of privately-owned land. Private land in Borsippa can be divided into two types: on the one hand, non-specified land that was identified on the basis of its geographic features or location and, on the other hand, land that was part of a so-called 'fifty' (*hanšû*). Much of the land owned by priestly families belonged to such *hanšû* units, which structured large parts of the green belt around the city. This chapter is therefore primarily devoted to a study of *hanšû* land.

My investigation unfolds in three parts, each part focusing on a different aspect of land ownership in Borsippa's priestly community. In Part 2.1. I start with a discussion of the historical origins of *hanšû* land in Borsippa. Based on

1 Jursa 2011: 187.
2 Zadok 2006. Cf. Cole 1994a, Cole and Gasche 1998: 51, Jursa 2004b, and Jursa *et al.* 2010: 360ff.
3 Zadok 2006: 391.
4 Zadok 2006: 447–449.

 | DOI:10.1163/9789004399969_004

administrative documents as well as literary texts, I show that *hanšû* land had a long history in Borsippa and originated as royal land grants in the eighth century BCE. After discussing the historical roots of the system, I reconstruct the identity of the schemes' first beneficiaries on the basis of the naming patterns of the *hanšû* estates. This sheds light on a large number of non-priestly families that have remained largely outside of our investigation so far. In the last section of Part 2.1, I assess the value the *hanšû* estates held for the descendants of the original beneficiaries during the long sixth century.

In Part 2.2. I turn to sales of *hanšû* land and real estate more generally. The primary aim is to examine whether any limitations of a social kind rested on selling and buying land in the priestly community of Borsippa. In particular, I reveal the subtle ways in which two major principles of social organisation in this priestly group, marriage and solidarity, influenced the circulation of land.

In the final Part 2.3. I take a closer look at tenancy and agricultural collaboration. Since much of their energy was presumably devoted towards their cultic duties and other affairs in town, many priests outsourced cultivation to others. By analysing the identity of tenants in conjunction with the identity of the landowners, new light can be shed on interfamily relations and the social organisation of the priestly community.

1 *Hanšû* Estates and the Ancestral Family

Evidence from various cities in the alluvium suggests that *hanšû* land, literally 'fifty'-land,[5] came into the possession of Babylonian families, and to a lesser extent into that of the temple institutions, as a result of land allotment schemes and related agricultural projects implemented by various kings of the past. The venerable history of this land, its distinct mode of identification, and its exceptional visibility in our sources suggest that it formed a crucial component in shaping the urban (priestly) elite in first millennium Babylonia. While it provided its owners with a stable source of income, *hanšû* land, perhaps more importantly, helped to underpin the social identity of the land-holding clans. It allowed them to lay claim to a share in the local topography, while at the same time tying them firmly into a shared local history.

In the following pages I trace the historical origins of landownership in Borsippa to the eighth century BCE and consider possible motivations behind the royal land grants. In order to better understand the function and impact of

5 Written 50^{e}, $50^{ú}$ or $50^{e/ú.meš}$.

these grants on the local community, I closely examine the evidence on the schemes' first beneficiaries contained in the naming patterns of the estates. This reveals that as the institution came into being, not only priests, but also many other segments from the urban elite benefited from these royal endowments. As a result, the local countryside turned into a stage where priests had to interact, cooperate, and compete with other sections of society that are too often left invisible in our priest-centred documentation. Interestingly, the *hanšû* institution turns out to constitute the single most important source of information on a large number of families that, while belonging to the local upper stratum, has remained largely outside of our purview. Based on their distinct family names, I argue that these families had a 'secular' (and at times, more specifically, a military) background. I conclude this section by asking what role the estates played and which value they still had for the descendants of the original beneficiaries in the long sixth century.

1.1 *The Nature of* Hanšû *Land*

Relatively little has been written on the subject of *hanšû* land, mainly because information is scarce and difficult to interpret.[6] However, *hanšû* estates are found in most Babylonian towns that produced cuneiform texts, including Borsippa, Babylon, Dilbat, Kiš, Nippur, Sippar, and Uruk.[7] The picture that can be drawn from this dispersed evidence suggests that *hanšû* lands were created as land allotments granted by various kings to individuals, groups, and temples at different times during the first half of the first millennium BCE.

Some scholars have argued that *hanšû*s represent a kind of feudal land allotment system in which designated plots were manned by groups of fifty individuals (in which case *hanšû* is held to refer to the unit size) and presided over by a headman called the 'commander of fifty' (*rab hanšê*) responsible for the communal obligations encumbered on the land.[8] At first, this led scholars to believe that the designation *hanšû* was related to 'military'-like organisation

6 See, for example, Cocquerillat 1968, Peat 1983, Brinkman 1964, Brinkman 1995, van Driel 2002, Zadok 2006, Zadok 2009, Jursa *et al.* 2010, Nielsen 2011, Janković 2013, and Nielsen and Waerzeggers 2016.

7 For an overview of the attestation of *hanšû*, see van Driel 2002: 300–305. For a more detailed discussion of the early attestations of *hanšû*, see Nielsen 2011: 46–49 (Babylon), 86–97 (Borsippa), 113–115 (Dilbat), and 144–147 (Kish).

8 See, for example, CAD H, which designated *hanšû* for the Neo-Babylonian period as 'a field held in feudal tenure by 50 men', or Brinkman 1984: 32–33, who understands it as a 'local agricultural administration … presided over by the 'Commander of the Fifty' (*rab hanšê*), who seems to have been … assigned responsibility for the unit and liable for the equivalent of feudal obligations for the land'. Cf. Peat 1983 and Beaulieu 1998: 315.

and occupation of the land in groups of fifty people, reminiscent of the land-for-service system known from the later Murašû archive.[9] However, this does not seem to apply to all the *hanšû* schemes in the Babylonian alluvium. Or, alternatively, the original (military) organisation became obsolete over time. Whereas various early documents from Uruk attest indeed to *hanšû* land being allotted to large groups of people,[10] sometimes designated as *rab hanšê*s,[11] no such evidence is available for other cities like Babylon and Borsippa. While a handful of references to *rab hanšê*s are known from various towns (usually as recipients of silver payments),[12] the small text group concerning Zēru-ukīn/Pir'u, a 'commander of fifty' from Nippur, suggests that he was a true military official who went on campaign (or performed corvée service) himself and bore the responsibility of mobilising his men when called for service or collect compensatory payments on behalf of the tax unit.[13] He is not mentioned, however, as the owner of *hanšû* land. Moreover, well-to-do men, like priests, usually did not perform the corvée obligation that rested on their landed property, but paid silver as compensation for substitutes.[14] Perhaps in this context the *rab hanšê* can best be seen as a military official and tax collector on behalf of the state, whose connection to the land in question was all but obliterated through the practice of substitution. Hence while in some cases there seems to be a link between the *rab hanšê*s and the land called *hanšû*, on the one hand, and the (military) group designated by the same term, on the other hand, more evidence is needed to accept it as a general rule.

Another idea is that the designation *hanšû* or fifty is related to the physical size of these plots or, alternatively, to the number of plots per land unit. This theory has found wider support.[15] As can be expected from lands originating

9 Stolper 1985: 70–103 and Jursa 2005: 113–114.

10 Ninety-one in AnOr 9 1 and NBC 4848, forty-five in YBC 11566, and thirty-two in BIN 1 159. See Janković 2013: 364–373 for a discussion of these texts and the structure of *hanšû* land in Uruk.

11 See, for example, AnOr 9 1.

12 See van Driel 2002: 297. Only three texts from Borsippa mention the official: BM 27781 (Cam 04) and BM 26693 (Dar 12) from the Atkuppu archive, and the private account BM 29230, undated and so far unassigned. See also Kleber 2008: 115f, for the role of *rab-hanšê*s in the organisation of the Eanna's building projects.

13 Jursa 2005: 115, Jursa *et al.* 2010: 649–650. This is also suggested by the text PSBA 7 148, from Babylon and dated to Dar 24. It reports on an individual who is said to have done one month of corvée work with his *rab hanšê*, who will not call on him again before the end of month VII, cf. van Driel 2002: 297.

14 See, for example, Jursa and Waerzeggers 2009 and Jursa *et al.* 2010: 647ff.

15 See, for example, Unger 1932: 412, San Nicolò 1951: 16, Weidner 1952: 37, Cocquerillat 1984: 67, van Driel 2002: 298, and Jursa *et al.* 2010: 321^{+1864}. Cf. Janković 2013: 365f.

in centralised division schemes, which presumably safeguarded fairness and equality, *hanšûs* belonging to the same unit shared a fairly regular size. In contrast to normal land, defined by both the length of the front (*pūtu*) and the side (*šiddu*), in dealing with *hanšû* land it sufficed the Babylonian scribes to give the frontage length only, which usually bordered on a canal. In a transaction from Babylon recorded in TCL 12 11, dating to the reign of Šamaš-šumu-ukīn (667–648 BCE), a *hanšû* unit with a frontage (*pūtu*) on the canal of 250 cubits is sub-divided into ten units (*ešertus*) of 50 cubits.[16] This seems to suggest that on principle the basic building block of *hanšû* divisions were 'units of fifty' cubits.[17] Perhaps the larger landholdings called 'thousand' (*līmu*), which were granted to institutions in the course of similar land allotment schemes, should be understood in similar terms.[18] However, even if *hanšû* land was originally at least occasionally allotted in standardised units of fifty cubits, the dynamics of inheritance and land alienation through sales and pledging, as well as the regrettable silence on the part of the Babylonian scribes in recording dimensions, make it generally impossible to substantiate the connection between the designation *hanšû* and the physical size of actual, documented plots.

More recently, G. van Driel tried to merge these two ideas by arguing for a connection between the *hanšû* schemes and the development of the Babylonian corvée and taxation system.[19] Family units of ten (*ešertu*), which could be established on the bases of residence patterns, professional affiliation, and/or social background, would have formed the basic component from which the state drew its resources.[20] What we see in these standardised *hanšû* schemes, according to van Driel, was an attempt by the Babylonian state to organise the taxable population on a higher level, namely, in standard blocks

16 Exceptionally, in this text also the length of the plot is given: one *bēru*, 21,600 cubits or 10.8 kilometres. While this extremely narrow plot is suggestive of centralised intervention it should perhaps not be ruled out that we are dealing here with some kind of legal/administrative fiction, not unlike the legally fragmented shares in the prebendary services, cf. Waerzeggers 2010: 201ff., for the calculation of prebendary shares in the baker's service in Ezida.

17 As has been noted by Janković 2013: 365[+1350], while none of the frontages recorded for *hanšû* units in Uruk are exactly 250 cubits, most of them are multiples of fifty (e.g. 400, 300, and 150).

18 Van Driel 2002: 298 and Jursa *et al.* 2010: 422[+2413]. See Janković 2013: 357–358, 364[+1348] for the allotment of *līmu* units (most of them feature a frontage of over 1,000 cubits) to the temple in Uruk.

19 Driel 2002: 295–300.

20 See, for example, Jursa 1999: 101–105, van Driel 2002: 295–305, and Jursa and Waerzeggers 2009: 294.

of fifty households/men.[21] This idea ties in neatly with the information found in texts such as TCL 12 11 (mentioned above), which organised *hanšû* land in units of ten and fifty. Even if evidence for a connection between the ownership of *hanšû* land and taxation based on units of *ešertu*s and *hanšû*s remains scarce,[22] van Driel's hypothesis so far best explains the nature of these *hanšû* schemes throughout Babylonia.[23]

In the end we have to realise that *hanšû* probably had different implications in different contexts. Its usage and operation were subject to local practice and might have changed over time. Land allotment schemes in Babylonia were created at various moments by various kings, presumably in an attempt to win over and cater to the needs of various elements in society. For example, in Sippar *hanšû* estates were allotted to the local temple institution,[24] in Borsippa the main recipients were urban families, whereas in Uruk there might be evidence that *hanšû*s were assigned to groups from the lower (perhaps rural) stratum of society.[25] It seems only likely that these allotments were subject to somewhat different arrangements.

1.2 *The Historical Origins of* Hanšû *Land in Borsippa*[26]

Regrettably, little is known about Babylonian society during the early centuries of the first millennium BCE. Most of our information comes from a scattering of 'boundary-stones' (*kudurrus*) that commemorate the endowment of land and prebends to state or temple officials by individual kings or from later (mainly) sixth-century chronicles.[27] The early second quarter of the first millennium BCE is somewhat better known thanks to the large letter corpus from the Assyrian state archives.[28] According to these sources, Babylonia witnessed a period of turmoil and disunity caused by internal as well as external political strife and ethnic friction. Not only was the country repeatedly threatened by its powerful Assyrian neighbour and at times incorporated into it, but

21 Van Driel 2002: 297f.

22 Janković 2013: 369.

23 Jursa *et al.* 2010: 247[+1455].

24 Jursa *et al.* 2010: 336[+1957], 338–340, 356.

25 Although a connection to the temple cannot be excluded, see Jursa *et al.* 2010: 421–422. Note that the city governor (*šākin-ṭēmi*), Nā'id-Marduk/Ūm-19-uṣur, is mentioned among the beneficiaries of *hanšû* land in two texts. See Janković 2013: 368f.

26 A similar investigation has been done by Nielsen and Waerzeggers 2016.

27 For studies on politics, society, and documentation from this period, see Brinkman 1968, Brinkman 1984, Brinkman and Kennedy 1983, Frame 1992, and Nielsen 2011. For a brief and critical overview, see Von Dassow 1999a.

28 See, for example, Cole and Machinist 1998 (SAA 13), Fuchs and Parpola 2001 (SAA 15), Dietrich 2003 (SAA 17), and Luukko 2012 (SAA 19).

Babylonia also had to deal with two influential foreign populations, the Chaldeans and the Arameans, that had settled in various parts of the alluvium during the late second and early first millennium BCE.[29] Due to a major dearth of everyday documentation, Assyriologists still lack a firm grasp of this period of Babylonian history. Nonetheless, some crucial innovations were introduced in Babylonia at this time, innovations that would turn out to characterise later Neo-Babylonian society.

It was in this period, in the late eighth and seventh centuries, that the basis for the typical, intensive form of agriculture of the sixth century was laid.[30] It was also in this period that the regular field systems, i.e. the *hanšû* schemes, were created on initiative of the state.[31] This agricultural restructuring was one of the beneficial factors that led to the economic growth that is documented in the long sixth century.[32]

The earliest attestation of the term *hanšû* in the Borsippa corpus dates from the reign of Šamaš-šumu-ukīn (667–648 BCE).[33] The picture we can draw from this and other early texts is, however, not as static as one would expect to find in case of a newly installed land scheme.[34] Rather, the landscape appears dynamic and already in an advanced stage of fragmentation. Hence, this suggests that Šamaš-šumu-ukīn was not the ruler who created a new land division scheme in Borsippa. Instead, his reign serves as the *terminus ante quem* based on the available local documentation. However, texts from other Babylonian towns provide more information on the existence of *hanšû*s pre-dating his reign.

Apart from Sippar, where *hanšû* land was introduced relatively late,[35] the material from most other cities in central Babylonia broadly corresponds to the picture seen in Borsippa. In Babylon, Kish, and Nippur, *hanšû* land is not attested before Šamaš-šumu-ukīn, the period that roughly forms the starting

29 See, for example, Brinkman 1968 and Frame 1992. For more on the presence and the role of these Aramean and Chaldean groups in Babylonia, see below and Chapter 6.4.

30 See, for example, van Driel 2002: 297.

31 See, for example, Jursa *et al.* 2010: 647.

32 See, for example, Jursa *et al.* 2010: 437–443, 754–772.

33 OECT 12 A 83 (Ššu 24-II-04). For the earliest reference to *hanšû* land in the first millennium Babylonian documentation see below.

34 See, for example, *RA* 10 no. 46 (Ššu 04), TCL 12 9 (Ššu 07), TuM 2/3 12 = BR 8/7 no. 9 (Ššu 10). These three land sales from the reign of Šamaš-šumu-ukīn record the sale or purchase of plots of *hanšû* land by individuals not belonging to the original beneficiary families. See Chapter 2.1.4.

35 See Jursa *et al.* 2010: 355–360.

point of the oldest Neo-Babylonian family archives.[36] The term is, however, attested slightly earlier in three property deeds from Dilbat, a town roughly fifteen kilometres southeast of Borsippa. Two texts are dated to the second regnal year of Bēl-ibni, an Assyrian puppet king appointed by King Sennacherib between circa 703 and 700 BCE,[37] and one text is dated to King Esarhaddon in 674/3 BCE.[38]

Earlier attestations of *hanšû* come from the southern town of Uruk. AnOr 9 1 and NBC 4848[39] record how the Chaldean King Merodach-Baladan (Marduk-aplu-iddin) II,[40] who was in power between circa 721 and 710 BCE, restructured land on his eponymous canal into *hanšû* units and allotted it to ninety-one *rab-hanšês*.[41] The oldest explicit reference to the institution of the *hanšû* thus dates to the 710s BCE. And unlike the mature state of *hanšû* land found in mid-seventh century Borsippa, the late eighth century divisions in Uruk seem to represent the system's inception.

The evidence from Uruk has led scholars to believe that the *hanšû* schemes in the south were generally older than those in the north.[42] But is this really so? The two texts from Uruk dated to Merodach-Baladan II were official records,[43] a text type generally missing from northern Babylonian towns. The Uruk texts were probably kept in the local temple archive[44] and copied repeatedly.[45]

36 Babylon: TCL 12 11 (Ššu 14); BM 64162 (Ššu 19); VS 5 3 (Kan 01); Kish: OECT 10 3 (Ššu 10); OECT 10 7 (Ššu 19); and Nippur: TuM 2/3 132 (Asb 36).

37 OECT 10 391 and OECT 10 392. For these texts belonging to the small archive of Marduk-šāpik-zēri//Egibi, see Jursa 2005: 100–101 and Nielsen 2015.

38 OECT 10 395 (Esh 07). For other somewhat later references to *hanšû* land in Dilbat, see Nielsen 2011: 112–115 and Nielsen 2015.

39 This seems to be a later copy as the scribe mentioned in the colophon is the same scribe who wrote BIN 1 159, a text concerning another *hanšû* scheme division during the reign of Kandalānu some fifty years later. See Jursa *et al.* 2010: 421[+2410] and Janković 2013: 364–373.

40 Known from 2 Kings 20:12 and Isaiah 39:1.

41 AnOr 9 1 tells us that a certain high royal official (*kerdippu*) was responsible for organising these land allotments; the same person is mentioned in NBC 4848 without a title. See Janković 2013: 367–368. Note that at least on two occasions a later king would emulate Merodach-Baladan's intervention in the countryside of Uruk. In his fourth and fifteenth regnal year King Kandalānu, who ruled between 647 and 627 BCE, allocated *hanšû* land to forty-two and forty-five individuals (BIN 1 159 and YBC 11566), cf. Jursa *et al.* 2010: 421[+2410].

42 See, for example, Jursa *et al.* 2010: 321–322.

43 See also van Driel 2002: 304–305.

44 Or in the archive of local temple scribes. BIN 1 159 and NBC 4848 have been copied by Nergal-ina-tēšî-ēṭer/Marduk-šākin-šumi who was a descendant of Sîn-leqe-unninnī, a prominent scribal family.

45 Note that NBC 4848 was copied perhaps fifty years later by the scribe of BIN 1 159. According to Goetze 1947: 352, who published parts of text NBC 4848, this text also has a duplicate known as 'fragment Crozer 201'.

Similar types of texts were still composed in Uruk in the later Achaemenid and even Hellenistic periods.[46] Moreover, private documents from Uruk referring to *hanšû* only start from the reign of Šamaš-šumu-ukīn, if not later, hence following the same pattern observed for the northern towns.[47]

In addition to the administrative record, there is evidence of a more vivid nature suggesting that land divisions took place in the Borsippa region in the late eight century as well.[48] VS 1 37 is a monumental stele composed at the occasion of a land grant to a high-ranking individual in 715 BCE.[49] In the introductory narrative, King Merodach-Baladan II describes his endeavours to expel intruders from the countryside of Babylon and Borsippa and to restore the land to its rightful owners:

> '[Merodach-Baladan] whose attention is set on restoring the lands to the sons of Sippar, Nippur and Babylon, and (all the other) cities of Akkad; and the old parcels of the Babylonians, ruined by an invading army,

46 AUWE 12, 223 presents a list of *hanšû* plots in the Uruk area presumably assigned to eleven individuals. This text was found in square U 18 in the southeast area on the site of Uruk/Warka. This find spot has been labelled the 'house of the exorcist', after the two consecutive families of exorcists who lived there in the early fourth (Šangû-Ninurta family) and late fourth to early third century BCE (Ekur-zakir family), respectively. Cf. Frahm 2002: 78–84 and Clancier 2009: 47–81. The two text assemblages consist of a large number of scholarly texts and a small number of private administrative documents. So far no convincing date has been suggested for AUWE 12, 223. Oelsner 1995: 386 assumes an earlier date and assigns it to the Šangû-Ninurta family based on the fact that *hanšû* can only be traced to the early fifth century BCE. The fact that none of the individuals mentioned in the text bear 'Anu' names, common in the Hellenistic period, also suggests an earlier date. In contrast, Beaulieu 1998: 315 believes that AUWE 12, 223 belongs to the archive of the Ekur-zakir and that it was kept out of an antiquarian interest. As we will see later, both families came from the urbanite circles that received *hanšû* lands in the early first millennium BCE, and both did potentially have a stake in this land. *Hanšû* might therefore have existed for over five hundred years in Uruk, if only in the memory of the scribal elite.

47 TCL 12 8 (Ššu 01). This seems to be a sale of possibly an entire irrigated sub-district (*ugāru*) of considerable size for 190 shekels of silver. See Zadok 2006: 390. However, it is doubtful whether one can classify this transaction as 'private'. The land was sold and said to be 'regarded as *hanšû* land of the Urukeans and possibly added to the Rudāya area (*kīma* 50$^{\acute{u}.me\check{s}}$ *ša Urukāya ana* <^{garim}>*Ruddāya uraddu*, ll. 9–10). According to Zadok 1985: 262, Rudāya was situated to the southwest of Uruk. Note also that the text is said to have been written 'at the time (*ina ūmišuma*) of Nabû-ušebši, the city governor of Uruk'. Other private texts from Uruk that mention *hanšû* land date to Nbk 17 (FLP 1533), Nbk 18 (Mich 9), and an unknown year (*Iraq* 59, no. 36).

48 Note that both VS 1 37 and ABC 24 (below) have been discussed in relation to the origins of *hanšû* estates by Nielsen and Waerzeggers 2016.

49 For a discussion of this text, see Leemans 1945: 444–448. For a recent edition of VS 1 37, see Paulus 2014: 693–703.

grazed off by foreigners like sheep – their borders were forgotten, their boundary marks were out of place, their estates were uncultivated and left unploughed – he restored the parcels and returned them to the sons of Babylon and Borsippa, not omitting a single person – he determined the parcels and made them take possession'

VS 1 37: col. iii 10–29

Admittedly, this text does not make any explicit reference to *hanšû* land. But then the question arises whether to expect the use of a legal-administrative term in this literary historical account in the first place? The manner in which it describes the king's effort – determining the boundaries of parcels and restoring them to the citizenry – is in keeping with a systematised, large scale land (re-)division project, the very context in which one expects to find the creation of *hanšû* schemes.

Moreover, the picture can be further adjusted if a related term of division is taken into consideration: (*šu*)*zu'uzti šarri*, 'royal (land) allotment', a term only attested a few times so far.[50] TuM 2/3 132, a text from Nippur dated to the 630s BCE, records a donation of a share in a *hanšû* unit located *ina zu'uzti šarri*, 'within the royal allotment'.[51] This passage shows that *zu'uzti šarri* and *hanšû* were not only compatible terms, but also that *hanšû*s were developed and made available in the course of royal land allotments.[52]

The earliest evidence for the *zu'uztu ša šarri* dates from the reign Erība-Marduk, a king of Chaldean origin who ruled over Babylonia in the 770s BCE.[53] A first reference is found in VS 1 37, the text discussed above. One of the two fields granted by Merodach-Baladan II, who coincidentally proclaims to be a descendant of Erība-Marduk,[54] is said to border on the 'royal allotment of Erība-Marduk, King of Babylon'.[55] A second reference is found in an unpublished legal text, BM 36479, written in the capital of Babylon and dated in year

50 Van Driel 2002: 297ff. Cf. CAD Z: 169 'field(s) apportioned by the king'.

51 See also van Driel 2002: 299. Note that BM 46799+, written in Ššu 12 at the city of Kish, mentions two *hanšû* plots located in the *zu'uztu* of Merodach-Baladan. See Nielsen 2010: 98, ll. 1–2.

52 Cf. Jursa *et al.* 2010: 248, 321[+1866].

53 Brinkman 1964. For *zu'uztu*s of the later kings Sargon II and Merodach-Baladan II, see van Driel 2002: 300 and Brinkman 1984: 49[+227].

54 Brinkman 1964: 29–30[+15, 18]. In VS 1 37, col. ii 40–44, Merodach-Baladan II calls himself the 'eternal royal scion who makes illustrious the name of his father who begot him, the offspring of Erība-Marduk'.

55 VS 1 37, col. iii 51–52: *zu'uztu ša Erība-Marduk šar Bābilī*.

13 of Šamaš-šumu-ukīn (ca. 665 BCE).[56] The text mentions two shares of *hanšû* land that are situated in the 'royal allotment of Erība-Marduk, the King'.[57]

The correlation between *hanšû* and *zu'uzti šarri* makes it possible to trace the origins of the *hanšû* system back to the early eighth century BCE, over a hundred years before it first appears in private administrative documentation. This early date is furthermore supported by the fact that the sacerdotal families of Borsippa themselves traced the origins of their (*hanšû*) landholdings back to the time of King Erība-Marduk.

C. Waerzeggers has argued that at least one of the genres of the Babylonian scribal lore was compiled in Borsippa: the chronicles.[58] While the capital city of Babylon had always been considered as the centre of chronicle writing, she demonstrates that many of the accounts of important historical and religious events were actually archived by the priestly families of Ezida in Borsippa. The chronicles usually reveal a particular orientation towards the god Marduk and his city Babylon, yet, there is at least one text that is clearly centred on Borsippa. Running from the Isin II period[59] (ca. eleventh century BCE.) to some point following the reign of Shalmaneser V (ca. 720s BCE), the so-called 'Eclectic Chronicle' (ABC 24)[60] zooms in on kings who have shown particular piety towards Nabû and the citizenry of Borsippa.[61] The following passage, reminiscent of VS 1 37, portrays how the Borsippean priests themselves understood the origins of their landholdings, which makes it an invaluable testimony for the present study:

> 'Erība-Marduk, son of Marduk-šākin-šumi took the hand of Bēl (i.e. Marduk) and the son of Bēl (i.e. Nabû) in his second year. He slew with the sword the Arameans who had taken by murder and insurrection the fields of the inhabitants of Babylon and Borsippa and brought about their defeat. He took the fields and orchards away from them and gave (it) to the sons of Babylon and Borsippa'
>
> GRAYSON 1975: 182–183; ABC 24, rev. 9–13

56 This document is mentioned in Brinkman 1964: 38[+12]. I thank John Nielsen, who kindly brought this to my attention.

57 BM 36479, ll. 17–18: *zu'uztu ša Erība-Marduk šarru*.

58 Waerzeggers 2012.

59 Pomponio 1978: 61.

60 Grayson 1975: no. 24 and Glassner 2004: no. 47.

61 See Waerzeggers 2012: 296–297, for the particular kings and their connection to Borsippa.

1.3 *The Motivations behind the Land Allotment Schemes*

Incidentally, the passages in ABC 24 and VS 1 37 tell us more about the historical background and the motivation behind the creation of these land allotment schemes. During the first half of the first millennium BCE Babylonia witnessed an exceptionally turbulent time. Weakened by political unrest, rebellion, and at times open war, the autochthonous population in the urban centres was economically paralysed and the country in a general state of decline. The kings that seized the Babylonian throne were not of old Babylonian stock,[62] but of Chaldean and Assyrian descent or indeed groomed at the Assyrian court, and could therefore not call on an established royal dynasty for legitimacy.[63] There can be little doubt that in this highly volatile political climate, rulers needed to consolidate their positions rapidly and for this the support of the local population was indispensable.[64] The episodes in ABC 24 and VS 1 37 seem to describe exactly such attempts. After a period of turmoil and encroachments, both kings claim (or are claimed) to have liberated the country from evil and returned the land to its rightful owners and original state. The analogy between them and Marduk, the divine king and conqueror of cosmic evil, who divided the fields and shares for the gods, is unmistakable.[65] Since Erība-Marduk and Merodach-Baladan II both belonged to the Bīt-Yakīn,[66] the Chaldean people based in the very southeast of Babylonia on the Persian Gulf,[67] it makes sense that much of their exploits were directed towards cities in central (Nippur) and northern Babylonia (Sippar, Babylon, and Borsippa). This area was far away from their natural power base in the south and close to

62 A very short-lived exception might have been Marduk-šākin-šumi II (ca. 703 BCE). If Brinkman is correct in identifying him as the (provincial) governor (*bēl pīhāti*) mentioned in VS 1 37: col. v. ll. 2–3, then he apparently came from the well-known Arad-Ea clan (1964: 24[+137]). Marduk-šākin-šumi was dethroned after only a few weeks.

63 Note, however, that Merodach-Baladan II did make an attempt to legitimise his position by claiming direct descent from the Chaldean and former King Erība-Marduk. See Brinkman 1964: 7[+5], 29f.

64 For a study of comparable political negotiations and power struggles between aspirant kings, warlords, and Babylonia's urban communities during the late Neo-Assyrian and the early Neo-Babylonian Periods, see Levavi 2017.

65 There are various references to Marduk as organiser of land in the Epic of Creation (*Enūma Eliš*), especially by his divine names such as 'Asarre, giver of arable land who established plough-land' (Lambert 2013: 125; see also the German translation of Kämmerer and Metzler 2012: 281 as 'der die Grundrisse (Feldfluren) fest gesetzt hat'), 'Gil...[t]he creator of grain and flocks, who gives seed for the land' (Lambert 2013: 129), and 'Zulum, who assigns meadows for the gods and divides up what he has created' (Lambert 2013: 129).

66 Brinkman 1964, Brinkman 1968: 221–224, and Brinkman 1984: 15[+61], 46–47.

67 Frame 1992: 40–42, Lipiński 2000: 419, and Beaulieu 2013a: 44–45.

the Assyrian border, and the need to win local favour there was arguably greatest.[68] Even if their self-serving claims to have 're-established the foundation of the land'[69] must be viewed critically, their initiatives were received favourably, at least by later generations,[70] and are to some extent corroborated by more contemporary references in the administrative records discussed above. One might think of a similar scenario concerning the *zu'uztu* allotment named after the Assyrian King Sargon II,[71] most likely brought into existence some time between 710 and 707 BCE. During a three-year stay in Babylonia, right after he pushed Merodach-Baladan II from the throne and defeated him at his capital of Dūr-Yakīn in 709 BCE,[72] Sargon II went to great lengths to present himself as a true Babylonian king and win the favour of the local population. His plan of action did not only involve the redistribution of land and related agricultural developments like the reopening of the Borsippa canal, but he also adopted traditional Babylonian royal titles, donated lavish temple gifts, and participated in the New Year's festival among various other measures.[73]

While certainly motivated by a wish to conciliate the local population, these royal land allotment schemes also served a greater economic purpose. Repeated wars, military campaigns, and incursions took a heavy toll on Babylonia's countryside. Remembering that the foundation of the Babylonian economy was at all times agrarian, the old urban centres were doomed without a solid basis in agriculture. Following G. van Driel, there can be little doubt that an important purpose of the land allotment policy of the kings of this period was the 'creation, or, minimally, strengthening of a town-based land holding group of people'.[74] Royal land allotments, including the *hanšû* schemes, were meant to reinvigorate the economy and spur the production of Babylonian cities. This can also be inferred from the fact that land schemes were not created in isolation but were usually part of much larger redevelopment projects, which beside (re)structuring (existing) estates also involved ambitious expansions of the hydraulic network and large-scale canal building. This allowed for the dual effect of opening up large areas of unexploited land as well as giving new impetus to local and regional trade, which could thrive by the improved waterway infrastructure. I already mentioned the canal named after Merodach-Baladan

68 Although one has to bear in mind that the geographical scope of VS 1 37 and ABC 24 depended at least in part also on the place of redaction in Babylon and Borsippa, respectively.
69 See VS 1 37 Col. ii: 41–44.
70 Brinkman 1964 and Brinkman 1968: 221–224.
71 See above, footnote 53.
72 Brinkman 1984: 50–54.
73 Brinkman 1984: 53.
74 Van Driel 2002: 297.

II, which served as the main water supply for newfound *hanšû* land in Uruk[75] and the opening of the Borsippa canal by Sargon II. A better example, however, is the major redevelopment in the hinterland of Sippar under Nabopolassar and Nebuchadnezzar II (ca. late seventh–early sixth centuries BCE), which can be examined in exceptional detail thanks to the Ebabbar temple archives.[76] As has been shown by M. Jursa, these royal projects involved the (re-)opening of various major canals, the reclamation of new land, the creation of *hanšû* units, and the allotment of landed estates to the temple administration and sacerdotal groups in the city's immediate vicinity but also further afield.[77] This royal intervention did not only set the parameters for general agrarian expansion and growth after a period of destruction caused by Nabopolassar's 'war of liberation' against the Assyrians, but it also played an important role in launching the trend towards a more intensive form of agriculture.[78] Moreover, the expanding agriculture and commerce in Sippar drew many newcomers to the city who further contributed to the region's prosperity.[79]

Besides gaining the support of the local population and boosting the economy, the land schemes generated tax income for the state.[80] As has been

75 Mentioned in AnOr 9 1, SAA 17 140, and YOS 3 74.

76 Jursa *et al.* 2010: 322–360. Another interesting case outside of Babylonia, although the political motivations behind it may have been different, is the massive agrarian development project in the Assyrian capital of Nineveh by King Sennacherib. He explains, 'to plant gardens, I subdivided the meadowland upstream of the city into plots of two *pānu* each for the citizens of Nineveh and I handed (them) over to them … I cut with iron picks a canal straight through mountain and *valley*, from the border of the city Kisiru to the plain of Nineveh. I caused an inexhaustible supply of water to flow there for a distance of one and a half leagues from the Husur River (and) made (it) gush through feeder canals into those gardens' (Grayson and Novotny 2012: no 1. ll. 88–90). Perhaps worthy of note is that this passage is followed by the following lines in inscription no. 16: 'I provided irrigation for 500 seeded field[s] in the *high* fields of Nineveh with (that) water (and thereby) [I made] grain and cereals grow high and luxuriantly on … an in furrows' (vol. viii. ll. 24–28). Not only is this clear evidence for the creation of regular size land schemes in the local countryside of Nineveh, but also the size of two *pānu* mentioned in the first passage coupled with the irrigation provided for five hundred fields in the latter invites a comparison with, if not the identification of, the so-called 'thousand' (*līmu*) land mentioned earlier. For the full-scale of Sennacherib's building activities and development project, see Frahm 1997: 275–276 and Grayson and Novotny 2012: 16–22 with references to the texts.

77 Jursa *et al.* 2010: 355ff.

78 The fruit of which could only be reaped by later generations. See Jursa *et al.* 2010: 358–360.

79 Waerzeggers 2014. See especially Chapter four in which she discusses the early activities of the Ṣāhit-ginês and other clans who migrated to Sippar in the first half of the sixth century BCE.

80 Note however that the evidence comes predominantly from the later Neo-Babylonian and Achaemenid periods. While the taxation system developed further in the course of

suggested by van Driel, the creation of regular field systems resulted from an attempt by the Babylonian state to (re)organise the taxable population in a more efficient way.[81] There is increasing evidence to suggest that the possession of land in *hanšû* schemes was indeed subject to tax and service obligations.[82] Moreover, the state coffers were replenished by fees for the use of hydraulic infrastructures[83] and tolls on the commercial transportation of goods on the waterways.[84] The expanded canal network was thus turned into a source of revenue.

Finally, we have to realise that besides a fiscal dimension the creation of land allotments allowed the king to bind the population on a more conceptual level. The king showed that he had the resources to undertake the construction of major new canals and other large-scale hydraulic complexes. Only he could make use of corvée labour on an appropriate scale to maintain the whole system but equally to shut it down.

1.4 *The Identity of the Beneficiaries*

Unlike other types of land, which was typically identified on the basis of its geographic features or location alone, *hanšû* lands were named after a person

---

the long sixth century and continued to do so afterwards, we can be sure that a rudimentary structure of taxation already existed before and assume that right from the beginning these holdings were encumbered with service and tax obligations. How this relates to the status of *kidinnūtu* (i.e. exemption from taxation and corvée labour) one often hears of in this early period is still in need of investigation.

81 Van Driel 2002: 294ff.

82 See the evidence presented by van Driel 2002: 297ff. This proposition has been embraced more recently by Jursa and Waerzeggers 2009: 240–251 and Jursa *et al.* 2010: 167, 247–249^{+1471}, 461^{+2543}, 647 where new conclusive evidence from Borsippa can be found.

83 In this respect the *gugallūtu* should be mentioned. It was a payment made on the basis of land ownership (found most often in harvest estimations, i.e. *imittu* texts) for the services of the *gugallu*. This office is usually translated as 'canal inspector' and the evidence, especially from Uruk, shows that he was responsible for the maintenance of canals and related hydraulic structures (van Driel 2002: 179ff., and Janković 2007). New evidence from Borsippa presented in Jursa and Waerzeggers 2009 suggests that from the reign of Darius I onwards, these *gugallus* turned into genuine tax collectors on behalf of the governor, and were put in charge of specific agricultural (*hanšû*) domains in return for a fixed payment.

84 Note that similar payments might have applied for the transportation via land routes. A number of related terms, including *kāru* (harbour tax), *miksu* (levy on goods), *mūṣû* (exit dues), as well as *nēbiru* and *maṣīru* (levy for…), can be mentioned in this respect. This complex cluster of taxation has been studied by van Driel 2002: 274–282. Cf. Jursa *et al.* 2010: 251f.

or a family.[85] Although there are a few units that were identified otherwise,[86] the vast majority of the *hanšûs* in Borsippa were known as 'fifty of the house of family so-and-so' (*hanšû ša bīt* (PN//)FN).[87] The dual application of family names for both local kin groups and their *hanšû* estates was especially deep-seated in Borsippa. Names were firmly attached to the land and there is no evidence that estates were ever renamed, even after the original 'eponymous' family let go of its property.[88] In the roughly 170 years documented in the private archive from Borsippa, around fifty-four different *hanšû* units are mentioned:

hanšû ša (*bīt*, henceforth: b.) …[89]
b. Abunāya
Nabû-remēni//Abunāya
b. Apkallu
b. Ašgandu (or: Šukandu)
b. Atkuppu
b. Bābāya
b. mār Bā'iru
b. Banê-ša-ilia

85 Zadok 2006: 420–447. Cf. van Driel 2002: 298–300, Nielsen 2011: *passim*. Note that some other geographical features could be called after a person or family. See, for example, the 'canal of the Damēqu clan' (*harru ša bīt-Damēqi*, BM 103458), 'village of Marduk-šumu-ibni(//Ilia)' (*ālu ša Marduk-šumu-ibni*, BM 25794) or 'irrigated district of Ša-Nabû-damqā' (*tamirtu ša Ša-Nabû-damqā*, BE 8 111).

86 See, for example, '50^{ú} *ina* garim *ba-he-e*' (TCL 12 11), '50^{ú} *i-na* ugu íd kiš^{ki}' (TCL 12 11), '50^{meš} *šá* ^{lú}tinr.tir$^{ki.meš}$ (RA 83: 153) '50^{ú} *ra-bu-ú*' (CT 56 44+), '50^{meš} *šá* ^{uru}du$_6$ *gub-bu*' (BM 79746), and '50^{ú} *qab-lu-ú*' (BM 74422).

87 See the list of *hanšûs* below.

88 Contra Zadok 2006: 426, 449. His only example of a *hanšû* changing its denomination and bearing the family name of the new owner (interchangeably: Rē'i-alpi, Mubannû, Kidin-Sîn), is based on a misreading and wrong interpretation. First, the dowry of ^{f}Nanāya-bulliṭiš//Mubannû, wife of Nabû-mukīn-zēri//Rē'i-alpi mentioned in BM 101980 is located in the *hanšû* Mubannû (like in the duplicate BM 82607, published in Roth 1990: 53f.) and not in the *hanšû* Rē'i-alpi. Second, contrary to Zadok 2006: 426, who claims that it subsequently changed from the *hanšû* Mubannû into the *hanšû* of the Kidin-Sîn family, this in fact concerns a second and different plot all together. These additional four *sūtu* of land are said to be on the canal (*harru*) of Nabû-šumu-līšir (or -ukīn?) in BM 26514, which in turn is said to be located in the *hanšû* of Kidin-Sîn in BM 26492//BE 8 108. Note incidentally that if the personal name should be read Nabû-šumu-ukīn, then this person might be identical with the individual who attached his name to parts of the *hanšû* of Kidin-Sîn described in BM 94697 (Cam 07), BM 82654 (Dar 01), and EAH 212 (Dar 02), among others.

89 The following list follows the alphabetical order of the family names whenever available. For the annotated lists of references, see Appendix 2.

Šumā//Banê-ša-ilia
Nabû-šumu-iškun//Bārû
b. Basia
b. Bēlāya
b. Bēliya'u[90]
b. Bibbê
b. Bitahhi[91]
Kāṣir//Ēdu-ēṭir
b. Esagil
b. Esagil-mansum
b. Gallābu
tamirtu humamātu
Ahu-ēreš//Huršanāya
b. Huṣābu
Iddin-Amurru[92]
b. Iddin-Papsukkal
Saggillu//Iddin-Papsukkal
b. (Ea-)ilūtu-bani
Illûa//(Ea-)ilūtu-bani
Nādin-ahi//(Ea-)ilūtu-bani
Suppê-Bēl//(Ea-)ilūtu-bani
b. Iššakku
b. Kidin-Sîn
Nabû-šumu-līšir//Kidin-Sîn
[PN]//Kidin-Sîn
b. Kudurru u b. ᶠLe'itu
b. Kurgarrê
b. Lahāšu
b. mār Lāsimu

90 This area is not explicitly designated as *hanšû*, yet the context in which it is mentioned and the fact that it is referred to as *bīt-Bēliya'u* strongly support such an assumption. See Appendix 2.

91 Note that this might be an alternative spelling for the better-attested family name Barihi. While the family name Bitahhi is only found twice in the entire corpus, one of these individuals, Nabû-mukīn-zēri/Nādin/Bitahhi (TCL 13 189), occurs on two other occasions with the family name Barihi (BM 85562 and BM 26635).

92 Contrary to Uruk, where the Iddin-Amurru clan is represented among the highest temple ranks, notably as *kalû*s, or cultic singers of the Lady-of-Uruk (Kümmel 1978: 147, 157), the family name is not found in Borsippa. Besides the geographic designation, Iddin-Amurru is found only once as a personal name in the corpus, VS 4 180 (Dar 36). That this specific *hanšû* derived its name from a personal rather than a clan name is also suggested by the lack of the designation 'house of' (*bīt*).

b. Mubannû
Nabû-mutakkil(?)
b. Naggāru
Nummuru//Naggāru
b. apil Nappāhu
b. Nikkāya
b. Pahhāru
mār Pa-ni-a-su-šu-du[93]
Nabû-ēṭir//Purattāya
Rabî
b. Rē'i-alpi
Nabû-zēru-ibni/Nabû-aplu-iddin/Rē'i-alpi
b. Rē'i-sisê
b. Rīšāya
b. Ṣillāya
Ša-Nabû-šū
b. Ṭābihu

At first glance, this list contains many of the families we have encountered in the previous chapter. Families like the Atkuppu, Ēdu-ēṭir, Esagil-mansum, Gallābu, Huṣābu, Iddin-Papsukkal, Ea-ilūtu-bani, Kidin-Sîn, and Rē'i-alpi all owned prebendary rights in the temples of Borsippa. They make up approximately a quarter of the list. Also found among the *hanšû* denominations are families whose prebendary status has not been revealed in the present state of the corpus (approximately 15%). As they were related to priestly families through marriage, however, it is not unlikely that they enjoyed a professional connection to the temple. This applies to, for example, the Bā'iru, Bārû, Kurgarrê, Pahhāru, and the Rišāya families. The fact that all these families had *hanšû* land named after them has led to the belief that, at least in Borsippa, the principal beneficiaries of this type of land were local priestly families.[94]

While this assertion is not wrong as such, it does fail to appreciate the complete landscape of *hanšû* names. The remaining nearly one-third of families, including the Abunāya (or Adnāya), Ašgandu, Bābāya, Bēlāya, Bibbê, Bitahhi,

93 This is probably an occupational family name because of the use of 'son' (*māru*) in front of the name; cf. *hanšû ša mār Bā'iru* (fisherman), *hanšû ša mār Lāsimu* (express messenger/scout) and *hanšû ša apil Nappāhu* (smith). According to R. Zadok, Pa-ni-a-su-šu-du is a name or term of Kassite origin (personal communication, 5-12-2012).

94 See, for example, van Driel 2002: 297–298, Nielsen 2011: 8–9, and Jursa *et al.* 2010: 322. But note the awareness in the latter publication that this picture might be a distorted one due the overall priestly nature of the Borsippa corpus.

Huršanāya, Iššakku, Lahāšu, Lāsimu, and Nikkāya, neither belong to the circle of prebendary families attested in the long sixth century nor do they seem to have been closely related to them.[95] Moreover, with attestations totalling eleven for Ašgandu, ten for Iššakku, nine for Abunāya, six for Purattāya, four for Bibbê, three for Lāsimu, and only one for Huršanāya, these families rarely appear in the Borsippa corpus. Nonetheless, these clans seem to have been indigenous to the Borsippa region, as they remain mostly absent from the corpora of other Babylonian towns.[96]

It thus seems that the range of families that traditionally attached their names to *hanšû* land in Borsippa can roughly be divided in two groups: sacerdotal families and closely allied clans who are generally well attested in the Borsippa corpus, and families who have remained largely unrecorded. As a consequence, this second group of families has escaped attention in the literature on *hanšû* land so far. Is it possible to illuminate their background despite the scarce documentation?

The most tangible evidence we have for the existence of these families is the names themselves, which serve as a starting point for this investigation. The majority of priestly families boasted a clan name that was in line with their professional identity. The Arkāt-ilāni-damqās, Ea-ilūtu-banis, Iddin-Papsukkals, Ilias, Ilī-bānis, Ilšu-abūšus, Kidin-Sîns, and Nabû-mukīn-aplis, for instance, all bear names with theophoric elements that reveal an explicit devotion to the gods in whose service they were enlisted as priests.[97] Other sacerdotal clans derive their names from a professional occupation: e.g. Atkuppu (reed-worker), Bā'iru (fisherman), Gallābu (barber), Itinnu (doorkeeper), Mubannû ('arranger-of-the-sacrificial-table'), Naggāru (carpenter), Nappāhu (smith), Rē'i-alpi (oxherd), and Ṭābihu (butcher). While some of these occupations could certainly be found in the secular domain outside of the temple, evidence from Borsippa and other temple cities like Sippar and Uruk has revealed that these jobs, and the families performing them, were well integrated into the prebendary system.[98]

If we now turn to the second group of families, important distinctions in naming practice can be observed. The first discrepancy is found in the

95 I only deal with *hanšû* estates identified after families here. The remaining thirty-two percent is made up of *hanšû*s named after institutions (*h. ša Esagil*), irrigation districts (*h. ša tamirtu humamātu*), personal names (e.g. *h. ša Iddin-Amurru* and *h. ša Ša-Nabû-šū*) or physical dimensions (*h. rabî*).

96 See Wunsch 2014 for the distribution of the most common Babylonian family names.

97 Note, however, that not all of the prebendary families from Borsippa bear names referencing a god. Examples of this include the Huṣābu, Ahiya'ūtu or the Mannu-gērûšu families. For the documented professions and their families in Borsippa, see Zadok 2012.

98 Kümmel 1979, Bongenaar 1997, Waerzeggers 2010: 38–42, and Zadok 2012.

evocation of the divine in these names, or rather the lack of it. The Ašgandu, Bābāya, Bibbê, Bitahhi, Huršanāya, Nikkāya, and Purattāya, among other families, from this cluster lack theophoric elements in their names. This, in my opinion, is a first clue that these families did not traditionally insist on a particular veneration of the gods. This finds further support if we examine the occupational family names in this group: Ašgandu ('messenger'),[99] Lāsimu ('express messenger', or '(military) scout'),[100] Iššakku (originally meaning '(city-)ruler' but also used as a designation for a 'class of privileged farmers'),[101] Pa-ni-a-su-šu-du (meaning unknown but presumably of Kassite origin),[102] and Rē'i-sisê ('horse-herder'). Contrary to the professions of, for example, the *mubannû* or the *atkuppu* that were integrated in the temple cult, these occupations are not attested as prebendary crafts but rather seem to belong to the army and state organisation.[103]

Apart from their name types, there is further evidence to support classifying the social or professional backgrounds of the families from the second group as not being tied to the temple. BM 28826, a text from Borsippa of unknown

---

99 Ašgandu is an Iranian loanword. See Powell 1972 and Zadok 2006: 440. It should be noted that a certain Gimil-Gula//Ašgandu is mentioned in a catalogue of texts and authors from the library of Assurbanipal, bearing the title [lú]maš.maš [lú]um.me.a tin.tir[ki], 'exorcist, scholar of Babylon' (K 9717+, col. VI: 8), see Lambert 1962: 66–67.

100 CAD/L: 106–108.

101 CAD/I-J: 262–266. Cf. Paulus 2014: 173.

102 Personal communication with R. Zadok (05-12-2012).

103 Note that the occupation of *lāsimu* is often found in a royal context among court officials in early Babylonian *kudurrus*. For references, see CAD/L: 106–108. Another case at hand might be the Bibbê (or Bibbûa) family, which attached its name to the homonymous *hanšû* (TuM 2/3 137). As we have seen above, this family is only attested four times in the entire corpus (BM 29180, BM 94872, BM 26633, and VS 5 92 dated between Nbk 17 and Dar 20). This suggests that the Bibbê family was not part of the traditional priestly stratum of Borsippa, or at least not sufficiently integrated to appear in its archives. According to Wunsch 2014: 304, the family is recorded in Babylon, Kish, and Sippar. While highly speculative, I wonder whether there is a link with Bibea, the leader of the Dakūrus who is mentioned among the royal magnates in the *Hofkalender* of Nebuchadnezzar II (Nbk 07; see Beaulieu 2013a: 34). The Dakūru people were located southeast of Borsippa (Lipiński 2000: 419) and a link to this city can thus be expected. The name was not uncommon among the Chaldean population, as indicated by the Assyrian letter ABL 1030, which mentions a certain Šumāya son of Bibê in the same breath with the notorious Merodach-baladan II (Radner 1999: 342). A group of Dakūreans might have been rewarded by the king with a share of *hanšû* land and named the property after its original beneficiary. The descendants might later have adopted the denomination as a family name in a similar scenario as the one described by Nielsen 2011: 278.

archival context,[104] presents a list of at least forty-four individuals bearing full filiation, including ancestral names, who are said to be, do or give of/for the king (*ša šarri*) (rev.: 9').[105] The following family names are preserved in order of attestation:

> Adad-nāṣir, Barihi, Ap-pa-en-na (?), Nabû-šemê, Rē'û, Huršanāya, Maṣṣār-abulli, Kidin-Nanāya (2x), Gallābu, Ea-bēl-ilāni, Nūr-Papsukkal, Pahhāru, Iddin-Papsukkal (2x), Ēdu-ēṭir, (Ea-)ilūtu-bani, Nikkāya, Iššakku, Naggāru, Ṣillāya, Bā'iru (2x), Huṣābu, Ninurta-ušallim, Kidin-Sîn, Mudammiq-[…], Rē'i-[…], Kidin-[…], Arkāt-ilāni(-damqā), Iddin-[…], Patāya, Ilšu-abūšu, Siātu, Nappāhu.

As one can see from this list, many of the recorded individuals were members of the well-known sacerdotal families: Kidin-Nanāya, Nūr-Papsukkal, Ilšu-abūšu, Huṣābu etc. However, the individuals who did not belong to these temple clans are of more interest to us. We encounter at least three '*hanšû* families' of the second group in this text, i.e. Nikkāya, Iššakku, and Huršanāya, perhaps even four if my assumption is correct that Barihi is the more common spelling for the name Bitahhi.[106] Other families in the list bear names that share the same characteristics as those of families of the second group, e.g. Ap-pa-en-na, Patāya, and Rē'û, which lack theophoric elements or describe non-prebendary professions.

A curious feature of BM 28826 is that none of its individuals is attested elsewhere in the Borsippa corpus. This either suggests that the text is of an early date, or, perhaps more likely, that it deals with a segment of the community that is not well-represented in our corpus. Even if it mentions priestly as well as non-priestly families, many of the latter individuals occur in the first part of the text, which, following Babylonian scribal conventions, should point to their relative importance in the transaction. BM 28826 can thus be taken as a piece of evidence in support of my consideration of the families of the second group as 'secular'.

The final testimony I would like to discuss here is perhaps the most compelling affirmation that the families of the second group came from a different social background than the priestly families. It concerns the remarkable

104 It belongs to the Borsippa sub-collection designated as 98-11-12, which is a mixture of texts belonging to the 'Bēliya'u' group and 'Rē'i-alpi' group according to Waerzeggers 2005.

105 The pertinent operational passage is lost.

106 See footnote 91.

rise of the Bābāya family. As said before, between 485 and 484 BCE large parts of the population supported two pretenders who challenged Xerxes' rule over Babylonia.[107] While they were successful for a short time, Xerxes prevailed over the rebels and retaliated by targeting the sacerdotal circles, bringing to an end a large part of the Neo-Babylonian documentation.[108] After the events of 484 BCE the well-known priestly clans of Borsippa all but disappear from the scene and only very few individuals bearing family names occur in the post-484 BCE documentation.[109] Yet, there are some pertinent exceptions. In the late Achaemenid governor's archive from Babylon, known as the Kasr archive, one finds a small dossier pertaining to a certain Bēl-uṣuršu and his father Ahušunu of the Bābāya family.[110] Additionally, the only known city governor (*šākin-ṭēmi*) of Borsippa after 484 BCE, who is known to have boasted a family name, is a descendant of the same Bābāya clan.[111] These circumstances suggest that this family, attested in Borsippa some thirty times between 614 and 484 BCE, had a profile and political agenda that contrasted strongly with that of the priestly families, as they were left untouched by the Persian retributions. Quite the opposite, the Bābāyas seem to have profited from the new political constellation and must have enjoyed the goodwill of the king, without which they would not have won the post of governor.

1.5 *The Value of* Hanšû *Land in the Sixth Century* BCE

How did families in the sixth century relate to the *hanšû* estates that their forebears obtained by royal favour in the eighth century BCE? Being in possession of an ancient estate that bore one's family name might have heralded proof of an established history and successful cross-generational continuity, while acquiring land in a *hanšû* named after another family might have been felt as an act of infringement, appropriation, and a likely source for resentment. In the following pages I examine the bond between families and their ancestral *hanšû* lands.

107 Kuhrt and Sherwin-White 1987, Rollinger 1998, Kessler 2004, Waerzeggers 2004, Oelsner 2007, Baker 2008, Kuhrt 2010, Henkelman, Kuhrt, Rollinger, and Wiesehöfer 2011, Kuntner, Heinsch, and Allinger-Csollich 2011, and Kuntner and Heinsch 2013.

108 Waerzeggers 2004.

109 For a study of the socio-economic situation in Babylonia post-484 BCE, readers are referred to the dissertation from Vienna University by J. Hackl, [*forthcoming* (b)].

110 See, for example, Stolper 1990, Jursa 2005: 61, and Clancier 2009: 156–157. A study of the Kasr archive is the subject of the forthcoming dissertation by A. Dix, Chicago University.

111 Waerzeggers 2010: 70.

The evidence on *hanšû* land in Borsippa reveals traces of continuity as well as discontinuity of ownership. Of the forty-one *hanšû*s named after a family, thirty-three were alienated at one point or another,[112] while only five estates remained in possession of their 'eponymous' clans.[113] This sobering picture can in part be explained by the nature of the sources at our disposal. Documentation on *hanšû* land (and real estate in general) typically comes into existence when the property is sold or otherwise transferred, giving rise to a rather unstable picture. However, there is additional evidence that helps us to put the data into proper perspective. While thirty-three *hanšû*s were alienated by their original beneficiaries, this divorce was seldom absolute. Only once was a *hanšû* unit sold in its entirety.[114] Families often held multiple *hanšû* plots in different areas that were named after them. A good example is found in the property portfolio of the Ea-ilūtu-bani family, which owned land in the *hanšû ša Illûa*//(*Ea-*)*ilūtu-bani*, *hanšû ša Nādin-ahi*//(*Ea-*)*ilūtu-bani*, and *hanšû ša Suppê-Bēl*//(*Ea-*)*ilūtu-bani*,[115] in addition to land in the *hanšû* named after the ancestral house, the *hanšû ša bīt* (*Ea-*)*ilūtu-bani*.[116]

Even if hardship and misfortune forced some families to sell their land, the emotional value attached to this type of property is illustrated by the fact that attempts were made to redeem lost estates, sometimes many generations later. The first case in point can be found in the archive of the aforementioned Ea-ilūtu-bani family. The *hanšû ša Nādin-ahi*//(*Ea-*)*ilūtu-bani* was sold to the Iddin-Papsukkal family around the 660s BCE,[117] only to be passed on to an individual of the Nappāhu clan a short time later.[118] The next episode remains undocumented, but the land eventually ended up in the possession of the Gallābus. In the reign of Nebuchadnezzar II, at least half a century later,

---

112 In eighteen instances (over half) of the known sales of *hanšû* from the original beneficiary family, this predates the reign of Nabonidus (555 BCE).

113 The following *hanšû* estates are mentioned in inheritance divisions or sale transactions within the lineage: *h. ša bīt Banê-ša-ilia*, *h. ša bīt Basia*, *hanšû Illûa*//(*Ea-*)*ilūtu-bani*, *h. ša bīt Kidin-Sîn*, and *h. ša bīt Rē'i-alpi*. The *h. ša Nikkāya* is mentioned only once as a neighbouring estate (TCL 12 30, Nbk 11) and since no owner is mentioned we cannot know whether it was still kept in the family at this point.

114 RA 10 no. 46 (Ššu 04) the *h. ša* Nummuru//Naggāru seems to have been sold as a whole to the Ilia family.

115 See, for example, YBC 11426 (Ššu 12), TuM 2/3 12 (Ššu 10), and TuM 2/3 23 (Ššu 12).

116 NBC 8362 (AmM 02). While families could own multiple *hanšû*s named after individual family members, there existed only one *hanšû* named after the ancestral house, i.e. '*hanšû ša bīt* FN'. Perhaps these estates represent the clan's original allotment from the eighth century BCE. *Hanšû*s named after individuals might have come into being later after inheritance, acquisition, and fragmentation.

117 See, for example, TuM 2/3 17, TCL 12 9, and TuM 2/3 11.

118 TuM 2/3 12.

members of the Ea-ilūtu-bani family re-assembled parts of their patrimony[119] and the land remained in the family's possession.[120]

Another, perhaps less successful, attempt of reclamation relates to the *hanšû ša bīt Gallābu*. This land was already lost to the eponymous family during or before the reign of Nebuchadnezzar II at which point it is found in possession of the Ea-ilūtu-banis.[121] After being divided and partly sold to the Iddin-Papsukkal family, a member of the Gallābu family was able to reclaim a portion of this *hanšû* in the time of King Nabonidus.[122] The Gallābus, however, were forced to sell again under King Cambyses, only a decade later.[123]

There is additional evidence, admittedly of a more circumstantial nature, of families attempting to regain their ancestral land through purchase or exchange or simply maintaining a keen interest in it. One example is the scribe of the Bābāya clan who recorded a cultivation contract for a plot in the *hanšû ša bīt Bābāya*.[124] Other examples involve individuals holding shares,[125] owning neighbouring land,[126] and acting as witnesses[127] in documents relating to their eponymous land.

A further illustration of the emotional attachment to these ancestral *hanšû*s is found in dowry transactions. We have seen in the previous chapter that the presentation of the dowry was an essential feature of Babylonian marriage. Among priestly families it typically consisted of slaves, silver, jewellery, household goods, furniture, and real estate, usually in the form of land.[128] In the majority of documented dowries in Babylonia this did not concern *hanšû* land,[129] but in Borsippa this was on the contrary quite often the case.[130] We know of ten *hanšû* estates that were transferred through dowry transactions.[131] This seems to indicate a limited attachment to this land. However, once we

119 OECT 12 A 163 (d.l.), OECT 12 A 98 (Nbk 08).
120 See, for example, NBC 8360 (Nbk 41) and TuM 2/3 153 (AmM 01).
121 YBC 9158.
122 BM 96351.
123 BM 29401.
124 BM 96291.
125 See, for example, VS 3 91 *h. ša bīt Basia*.
126 See, for example, TCL 12 30 *h. ša bīt Atkuppu*; BM 17599 *h. ša bīt Ēdu-ēṭir*; OECT 12 AB 241 *h. ša bīt Iddin-Papsukkal*; and BM 82656 *h. ša Nabû-šumu-līšir//Kidin-Sîn*.
127 See, for example, BM 25630//BM 25653 *h. ša bīt Naggāru*.
128 Roth 1989b, Roth 1990, and Oelsner, Welsch, and Wunsch 2003: 940–944.
129 For relevant sources, see Roth 1990: 10–12.
130 This is in all likelihood thanks to the widespread existence of *hanšû* land in the Borsippean countryside.
131 BM 82629 (Roth 1990 no. 13), BM 96313, BM 96186, BM 26487, OECT 12 AB 241, BM 26576 = AH XV no. 192, BM 82609 = Roth 1989 no. 22, BM 101980//BM 82607, BM 96315, BM 29375, BM 103458. Note that five more ambiguous transfers might be added. See the Appendix

take a closer look at these transactions, the opposite seems true. In the majority of the endowments the *hanšû* plot did not bear the ancestral name of the bride's family. There is in fact only one example in which land was named after the wife-giver's family.[132] This suggests that families preferred to endow their daughters with *hanšû* land that did not belong to their original allotment.

Hanšû land was meant to stay in the patrimony to be passed on to future generations. Evidence suggests that families held on to their ancestral land for a long time indeed. A case in point is the *hanšû ša bīt Lāsimu*. A member of the Lāsimu family sold part of it to the Bēliya'u family in the reign of Darius I (ca. 512 BCE), implying that the family had been able to hold on to their ancestral property for over two hundred years since its supposed endowment in the eighth century BCE.[133] The same is true for the Iššakku family. While evidence on their *hanšû* also came into being at a moment of crisis (it was being held as pledge), BM 29007 dates to the twenty-seventh year of Darius I (ca. 495 BCE), thus showing that the land had probably been handed down within the family for as many as three hundred years. Yet, a note of caution should be voiced here. The evidence reviewed above suggests that the *hanšû* schemes in Borsippa originate from the late eighth century BCE, yet one should allow for the possibility that some schemes were created at a later date. If my understanding of the land described as *bīt Bēliya'u* in BM 28904 (Nbk 33) is correct, it shows that new *hanšû* units could be created out of existing ones well into the Neo-Babylonian period.[134]

2 Land Sales and the Circulation of Property

Land was an essential component of the subsistence strategy of priests. Yet, despite its economic value, the devolution of landed property can and should not be interpreted in terms of maximisation of profit alone.[135] Beneath the

2 for: *h. ša bīt* Basia, *h. ša bīt Nabû-šumu-iškun//Barû, h. ša bīt Esagil-mansum, h. ša Saggillu//Iddin-Papsukkal*, and *h. ša bīt Ṣillāya.*

132 This might be deduced from text BM 101980//BM 82607. Early in the reign of Darius I (ca. Dar 05–09) Nabû-mukīn-zēri//Rē'i-alpi tried (the attempt was later contested and nullified) to assign the dowry field in the *hanšû ša bīt Mubannû* of his wife ᶠNanāya-bulliṭiš//Mubannû to his daughter and grandson. This suggests that ᶠNanāya-bulliṭiš brought part of her family's land into the conjugal household when she married into the Rē'i-alpi family.

133 BM 96289. The *hanšû* name is not mentioned in the sale contract but restored from a follow-up document (BM 96299).

134 See Appendix 2.

135 Very inspirational in this respect has been the pioneering study by the Italian microhistorian G. Levi 1985, *L'eredità immateriale: carriera di un esorcista nel Piemonte del*

apparent market functioning of land sales lie social mechanisms of, for example, patronage, charity, power, reciprocity, neighbourhood networks, and political affiliation.[136] This raises the question whether any limitations of a social kind rested on selling and buying land in Borsippa's priestly community. In this part I examine whether two major principles of social organisation in this group, the hypergamous marriage system and professional solidarity, somehow influenced the circulation of this kind of property within the community. In both analyses I add the sales of other immovable properties, non-*hanšû* land and urban real estate, in order to determine whether *hanšû* land was treated differently from other types of real estate.

2.1 *Marriage Alliances*

Earlier in this study I demonstrated that the hypergamous marriage system of Borsippa's priests assigned all participating families a certain set of rights and duties *vis-à-vis* one another. Did these arrangements regulate other types of interactions as well? In this section I examine the relation (if any) between marriage alliances and the ways in which families managed their *hanšû* estates. More specifically, I analyse whether marriage ties regulated the patterns of sale and purchase of this property.

So far the Borsippa corpus references a total of twenty-eight sales of *hanšû* land.[137] While this number is relatively modest, the diachronic distribution is quite satisfactory: three sales (10%) date before the advent of the Neo-Babylonian Empire (ca. 620 BCE), six (21%) before the reign of Nabonidus (555 BCE), ten (36%) until the end of Cambyses' rule (555–522 BCE), and nine (32%) in the final phase of the documentation (until 484 BCE). The information about marriage ties of the clans involved in these transactions is also reasonably substabtial. In sixteen cases, there is information on marital alliances of both parties (approximately 57%); in eleven cases there is information for one of the parties (39%). Only in once case are we completely ignorant on marital ties of both parties.

In the following analysis I adopt the same methodology as in the previous chapter and use the individual clan as basic unit of analysis. This means that the clan or family is understood as a corporate entity whose individual members were to a certain extent subject to the same rights, obligations, social

Seicento. In this work he attempts to reconstruction the 'peasant-specific rationality' in seventeenth-century CE Italy, based on the study of a specific individual (a local exorcist) and his locality. Of special interest for the present study is his endeavour to do away with the widespread misconception among medieval historians (and historians in general) that all transactions of land should be interpreted in terms of economic motivation.

136 Levi 1985: 113–132.

137 See Appendix 3 for a list of all the sales of *hanšû* land.

agenda, and professional identity, and, following the alliance system, shared a collective disposition towards the rest of the community.

Let us compare the constellation of wife-givers and wife-takers (figure 6 above) and the dissolution pattern of *hanšû* land. The transactions most relevant here are those from the first category, where information on the marriage ties of both parties is available. In almost half (44%) of these transactions, no marital tie between the parties is attested so far. Sales of *hanšû* by a wife-taker family to a wife-giver family are attested in five instances (31%). In three instances a wife-giver sold *hanšû* property to his wife-taker.

This does not seem to suggest a particular preference when it comes to finding a suitable buyer of *hanšû* land. However, the picture changes once we take the chronological arrangement of the transaction *vis-à-vis* the marriage into consideration. The following re-evaluation suggests that the priestly families tended not to engage in land transactions anymore once they established a marital tie among them. Of the five land sales by a wife-taker to his wife-giver (twice direct and three times indirect), four transactions predate the marriage settlement.[138] The fifth wife-taker was involved in the transaction only as proxy.[139] The same is true for sales by wife-givers to wife-takers. Two of the recorded transactions were settled long before the marital tie was established.[140] There is only one instance where a wife-giver sold *hanšû* land to his direct

138 First, in Ššu 07 (TCL 12 9) the Ea-ilūtu-bani family sells *hanšû* land to the Iddin-Papsukkal family, whereas the marriage alliance between these two families was established around Dar 25 (VS 5 96). Second, in Cyrus 06 (OECT 12 AB 241) an individual from the Aqar-Nabû family and his wife from the Huṣābu family sold a piece of *hanšû* land to the Ahiya'ūtu family, but only in the reign of Darius I did the latter give a daughter in marriage to the Nūr-Papsukkal family, making the Huṣābus indirect wife-givers of both sellers. Third, in the fourteenth year of Nabonidus (BM 96351), a piece of land in the *hanšû* of the Gallābu clan is sold by the Ea-ilūtu-banis to an individual of the Gallābu clan. It is, however, only by marrying a daughter to the Kidin-Sîn family some thirty years later (BM 85447, Dar 06) that the Gallābu clan became indirect wife-givers of the Ea-ilūtu-banis. Fourth, according to BM 82656, the Kidin-Sîn family sold a plot of *hanšû* to the Rē'i-alpi family at the beginning of Darius I's reign. Only several decades later did the Rē'i-alpi family become an indirect wife-giver of the Kidin-Sîn family (via the Gallābus).

139 According to BM 25627 (Nbn 00) Nabû-mukīn-apli/Apla/Rē'i-alpi bought land in the *hanšû ša Rē'i-alpi* from an individual of the Arkāt-ilāni-damqā clan. While the families were intermarried, the text explains that the seller had previously bought it from ᶠAmat-Ningal//Rē'i-alpi, on behalf of Nabû-mukīn-zēri//Rē'i-alpi (the eventual buyer). It thus represents a sale within the Oxherd family.

140 According to the available evidence the Naggāru family only became an indirect wife-giver of the Ilia clan (via Ilšu-abūšu) at the beginning of Nabonidus' reign (BM 28863 = AH XV no. 115). The sale of *hanšû* land, following the direction of marriage, took place almost 100 years earlier (*RA* 10 no. 46, Ššu 07). Also, OECT 12 A 163, dated to the early Neo-Babylonian period (ca. Npl – early Nbk), records a transaction of land sold by Gallābu to

wife-taker after arranging a marriage alliance. But here the sale did not stand on its own, being part of a belated dowry transaction, inter-family property transmission or debt settlement.[141]

This closer assessment of the evidence thus reveals that ninety-four percent of *hanšû* land transactions was concluded between parties that were not related by close or more distant marriage. Whether we can talk about a genuine pattern or preference is hard to decide, however. The amount of data is too meagre to support a compelling quantitative analysis. Nonetheless, the same pattern is obtained after we incorporate more data into our analysis. In the following statistics all eighty property sales from Borsippa including *hanšû* land sales, non-*hanšû* land sales, and house sales have been subjected to the same examination.[142] This shows that property was sold sixty-two times (77.5%) between families not related by marriage; ten times (12.5%) by a wife-taker to his (in-)direct wife-giver; and eight times (10%) by a wife-giver to his (in-)direct wife-taker. The number of sales in the latter two categories can be further reduced once we take the time of sale into consideration. In eight out of ten cases in which a wife-taker sold property to his wife-giver the transaction predates the marriage alliance.[143] This also applies to at least four of eight

(Ea-)ilūtu-bani. The former only became a wife-giver of the (Ea-)ilūtu-bani family (via Kidin-Sîn) during the reign of Darius I (ca. 520s BCE).

141 The issue at hand concerns the Rē'i-alpi and the Šarrahu families, more specifically ^{f}Inbā/Nabû-mukīn-apli/Rē'i-alpi and her husband Rēmūt-Nabû/Nabû-šumu-uṣur/Šarrahu. While the exact date of their marriage is unknown it must be dated between the reigns of Nabonidus and Darius I since they already had two children by Dar 05. In that year an extensive property transfer was initiated. Nabû-mukīn-zēri//Rē'i-alpi (father of ^{f}Inbā) bequeathed his two grandchildren (by ^{f}Inbā and her husband of the Šarrahu family) with large parts of his property, thereby effectively bypassing his own son, Rēmūt-Nabû (Waerzeggers 2010: 561–562). While the date of the sale of *hanšû* land by a certain Nabû-râm-nīšīšu//Rē'i-alpi to Nabû-šumu-uṣur//Šarrahu (father-in-law of ^{f}Inbā//Rē'i-alpi) is missing (BM 94552), it is very likely that it was concluded in the same period of property transmission. Nabû-râm-nīšīšu was involved in several transactions with Nabû-mukīn-zēri and his son (BM 94653 = AH XV no. 160, Cam 01; BM 26671, Dar 00; BM 94676 = AH XV no. 171, Dar 01; BM 26535 = AH XV no. 199, Dar [x]). This whole dossier is quite complex and it is not unthinkable that this last transaction of *hanšû* land represents the settling of debts between Nabû-râm-nīšīšu, Nabû-mukīn-zēri, and Nabû-šumu-uṣur.

142 See Appendix 3 for a list of sales of housing plots and non-*hanšû* land. In the analysis I left out those transactions that took place within the same clan (Bēliya'u: BM 25100; (Ea-)ilūtu-bani: OECT 12 A 131, TuM 2/3 14, YBC 11426; Gallābu: BM 96343; Lā-kuppuru: VS 5 91; Rē'i-alpi: BM 82632) and those in which the names of the parties have not been preserved.

143 For the *hanšû* sales, see above. For the other types of property sales, see the following instances. First, the Gallābu family sold property to the Ilia family early in the reign of Nabonidus (BM 82679); the latter is only attested as wife-giver of Gallābu in Nbn 15 (BM 85570). Second, Ea-ilūtu-bani sold a house to Ilia D (BM 82740). Based on prosopography

occasions when property was sold by a wife-giver to his wife-taker.[144] Finally, in two out of three cases in which one can confidently assert that a family sold property to his wife-taker (in all three cases the Rē'i-alpi family is involved),[145] the transactions were part of a larger property transfer presumably caused by indebtedness and cannot be seen as ordinary sales.[146] Hence, in the vast majority, sales took place between parties that were not related through marriage. Even if the available evidence is somewhat scarce, one could propose, as a general rule, that in the priestly community of Borsippa marriage alliances usually excluded property sales.

A possible rationale behind this restriction may be sought in the hypergamous alliance system. I demonstrated in the previous chapter that by intermarriage two clans engaged in a mutual alliance that involved specific rights and obligations towards each other. Marriage re-confirmed or indeed triggered a relative status difference in which the wife-taking family assumed a superior position. Yet, this (marriage) hierarchy was not always clear-cut and perhaps even fragile. Hence, if two clans related through marriage sold land to each other, this could have set a new flow of property in motion, compelling the parties to re-evaluate and renegotiate their relative status. It is in my opinion precisely the avoidance of this effect that underlies the pattern of property sales. Families ranked by marriage did not want to disturb the established hierarchy by entering into a new contract. Moreover, buying each other's property might have been perceived as an unfriendly act or an infringement on the patrimony;

---

this took place between Nbn 04 and the reign of Cambyses. According to the available documentation the Ilias only became wife-givers of the Ea-ilūtu-bani clan in Dar 25, via the Iddin-Papsukkal family (VS 5 96). Third, according to BM 85542, dated Nbn 16, the Ea-ilūtu-bani family sold land to the Gallābu family. It was however only by marrying a daughter to the Kidin-Sîn family some 30 years later (BM 85447, Dar 06) that the Gallābus became indirect wife-givers of the Ea-ilūtu-banis.

144 For *hanšû* sales, see above. For the other types of property sales, BM 87358 (Nbn 13) records the sale of a house by the Nūr-Papsukkal to the Ilia (D) family. It was only some eighty years later that the Nūr-Papsukkal family became an indirect wife-giver of the Ilias via the Ilšu-abūšu family (Smith Coll. no. 92, Dar 30). Also, in Nbn 12 the Gallābus finalised their payment to the Ša-nāšišu family for land they had received from the latter. The Ša-nāšišus only became wife-givers of the Gallābus a couple of years later through an alliance with the Ilia family (BM 85570).

145 In the case of the Arad-Ea and Ilia families this cannot be answered with certainty. While the former became an indirect wife-giver of the Ilias (through Rē'i-alpi) around Dar 01 at the latest, the date of the transaction is lost (BM 94557). There are no prosopographical leads that help us date the text more precisely.

146 BM 25712//BM 82790 and BM 26656//BM 26687. These texts belong to a dossier discussed by Waerzeggers 2010: 555–556, which concerns the insolvent Nabû-ušebši/Marduk-šākin-šumi/Rē'i-alpi who relinquished property to several relatives to pay off his debts.

it could easily lead to friction and legal contestation between related and befriended clans. The priestly families from Borsippa preferred to preserve the *status quo* established by direct or indirect marriage[147] and searched for a neutral buyer instead. This accentuates the cardinal importance of marriage in this sacerdotal community as its repercussions reached well outside of the temple fabric, effectively modulating the dissolution of property among the local families. The above evidence also confirms that the phenomenon not only had an impact on direct marriage partners but also on families that were related by indirect marriage through the principle of transitivity. One can only hope that more evidence on sales, but also on marriages comes to light to substantiate or annul this hypothesis.

2.2 *Professional Solidarity*

In addition to marriage ties, it seems that professional affiliation, perhaps better described as group solidarity, may have had an effect on the circulation of property in this community. Beginning my analysis with *hanšû* land, it appears that of eighteen instances[148] in which a priestly family sold such land, four buyers (22%) belonged to the same prebendary group,[149] eleven buyers (61%) to another prebendary group,[150] and three buyers (17%) to non-priestly clans.[151] This suggests that there was a tendency among Borsippean priests to sell this type of land outside their own prebendary group but within the circle of prebendary families. Eighty-five percent of all sales were realised within the broader prebendary circle. If we now change the focus and examine the purchase of *hanšû* land by priestly families, an interesting facet is revealed. Out of twenty-two cases in which a sacerdotal clan acquired *hanšû* land, seven sellers (32%) belonged to a non-prebendary family.[152] This suggests that sacerdotal families from Borsippa bought *hanšû* land *from* 'outsiders' more often than they sold it *to* them: once this land entered into the possession of the sacerdotal families, it rarely left their social circle.

147 This is perhaps further supported by the fact that when intermarried clans did engage in property sales, it was sold more often than not by the wife-giver to the wife-taker family, thus following the existing direction of marriage and the related flow of property.

148 See Appendix 3 for a list of *hanšû* land sales.

149 Group specific: once baker, once brewer, twice temple-enterer.

150 More specific, land sold by **Baker**: twice oxherds; by **Barber**: twice temple-enterers, and once brewers; by **Brewer**: once oxherd; by **Butcher**: once baker; by **Temple-enterer**: twice brewers, and once barber.

151 Land was sold to a member of the Adad-ibni, Mudammiq-Marduk, and Šarrahu families.

152 Ša-ṭābtišu (VS 5 140), Lāsimu (BM 96289), Šagimmu (BE 8 43), Damēqu (TuM 2/3 15), Asaluhhi-mansum (VS 5 48), and individual without clan affiliation (BM 26510).

This trend was not restricted to *hanšû* property; it applied to all types of real estate.[153] Based on the entire data set it appears that in fifty-five percent of cases real estate circulated within the larger prebendary group,[154] but almost as much (45%) was bought from outside families. But no more than twenty percent of property sales (perhaps as little as 13%) was made by priestly families to non-prebendary outsiders.[155] It is also interesting to note that the Rē'i-alpi family was involved in most sales in the last category. As I have shown earlier, this prebendary group occupied a lower rung in the temple hierarchy and in comparison to the other (higher-ranking) priestly families adopted an outward-looking attitude in the local alliance system by intermarrying with outsiders.

These figures suggest that the priestly stratum in Borsippa worked as a centripetal force, steadily acquiring new property and releasing only very little from its control. This may be seen as a form of solidarity, not *per se* within one's own professional group, but towards the prebendary circle at large. Yet, a note of caution is at place here. The numbers drawn from this quantitative analysis are likely to be a result of the biased nature of our documentation, consisting mainly of archives of priests. While the patterns of dissolution among priestly families may well be representative, this cannot be said with the same degree of certainty for sales outside the prebendary circle. Babylonian archival practice dictates that together with the sale of property all documents relating to the sold property were transferred.[156] This renders the twenty percent of property sales made by priestly families to non-priestly families questionable, since most of the property that was sold in such transactions has become largely untraceable. One has to maintain the possibility that there was much more transaction from this category. In order to validate these findings, we need additional archives of at least some outside families to see whether their dynamics of dissolution agree with the ones reconstructed above for the prebendary circles.

153 See Appendix 3 for a list of all property sales from Borsippa.

154 Of the fifty-five transactions in which sacerdotal families were involved as buyers, seven times (13%) was intra-prebendary, twenty-three times (42%) inter-prebendary, and twenty-five times (45%) extra-prebendary (i.e. from outsiders).

155 Of the forty transactions in which sacerdotal families are found as sellers: seven times (18%) was intra-prebendary, twenty-five times (63%) inter-prebendary, and eight times (20%) extra-prebendary. But note that at least three sales from this last category were between direct marriage partners. It is thus perhaps not entirely correct to label these as 'extra-prebendary'.

156 Oelsner, Wells and Wunsch 2003: 923–924.

3 Tenancy and Agricultural Collaboration

Land ownership was not only a marker of wealth and prestige, but it also guaranteed a livelihood for its owner. In the waterlogged region of Borsippa, agriculture was geared largely towards date palm cultivation.[157] Besides the yearly harvest of dates, owners could extract a set of by-products from the trees, among which various baskets, processed dates, palm-fibre, and firewood.[158] In order to reach and maintain productivity of the land, continuous labour and care were required.[159] Besides the obvious tasks of planting and harvesting, the sources inform us about a range of activities such as maintaining the irrigation channels, watering, breaking up soil clods, weeding, tending to palm-trees, palm-shoots and the subculture, erecting fences and walls, and the protection of the land in general.[160]

Since much of their attention was centred towards their cultic duties in town, priestly families did not usually cultivate their own land, but, with a few exceptions, outsourced agricultural labour to others.[161] This practice has left an extensive paper trail in the archives of Borsippa's priests, in the form of cultivation contracts, harvest estimations, field-rent payments, debt notes, and receipts.[162] On the basis of these sources, patterns of tenancy can be reconstructed. While some information on tenants of private land can be found in the literature,[163] existing studies are usually concerned with economic matters,

157 Jursa *et al.* 2010: 360–385. While there is evidence for the cultivation of barley, and to a lesser extent, also sesame (NBC 8362 (AmM 02), BM 29473 (Dar 19), and Bellino Q (Dar II 14)), wheat (BM 94716 (Dar 10)) and emmer are underrepresented in Borsippa. The latter is so far only attested in the cult (BM 96320 (Dar 15)). The trend towards a more intensive form of date-palm horticulture, partly at the expense of arable farming, was well advanced in sixth century Borsippa, cf. Jursa *et al.* 2010: 437–443.

158 For secondary products from date-palm cultivation, see Landsberger 1967: 42ff. It was not uncommon to grow other fruits and vegetables in separate tracts or as subculture between the palms. In Borsippa one hears occasionally of grapevines (BM 29004 (Dar 10), RA 10 no. 40 (d.l.)), figs (e.g. BM 103637 (Dar 13)), pomegranates (e.g. BM 102012 (Dar 08)), and onions (e.g. BM 94688 (Cam 02), BM 82660 (Cam 03), BM 17683 (Dar 06)).

159 See Ries 1976, van Driel 1990, and Jursa 2004a, for Neo-Babylonian cultivation and its technicalities. Extensive references and bibliography can be found in these publications.

160 Cf. Jursa 2004a.

161 There are a few attestations in which young members of prebendary families are found working on their patrimonial land or at least assuming management over it. It has been suggested by Jursa *et al.* 2010: 182ff., that this might have been a temporary occupation for individuals of priestly families before they were enrolled in the priesthood.

162 Of particular interest are those debt notes and receipts that mention typical agricultural terms like *imittu*, *sūtu*, *šibšu*, *ebūr eqli* or *sissinu*. On these terms, see Jursa 1995.

163 Specific prosopographies of tenants can be found in archival studies, such as, Joannès 1989: 65–96, Wunsch 2000: 54–58, and Baker 2004: 65–68. One finds general statements

technicalities of agriculture, and the legal position of the tenants in terms of income rights and contract durations. Social aspects of tenancy have received little attention thus far.[164]

In the following pages I take a closer look at the tenants who were employed in the cultivation of the landholdings of our priests. By analysing the identity of these tenants in conjunction with the identity of the landowners, new light can be shed on interfamily relations in the agricultural sphere and the social organisation of the priestly community vis-à-vis other social groups in Borsippa. Tenants can be divided into three groups: tenants of unfree status, free tenants without family names, and free tenants with family names. These three groups are discussed in said order.

3.1 *Unfree Tenants*

The first group of tenants employed by the priests, the group that appears least frequently in the documentation, are unfree individuals: *širku*s and private slaves. A *širku*, literally 'oblate', was a serf bound to the temple.[165] While usually retained by the institution, *širku*s did enjoy some freedom as they were, for example, allowed to marry and to acquire property, which they could dispose of freely. Even if they never became fully independent actors, some *širku*s acquired substantial personal wealth.[166]

Tenants of *širku* status are attested a dozen times in Borsippa. They occur as debtors of harvest estimates (perhaps as seasonal workers),[167] as well as fully fledged gardeners in cultivation contracts.[168] Normally, they seem to have been employed independently, but on at least one occasion a *širku* was hired for the cultivation of an onion field in addition to a well-established tenant of the Naggāru family.[169] Most *širku* tenants occur only once in the documentation,

concerning the use of free labour in Neo-Babylonian agriculture, such as, 'the labor of free farmers and tenants was the basis of agriculture' (Dandamaev 1996: 208) or '[t]he urban upper class tended to lease their land to free tenants rather than farm it themselves or with slaves' (Jursa *et al.* 2010: 31).

164 Management and tenancy of temple land have received more thorough analysis. Note especially Jursa 1995: 7–47 where the social status and background of the temple farmers are examined.

165 On the status of the Neo-Babylonian *širku*, see, for example, Kleber 2011, and the 2007 Harvard dissertaton by A. Regan.

166 A well-known example is Gimillu, a high-profile *širku* from Uruk, discussed by Jursa 2004c.

167 See, for example, BM 85649 (Cam 05), BE 8 111 (Dar 16), and VS 3 128 (Dar 21).

168 See, for example, BM 94688 (Cam 02), BM 29499 (Dar 14), and BM 26524 (Dar 15).

169 The cultivation contract in question is BM 94688 (Cam 02) and belongs to the Ilia (A) archive. One year earlier the same Lâbâši//Naggāru leased a field from the Ilia family (BE 8 79).

which suggests that they were hired on an *ad hoc* basis, perhaps only when the temple could spare their labour and temporarily allowed them to work elsewhere. Yet, there is at least one instance where a *širku* enjoyed a longer relationship to the land and its owner. The case in question comes from the Bēliya'u archive. In Dar 20, Šaddinnu//Bēliya'u bought an orchard located in the *hanšû ša bīt mār Lāsimu*.[170] The three ensuing harvest estimations, dated Dar 21, 22 and 23, were all due from Haddā/Guzānu, a *širku* of Nabû.[171] He tended to this garden for at least three years. There is one further *imittu* text concerning the same plot, which dates to Xer 01, some fifteen years later. In BM 28972, the debtor is not Haddā, however, but a certain Šamaš-ibni//Arad-Nergal. Even so, two details suggest that Haddā was associated with this land. First, Šamaš-ibni//Arad-Nergal witnessed all previous *imittu* estimations due from Haddā, raising the possibility that he had always superintended Haddā. Second, BM 28972 is written by a certain Bēl-ēṭir/Haddā. While he is not identified as a *širku*, it seems likely that he was the son of Haddā. Not only does this indicate that Haddā's tenancy spanned well over a decade, but also that he passed some of his charges on to the next generation.[172]

Another point of interest is the fact that temple oblates are only found on land held by members of the Bēliya'u, Iddin-Papsukkal, Ilia, and Gallābu families, all priestly families.[173] Although this could be a coincidence of discovery, in the archive of the non-priestly Egibi family from Babylon, which is our most extensive source on private landowning in Babylonia, temple oblates are not attested as tenants.[174] Perhaps thanks to their association with the temple, priestly families were more likely to profit from or perhaps had better access to this source of institutional manpower.

The second group of unfree tenants is made up of privately-owned slaves. Virtually all prosperous urban families owned slaves.[175] They were the absolute property of their masters and could thus be disposed of freely, but slaves did occasionally enjoy a greater degree of freedom.[176] We find them married,

170 BM 29113.

171 VS 3 128 (Dar 21), BM 96299 (Dar 22), and BM 96221 (Dar 23).

172 Also note that in BM 96303 (Dar 10) Šaddinnu//Bēliya'u rented a house to a *širku* named Guzānu/Nergal-iddin. If this person should be identified as the father of Haddā the association between the two families spanned three generations and as many decades.

173 The latter does not concern the non-prebendary Gallābu family whose archive we have. Note, however, that the above-mentioned Haddā or his brother might also have cultivated the land for the Lāsimu family before it entered the Bēliya'u archive. This idea is based in the fact that he received part of the purchase price. Yet, the background of this compensation is not made explicit in BM 29113 (Dar 20).

174 Wunsch 2000: 54–58.

175 Jursa *et al.* 2010: 233ff.

176 See Oelsner, Wells and Wunsch 2003: 928–993 on the Neo-Babylonian (chattel) slave.

running important business affairs of their masters, and acquiring property, while some slaves were allowed to set up businesses of their own.[177] However, keeping with the general trend slaves are mentioned less than a dozen times in the Borsippa corpus in relation to agricultural activities.[178] While most of them are found as debtors of *imittu* estimates, suggesting that they were put to work during harvest time when extra hands were required,[179] at least one slave was responsible for the actual cultivation of a field.[180] In seven out of ten known cases of slaves being employed as tenants, they were working the land of their own master, sometimes in tandem with a free gardener.[181] Families who used their own slaves for agricultural purposes are the Ea-ilūtu-bani, Ilī-bāni, Ilia (A), and Ilia (D) families.

3.2 *Tenants without Family Names*

The use of a family name functioned as a marker of established descent and affiliation to the urban elites. Individuals lacking this nominal affiliation presumably constituted the greater part of the Babylonian population. In the Borsippa corpus there are, however, only slightly over fifty references to such individuals, some of who may be of foreign (West-Semitic) extraction,[182] employed on the land of priestly families. This group of tenants accounts for less than twenty percent of the entire (recorded) labour force.

The labour of these tenants was often secured on a contractual basis by means of cultivation contracts. While generally employed for unspecific 'gardening' (*ana nukuribbūti*)[183] and 'cultivation' (*ana errēšūti*),[184] some tenants

177 In which case they were obliged to pay their owner a quit-rent (*mandattu*). Best-known in this respect are the agent-slaves of the Nūr-Sîn and Egibi families. See, for example, Dandamaev 1984: 345ff., 365ff. and Wunsch 1993: 42–50. An interesting example from the priestly circles from Borsippa is the slave Balāṭu. Besides being active as agent for his masters of the Ilšu-abūšu (A) family, Balāṭu helped him with the brewing of beer for the offerings, thereby clearly making a small profit of his own. Interestingly, the documents from Balāṭu seem to have been discovered separately from those of his master, suggesting that he kept his own archive. See Jursa 2005: 88–89 and Waerzeggers 2010: 437–441, which includes the publication of some of his documents.

178 Dandamaev 1984: 252ff., 277; Jursa *et al.* 2010: 234–235.

179 See, for example, OECT 12 A 92 (Nbk 34), TuM 2/3 156 (Ner 01), BM 26548 (Dar 13).

180 BM 29489 (Cyr 05) from the Ibnāya archive.

181 See, for example, TCL 12 52 (Nbk 35), TuM 2/3 156 (Ner 01), BM 102178 (Dar 02), and BM 94816 (Dar 22).

182 See, for example, Digiria in TEBR 74 (Dar 21), Napsānu in BM 17648 (Cam 07), and Šenduri in YBC 9191 (Nbk [x]).

183 See, for example, TuM 2/3 133 (Kan 04), BM 29487 (Dar 12), and BM 29020 (Xer 02).

184 See, for example, NBC 8362 (AmM 02) and BM 28954 (Dar [x]).

obtained the lease of a field against a fixed rent (*ana sūti*).[185] The latter is suggestive of a more professional, business-oriented enterprise from the perspective of the gardeners.[186]

Without the help of family names, it is difficult to keep track of these tenants in the documentation. The widespread use of nicknames and the occasionally lacunal documentation make it often impossible to establish whether references concern the same person or not. The initial impression is that priests, who needed their services mainly around harvest time or as seasonal workers, employed these tenants only periodically. However, taking a closer look at the available evidence enables the identification of priestly families who did enjoy more stable business relations with tenants of lower strata. The first clue comes from the cultivation contracts mentioned above. While the duration of employment is usually not specified in these cultivation contracts (a lease of one year minimum is to be expected), at least five agreements were made for either three or five years, all of them belonging to the Bēliya'u archive.[187] Another example of a long and stable tenant-landowner relationship is found in the Ilia (A) archive. Marduk-šumu-ibni//Ilia inherited a plot located in the *tamīrtu Hamar* area, which he kept undivided with his two younger brothers. The first harvest estimation (*imittu*), recorded in Dar 03, was due from a certain Šumu-ukīn/Nabû-ēṭir, who also delivered the dates in Dar 07 and Dar 09.[188] While Šumu-ukīn was replaced by another tenant in Dar 16,[189] he was back in business together with a colleague two years later.[190] His final attestation as tenant occurred in Dar 26 when he is identified by his full name, Nabû-šumu-ukīn.[191] Other examples can be found in the Ea-ilūtu-bani, Ilī-bāni, and Rē'i-alpi family archives.[192]

185 See, for example, TuM 2/3 137 (Cam 02) and BM 94826 (Dar 11).
186 For the different types of cultivation contracts, see Jursa 2004a.
187 BM 29004 (Dar 10), BM 29487 (Dar 12), BM 96190 (Dar 20), BM 28954 (Dar [x]), and BM 29020 (Xer 02).
188 BM 109868 (Dar 03), BM 87275 (Dar 07), and VS 3 105 (Dar 09).
189 VS 3 121 (Dar 16?).
190 BM 27797 (Dar 18).
191 KVM 59 (Dar 26).
192 Ea-ilūtu-bani: in BM 94600 (AmM [x]) a certain Nabû-ahu-iddin has to deliver the harvest of a field to Zēru-Bābili//Ea-ilūtu-bani. By Nbn 13 Zēru-Bābili was succeeded by his son Mušēzib-Marduk and the same seems to have happened to Nabû-ahu-iddin. TCL 12 105 (Nbn 13), BM 94780 (Nbn 13), NBC 8347 (Nbn 13), and BM 94851 (Nbn [x]) report on the agricultural activities of Rēmūt and Kalbā, sons of Nabû-ahu-iddin. It stands to reason that these are indeed the sons of the former tenant. Ilī-bāni: L 1637 (Nbn 09) is an *imittu* debt that was due from Itti-Nabû-balāṭu/Bullissu. 20 years later we meet the same tenant cultivating a different field for the same family (TuM 2/3 127, Cam 02). Rē'i-alpi: BM 94684 (Dar 12) is a debt note for dates and palm-fibres, which had to be delivered by Nabû-ittannu/

Finally, it is worth considering which of the priestly families employed lower-stratum individuals. Although such tenants were employed by all of the priestly families, from the highest temple-enterers to the lowest reed-workers, there is one priest who seems to have availed himself of their labour on a much larger scale. Whereas in most priestly archives these individuals represent around twenty percent of the tenants,[193] in the archive of Šaddinnu//Bēliya'u they are found almost half of the time (twenty out of forty-two instances). Whether this should be explained in light of Šaddinnu's particular background needs further study.[194] One should, however, remember that Šaddinnu was the only priest who according to the available sources employed these tenants explicitly for three to five years through binding cultivation contracts.

3.3 *Tenants with Family Names*

The second group of free individuals employed on the land of priests is made up of persons identified by a three-tier genealogy ('PN, son of PN, descendant of FN'), i.e. individuals with family names. With close to two hundred attestations, they make up the lion's share (75%) of the tenants.[195] Like lower stratum tenants, these individuals are found both engaging in prolonged cultivation by contract and delivering the produce of the field around harvest time. While usually operating alone, they could also team up with colleagues to perform the work in pairs (sometimes alongside tenants without family name or slaves).

Taking a look at the clans whose members assumed agricultural responsibilities, it appears that a very wide range of names is represented. Once again, these can be divided into roughly two groups. On the one hand, there are families that did not belong to the priestly circle of Borsippa like the Agru, Babūtu, Hunzû, Hulamišu, Itti-enši-Nabû, Maṣṣār-abulli, Raksu, Ṣilli-ahi, Ša-haṭṭu-ēreš, and Zērāya families. Besides being underrepresented in our priestly corpus, these names are found predominantly in documents relating to land management, frequently drafted in the countryside itself. This suggests that these families did not belong to the core of Borsippa's urban elite, but concerned

Arrabi to Rēmūt-Nabû//Rē'i-alpi. The same tenant was responsible for *imittu* six years later in BM 94675 (Dar 18).

193 Ilia (A+D): thirteen out of sixty-six tenants; Ea-ilūtu-bani, Ilī-bāni and Nannāhu: sixteen out of sixty-five tenants; Atkuppu: three out of nine tenants; Rē'i-alpi: three out of twelve tenants.

194 For Šaddinnu//Bēliya'u, see Introduction 7.3.

195 In comparison, tenants without family names make up approximately seventeen percent and unfree tenants only eight percent.

themselves primarily with (agricultural) activities outside of town.[196] On the other hand, most of the tenants were affiliated to temple-based families such as temple enterers (e.g., Aqar-Nabû, Ilī-bāni), brewers (e.g., Ilia, Ilšu-abūšu,), butchers (e.g., Ibnāya, Eppēš-ilī), bakers (e.g., Esagil-mansum, Kidin-Sîn), and reed-workers (Atkuppu). These tenants, like their non-priestly counterparts, seem to have lived outside of Borsippa.[197] Whether these individuals performed the labour in person or hired tenants and/or employed unfree labour is something we cannot determine from the present documentation, but the latter seems not unlikely.[198]

Let us now have a look at the families who cooperated in the agricultural sphere. This is best done by looking at our main sources individually, notably the Ea-ilūtu-bani, Ilia (A), Bēliya'u, and Atkuppu archives.[199] The Ea-ilūtu-bani archive cluster provides us with evidence pertaining to families of the highest temple status.[200] Many different families were engaged in the cultivation of their private land, both priestly and non-priestly in nature. The overall impression is that of fairly stable tenancy relations. Several individuals are repeatedly found in their employment. For example, in Ner 03, Zēru-Bābili//Ea-ilūtu-bani hired a certain Nādin/Nabû-šumu-ibni/[x]-matu for the cultivation of a field for the duration of five years.[201] In Nbn 04, this contract was extended for another three years.[202] There are at least five other individuals, respectively from the Ibnāya, Iddināya, Siātu, Šangû-Ninurta, and Širikti-Nabû families, who were hired in more than one year for harvesting purposes.[203]

---

196 BM 28933 (AmM 01) might serve as a case in point. In this contract an individual of the Šahaṭṭu-ēreš family is found leasing the office of *gugallu*, an agricultural office often translated as 'canal inspector', from the city governor (*šākin-ṭēmi*) of Borsippa for the yearly sum of two minas of silver. See Jursa and Waerzeggers 2009: 242f. Yet, the lucrative post of *gugallu* was equally coveted by local families with a temple-based background, cf. BM 29035//BM 96285 (Ner 00).

197 This is because the majority of these tenants do not resurface elsewhere in the documentation. A unique archive of such a 'country dweller', namely the small archive of ᶠInṣabtu//Naggāru, is published in Waerzeggers 1999/2000.

198 Perhaps one could postulate that for those well-to-do country dwellers an honourable way of making a living and maintaining their patrimony was to take on agricultural management for third parties presumably in addition to their own land. This idea needs further study.

199 Information from other priestly archives comes in much smaller amounts. Especially, the information on land management in the Rē'i-alpi archive is exceptionally sparse.

200 For this archive, see Introduction 7.1.

201 TuM 2/3 135 (Ner 03).

202 TuM 2/3 136 (Nbn 04).

203 Nabû-šumu-iškun//Iddināya: TCL 12 56 (Nbk 30⁺) and OECT 12 A 180 (Nbk 40); Itti-Šamaš-balāṭu//Ibnāya: TuM 2/3 155 (Nbk 40) and TuM 2/3 154 (Nbk 41); Nabû-ahhē-ušallim//

More interesting, however, is the fact that in this tight-knit family cluster much of the collaboration took place within the prebendary group. There are at least three members of the wider Ea-ilūtu-bani clan who engaged in the cultivation of land. In the first case, the employer was Mušēzib-Bēl//Ea-ilūtu-bani[204] while the two remaining tenants were hired by the Ilī-bāni family.[205] Hence, all three tenants were working either for a member of their own clan or for a family to which they were associated by marriage and professional affiliation. The same is true for the temple-enterer families of the Ilī-bāni and the Aqar-Nabû. Of the five Ilī-bānis who were employed as gardeners, four worked on land owned by the same clan.[206] Three tenants from the Aqar-Nabû family were hired by the Ilī-bānis and the Nannāhus.[207] In at least one case, collaboration proceeded from the fact that the tenant owned neighbouring land. In light of inheritance and close intermarriage this might have been the primary motivation behind other collaborations as well. Yet, one cannot escape the impression that in the group of temple-enterers, patterns of tenancy were also motivated by clan membership, intermarriage, and professional affiliation. In fact, a similar attitude of solidarity towards the own professional group is found in their credit operations (see Chapter 3.1).

The Ilia (A) archive is our largest source on agricultural management by the brewers of Ezida. Marduk-šumu-ibni//Ilia held a number of small plots in various locales, some of which together with his younger brothers. Although individuals employed by Marduk-šumu-ibni came from a limited number of families, he was able to secure their services on a longer basis than his senior temple colleagues. Besides members of his own clan, most of the tenants were recruited from the Esagil-mansum, Iddin-Papsukkal, Ilšu-abūšu, Naggāru, Ša-haṭṭu-ēreš, and Ṣilli-ahi families.[208] If we compare these families with the marriage network (figure 6, above), it appears that most of them qualify as direct or indirect wife-givers of the Ilias. Not only is this in line with the pattern of

Siātu: TuM 2/3 159 (Cyr [x]) and L 1668 (Cyr 07); Nabû-ēṭir//Šangû-Ninurta: L 1647 (Nbn 13) and OECT 12 A 178 (Nbn [x]); Arad-Nanāya//Širikti-Nabû: TuM 2/3 162 (Cam 03) and TuM 2/3 163 (Cam 06).

204 BM 94692 (Cyr 06).

205 TuM 2/3 77 (Nbk 38) and NBC 8338 (Nbn 15).

206 TCL 12 97 (Nbn 10), TCL 13 128 (Cyr 03), NBC 8361 (Cyr 04), and BM 94608 (Dar 26). According to BM 96306 (d.l.) Ṭābia//Ilī-bāni was working for Šaddinnu//Bēliya'u together with another gardener of the Pahhāru clan.

207 Ilī-bāni: TuM 2/3 158 (Nbn 09) and TCL 12 97 (Nbn 10); and Nannāhu: TuM 2/3 165 (Dar 03).

208 Among the most notable tenants are Šumu-ukīn//Esagil-mansum, BM 102278 (Cam 01); Nidintu//Iddin-Papsukkal, BM 17686 (Dar 05); Lâbâši//Naggāru, BM 94688 Cam 02); Nabû-tabni-uṣur//Ša-haṭṭu-ēreš, LB 863 (Nbn 15); and Nabû-uṣuršu//Ṣilli-ahi, BM 95194 (Cam/Cyr 01).

tenancy observed among the temple-enterers, this correlation gives further weight to the importance of marriage in this community. Priestly marriage in Borsippa did not only entail the transfer of a woman and her property, it also implied that the wife-giver family provided certain services to its wife-taker. Note in this respect that both the Ilšu-abūšus and the Naggārus acted as 'cultic performer' (*ēpišānūtu*) for the Ilia clan and thus provided their wife-taker with cultic support as well (see Chapter 1.6).

Additional evidence comes from the baker's archive of the Bēliya'us. We have seen already that half of Šaddinnu's tenants were recruited from the lower and unfree strata of society. Turning to the tenants with family names, it seems that he enjoyed particularly strong collaborations with tenants from the Bā'iru, Pahhāru, and Esagil-mansum families.[209] While the first family does not figure prominently in Šaddinnu's affairs, his relationship with the Pahhārus and the Esagil-mansums was well-established. An individual from the Pahhāru clan had married his mother after her husband's death.[210] The Esagil-mansums were immigrants like the Bēliya'us and also belonged to the ranks of the temple bakers. Moreover, they had committed themselves as wife-givers to Šaddinnu's family and acted as Šaddinnu's 'cultic performer' (*ēpišānūtu*). This gives additional credence to the idea that intermarriage regulated patterns of tenancy. Incidentally, the Pahhāru family was also an indirect wife-giver of the Bēliya'u clan.

The Atkuppu family was located on the lowest fringes of the priestly community in both economic and professional terms. Accordingly, their pattern of tenancy, which differs from what we have observed among more senior temple colleagues, is congruent with their modest position. First of all, it appears that none of their tenants came from priestly families. With the exception of gardeners from the Atkuppu family itself, collaboration took place with the Ašgandu, Maṣṣār-abulli, Rēmūt-Ea, and Zērāya families. Second of all, as opposed to their senior colleagues, the archive holding branch of the Atkuppu family engaged frequently in agricultural management themselves. They are found in the employment of the Gallābu, Ilia, and Kidin-Nanāya families (all

209 Most notably, Habaṣīru (aka. Ṣiṣiru)//Bā'iru, BM 29474 (Dar 20?); Bēl-uballiṭ (aka. Bibānu)//Pahhāru, BM 96306 (d.l.); Iddin-Nabû//Pahhāru, BM 29432 (Dar 21); Lâbâši// Esagil-mansum, BM 96277 (Dar 22); and Mār-bīti-ahhē-iddin//Esagil-mansum, VS 3 91 (Dar 02).

210 Šaddinnu's father died early in the reign of Nabonidus and his mother had presumably remarried Nādin//Pahhāru by Nbn 07 (BM 29067). In his last testament, dated to Cyr 08 (BM 28861), Nādin specifies that his new wife should live in his main residence for the rest of her life, which might suggest that she had moved there already before presumably together with her child Šaddinnu.

senior temple families),[211] although most of the Atkuppu's labour force was invested within the extended family. Hence, out of eleven tenants from the Atkuppu family, seven worked on land owned by the Atkuppus themselves or by members of the Adad-nāṣir family to which it was linked through marriage.[212]

Conclusion

In the first part of this chapter I traced the creation of *hanšû* land in Borsippa and the surrounding region back to the reign of Erība-Marduk, the Chaldean king who ruled in the first quarter of the eighth century BCE. The motivations behind these royal land allotment schemes were multiple. Economically, they enabled the state to (re)organise the taxable population in a more systematic way, to reinvigorate the agricultural output and the mercantile potential of the urban centres, and to turn the hydraulic infrastructure into a more lucrative source of revenue. Ideologically, they allowed the kings to walk in the footsteps of Marduk who, as king of the gods, had established boundaries and granted land to his divine subjects. Yet, there can be little doubt that in the extreme political volatility of the early first millennium BCE, the need to conciliate the local population was great for any king.

My enquiry has made it clear that in Borsippa the ownership of this type of land was not a specifically priestly prerogative. In addition to *hanšû*s that were named after an individual, temple or geographic location, a far larger number was named after local families. Only forty percent of these *hanšû* names refer to sacerdotal families and families associated to them by marriage. Of the remaining *hanšû* names, twenty-eight percent refer to families who did not belong to this circle. Based on a number of arguments, I proposed to label the latter collectively as having a secular and, perhaps more specifically, a military background.

These results are important for several reasons. First and foremost, they show beyond doubt that the local upper stratum was not restricted to priestly families but included families with different social backgrounds (e.g., royal, military or commercial). It has to be seen whether future investigation can improve and refine the characterisation of individual families within this group. Second, as the *hanšû* grants benefitted priestly as well as non-priestly families,

211 Gallābu: BM 26627 (Dar 26); Ilia (D): BM 26736 (Dar 24); and Kidin-Nanāya: BM 25713 (Dar 14).

212 BM 87327 (Cyr 05), BM 87348 (Cam 01), BM 27781 (Cam 094), BM 17706 (Dar 04), BM 17694 (Dar 05), BM 94787 (Dar 11), and BM 28897 (Dar 18).

the local countryside became an arena in which the larger Borsippean elite stratum had a stake. Yet, even here, Borsippa's priestly families kept interaction with non-priestly outsiders to a minimum. These findings thus provoke a more weighty impression of the priestly stratum as a social group. Having demonstrated that the Borsippean elite community consisted of a far larger group of families than only the prebendaries, it is striking how little these 'others' are attested in the documentation. Certainly, large parts of the priestly archives deal with temple affairs in which non-priestly families are not likely to have been involved. But an equally large part of their archives deals with land management, monetary transactions, family affairs, and other non-religious subject matters. The absence of 'others' in these transactions adds further weight to my working hypothesis that the priestly stratum in Borsippa (and presumably Babylonia at large) formed a close-knit community that was effectively shielded off from external influence and can thus be perceived as a distinct segment of the Babylonian population.

The final inquiry of Part 1 dealt with the bond between the local families and their ancestral *hanšû* land in the long sixth century. At first sight this bond seemed to have been marked by discontinuity. Much of our evidence on *hanšû* land came into existence when the property was sold. Yet, this rarely meant complete alienation of the ancestral land. First of all, families owned multiple *hanšû* estates. In addition to the *hanšû* named after the clan as a whole, which can perhaps be identified with the original eighth century endowments, there also existed estates linked to individual family members. Second of all, sales usually involved shares in a *hanšû* unit; the sale of a *hanšû* in its entirety is attested only once so far. However, even if they had somehow lost control of (parts of) their land, families kept an active interest in it. Descendants can be found as tenants, scribes, and/or witnesses in matters concerning their land, while others endeavoured to buy back their land and re-accumulate the patrimony, sometimes centuries after it had been sold.

Finally, while *hanšû* land could be bought and sold just like any other private property, the special attachment to this 'eponymous' land transpires from the composition of dowries. Dowries played an important role in the priestly marriage in Babylonia, and land is an often-reoccurring component of them. While there are a fair amount of instances in which priestly families from Borsippa transferred *hanšû* land through marriage settlement, in only one case did this involve the family's own *hanšû* land.

All this makes it clear that the sixth-century descendants of the original beneficiaries still greatly valued the land that their forebears had obtained centuries before. This ancestral land was clearly meant to stay in the patrimony, even more than any other type of landholding. We can assume that being in possession of one's original *hanšû* signalled successful cross-generational continuity and gave its owners a place in the established local history.

In the second part of this chapter I explored possible social restrictions on the circulation of *hanšû* land. I started by comparing the transaction patterns of *hanšû* with the marriage network reconstructed in the previous chapter. It turned out that there is only very limited overlap between the constellation of wife-givers and wife-takers and that of sellers and buyers of *hanšû* land. On the contrary, priestly families of Borsippa tended to acquire this property from, and sell this land to, families that were not part of their direct or indirect marriage network (94%). The same tendency was found for other types of real estate. Almost eighty percent of the transactions were carried out between families that could not be linked by marriage according to the current state of documentation. Besides the fact that the acquisition of someone's property could be seen as an unfriendly act and an infringement on the patrimony, I proposed that this could perhaps best be explained by the dynamics of marriage. After all, intermarriage meant that two clans engaged in a mutual alliance, assigning each of them a specific set of rights and obligations. Marriage reconfirmed or indeed triggered a relative hierarchy, ranking the family of the wife-taker over the wife-giver. I suggested that rather than upset the (fragile) status quo reached through marriage, the families preferred to look for suitable buyers or sellers among the families to which they were not yet related. I tentatively formulated the general rule that in the priestly community of Borsippa marriage ties excluded property sales.

The following issue I addressed was the possibility that the patterns of *hanšû* land (and other real-estate) transactions were regulated by a particular solidarity towards the professional group. I have shown earlier that at the time of its inception *hanšû* land was given to the wider elite stratum of Borsippa and that it, as a consequence, did not circulate in the group of sacerdotal families alone. As the professional affiliation of many of the non-priestly families is not clarified in the corpus, it posed a serious limitation to this analysis. Yet some patterns were still discernible. The available evidence suggests that there was no clear preference to sell land to and buy land from families that traditionally belonged to the same prebendary group. Rather, there was a tendency to circulate *hanšû* land mainly among the wider priestly stratum. Moreover, it appeared that there was a steady influx of newly acquired land from outsiders to whom only relatively little land was sold in return. This trend was not limited to *hanšû* property: half of all sales were made between priestly families. In forty percent of the transactions one finds priestly families buying up property from non-priestly families. Of all the sales made by sacerdotal families probably less than one-fifth were made to 'outsiders'. It seems that the priestly stratum of Borsippa worked as a centripetal force, steadily acquiring new property and releasing only very little from its control.

While this might point to an attitude of solidarity among priests, a note of caution must be made. The numbers drawn from the statistical analysis are likely to be a result of the biased nature of our documentation, which consists mainly of temple-based family archives. The number of sales made by priestly families to non-priestly families particularly remains difficult to gauge since most of the property that was sold in these transactions has become untraceable for us. It should thus be clear that more evidence is needed in order to validate my hypothesis concerning solidarity of sales within the prebendary circle of Borsippa.

In the final part of this chapter I investigated the pattern of tenancy and agricultural collaboration. My point of departure was the notion that priests did not cultivate their land themselves. Since most of their energy was devoted towards their cultic duties in town, priests outsourced cultivation either to tenants of unfree status, to free tenants without family names or to free tenants with family names.

Tenants of unfree status, including temple serfs (*širkus*) and privately-owned slaves, are the smallest group and represent only eight percent of the labour force employed by priests from Borsippa. A small note of caution should be sounded, however. It is not unlikely that slaves were used on a more regular basis and the fact that they appear only infrequently in the documentation should be seen in the light of their status. The same might apply to the next group of tenants.

While individuals lacking family names must have constituted the vast majority of the Babylonian population, they make up for only seventeen percent of the tenants in Borsippa. Only Šaddinnu//Bēliya'u recruited his tenants from amongst this group on a more regular basis – almost half of the time. Whether this should be assigned to Šaddinnu's keen entrepreneurship or to the fact that, due to his immigrant background, he was unable to rely on social conventions in matters of tenancy to the same degree as established priestly clans remains uncertain.

Three-fourths of the tenants with family names represent the dominant group in this domain. While I designate them as tenants, it is likely that these upper-stratum individuals only assumed managerial responsibilities of the land, while outsourcing the actual labour to a (subordinate) third party. The vast majority belonged to temple-based families. By analysing the identity of these tenants in conjunction with the identity of the landowners, I was able to reveal some underlying principles of tenancy and to assign agricultural collaboration a sound place in the social organisation of this priestly community.

Tenancy among the priestly families of Borsippa was in large part based on the intricate web of social rules or conventions that was being spun together since long before the start of our documentation. Although, in the light of sale, inheritance, and intermarriage, neighbourship might have been an important motivation for collaboration on the countryside as well, there is only very little direct evidence for this. I showed that the particular arrangements of tenancy and agricultural collaboration could perhaps better be understood as deriving from professional solidarity (e.g. temple-enterers) and intermarriage (e.g. brewers). In fact, the pattern of tenancy neatly follows the organisation of this priestly community, which has been outlined first and foremost by the hypergamous marriage system. Moreover, the fact that priests relied primarily on individuals from fellow priestly families in agricultural matters lends further weight to my hypothesis that the priestly circle in Borsippa formed a close-knit community that effectively shielded off external influences and perceived of and maintained themselves as a discrete social unit.

CHAPTER 3

Silver Lending

In this chapter I investigate the practices of silver lending in the priestly community of Borsippa. In the previous chapters I drew on a wide range of documents kept by the sacerdotal families including marriage and dowry contracts, sales of property, and documents related to the management of urban and rural property. However, a large part of the corpus is made up of debt notes of silver and related receipts. They make up the sources examined in this chapter.

Existing studies of lending practices focus mainly on the technicalities of the Babylonian debt note (*u'iltu*).[1] Composed in an abstract and versatile phraseology, this type of document enabled the Babylonian scribe to record a wide range of transactions.[2] In her recent article on the Neo-Babylonian credit system, C. Wunsch identified no less than fourteen different transactions that could be rendered through the *u'iltu*:[3] from the investment of money for business ventures and the deferred payment of acquired property to rents of fields and houses, and genuine loans of money or in kind.[4] With regards to silver loans, one can distinguish three general types. The interest-free loan usually involved modest sums of silver to be repaid on a set date; this can be considered a 'friendly' loan. The interest-bearing loan usually charged a rate of twenty percent *per annum*, which, although high to modern standards, was the norm during the Neo-Babylonian period.[5] Loans secured by a pledge ensured that

1 The most important study on the legal issues of loans in first millennium Babylonia is still Petschow 1956. More recent studies include Oelsner 2001, Jursa 2002, Wunsch 2002, Oelsner, Wells and Wunsch 2003: 949–953, Jursa 2004d: 451–454, and Jursa 2005: 41–42. More general surveys of moneylending and the role of silver in Neo- and late-Babylonian society include Bongenaar 1999, Powell 1999, Varygas 2000, van Driel 2002, Jursa 2009, and Jursa *et al.* 2010: 240–245.

2 The operative clause in these debt notes reads: (object) *ša* A *ina muhhi* B, '(object) is owed by B to A'. Receipts read simply: (object) A *ina qāt* B *eṭir* (*mahir*), 'A has been paid (has received) (object) from B'. Cf. Oelsner 2001: 290–292, Wunsch 2002: 229–234, and Jursa 2005: 41–42.

3 Derived from the verb *e'ēlu* (CAD E, p. 40 meaning 2: 'to bind') it has been rendered as 'binding obligation'.

4 Wunsch 2002: 224–229.

5 Jursa *et al.* 2010: 490–500. Interest is expressed in the sources by saying that per mina (= 60 shekels) of silver, one shekel accrues per month, i.e. twelve shekels per mina per year. Higher and lower interest rates are attested.

 | DOI:10.1163/9789004399969_005

the creditor could retrieve his capital even in the event of non-payment. Slaves, houses, fields, and prebends are the most frequently found pledges. Creditors could also be allowed antichretic usage of the property in lieu of interest. In archival studies these different loans are usually dealt with in synoptic terms.[6] Besides an attempt to assign individual debt notes to existing dossiers, these texts are commonly reduced to tabulated summaries.

What is still largely missing is an investigation of the individuals and families who interacted with each other in this domain and under what conditions. A pioneering study in this respect was M. Jursa's 1999 monograph on the archive of Bēl-rēmanni, a priest who worked in the Eḫabbar temple of Sippar in the early Persian period. Jursa used debt notes and receipts to examine the social field of this man's lending activities. It turned out that the majority of his loans were contracted with individuals who were not enrolled in the temple organisation and who thus stood outside of his intimate social network. In the following pages I apply this methodology not to one man but to a cross-section of the Borsippean priesthood. Moreover, my focus is on silver loans. Advancements in kind (normally dates or barley) are left to future research since such transactions arose primarily from agricultural and prebendary activities.[7]

Crucial to the following analysis is the division of families into priestly and non-priestly categories. Did a certain debtor/creditor belong to a prebendary family of Borsippa or was he or she a descendant of a non-priestly 'outsider'? While Borsippa's priests kept their marriage system closed to outsiders, interaction with non-priestly families was more commonplace in the domain of land management and property sales, as we have seen. Determining the social pattern of silver lending tells us in which circumstances and to what degree priestly families of Borsippa adhered to the boundaries of their prebendary in-group or whether they interacted with a greater section of society in the domain of moneylending.

Before I start my investigation, some words of caution are in place. In view of the versatile nature of the debt note, it is notoriously difficult to determine whether or not a debt note represents a genuine silver loan.[8] I do not provide a ready solution for this problem in the present chapter. In order to keep the data-set as clean as possible, I excluded all the credits that were part of existing contracts and agreements like tenancy, dowry transfer, *harrānu*-enterprises,

6 See, for example, Joannès 1989: 103–104, 114–118, Kessler 1991: 118–120, Wunsch 1993: 56–57, Waerzeggers 2000/2001: 115–125, Baker 2004: 77–82, and Frame 2013: 68–70.

7 This also stands to some degree for silver loans. See Jursa *et al.* 2010: 522–524.

8 See, for example, Joannès 1989: 103–104, 114–118, Kessler 1991: 7, Wunsch 1993: 7, Joannès 1995: 1476–1477, Jursa 1999: 111–125, Waerzeggers 2000/2001: 115–125, Wunsch 2002, Jursa 2002, Baker 2004: 77–82, and Frame 2013: 68–70.

and make reference to a previous transaction such as the acquisition of property or any other type of object.

1 Temple-Enterers

Let us start with the credit operations of the Ea-ilūtu-banis, a family of temple-enterer status.[9] The family archive contains a total of twenty-two silver loans. They date from the second generation, in the 640s, and continue until the sixth and final generation in the early fifth century BCE. In this timespan, members of the Ea-ilūtu-bani family are attested fourteen times as debtors and eight times as creditors of an amount of silver. I start with the former operations.[10]

The creditors of the Ea-ilūtu-banis belonged to priestly as well as non-priestly families. Whereas only four of them had no apparent connections to the temple institution,[11] ten of them did.[12] More specifically, it appears that the Ea-ilūtu-banis preferred to appeal to fellow temple-enterer clans and kin when in need of cash: three loans came from the Ahiya'ūtu, Arkāt-ilāni-damqā, and Nūr-Papsukkal families, and five from within the Ea-ilūtu-bani clan itself.[13] In short, members of this family only rarely turned to 'outsiders' for silver loans. Rather, they appealed to peers. Moreover, most of these loans were either small and interest-free or secured by a pledge.

A similar arrangement is found in the eight silver loans that the Ea-ilūtu-banis extended to others.[14] The majority of their debtors came from families belonging to the ranks of temple-enterers or from kin (e.g. Ēdu-ēṭir, Ilī-bāni).[15] Only once did the debtor come from a non-priestly family, the Iddināya.

9 For this family, see Introduction 7.1.

10 Here follows the list of silver loans taken out by the Ea-ilūtu-banis in chronological order: OECT 12 A 127 (Nbk 00), OECT 12 F 6 (Nbk 09), L 1661 (Nbn 03), NBC 8407 (Nbn 11), TuM 2/3 116 (Nbn 11), OECT 12 A 108 (Nbn 16), TuM 2/3 55 (Cyr 6), BM 94501 (Cam x), TCL 13 202 (Dar 02), TuM 2/3 61 (Dar 04), TuM 2/3 120 (Dar 08), OECT 12 A 130 (d.l.), OECT 12 A 165 (d.l.), and TuM 2/3 62 (Dar 28).

11 Abunāya (or Adnāya), Patāya (2x), and Sîn-šadûnu families, the latter two were represented by female members. See OECT 12 F 6 (Nbk 09), L 1661 (Nbn 03), OECT 12 A 108 (Nbn 16), and TuM 2/3 55 (Cyr 06).

12 OECT 12 A 127 (Nbk 00), NBC 8407 (Nbn 11), TuM 2/3 116 (Nbn 11), TCL 13 202 (Dar 02), TuM 2/3 61 (Dar 04), TuM 2/3 120 (Dar 08), OECT 12 A 130 (d.l.), OECT 12 A 165 (d.l.), BM 94501 (Cam [-]), and TuM 2/3 62 (Dar 28).

13 The two remaining loans were extended by members of the Ilia and the Ašlāku, respectively.

14 Here follows the list of silver loans advanced by the Ea-ilūtu-banis in chronological order: BM 95091 (Kan 07), TCL 12 41 (Nbk 27), YBC 9631 (Nbk 29), BM 94839 (Ner 00), TuM 2/3 115 (Nbn 6), NBC 8342 (Cyr 02), TuM 2/3 54 (Cyr 04), and L 1657 (Nbk IV 01).

15 One loan was taken out by an individual of the Gallābu family (prebendary barbers).

TABLE 1 Silver loans of the Ea-ilūtu-bani archive (kin 8x)

Distribution of silver loans[a]	No interest	With interest	Interest + Pledge or Antichresis	Total:
Prebendary family	10	3	4	17
Non-prebendary family	2	1	2	5

a The layout of the following tables is borrowed from Jursa 1999: 125. For the sake of convenience, loans that the archive-holders borrowed as debtors and extended as creditors are merged. The purpose is to provide a general overview of the type of families (priestly/non-priestly) involved in the lending partners of the Borsippean priests and under what conditions silver was being loaned. For example, three interest-bearing loans were contracted between the Ea-ilūtu-banis and priestly families, while only one was with non-priestly outsiders. Moreover, eight loans were contracted with members of their kin-group.

The evidence of the known credit operations from the Ea-ilūtu-bani archive is summarised in table 1.

The two most striking features one can observe in this graph are, first, the fact that the Ea-ilūtu-bani family mainly dealt in (smaller-sized) loans without interest or security and, second, the fact that temple-based families prevailed in this sphere of their business. Seventeen out of the total twenty-two silver loans (77%) were contracted between the Ea-ilūtu-banis and individuals from local priestly families. Closer examination of their professional identity reveals that in fourteen cases the family can be classified as temple-enterer, i.e. as belonging to the same professional group as the archive-holders.[16]

The evidence we have for the credit operations of other temple-enterer families from Borsippa suggests that the predisposition to engage with kin and temple families of equal rank was not confined to the Ea-ilūtu-banis, but that it constitutes a practice shared more widely in this group. The first family to be discussed is the Ilī-bāni family, which was associated to the Ea-ilūtu-bani clan by marriage.[17] Of the twelve silver loans recovered from their archive, at least seven were contracted with kin or members of temple-enterer families (e.g. Nūr-Papsukkal, Arkāt-ilāni-damqā, and Ea-ilūtu-bani).[18] Moreover, the

16 Many of which, however, came from the Ea-ilūtu-bani clan itself.

17 For this family, see Introduction 7.1.

18 OECT 12 A 152 (Nbk [-]+04), YOS 17 327 (Nbk 11), OECT 12 A 84 (Nbk 18), YBC 9154 (Nbk 26), OECT 12 A 89 (Nbk 28), OECT 12 A 91 (Nbk 31), TuM 2/3 128 (Nbk 37) L 4731 (Nbk 41), BM 94818 (Nbn 07), BM 94885 (Nbn 08), TuM 2/3 52 (Nbn 13), TuM 2/3 57 (Cyr 07), TuM 2/3 60 (Cam 06), and TuM 2 122 (Dar 32). Of the remaining five loans, three are contracted with women (twice of the Bā'iru family, once with a woman lacking a family name), one

fact that some of these loans concerned substantial amounts of silver at a reduced interest rate is suggestive of a sense of solidarity within this professional group.[19]

The next family is that of Nannāhu.[20] Six loans involving members of the Nannāhu family have been recovered in which they appear as debtors.[21] Examining the background of the creditors reveals the same pattern as before: twice a loan was received from the Ahiya'ūtu family (temple-enterer and brewer family, on both occasions from a woman), and four times from within the Nannāhu family.[22]

The last piece of evidence that should be evaluated here concerns the Iddin-Papsukkal (B) family.[23] This small archive of a temple-enterer of Mār-bīti and Ištar contains five debt notes.[24] In at least four of the loans contracted by the archive holder, the silver was due to a fellow temple-enterer or kinsman.[25] A note of caution should be sounded, however. As has been observed before by M. Jursa, the loans found in this small text group are likely to have their background in the prebendary sphere based on the fact that for three loans prebendary income was pledged as security or interest.[26]

In summary, there are strong indications that the temple-enterers of Borsippa maintained an inward-looking mentality in terms of silver lending: they preferred to get silver *from*, and lend silver *to*, the extended kin-group and individuals from within the same prebendary group. It is likely that this pattern stems from a sense of solidarity towards the in-group, which also transpired from their agricultural collaboration, as was discussed in the previous chapter.

---

with an individual of the Patāya clan (same creditor is found in Ea-ilūtu-bani archive), and thrice with related members from the Balāṭu clan. In the first debt note, YBC 9154, the creditors were Bēl-lē'i//Balāṭu and his son Ṣillā. In TuM 2/3 128 and L 4731, receipts of silver and interest dated some ten and fifteen years later, respectively, Ṣillā's son Nabû-šumu-iškun acted as creditor while his father was present as a witness. These documents probably concern the same loan and might well be related to the running of a business venture.

19 For example, OECT 12 A 152 (four minas, 10% interest), YOS 17 327 (two minas, 10% interest), and OECT 12 A 89 ([x] shekels, 12.5% interest).

20 For this family, see Introduction 7.1.

21 L 1641 (Cam 02), OECT 12 A 119 (Dar 15), OECT 12 A 120 (Dar 17), NBC 8405 (Dar 18), OECT 12 A 123 (Dar 23), and BM 94549 (Dar [-]).

22 The loans are generally high, between twenty-seven shekels and two minas of silver, and are usually extended under interest and security.

23 For this archive, see Jursa 2005: 85.

24 BM 85448 (Dar 23), BM 85443 (Dar 27), BM 85375 (Dar 31), VS 4 187 (Dar x), and BM 85562 (Dar 22).

25 In BM 85562 the family name of the creditor is not given.

26 Jursa 2005: 85.

2 Brewers

Our main source on prebendary brewers is the archive of Marduk-šumu-ibni// Ilia (A), although this man rarely engaged in money lending.[27] His archive contains only thirteen silver loans. Six of these mention Marduk-šumu-ibni as debtor.[28] The amounts range from sixteen to sixty-six shekels, mostly interest bearing and at least once secured by a pledge. When taking the identity of the creditors into account, an interesting pattern emerges. Marduk-šumu-ibni contracted all of these loans from families who were either married to his own clan (i.e. Gallābu, Iddin-Papsukkal, and Ilšu-abūšu)[29] or who belonged to his direct temple associates.[30]

Marduk-šumu-ibni is himself attested seven times as creditor of silver.[31] The amounts of these loans were rather small, rarely exceeding five shekels of silver.[32] His debtors belonged to a somewhat wider and less homogeneous circle. Twice he extended a loan to kin (i.e. descendants of the Iddin-Papsukkal and the Ilia families; the latter was his paternal cousin) and once to a family of temple-enterers (i.e. Aqar-Nabû). The remaining loans were contracted by individuals with no apparent temple background. The evidence of the credit operations of Marduk-šumu-ibni is summarised in table 2.

It is clear from this table that Marduk-šumu-ibni most often contracted loans from fellow prebendary families (69%). Moreover, eight out of these nine individuals were related to Marduk-šumu-ibni either by blood or marriage. The high presence of fellow priests and kin involved in the loans of Marduk-šumu-ibni is comparable to what we have seen among temple-enterers. I suggested that it could point to an attitude of group solidarity, and this might equally be

---

27 For this individual, see Introduction 7.2.

28 The silver loans in which Marduk-šumu-ibni acts as debtor are BM 102311 (Nbn 10), BM 102342 (Cyr 04), BM 94640 (Cam 00), BM 17651 (Cam 01), VS 4 75 (Cam 04?), and VS 4 101 (Dar 04).

29 For example, at one point or another, ᶠAmtia//Ilšu-abūšu (creditor in BM 102342) became his sister-in-law. Nabû-zēru-līšir//Ilšu-abūšu was the brother-in-law of the original debtor and cousin of Marduk-šumu-ibni, whose debt he pays off in VS 4 101.

30 Nabû-uballiṭ/Nabû-šumu-iddin/Ilšu-abūšu is a well-known temple brewer (BM 96504 and BM 96508 = AH XV no. 55). He was also present at the stipulation of the *ēpišānūtu*-contract between Marduk-šumu-ibni and his great-nephew Bēl-iddin (BM 102033 = AH XV no. 17). Nabû-zēru-līšir//Ilšu-abūšu (mentioned above) and his brothers were associates of Marduk-šumu-ibni and the Ilia family in the cult (BM 24480 = AH XV no. 10, BM 102308 = AH XV no. 18, and BM 29441 = AH XV no. 50). They might well have a background in the cult or temple-related debts.

31 Loans that Marduk-šumu-ibni extended are BM 17640 (Nbn 11), BM 94922 (Nbn 14), BM 27899 (Nbn 17), BM 17676 (Cam [-]), VS 4 83 (Cam [-]), BM 26723 (Dar 15?), and BM 26708 (Dar 10⁺).

32 With the exception of a one-mina loan recorded in BM 17676.

TABLE 2 Silver loans of Marduk-šumu-ibni//Ilia (A) (8x kin)

Distribution of silver loans	No interest	With interest	Interest + Pledge or Antichresis	Total:
Prebendary family	6	2	1	9
Non-Prebendary family	2	1	1	4

the case for Marduk-šumu-ibni, perhaps even more so since the latter seems to have suffered from a chronic lack of liquid cash, i.e. silver.[33] It is therefore not surprising that Marduk-šumu-ibni turned to individuals who were likely to be more mindful to his needs and abilities, namely temple colleagues and members of his extended family (two of whom were women).

There are eight more silver loans involving individuals of the wider Ilia kin group. These include two loans of Marduk-šumu-ibni's father Šulā,[34] two loans of his great-nephew Bēl-iddin//Ilia (B),[35] one loan of Nabû-ēṭir//Ilia (C),[36] and three loans of the Ilia (D) family.[37] Except for Šulā, who contracted both of his loans from women of non-prebendary families, all other members dealt with

33 As the first son from a second marriage, Marduk-šumu-ibni (together with his two younger siblings) saw the paternal estate divided in favour of the offspring of his father's first marriage who received a share of two-thirds. Although not all the family possessions are mentioned in the inheritance documents (e.g. no mention of silver is made), there is further evidence that suggests that Marduk-šumu-ibni was not left with large amounts of cash. In order to improve his inherited estate Marduk-šumu-ibni most frequently resorted to exchange. The few acquisitions found in the archive were minor and probably bought with the money from his wife's dowry (LB 874). The paucity of silver is further suggested by the compositions of the dowries of his daughters. On one occasion, Marduk-šumu-ibni converted five minas of silver belonging to his daughter's dowry into real estate (BM 26483). There is so far no evidence that he spent any silver on the dowries of his two other daughters. Moreover, as a whole, the texts of Marduk-šumu-ibni contain only very few payments made in silver (exceptions include forty-five shekels for *qaštu*-tax in BM 27779 = AH XV no. 25 and sixty shekels for *qaštu*-tax in BM 102031). Finally, it is worth pointing out again that the amounts of silver Marduk-šumu-ibni borrowed were higher than the credits he extended himself. Evidence for Marduk-šumu-ibni's monetary situation has previously been collected by C. Waerzeggers, who kindly allowed me to draw on this material.

34 BM 94604 (Nbk [x]$^{+3}$, no family name) and BM 102286 (Nbk 27, Adad-šumu-ēreš). I do not think that the debt of eighty shekels that Šulā had to pay to the *rēš-šarri šá kurummāt šarri* qualifies as a genuine loan (BM 25858).

35 *JCS* 39 (Cam 06, Bābāya) and BM 102257 (Dar 18, Nūr-Papsukkal).

36 BM 17656 (Nbk 38, Ea-ilūtu-bani). The slave taken as antichresis belonged to the dowry of Nabû-ēṭir's wife.

37 BM 94624 ([Dar?] 05, Šikkûa) and BM 94714 (Dar 12, Suhāya; for the restoration of debtor's filiation, see Sandowicz 2012: 340–341), and BM 87315 (Dar 20, Ilia).

fellow priests (on two occasions within the group of brewers), which brings the total distribution of credit partners of the Ilias to 12:8 in favour of temple-based families. It seems that the evidence of the wider Ilia clan is only roughly in line with the lending pattern observed for Marduk-šumu-ibni. Yet, the evidence pertaining to these other members is scant and less forceful from a quantitative point of view. The same stands for the information on silver lending for other brewers from Borsippa. There is only one loan from the Ahiya'ūtu,[38] three from the Ilšu-abūšu (B),[39] one from the Kudurrānu,[40] two from the Lā-kuppuru,[41] and three from the Mannu-gērûšu archives.[42] Integrating the heterogeneous evidence on moneylending among the brewers from Borsippa, one arrives at the figures given in table 3.

Carefully summarising this information, it seems that the remaining evidence of the Ilia and other brewer clans is only partly in line with the lending pattern observed so far. Moneylending with non-priestly members of the community more often than not assumed the form of an interest-bearing or collateralised debt obligation, whereas loans within the prebendary group were often extended under more lenient conditions, which betrays an attitude of mutual support towards the sacerdotal in-group. If so, it should not come as a surprise that brewers preferably called on (extended) kin and fellow brewers when in need of cash, though again, the idea that these loans could have a background in the cultic logistics should not be dismissed altogether. There

38 Nabû-ana-mērehti//Ahiya'ūtu once gave a loan of fifty shekels according to Amherst 246//RBC 734 (Xer 01). The debtor came from the Kidin-Sîn family and pledged his cultic storeroom (*bīt-šutummi*) against the silver.

39 In VS 4 153 (Dar 20) Nabû-uballiṭ//Ilšu-abūšu (B) is found as a debtor of an interest-free loan of twenty shekels, borrowed from the Ibnāyas, a family of prebendary butchers. Nabû-uballiṭ extended loans on two occasions: in BM 29038 (Dar 12) a sum of fifty shekels to his kinsman from the Ilšu-abūšu family and in BM 28994 (Dar [-]) a loan of four minas to a member of the Ir'ani family. There is, so far, no evidence that the Ir'anis belonged to the prebendary ranks of Borsippa.

40 In Nbk 34 Nabû-ahhē-iddin//Kudurrānu provided ten shekels of silver, the interest of a principal loan of one mina (BM 29103). The silver was due to a minor and his mother, neither of whom bore a family name.

41 Nabû-ušallim (aka. Šullumā)//Lā-kuppuru is found twice involved in silver lending: VS 4 173 (Dar 27) and OECT 12 A 160 ([-]). The first was contracted at Babylon and was interest bearing. The second concerns a short-term, interest-free loan of about twenty shekels. None of the credit partners seem to have belonged to the prebendary circle of Borsippa.

42 As debtor Nabû-ahu-ittannu//Mannû-gērûšu contracted two loans of around ten shekels: VS 4 179 (Dar 23) and Amherst 245 (Xer 01). The first was borrowed without interest from a couple that lacked family names. The second was extended by a fellow brewer of the Ilia clan and was interest-bearing. As creditor Nabû-ahu-ittannu once issued an interest-bearing loan of one mina of silver to a descendant of the non-priestly Širikti-Marduk clan.

TABLE 3 Silver loans of all brewer archives (Ilia (A-D), Ahiya'ūtu, Ilšu-abūšu (B), Kudurrānu, Lā-kuppuru, and Mannu-gērûšu)

Distribution of silver loans	No interest	With interest	Interest + Pledge or Antichresis	Total:
Prebendary family	10	3	4	17
Non-Prebendary family	6	4	4	14

are in total twelve loans extended between kin and fellow temple brewers. Yet, on the whole, compared to the temple-enterers, the reliance on these people is less numerically significant among brewers. Of a total of thirty-one loans, fourteen were contracted with outsiders, and only slightly more than half (i.e. 55%) between prebendary families.

3 Bakers

The largest and most important source pertaining to the bakers of Ezida is the archive of Šaddinnu//Bēliya'u.[43] Because the archives of other baker families such as the Kidin-Sîn, Nabû-mukīn-apli, Šēpê-Ilia, and the Esagil-mansum still need to be recovered, the lending patterns of this group can only be reconstructed partially. Moreover, while the evidence on Šaddinnu's credit operations is relatively generous, it seems that he might have behaved differently in this domain than his fellow bakers did.

The archive contains a total of twenty-six loans of silver.[44] One finds Šaddinnu extending credit twenty-two times, while taking out loans on only four occasions. According to the archival practices of the time, paid debt notes were returned to the debtor as proof of his or her discharge of obligation.[45] There might be various explanations for the relatively high number of loans in which Šaddinnu acted as creditor,[46] but in his case it can probably be taken as an approximate reflection of actual practice. His financial position was such

43 For this individual, see Introduction 7.3.
44 See Jursa *et al.* 2010: 243 for an overview of these loans.
45 Jursa *et al.* 2010: 241.
46 For example, these debt notes might have been written off as 'bad loans', i.e. losses, or Šaddinnu could simply have kept copies for administrative purposes.

that he could afford to lend money more often than he needed it for himself[47] and presumably he engaged in moneylending as a business pursuit.

Let us have a closer look at the four loans that Šaddinnu contracted as debtor. The first two were borrowed from non-prebendary families, Imbu-īnia and Rē'û, and amounted to twenty-two and thirty-three shekels of silver, respectively.[48] Both were short-term loans without interest or security. The two other loans were obtained from Bēl-iddin//Ibnāya and his brother Bēl-ušallim.[49] These brothers might have engaged in the moneylending business on a more professional basis as well, acting as creditors in other archives too. The first loan amounted to one mina of silver and was interest-bearing. The second loan, slightly below five minas of silver, required repayment within the month. We do not know what the consequences were for Šaddinnu in case of default. It is, however, interesting to note that some time earlier, Bēl-iddin//Ibnāya bought a field from Šaddinnu. Under what circumstances this field was sold is not clear, but that this Bēl-iddin was a strict moneylender can be deduced from the fact that he extended loans in return for pledges that were automatically forfeitable on due date (i.e. *Verfallspfand*).[50]

Let us now turn to the twenty-two loans that were extended by Šaddinnu.[51] The amounts range from less than ten shekels to more than 300 shekels of silver.[52] There are only two instances in which Šaddinnu lent money at interest. More frequent are the 'friendly' loans on short term (11) and loans that were covered by a pledge or lent under antichresis (9).

Dividing Šaddinnu's debtors in the two familiar groups yields the following figures: twelve of the twenty-two loans (55%) were taken out by individuals of local prebendary clans.[53] The remaining loans were contracted

47 Note that his four debts had to be repaid on the short term, which means that Šaddinnu was able to raise the silver at short notice.

48 BM 29174 (Cam 03) and BM 96266 (Dar 09). Note that the former might have resulted from a house sale. See BM 29019 (Dar 06?).

49 BM 96150 (Dar 21) and BM 29116 (Dar [-]).

50 BM 26650//BM 27857 (Dar 13) records a silver loan from the Rē'i-alpi archive in which the creditor, Bēl-iddin//Ibnāya, holds a field of the Rē'i-alpi family as a *Verfallspfand*.

51 VS 4 64 (Cyr 07), BM 29190 (Cam 0), BM 96177 (Cam 06), BM 28973 (Cam [-]), BM 96334 (Dar 09), BM 29494 (Dar 09), VS 4 130 (Dar 10), BM 29484 (Dar 12), BM 96248 (Dar 12), BM 96187 (Dar 12), BM 29716 (Dar 14), BM 29416 (Dar 15), BM 28988 (Dar 15), BM 96271 (Dar 15), BM 28912 (Dar 21), BM 29433 (Dar 21), BM 25644 (Dar 25), BM 96234 (Dar 26), BM 96331 (Dar 30), BM 28864 (Dar 34), BM 28931 (Dar 36), and BM 29010 (Dar [-]).

52 Six times the amount was sixty shekels or more, five times between twenty and sixty shekels, and six times less than twenty shekels of silver.

53 Kidin-Nanāya, Eppēš-ilī, Naggāru, Lā-kuppuru, Bēliya'u (twice), Ilī-bāni, Itinnu (twice), Ilšu-abūšu, Allānu, and Esagil-mansum.

TABLE 4 Silver loans of Šaddinnu//Bēliya'u (4x kin)

Distribution of silver loans	No interest	With interest	Interest + Pledge or Antichresis	Total:
Prebendary family	6	2	7	14
Non-Prebendary family	8	1	2	12

by non-prebendaries.[54] Cooperation with fellow priests was clearly limited compared to the brewers and, especially, the temple-enterers. Moreover, most of the loans Šaddinnu extended to prebendary families were secured with a pledge.[55] Table 4 summarises the silver loans found in the Bēliya'u archive.

More revealing aspects of Šaddinnu's attitude towards his immediate environment become apparent once we take a closer look at the identity of the families concerned. In the first place kin and affinal relatives played only a minor role in his lending activities. They appear in only four (15%) of the twenty-six silver loans preserved in the archive. Twice, a loan was extended to a member of the Bēliya'u family: first, for a sum of sixteen shekels and, second, for the staggering sum of 320 shekels of silver for which a kettle and a field were taken as pledge, respectively.[56] The remaining two loans were taken out by clans who were connected to the Bēliya'us through marriage: Kidin-Marduk (alias Kidinnu)//Ṣillāya, a well-known scribe in the archive, borrowed the sum of thirty-six shekels,[57] and Mār-bīti-ahhē-iddin//Esagil-mansum received a loan of twenty shekels.[58] The limited appearance of relatives in Šaddinnu's

54 Mudammiq Adad, Sîn-tabni (2x), Ea-ibni, Idinnāya, Bābūtu, Sîn-damāqu, Ṣillāya, and Sîn-šadûnu.

55 VS 4 64 (Cyr 07), BM 96177 (Cam 06), BM 29716 (Dar 14), BM 29416 (Dar 15), BM 28912 (Dar 21), BM 96331 (Dar 30), and BM 28864 (Dar 34). The pledged properties, which, as far as I can judge, were of equivalent value as the borrowed sums ranged from houses and fields to slaves, kettles, and at least once a garment of a god (presumably derived from a domestic shrine).

56 BM 29716 (Dar 14) and BM 28912 (Dar 21). Note that the second debtor, Nabû-ahhē-iddin/Nabû-mukīn-apli, was Šaddinnu's nephew. See Waerzeggers 2010: 732. Nabû-ahhē-iddin also occupied the position of 'canal inspector' (*gugallu*) of Borsippa around Dar 18 (BM 21965).

57 BM 96271 (Dar 15). He probably also sold a field to Šaddinnu (BM 29404//BM 28914, Dar 16), as well as a slave (VS 5 85, Dar 08?).

58 BM 29010 (Dar [-]). He also owed Šaddinnu dates from the harvest estimation (VS 3 91, Dar 02).

moneylending contrasts strongly with the practices observed among temple-enterers and brewers, where the majority of the loans were contracted with kin and temple families, especially from the same prebendary profession.

This brings us to the second peculiarity of Šaddinnu's moneylending practices: the absence of fellow bakers. According to the available documentation, Šaddinnu contracted only one loan with an individual of a baker family. It concerns the aforementioned loan taken out by Mār-bīti-ahhē-iddin//Esagil-mansum. It is remarkable that neither the Nabû-mukīn-aplis nor members of the prominent Kidin-Sîn and Šēpê-ilia families figure in these interactions, especially given the significant role played by fellow priests among the more senior prebendary groups. Could there be a specific reason behind the absence of interaction?

It seems that the bakers of Ezida were divided in two opposing camps: the Kidin-Sîn and Šēpê-ilia families represented an older group, while the Bēliya'u and Esagil-mansum families represented a younger one.[59] That these families constituted two distinct groups is seen, first of all, in the fact that while marriages were settled between Kidin-Sîn and Šēpê-ilia, and between Bēliya'u and Esagil-mansum, there is so far no evidence for alliances established between these two family clusters.

Additional evidence is found in a series of property sales. In a short period during the early years of Darius I (probably during the third and fourth regnal years) at least five important transactions were negotiated between these two groups: three sales of prebends and two sales of real estate.[60] On four occasions property was sold by the Kidin-Sîns to the Bēliya'u family; once the Bēliya'us sold a prebend to the Šēpê-ilia clan. That these sales did not always run smoothly is demonstrated by the acquisition of a plot of land by the Bēliya'us, which required a further document (*mukinnūtu*) preventing the alienating family from contesting this transaction in the future. An even more compelling testimony transpires from the fact that the acquisition of the prebend by the Šēpê-ilias was eventually nullified by the Bēliya'u clan, which successfully reclaimed their cultic rights.[61]

It is hard to determine how the various parties perceived these sales, but Šaddinnu's reluctance to loan silver to members of the opposing camp is further evidence of a lack of solidarity, trust, and inner-group collaboration

59 See Introduction 7.3.

60 Prebend sales: BM 96286 = AH XV no. 75, BM 96163 = AH XV no. 77, and BM 96194. Sales of real estate: BM 25589 and BM 96218.

61 That Šaddinnu had a personal hand in this affair is clear from the fact that he acquired half of the prebend in the course of these events.

among the bakers of Ezida. If their relationship can indeed be described as antagonistic, the situation seems to have deteriorated over the years, culminating in Dar 33 when two high-profile lawsuits were filed against Šaddinnu. In the first case a member of the Kidin-Sîn contested the sale of a housing plot, a field, and a baker's prebend to Šaddinnu – the matter was settled to the latter's advantage.[62] The second case, adjudicated some five months later by the same judge, deals with the rights to prebendary income and was decided in favour of the Šēpê-ilia clan.[63]

A possible explanation for this rift may be found in the background of Šaddinnu's family. The Bēliya'us were part of the larger group of families that moved from the capital of Babylon to the burgeoning provincial towns during the reign of Nebuchadnezzar II.[64] This meant that Šaddinnu and his relatives were left out of much of the local social organisation that had been evolving since at least the eighth century BCE.[65] Consequently, it can be argued that the Bēliya'u clan was not tied to the same customary rights, obligations, and moral restrictions as were the indigenous priestly families. Presumably, Šaddinnu and his kin could act more independently from this close-knit priestly community and thus also deviate more easily from the established social norms in pursuit of their fortunes. Not only does the near absence of kin and fellow bakers families in Šaddinnu's lending practice become less surprising, Šaddinnu's family background and social position in this community could also explain, at least in part, his active engagement in entrepreneurial activities such as the acquisition of (vacant or dilapidated) urban plots with the aim of renting them out.[66] There is no doubt that Šaddinnu's involvement in this sector can to a large extent be ascribed to his personal entrepreneurial mentality, but it might have been his lack of deep roots in Borsippa's sacerdotal community that allowed him to pursue this line of work on an 'un-priestly' scale.

Finally, Šaddinnu's implication in the housing business might help to elucidate further aspects of his lending practice. If we compare the families who contracted loans from Šaddinnu with the families who appear in the housing dossier, there seems to be some overlap: Kidin-Nanāya, Imbu-īnia, Eppēš-ilī, Ea-ibni, Šigûa, and Sîn-šadûnu, among others, all appear in both dossiers.

---

62 BM 25629. Note that a member of the Purkullu family joined the claimants.

63 BM 25633.

64 See Introduction 7.3. It is not unlikely that Šaddinnu's forebear only settled in Borsippa as late as Nbk 33 (BM 28904). For similar immigrant families in Sippar, see Waerzeggers 2014.

65 I have argued earlier that local landownership (Chapter 2.1.2) as well as the marriage system (Chapter 1.5) went back several centuries before our documentation and brought with it various side effects in the social organisation of this community.

66 Jursa *et al.* 2010: 170f.

In some cases it concerns the same individuals. For example, Bēl-ēṭir//Šigûa, one of Šaddinnu's most trusted contacts,[67] collected some of his rents,[68] but also contracted a loan from Šaddinnu.[69] Libluṭ/Nabû-ušebši, an individual who leased rights to temple revenue to Šaddinnu, at least once took out a loan. In return he pawned his house to Šaddinnu who consequently cashed in the house rent.[70] Yet, in most cases the overlap is only in the families concerned and not in the individual persons. Still, it seems not too far-fetched to suggest that some of the loans have their background in Šaddinnu's housing business. Some of the moderate-sized loans that were extended on short term and without interest might actually represent house rents. If nothing else, his activities as multi-landlord must have brought him in contact with various tenants, their neighbours, and families who were likely to appeal to a propertied man, a patron, like Šaddinnu when in need of cash.

In summary, Šaddinnu's peculiar moneylending practices can be explained in their proper context. Disunity among the ranks of Ezida's bakers divided them in two seemingly opposing camps. While collaboration in the cult was inevitable, their interaction outside the temple was marked by mutual exclusion (in marriage and silver lending) and discord (in property sales and lawsuits). Even if Šaddinnu was able to maintain more intimate relationships with members of the Kidin-Sîn family, I show in the next chapter that such ties were completely absent with the Šēpê-ilias. I argue that some of this could be related to the fact that Šaddinnu and his family were not indigenous to Borsippa. There is no question that Šaddinnu took part in the local priestly community, indeed quite successfully, but his lack of deep roots meant that he was less thoroughly embedded in it, and perhaps more importantly, not restrained by the social norms that indigenous families tended to respect.

4 Oxherds

Counting well over four hundred documents, the Rē'i-alpi family archive informs us in great detail about the family's main occupation as cultic oxherds.[71] The majority of the documents concerns Nabû-mukīn-zēri/Aplāya and his son Rēmūt-Nabû of the third and fourth generation, respectively. The family was

67 See Chapter 4.2.3.
68 BM 25690 (Dar 21).
69 BM 25644 (Dar 25).
70 BM 29433 (Dar 21).
71 For an overview of this archive, see Introduction 7.4.

obviously rich and there is ample information on the acquisition of property as well as on moneylending. Together, Nabû-mukīn-zēri and Rēmūt-Nabû appear in no less than eighty-three silver loans (a further seven were contracted by Rēmūt-Nabû's son, Bēl-ittannu), making their transactions the largest dataset on lending in the Borsippa corpus.

Let us begin by evaluating the silver loans of Nabû-mukīn-zēri and his son individually. Of the ninety loans found in the archive, thirty-four belong to Nabû-mukīn-zēri (nineteen as debtor, fifteen as creditor).[72] He tended to borrow modest sums of silver (ten times under twenty shekels), while himself extending more substantial ones (eight times over sixty shekels of silver). Nabû-mukīn-zēri did not usually pay interest or provide pledges to his creditors, yet he did receive such benefits from his own debtors on multiple occasions. On the whole, Nabû-mukīn-zēri's financial situation seems to have been favourable.

There are forty-nine loans contracted by his son Rēmūt-Nabû (thirty-one as debtor, eighteen as creditor).[73] However, Rēmūt-Nabû's lending pattern differs from that of his father. He tended to borrow substantial sums of silver: he asked for amounts between twenty and sixty shekels on twelve occasions, but at least as often for more than one mina of silver. His creditors usually demanded security. The loans he extended were modest in comparison: only

72 Loans Nabû-mukīn-zēri contracted as debtor: BM 102320 (Ner 03), BM 94824 (Nbn 02), VS 4 38 (Nbn 04), BM 25856 (Nbn 05), BM 94841 (Nbn 08), BM 94830 (Nbn 08), BM 17664 (Nbn 09), BM 94811 (Nbn 10), BM 94730 (Nbn 12), BM 82678 (Nbn 12), BM 82778 (Nbn 14), BM 94758 (Nbn 16), BM 94873 (Nbn [-]), Smith Coll. 82 (Cyr 02), BM 26664 (Cyr 06), BM 26608 (Cyr 06), VS 4 111 (Dar 06), BM 82627 (Dar 07) (this loan was later cancelled), and BM 26490 (Dar 11). Loans Nabû-mukīn-zēri extended as creditor: BM 94698 (Nbn 14), BM 94977 (Cyr 01), VS 4 70 (Cyr 01), BM 102028 (Cyr 02), BM 94689 (Cyr 03), BM 102013 (Cam 01), VS 4 76 (Cam 04), BM 94718 (Cam 04), VS 4 100 (Dar 01), BM 102003 (Dar 01), BM 27858 (Dar 04), BM 26697 (Dar 06), BM 101994 (Dar 08), BM 94648 (Dar 09), and BM 102018 (Dar [-]).

73 Loans Rēmūt-Nabû contracted as debtor: BM 26680//BM 26754 (Cam 06), BM 82787//BM 82653 (Dar 08), BM 102254 (Dar 09), BM 26654 (Dar 09), BM 82728 (Dar 09), BM 94667 (Dar 09), BM 26642 (Dar 09), BM 25717 (Dar 10), BM 26542 (Dar 11), BM 26490 (Dar 11), Mich 403 (Dar 12), BM 26650//BM 27857 (Dar 13), BM 26547 (Dar 14), BM 26678 (Dar 14), BM 26584 (Dar 15), BM 26554 (Dar 17), BM 27793 (Dar 17), BM 82625 (Dar 18), BM 26618 (Dar 18), BM 26617 (Dar 19), BM 94685 (Dar 19), EAH 225 (Dar 21), BM 94708 (Dar 21), BM 26534 (Dar 26), KVM 60 (Dar 28), BM 26521 (Dar [-]), BM 82701 (Dar [-]), BM 26486 (Dar [-]), BM 25668 (Dar [-]), BM 82694 (d.l.), and BM 102014 (d.l.). Loans Rēmūt-Nabû extended as creditor: VS 4 107 (Dar 05), BM 17693 (Dar 06), BM 26696 (Dar 08), BM 82727 (Dar 08), BM 26622 (Dar 10), BM 94872 (Dar 13), BM 25724 (Dar 13), BM 26581 (Dar 13), BM 27845 (Dar 15), BM 26529 (Dar 16), BM 25844 = AH XV no. 189 (Dar 16), BM 27873 = AH XV no. 190 (Dar 16), BM 94808 (Dar 19), BM 82730 (Dar 20), BM 29413 (Dar 21), EAH 226 (Dar 24), BM 94687 (Dar 26), and BM 26555 (Dar 28).

three of eighteen loans exceeded thirty shekels of silver. At least half of these were interest-bearing or secured by a pledge. This suggests that Rēmūt-Nabû tried to make a profit on the small amounts of silver at his disposal. On the whole, however, his finances were unbalanced: he borrowed at a far greater speed than he was able to raise money. This situation clearly derailed in Dar 20 when Rēmūt-Nabû was charged with paying close to one talent of silver (BM 26576 = AH XV no 192). One possible explanation for Rēmūt-Nabû's financial difficulties is tax pressure.[74]

Let us now turn to the individuals and the families with whom the Rē'i-alpis engaged in moneylending. Nabû-mukīn-zēri contracted most of his loans with fellow temple-based families (approximately 70%).[75] Rēmūt-Nabû, by contrast, turned more often to non-priestly families (approximately 43%), especially when in need of larger sums of silver.[76] Another point of interest is that he appealed to a number of families more than once, which could indicate particular relations of trust between him and these families.[77] Turning to the loans he provided as creditor, it seems that here Rēmūt-Nabû's practices resembled more those of his father: six loans went to non-priestly families, whereas twelve were given to priestly families.[78]

---

74 Tax payments are amply documented in the archive. See, for example, BM 94970 (Dar 05), BM 94620 (Dar 10), BM 94545 (Dar 11), BM 102259 (Dar 13?), HSM 1899.2.145 (Dar 15), BM 82666//BM 102010//BM 102262 (Dar 16), BM 82716 (Dar 18), VS 6 150 (Dar 27), and BM 26557 (Dar 29). Note that Rēmūt-Nabû contracted at least four loans with members of the Naggāru family (see below). The fact that a certain Nabû-balassu-iqbi//Naggāru was the '*ziqpu*' of the Rē'i-alpis, i.e. the person in charge of their tax-group supports the idea that at least some of Rēmūt-Nabû's loans had their background in taxation. See Jursa and Waerzeggers 2009: 244ff.

75 The priestly families were the Arkāt-ilāni-damqā (twice), Atkuppu, Ea-ilūtu-bani (twice), Gallābu, Iddin-Papsukkal (twice), Ilia (three times), Kidin-Sîn, Kudurrānu, Lā-kuppuru, Nūr-Papsukkal, Rē'i-alpi (six times), and Ṣāhit-ginê. The non-priestly families were the Adad-nāṣir, Bā'iru, Damēqu, Mallāhu, Maṣṣār-abulli, Rēš-ummāni, Sippê, Šagimmu, Šamaš-ilāni, and Zērūtia. The Rēš-ummāni is so far not attested as prebendary of Ezida and the family is in this study classified as non-priestly. Note, however, that in this debt Nabû-nādin-ahi//Rēš-ummāni pledges his right to twelve pieces of meat belonging to a (butcher's?) prebend before the god Sîn (BM 94977).

76 Creditors from priestly families were the Arkāt-ilāni-damqā (twice), Ea-ilūtu-bani (twice), Esagil-mansum, Ibnāya (twice), Ilia (twice), Ilī-bāni, Kudurrānu, Naggāru (twice), and Rē'i-alpi (twice). Creditors from non-priestly families were the Amēl-Ea, Balāṭu, Banê-ša-ilia, Ea-imbi, Dannēa (three times), Imbu-īnia, Mallāhu, Rīšāya, Šangû-Ninurta, and Šarrahu (twice).

77 These relations might have originated with his father who had dealings with the same (priestly) families.

78 The priestly families were the Ahiya'ūtu, Allānu, Gallābu, Ilšu-abūšu (twice), Naggāru (twice), Nūr-Papsukkal, and Rē'i-alpi (three times). The non-priestly families were the Adad-šamê, Balāṭu, Dābibī, Rēmūt-Ea, and Sîn-šar-ilāni.

TABLE 5 Silver loans of the Rē'i-alpi archive (kin 28x)

Distribution of silver loans	No interest	With interest	Interest + Pledge or Antichresis	Total:
Prebendary family	22	14	25	61
Non-Prebendary family	14	7	8	29

Finally, Bēl-ittannu, Rēmūt-Nabû's son was engaged in seven silver loans, always as creditor.[79] None of the loans exceeded half a mina of silver. Most of his debtors belonged to the Rē'i-alpi family (4 members) or to other priestly families (2 members).[80] He once extended a loan to an individual from the lowest stratum of the community, i.e. a *širku* of Nabû.

When combining the data of the ninety silver loans from the Rē'i-alpi archive, the following figures emerge in table 5.

With a ratio of 2:1, the Rē'i-alpis engaged most often with individuals from fellow priestly families. While the social patterns of moneylending become less centred on the prebendary in-group the further down we move in the temple hierarchy, the high overall number of priestly families in the credit operations of the Rē'i-alpis resembles the practices observed among the Ea-ilūtu-banis and other temple-enterers more than those of the middle-high ranking brewers or bakers.

The Rē'i-alpis share another feature with their more senior temple colleagues: a strong reliance on kin. Twenty-eight of their lending partners can be identified as relatives. Of these, fifteen individuals belonged to the Rē'i-alpi clan while the others were related by marriage. Taken together, close kin and extended family members accounted for thirty percent of the loans contracted by Nabû-mukīn-zēri, his son, and grandson. If one includes indirect marriage partners, then nearly half of all their loans were contracted with kinsmen.

Solidarity within the Rē'i-alpi clan transpires from the many and, at times, favourable loans extended to one another. Many loans were non-interest-bearing (e.g. BM 94626), extended under a reduced interest rate (e.g. BM 17664) or interest-free until default (e.g. BM 94689). Moreover, after his crisis of Dar 20, Rēmūt-Nabû turned mostly to his own kin for financial support.[81] Kith and kin clearly functioned as an ultimate safety net.

79 BM 94553 (Dar 34), BM 26541 (Dar 35), BM 94690 (Dar 35), BM 102026 (Dar 36), BM 26599 (Xer 01), BM 94626 (Xer 01), and BM 26646 (Xer 02).

80 The Aḫiya'ūtu and the Arkāt-ilāni-damqā families.

81 See, for example, BM 94708 (Dar 21), BM 26534 (Dar 26), and KVM 60 (Dar 28).

5 Reed-Workers

The final case study of this chapter concerns the lending practices of the lowest-ranking group of prebendaries available in the corpus: the prebendary reed-workers.[82] Most of the evidence from the Atkuppu archive pertains to Marduk-šumu-ibni's sons Nabû-šumu-uṣur, Nabû-iddin, Murānu, and Iqīša.

Together, the four brothers contracted twenty-five silver loans, primarily as debtors.[83] Even though they preferred to borrow modest sums of silver,[84] all but two loans received from their two closest moneylenders, were interest-bearing or covered by a pledge. This picture corroborates the idea that their financial situation was not particularly strong.

While most of their creditors are known from the archive or are attested elsewhere in Borsippa, two families were particularly closely associated to the Atkuppus: the Rēš-ummāni family who provided four loans and the Ahiya'ūtu family who provided three. On two occasions the brothers turned to their in-laws from the Nappāhu family for financial support[85] and once even to each other.[86] The remaining loans were received from individuals who were not closely associated with the Atkuppus: Agru, Banê-ša-ilia, Ea-ibni, Ea-ilūtu-bani, Gallābu, Ibnāya (two times), and Sîn-imittī. The ratio between priestly and non-priestly families seems to have been more or less equal. The same applies to the loans in which the Atkuppu brothers acted as creditors.[87] Sums are usually modest[88] and prebendaries and non-prebendaries are more or less equally represented among their debtors.

Four loans contracted by earlier generations of Atkuppus should be mentioned briefly here. Two interest-bearing credits of about ten shekels of silver were lent by Nabû-mušētiq-uddê, great-grandfather of the Atkuppu brothers,

82 For this family, see Introduction 7.5.

83 VS 4 97 (Dar 03), BM 26655 (Dar 06), BM 29678 (Dar 11), BM 102309 (Dar 14), VS 4 140 (Dar 14), BM 26665 (Dar 18), VS 4 150 (Dar 18), VS 4 149 (Dar 18), BM 102256 (Dar 19), BM 94733 (Dar 19), VS 4 156 (Dar 20), BM 87282 (Dar 24), BM 26649 (Dar 25), BM 26724 (Dar 26), BM 102314 (Dar 27), BM 87297 (Dar [-]), and BM 102252 (Dar [-]). Note that BM 94722 (Dar 27) records the loan between two of the brothers.

84 Only two loans exceeded one mina of silver (seventy and seventy-eight shekels). Fourteen loans ranged between three and twenty shekels of silver.

85 Nabû-šumu-uṣur was married to a daughter of the Nappāhu family.

86 BM 94722 (Dar 27).

87 BM 17680 (Dar 05), BM 17698 (Dar 05), BM 26605 (Dar 06?), BM 26631 (Dar 10), BM 26693 (Dar 12), BM 26704 (Dar 15), and VS 4 174 (Dar 28). Note that BM 26631 (Dar 10) involves onions and two debtors which could indicate that this was part of the management of a *harrānu* venture. BM 26693 (Dar 12) involves the payments of tax to the *rab-hanšê* for a third party.

88 Only twice exceeding twenty shekels of silver.

TABLE 6 Silver loans of the Atkuppu archive (3x kin)

Distribution of silver loans	No interest	With interest	Interest + Pledge or Antichresis	Total:
Prebendary family	4	6	3	13
Non-Prebendary family	2	6	8	16

to individuals of the Ša-haṭṭu-ēreš and the Mallāhu families. Their grandfather, Nabû-ēṭir, once extended a minor loan of one shekel to an individual of the Mudammiq-Marduk clan and his wife, for which they pawned their house. Finally, their father Marduk-šumu-ibni is attested once as debtor of two shekels in return for which the creditor of the Pahhāru family received his field as pledge. The evidence is summarised in table 6.

The pattern of silver lending observed in this archive confirms the correlation between temple rank and reliance on temple-based families that I have observed earlier in this chapter. The Atkuppus relied relatively less on temple relations in terms of moneylending than did the temple-enterers, brewers, bakers, and oxherds. Moreover, they also relied less strongly on kin.[89] Also, in other aspects of their interaction (most notably in marriage and tenancy) it has been shown that the Atkuppu family relied less on priestly families compared to their more senior colleagues.

Conclusion

In this chapter I investigated the pattern of silver lending in the sacerdotal community of Borsippa. My primary aim was to examine the extent of the priests' social field in this area of interaction. Did they abide strictly by the boundaries of the prebendary in-group? Or did they turn to a larger segment of the community when in need of cash? Is it possible to reconstruct a typical lending practice shared by all priests? These questions have proven difficult to answer. There many pitfalls in using the highly versatile genre of the Babylonian debt

89 Of the twenty-nine silver loans, only three (10%) were contracted with relatives. The two loans for which both amount and terms are preserved suggest that there was no particular trust or solidarity between the parties. The ten shekels borrowed from the in-laws of the Nappāhu family were extended in return for the usufruct of their house. Nabû-šumu-uṣur once lent his younger brother Murānu five shekels of silver. This amount, however, bore an above-average interest rate of twenty-five percent per annum.

note as a primary source. Nonetheless, this investigation has made it clear that a range of social factors influenced the way in which Borsippa's priests lent and borrowed, leading to divergent credit profiles.

Nabû-mukīn-zēri//Rē'i-alpi's favourable monetary circumstances, for example, allowed him to extend large sums on many occasions and borrow only modestly himself whereas Marduk-šumu-ibni//Ilia's chronic lack of silver made him contract loans primarily with his closest relatives and temple colleagues, while keeping his overall involvement in moneylending limited at the same time. Solidarity and co-operation enabled the Rē'i-alpi family to successfully manage its prebendary patrimony. It also motivated Rēmūt-Nabû to appeal to his innate network of kin and in-laws for financial support after his crisis in Dar 20. This network functioned both as a community of interest and an ultimate safety net. Finally, I argued that the Bēliya'u family's immigrant background, if not also a reason for other indigenous bakers to dissociate themselves from this family, may have led Šaddinnu to pursue a more active career as entrepreneur and moneylender in addition to his obligations as priest of Nabû.

While other examples could be provided to illustrate the influence of personal circumstances and family background in this area of interaction, another factor that seems to have patterned the practices of moneylending in significant ways, albeit on a more general level, is professional affiliation. In fact, the available evidence reveals a faint correlation between temple rank and lending pattern. Priests in the higher echelons of the temple hierarchy adhered to a more inward-looking lending practice, geared towards fellow prebendary families and kin (i.e. Ea-ilūtu-bani and others), while families located in the lowest fringes of the temple institutions engaged with a much more diverse set of families and relied less on fellow prebendary clans (Atkuppu). This development could be traced from the temple-enterers to the brewers, the bakers, and the reed-workers. Only the Oxherd family, with its strong sense of solidarity and close collaboration with fellow priests, deviates from this trend.

Still, this observation has been important for a couple of reasons. Not only does it indicate that with the reed-workers we are indeed reaching the outer fringes of the temple community, but at the same time it provides additional support for my working hypothesis that the temple fabric loses its influence on its participants the further one descends in the temple hierarchy.

Moreover, the fact that priests adopted a lending practice that was, overall, geared towards the prebendary in-group becomes clear once all the loans incorporated in this study are added together. Dividing the lending partners into priests and non-priestly 'outsiders', the grand total is 138:80 in favour of the former. This means that out of the 218 silver loans found in the archives of Borsippa's priests, nearly two-thirds were contracted with individuals from temple-based families.

The preponderance of priestly families should perhaps not surprise us. Many lending partners met in the temple on a daily basis. Additionally, loans contracted within the prebendary in-group often took the form of modest interest-free loans. One cannot fully dismiss the possibility that they were extended to cover prebend-related expenses and were therefore part of the cultic organisation, although the absence of temple colleagues in the credit operations of Šaddinnu//Bēliya'u speaks against this. Moreover, in contrast to what has been observed in the organisation of tenancy, most of the debtors and creditors of silver loans resurface outside of these encounters. Among the twenty-six lending partners of Šaddinnu, for example, four remain unattested; one is found elsewhere in the corpus while the rest is known from his archive in other capacities. Of the forty-two credit partners of Rēmūt-Nabû who are identified by a three-partite filiation, no less than thirty reoccur in the Rē'i-alpi archive. The same stands for Marduk-šumu-ibni: only three of his thirteen partners remain otherwise unknown, while the rest are either attested in the Ilia (A) archive or elsewhere in the corpus. All this suggests that moneylending took place in a restricted geographic space and that the priests from Borsippa found their lending partners in their immediate environment.

Perhaps more remarkable, then, is the relatively high involvement of non-prebendary families (37%). There could be many reasons why priests engaged with 'outsiders'. One simple explanation is that priestly and non-priestly families inhabited the same neighbourhoods, presumably those located closest to the temple complex (see Chapter 6.2.1 for more on residential patterns). Nonetheless, the high participation of these members of the community in moneylending contrasts strongly with their near exclusion in the hypergamous marriage system. Whereas marriage was something that was planned well in advance, the motives underlying individual credits are far more convoluted. Many of the loans must have been contracted quickly in moments of crisis or on an *ad hoc* basis.

It should be clear that more work is needed to fully unravel the social dimensions of silver lending in ancient Babylonia. It remains extremely difficult to qualify loans, let alone establish their correct background. While I have been careful to only use credits that make no reference to existing contracts, agreements, and sales, perhaps a finer methodology is advisable for future research. A more fruitful approach might be to focus primarily on advancements involving lower sums as they are more likely to represent genuine loans than credits of several minas of silver. It remains to be seen in the future how patterns of loans in kind relate to the ones in silver.

CHAPTER 4

Circles of Trust and Intimacy

The previous chapters of this study were devoted to social interactions in which the priests from Borsippa and their families engaged on a more or less regular basis. Far from happening at random, we have seen that marriage alliances, professional affiliation, kinship ties, and family background, among possible other factors, played an important role in configuring these interactions.

This chapter examines the priests' personal networks, more precisely, their circles of trust and intimacy. Which individuals belonged to their immediate entourage, whom did they trust and bring along to important transactions, and whom did they choose as business partners? It seems reasonable to suggest that in these intimate and confidential matters priests enjoyed much more freedom from social convention and custom than in any of the interactions studied so far. Exploring these relationships of trust and intimacy, which perhaps even included friendship, provides a unique insight into their most immediate social environment.

Apart from a handful of short proverbs, no diaries, letters, poems or other textual sources bearing a personal account on friendship were composed during 3000 years of Mesopotamian history.[1] Nor is there a Babylonian equivalent of the *Nicomachean Ethics*, Aristotle's most famous work on ethics, which provides us with a philosophical exegesis on the different forms of friendship (φιλία; *philia*), according to a prominent Athenian intellectual in the fourth century BCE.[2] Even if friendship represents a major leitmotif in the celebrated epic of Gilgamesh,[3] no expressions of amity have entered the business archives

1 See Alster 1997: SP 2.33, SP 2.62, SP 3.16, SP 3.17, SP 3.64, SP 3.159, SP 4.9, SP 9 Sec. E 5 and UET 6/2 276, among others, for Sumerian sayings concerning friends (ku.li) or friendship (nam. ku.li). Implicit expressions of friendship and intimacy from the Neo-Babylonian period can occasionally be found in private letters. See Jursa, Hackl, and Schmidl 2014. One may also consider the optional piggyback messages on letters through which fellow temple officials inquired about each other's well-being. See Levavi 2018: § 4.2.3.3. In this context the correspondence between the deputy of the Sealand and the chief temple administrator of the Eanna temple in Uruk merits special mention as their particularly congenial relationship is noticeable throughout their letters. See Levavi 2018: § 4.2.4.3.4.1.

2 Irwin and Fine 1996 and Cooper 1980.

3 Sallaberger 2008: 69–72 and George 2003: 140–142.

 | DOI:10.1163/9789004399969_006

of the Borsippean priesthood.[4] One might therefore rightfully ask whether it is at all possible to capture ties of intimacy, let alone friendship, in the administrative texts, which are the products of conservative legal practice and scribal conventions. Moreover, we have to bear in mind that the written record represents only a small proportion of the transactions that took place in actual daily life, and that meeting one's friends surely did not require a written testimony.

Hence, how can ties of friendship in this ancient priestly community be reconstructed? Following notions found in the socio-anthropological literature, friendship could be paraphrased in the most basic terms as 'a more or less informal social relationship, based on choice, trust, and voluntariness'.[5] Research into these ties, how they materialise and structure society, has a long tradition in the social sciences. Among the pioneering studies that focus on intimacy and friendship in the urban setting one should mention Lazarsfeld and Merton 1954, Laumann 1966, Verbrugge 1977, Fischer *et al.* 1977, and Fischer 1982. These studies remind us of the fact that friendship comes in many forms and intensities and may vary from person to person, context to context, and place to place. Yet, they also reveal that in addition to psychological characteristics commonly associated with friendship, one can find structural features that form the basis for, or alternatively, result from intimate relationships such as friendship. Thus, leaving aside psycho-emotional aspects, which transcend the scope of our legal documentation, I approach the issue of friendship in Borsippa through the structural features evident in the corpus.

The principal concept in this respect is that of the 'strength' of ties, introduced most clearly by the sociologist M. Granovetter. In his seminal 1973 article on the strength of weak ties, Granovetter proposed that 'the strength of a tie is a (probably linear) combination of the amount of time, the emotional intensity, the intimacy (mutual confiding), and the reciprocal services which characterise the tie'.[6] Even if he left a more precise definition for future research, many subsequent scholars (most notably among network analysts) have since

---

4 The term found in the Borsippa corpus that comes closest to expressing an attitude of intimacy or friendship is 'brother' (*ahu*). Besides referring to someone's sibling, i.e. a son of the same father, the term was also applied, fictively, to individuals of different parents. Yet, as has been shown by C. Waerzeggers 2010: 85–90, in Borsippa the latter use was reserved for individuals belonging to the same paternal family, the so-called *bīt-abi* (see Chapter 6.1.1 and 6.1.5), and is thus far only found in the context of prebend transfers.

5 This definition is adopted from Beer 2001, an overview article on the anthropology of friendship.

6 Granovetter 1973: 1361.

integrated the concept of tie strength in their analysis and expanded the list of its dimensions with other structural, emotional, and social factors.[7]

One of the most basic and commonly applied indicators for tie strength is the frequency of interaction. Do actors have contact daily, weekly, and/or monthly? Or do they meet only on very rare occasions? Even if contiguity cannot be taken as an absolute yardstick for friendship or intimacy, repeated contact between individuals facilitates the process of conversion from strangers into acquaintances, and from acquaintances into friends.[8] Moreover, we tend to spend more time with our closest friends. Hence, by examining the people who figure most frequently in the archives of Borsippa's priests, it is possible to obtain a basic idea of who belonged to their intimate circles. The following investigation begins with a purely quantitative approach, which inform us on a general level about possible structural differences and similarities between the personal networks of priests.

Yet, results gained from an analysis based solely on frequency can be misleading. The inclusion of, for instance, stubborn debtors or tax collectors contaminate the results,[9] while the strength of ties between close kin are bound to be overestimated.[10] Even if there is no doubt that priests have enjoyed intimate (and perhaps even their strongest) relationships with immediate kinsmen, the 'strength' of such ties are based more on specifics of family demography and division of property than anything else. Moreover, kin relations are, so to speak, given to, rather than chosen by, a person. Following the notion of friendship as a relationship based on choice, close relatives should be set apart from the discussion.[11] This requires a more qualitative appraisal. In the second part of this chapter I therefore focus on the individuals who occur most frequently in the archives and examine which of them were involved in relations of trust and intimacy by introducing additional factors of tie strength. These include duration, multiplexity, and intensity.

The notion of duration refers to the possible time spent in a relationship. Even if the duration of a relationship cannot automatically be taken as

7 For some of the older studies that have invoked the concept, see Granovetter 1982. Cf. Gilbert and Karahalios 2009 for a brief overview of different factors of 'strength' with special relevance to its application in modern social media.

8 Verbrugge 1977: 577–578, Fischer *et al.* 1977, *passim* (especially Chapter 3), Scott 1991: 44–46, and Wasserman and Faust 1994: 44–45.

9 A similar observation has been made by C. Waerzeggers 2014: 12.

10 See Marsden and Campbell 1984 for the problems of using frequency as a measure of tie strength.

11 This does not apply to more distant (consanguine and affinal) relatives who cannot be linked immediately to the protagonists and certainly came from outside the latter's household.

benchmark for its strength, prolonged contact does increase the probability of forming an intimate relationship.[12] It has been noted that over a prolonged period of interaction individuals develop more efficient ways of communication, thus raising the intrinsic value of their relationship, provided it is a positive one.[13] Hence, in the following investigation a relationship sustained over a longer period of time can be considered stronger and more robust than a short-lived one with a similar degree of frequency.[14]

Multiplexity refers to the idea that interpersonal ties are stronger if they involve different forms (and different contexts, see Chapter 4.2).[15] In essence, multiplexity is a measurement of the diversity of shared activity. This means that an individual who, for example, only acts as somebody's witness does not enjoy an equally strong relationship as someone who acts as creditor, guarantor, scribe, and witness. Rather than requiring a new contact for every new transaction, a multiplex relationship between two individuals makes it possible to fulfil a much broader range of needs and can thus be seen as indicative of interpersonal intensity. As opposed to other kinds of relationships, ties of friendship are usually more multiplex, a quality that is often developed over time.

Intensity is the final factor taken into account. While this dimension of tie strength usually refers to emotional aspects, it is more important for us to take notice of the exact nature and context of interaction. There is a difference between people living in the same neighbourhood who enjoy a 'nodding' relationship in passing, and people who acted as each other's groomsman. While the former might see each other more often, the relationship that exists between the latter is far more ritualised and emotionally charged, and hence more intensive. In the second part of this investigation I pay special attention to important, personal events of Borsippa's priests like marriage, adoption, and property sales as well as other momentous transactions like substantial loans and business enterprises.

12 Fischer *et al.* 1977: Chapter 3, Fischer 1982, and Marsden and Campbell 1984.

13 Hruschka 2010: 156–159.

14 One has to realise that an intimate relationship like friendship is not static but in a continuous process of change. See Lazaresfeld and Merton 1954 and Hruschka 2010. At the particular moment when we capture intimate relations in the sources, some might still be in the early stages of formation, while others might be already well established or even on their way towards dissolution. While it need not be the case, whenever the evidence for such a relation breaks off, it could point to the dissolution of the bond.

15 For the concept of multiplexity (earlier known also as *multistrandedness*) see Fischer *et al.* 1977, *passim* (especially Chapter 3), Verbrugge 1979, Fischer 1982: 139–144, Scott 1991: 65–67, Prell 2012: 138–140, and Hruschka 2010: 157. See also Waerzeggers 2014 who engaged in a similar investigation of interaction frequency and multiplexity for the Sipparean priests-entrepreneur Marduk-rēmanni.

In the end a strong tie should be understood as the result not of a high degree in any single one of these dimensions, but rather as the cumulative result of all these criteria together. While the application of tie strength deeply refines our appraisal of the circles of trust and intimacy, it equally enables us to reconstruct parts of the network that were not captured adequately by straightforward quantitative analysis.

1 Formal Quantification of Personal Networks

Let us now examine the sources from Borsippa from a quantitative perspective. The purpose of this investigation is to see whether a purely quantitative analysis of the priestly archives can tell us more about the personal networks of trust and intimacy as well as the general (interactional) attitude of the protagonists. The underlying idea is that lifestyle correlates with specific social networks or, conversely, that specific network properties reflect particular modes of behaviour. Hence, the more conservative and inward-looking attitude of a priest translates into an ego-network with fewer individuals but a higher number of frequent contacts compared to the network of an outgoing and entrepreneurial merchant, which consists of a larger (and more diverse) set of contacts yet holds a smaller number of frequent contacts.[16] Moreover, the network of the merchant is, on the whole, less dense than that of the priest who is secluded in his tight-knit temple community where everybody knows everybody.[17]

The focus is on the main protagonists of the Ea-ilūtu-bani (including Ilī-bāni and Nannāhu), Ilia (A), Bēliya'u, Rē'i-alpi, and Atkuppu family archives. It has been noted that the structures of these archives differ greatly. On the one hand, the documents of the Ea-ilūtu-bani and the Atkuppu archives are distributed more evenly over the long sixth century and often report on the activities of contemporary siblings and in-laws, thus providing a broader but less dense account. On the other hand, the Bēliya'u, the Ilia (A), and the Rē'i-alpi archives have been classified as single-generation archives since the great majority of their texts were produced by one, or in the case of the Rē'i-alpis, two consecutive individuals. The latter archives are most suitable for this ego-centred examination. The Ea-ilūtu-bani and the Atkuppu archive, in contrast,

16 A convincing example from Sippar has been presented by Waerzeggers 2014: 10–14.

17 In social network theory 'density' measures how many ties (between the actors) of all the ones possible are actually present in the network. In the words of C. Waerzeggers, 'a dense network is indicative of a cohesive world where everybody knows everybody'. See Waerzeggers 2014b: 212.

lack a similar density of information, making quantification less meaningful. In order to incorporate them into the following analysis some arbitrary measures are in order. The Ea-ilūtu-bani archive cluster, for example, is taken as one single unit. In the Atkuppu archive the focus is on the fourth generation, represented by the four sons of Marduk-šumu-ibni, who carried out much of their business collectively.

Let us start with fleeting contacts. The vast majority of the individuals mentioned in the archive are attested only one time. There is little doubt that the archive holders actually met some of these contacts more than once (especially those with whom they entered into a formal contract),[18] yet the figures are consistent between the archives and seem to present a fair reflection of reality. Of the 810 individuals mentioned in the network of Marduk-šumu-ibni//Ilia (A), 658 (81%) are attested only once.[19] A very similar figure is found in the network of Rēmūt-Nabû//Rē'i-alpi in which 497 (79%) of his 627 contacts appear not more than once. Also, Šaddinnu//Bēliya'u, who otherwise displayed a more entrepreneurial attitude compared to his fellow priests, had the same percentage of fleeting contacts (1,013 of 1,248 individuals or 81%). The only ego-network that deviates from this pattern is that of Nabû-mukīn-zēri//Rē'i-alpi: only seventy percent of his contacts occurs once. In other words, nearly one-third of all the individuals mentioned in his texts reappear, which might indicate that Nabû-mukīn-zēri conducted his business in a somewhat more restricted and perhaps more intimate circle. Even if the full implications of this result remain unclear in the present state of research, the Rē'i-alpis did exhibit a noticeable attitude of solidarity towards their own clan and a number of related families in other settings, which might serve as a partial explanation.

At the other edge of the spectrum we find the archives of the Atkuppu archive. Slightly more than ninety percent of the 355 individuals attested in the documents of the fourth generation occurs only once. However, as the sample taken from this archive is the smallest of our corpus (consisting of only eighty-three documents) and as it concerns the affairs of four brothers, it is likely that this high percentage is a result of the scarcity of information rather than a representation of reality. Somewhat less pronounced but still higher than the figures from the single-generation archives is the number of fleeting contacts found among the Ea-ilūtu-banis and their connected families. Of the total

18 Remember that the textual evidence at our disposal is far from complete. Moreover, the widespread use of nicknames in Borsippa makes it inevitable that some individuals have escaped correct identification.

19 Not included in this and the following numbers are those individuals whose name are damaged and cannot be identified with any certainty.

1,320 individuals, 1,138 (86%) appear only once. Again, this should probably not be taken as a fair reflection of reality since this figure is derived from a multi-generational archive lacking adequate ego-networks. Still, it might reveal a more structurally inherent feature of the family. Taking only the texts of Mušēzib-Bēl/Zēr-Bābili/Ea-ilūtu-bani, who with sixty-five attestations is the best-documented protagonist in this archive cluster, we arrive at the same eighty-six percent.[20] Very similar figures are found for some of his relatives.[21]

Let us now move on to the most frequently attested contacts. Five or more (≥5) attestations of the same individual was my cut-off point for determining who could be considered an intimate contact.[22] As expected, in contrast to the high number of one-timers, we find only a very small number of intimates in the archives under investigation. The highest figures are found in the networks of Marduk-šumu-ibni//Ilia (4% or 29 of 810) and Nabû-mukīn-zēri//Rē'i-alpi (3.5% or 24 of 688). While this seems high at first, in the case of Marduk-šumu-ibni many of these contacts represent close relatives. Leaving these out of the analysis reduces his intimate network to merely eighteen individuals (2.2%). This group is slightly more diverse for Nabû-mukīn-zēri, including only three close relatives (but still a relatively large number of clan members, as shown below). In contrast, this number (13 out of 627 or 2%) is somewhat smaller for the latter's son, Rēmūt-Nabû, and becomes even smaller (1.4%) if we exclude his close relatives. A slightly higher figure is found in the network of Šaddinnu//Bēliya'u where thirty of 1,248 (2.5%) qualify as intimate contacts. He does not seem to have relied much on close kin.

When turning to the final two archives, one finds the lowest figures. In the documents of the Atkuppus' fourth generation only four individuals are attested five times or more (1.2%). Even if the number seems higher in the collective network of the Ea-ilūtu-bani cluster (2.5%), many of these close contacts can be identified as one of the many archive holders; once we exclude them barely one percent qualifies as a close contact.

20 232 of his 270 contacts occur only once.

21 Mušēzib-Bēl's father, Zēru-Bābili/Nabû-šumu-ukīn/Ea-ilūtu-bani, is attested forty-six times. Of the total of 174 contacts found in his documents, 154 (88.5%) occur one time only; 87% for Nādin (aka. Dadia)//Ilī-bāni; 84% for Ahušunu//Nannāhu; and 86% for Zēru-Bābili/Šumā/Ea-ilūtu-bani. However, these latter three men are poorly attested.

22 The cut-off point of five or more attestations, which is also used by Waerzeggers 2014: 10–14 in a similar analysis, seems to offer a suitable middle ground. Lowering the cut-off point to four attestations drastically inflates the number of individuals involved, making our dataset a questionable tool for studying circles of trust and intimacy, let alone networks of friendship. Raising this point above five attestations, on the other hand, would have nearly excluded the Atkuppu archive, which mentions only three individuals more than five times.

As I said earlier, the figures from the latter two archives should not be taken at face value as they are probably a result of a lack of information. The figures established for the other archives seem, however, more reliable and these ego-networks can be compared more adequately with one another on a quantitative level. The relatively larger presence of intimate contacts in the network of Marduk-šumu-ibni could point to a particular reliance on family. Equally interesting is the contrast between the networks of Nabû-mukīn-zēri and his son Rēmūt-Nabû. With a relatively low frequency of fleeting contacts (70%) and a relatively high number of close contacts (3.5%), the former seems to have maintained a closer grip on his social environment compared to his son (75% fleeting and 2% close contacts). Whereas Nabû-mukīn-zēri's business activities are marked by prosperity and property acquisition, Rēmūt-Nabû faced times of austerity and crisis. One wonders whether their respective networks can account for these events; that is to say, whether their different levels of connectivity could be linked to their prosperity and hardship, respectively.

Before we investigate the identity and contexts of the closest contacts of the Borsippean priesthood in a more qualitative manner, let us briefly turn to a recent study on an influential man from Sippar and his social environment by C. Waerzeggers.[23] In her archival study of the entrepreneur-priest Marduk-rēmanni//Ṣāhit-ginê, Waerzeggers begins her investigation by submitting this man's archive to a similar quantification. Marduk-rēmanni, whose recent ancestors had migrated from the capital of Babylon, was both active in the temple and on the harbour of Sippar and he had contacts all over Babylonia. Waerzeggers shows that this man's ego-network reflects his broadly connected and dynamic lifestyle by comparing it with the contemporary network of Bēl-rēmanni, a more conventional priest of Šamaš. The network of Marduk-rēmanni was relatively less dense (84% fleeting and only 2% close contacts) than the one of his fellow townsman Bēl-rēmanni (74% vs. 4%). How exactly these figures relate to the networks from Borsippa remains unclear as the latter seems to oscillate between the two (see table 7). While affinity between the networks of Bēl-rēmanni and Nabû-mukīn-zēri//Rē'i-alpi seems right on an intuitive level, the fact that we have similar figures for Marduk-šumu-ibni//Ilia and the entrepreneur Marduk-rēmanni is surprising to say the least.

Not much can thus be said based on this rudimentary quantification. While the Ea-ilūtu-bani and the Atkuppu archives do not provide us with ideal data sets, the remaining archives generate nearly identical results. Other than a few general observations, the numbers do not seem to reveal any clear differences in terms of social behaviour of individual priests. Nor do they help us to

23 Waerzeggers 2014: 10–14.

TABLE 7 Contacts in Borsippa archives vs. Sippar archives

	Ilia (A)	Bēliya'u	Nabû-mukīn-zēri//Rē'i-alpi	Rēmūt-Nabû//Rē'i-alpi	Marduk-rēmanni	Bēl-rēmanni
1x contacts	81%	81%	70%	79%	84%	74%
≥5 contacts	4%	2.5%	3.5%	2%	2%	4%
(figures without close-kin)[a]	(2.2%)		(3%)	(1.4%)		
			Ego-networks from Borsippa		Ego-networks from Sippar	

a Note that the figures given for Bēliya'u, Marduk-rēmanni, and Bēl-rēmanni do not include close kin.

pinpoint their position in this community more precisely. Nevertheless, all ego-networks belong to priests, and even if different attitudes or mentalities have been observed in previous chapters, they essentially shared very similar social positions and lifestyles. Hence, homogeneity rather than heterogeneity must be expected. It is clear that much more work is needed on Babylonian ego-networks before we can fully grasp the meaning of these figures. Ideally, one should be able to compare these priestly ego-networks with the non-priestly networks from Borsippa with similar parameters (e.g. archive size, chronology, etc.).[24] Moreover, I believe that it is necessary in the future to examine how factors like time-span of the archive, size of the archive, text genre, and perhaps even community size influence the nature of these ancient networks.

2 Qualitative Analysis of Tie Strength and Friendship

The formal quantitative analyses of the previous part helps us to delineate, at least in preliminary form, the priests' networks of trust and intimacy as they supply us with the names of their most regular contacts. Following the order of the subsequent discussion, these networks consisted of thirty-one individuals

24 The only non-priestly archive from Borsippa that might be used to carry out a comparative study is the Gallābu archive. The texts from Nabû-zēru-ukīn//Gallābu contain 89% fleeting contacts vs. 1.6% of five or more contacts. The fact that these figures resemble the results gained from the Atkuppu and Ea-ilūtu-bani archives supports the idea that they are linked to the limited size of the archives.

in the Ea-ilūtu-bani archive cluster, twenty-nine for Marduk-šumu-ibni//Ilia (A), thirty for Šaddinnu//Bēliya'u, twenty-four and thirteen for Nabû-mukīn-zēri and his son Rēmūt-Nabû//Rē'i-alpi, respectively, and four for the Atkuppu brothers. These figures, however, include close members of the family and individuals whose relationship with the protagonist cannot be qualified as one based primarily on voluntariness or involving intimacy. Even if frequency of interaction is an important dimension of the strength of ties, it is clear that these numbers give at best a very crude representation of the actual networks of friendship. Hence, in the following I present a more qualitative appreciation of the circles of trust and intimacy by introducing the additional factors of tie strength: duration, intensity, and multiplexity. While the first two dimensions do not need further explanation, some words need to be said about multiplexity in our sources. As we see in the following, individuals attested most frequently in the personal networks of our priests can only rarely be described as multiplex in terms of roles because they usually appeared in only one or two functions on a regular basis. While the traditional sense of multiplexity is applied in our investigation, I would like to introduce a further notion that might be more useful in our case, namely, that of multiplexity of context. In the following survey I have divided the activities of our priests according to socio-economic contexts: temple-related activities including prebendary management, agricultural management, family affairs, property sales and acquisition, money-lending, housing management, *harrānu* business enterprises, and taxation. Undoubtedly, some of these overlap. For example, the transfer of a prebend within the Rē'i-alpi clan could be a matter of cultic management, a property acquisition, and a family affair. Yet, these social settings were to a certain extent structurally (and sometimes also culturally) circumscribed areas of activities, which may be associated with specific physical settings, in case of agricultural or temple affairs, and with specific sets of people such as colleagues, kin, tax collectors, and tenants. Hence, a relationship with an individual who accompanied someone to a wide range of settings can be qualified as more robust and involving a higher degree of trust and intimacy than a relationship that is found in a small range of contexts only. Even if these contexts were not isolated social worlds, I believe that this additional notion of 'multiplexity of context' can offer us an informative dimension of tie strength in Borsippa.

The following investigation adopts a descriptive approach, evaluating the individuals most frequently attested in the networks in terms of the various dimensions of tie strength. However, in light of the size of some of these personal networks reconstructed through quantification (some of which consisted of approximately thirty individuals), it would be impractical and rather needless to discuss all of them at full length. Instead, for each network I focus on a couple of individuals who seem to have enjoyed a particularly close relationship with the archive holder. These accounts provide much information about the types of trust and intimacy that transpire from the sources, offering us the most likely cases of friendship among individuals of this priestly community. All the information about the multiplexity of roles, contexts, and duration of interaction is summarised in tabulated form at the end of each section.[25] Rather than an attempt to rank individuals in absolute terms, these tables serve as a convenient overview of the relations of trust and intimacy, and place them only on a very relative scale. Finally, while these tables are made for the larger single-generation archives of the Ilia (A), Bēliya'u, and Rē'i-alpi, they are lacking for the Ea-ilūtu-bani and the Atkuppu archives. The information in these archives is simply not adequate enough to warrant such an overview either because the number of frequent contacts is too small or because the protagonists are found in only a handful of different contexts.

2.1 *Ea-ilūtu-bani*

While the make-up of the Ea-ilūtu-bani archive cluster was not ideally suited for the quantifying analysis, it is still useful to take a closer look at the identity, attestations, and roles of the close contacts of these temple-enterer families. In the following I look at the various archive holders and their intimates individually.

Let us start with Nabû-šumu-iškun/Puhhuru from the third generation of the Ea-ilūtu-bani family who lived roughly between the 610s and 560s BCE.[26] There is relatively little information on this protagonist and only one of his contacts deserves a closer look. Although Nabû-šumu-iddin//Ahiya'ūtu is attested only four times, and always as a scribe, the variety of events that he recorded appears to distinguish him as an intimate contact. Other than an ordinary debt note for vats,[27] he composed the inheritance division between Nabû-šumu-iškun and his two brothers,[28] a sale contract of *hanšû* land,[29] and a record pertaining to the marriage arrangements of Nabû-šumu-iškun's son.[30]

25 I include some additional individuals in these tables, which have not been discussed in this study. Their inclusion helps to provide a more complete picture of the personal networks but may also serve as examples of individuals who are well attested yet enjoyed an overall weaker connection to the protagonists in terms of tie strength.

26 For more information on this individual, see Joannès 1989: 31–35.

27 BM 94819 (Nbk 08).

28 TuM 2/3 5 (Npl 16).

29 OECT 12 A 98 (Nbk 08). Nabû-šumu-iškun bought the land from a member of his own clan.

30 TuM 2/3 48 (Nbk 25). It concerns silver from the dowry of his daughter-in-law that was still due to him.

In view of the fact that scribes of such documents usually represent intimate relations in other archives, Nabû-šumu-iddin//Ahiya'ūtu can be considered a close contact, even if the number of attestations falls under the threshold applied elsewhere in this study.

Nabû-šumu-iškun's son Zēru-Bābili//Ea-ilūtu-bani appears to have had only one contact who appears more than five times in the available sources.[31] Nabû-lē'i/Marduk(a)/Ur-Nanna is attested eight times as a witness between 565 and 558 BCE.[32] The majority of these transactions took place in an agricultural context, once even in a village outside of Borsippa.[33] He also witnessed a work contract for the manufacture of bricks (i.e. taxation),[34] a loan of silver,[35] and a house rent contract for Zēru-Bābili.[36] That he enjoyed an intimate relationship with Zēru-Bābili might be further deduced from the fact that he usually appears as first witness in his records.

Iqīša-Marduk/Šumu-ukīn/Ea-ilūtu-bani was a distant relative and frequent contact of Mušēzib-Bēl, son of Zēru-Bābili//Ea-ilūtu-bani.[37] Besides acting as a witness for Mušēzib-Bēl on four occasions (twice as first witness),[38] he also exchanged land with him.[39] One year after the exchange, he also took out a loan of silver from Mušēzib-Bēl.[40]

The last protagonist of the Ea-ilūtu-bani clan to be discussed here is Zēru-Bābili/Šumā who is frequently identified as a temple-enterer of Nabû.[41] In the twenty-five documents that have entered the archive, most of which dealt with the management of his agricultural property, there is one individual who stands out: Šulā/Arad-Nabû/Ea-ilūtu-bani. Attested some ten times between circa 584 and 562 BCE, he is Zēru-Bābili's best-attested witness (usually

31 For more information on this individual who can be followed in the documentation between roughly 580 and 540 BCE, see Joannès 1989: 35–36.

32 OECT 12 A 88 (Nbk 40) and NBC 8378 (Ner 02)

33 TuM 2/3 156 (Ner 02) is an *imittu* text written in Bāb-kirāti. Others texts include OECT 12 A 88 (Nbk 40), L 4735 (Nbk 41), and TuM 2/3 80 (Nbk 42).

34 L 1632 (Nbk 40).

35 L 1625 (Nbk [x]).

36 NBC 8378 (Ner 02).

37 See Joannès 1989: 39–45 for more information on this protagonist who is found in the texts between circa 560 and 510 BCE.

38 TuM 2/3 6 (Nbk IV 00), TuM 2/3 166 (Dar 07), NBC 8376 (Dar 07), and OECT 12 A 165 ([-]).

39 NBC 8366 (Cam 07) is a debt note of silver referring to the earlier exchange of land with Mušēzib-Bēl.

40 L 1657 (Nbk VI 01).

41 For more on this individual, whose texts date between circa 587 and 550 BCE, see Joannès 1989: 36ff. As Joannès shows (following an earlier observation by San Nicolò 1947: 155) he should not be equated with Zēru-Bābili/Nabû-šumu-iškun in spite of the onomastic similarities.

as first witness).[42] In this capacity he accompanied him to eight *imittu* harvest estimates,[43] a sales contract for a donkey,[44] and a debt note for silver resulting from a work obligation.[45] Moreover, according to TCL 12 52 (Nbk 35), Šulā's slave was to deliver the harvest from a field belonging to Zēru-Bābili, presumably by virtue of his activities as tenant. This last piece of evidence indicates that Šulā and Zēru-Bābili enjoyed a more complex relationship. Finally, although Šulā's exact patrilineal connection to the family is not elucidated in the present state of the documentation, it is interesting that he appears in connection with other protagonists of the archive: once in connection with Nabû-šumu-iškun/Puhhu-ru[46] and two times with Lūṣi-ana-nūri-Marduk/Nabû-mukīn-zēri/Ilī-bāni.[47] Additionally, Šulā's son, Nabû-nādin-ahi, is frequently attested as scribe (see below).

Shifting our focus to the Ilī-bāni family branch and its first protagonist, Lūṣi-ana-nūri-Marduk/Nabû-mukīn-zēri,[48] it turns out that his closest contact, Marduk-šākin-šumi/Bēlšunu/Rē'anu, is also found in documents of Zēru-Bābili/Šumā (see above). In the relatively short period of twelve years,[49] Marduk-šākin-šumi wrote ten documents of the archive, six for Lūṣi-ana-nūri-Marduk[50] and four for Zēru-Bābili/Šumā,[51] all related to the management of agricultural holdings or silver debts. Admittedly, this contact seems not to have been particularly influential (neither in terms of roles nor in terms of contexts in which he appears), and apart from the fact that he was connected to various protagonists of the archive, not much can be said about him.

We learn a great deal more about the close associates of Nādin (aka. Dadia), son of Lūṣi-ana-nūri-Marduk//Ilī-bāni,[52] most notably about the three scribes Nabû-kāṣir/Itti-Marduk-balāṭu/Ea-ilūtu-bani, Nabû-nādin-ahi/Šulā/Ea-ilūtu-bani, and Nabû-mukīn-apli/Nabû-nādin-ahi/Gahal. While the majority of

42 His earliest and latest attestations are, respectively, YBC 9194 (Nbk 21+) and TuM 2/3 112 (Nbk 42).

43 YBC 9194 (Nbk 21+), TuM 2/3 152 (Nbk 28), YBC 9158 (Nbk 32), and TuM 2/3 155 (Nbk 40).

44 OECT 12 A 90 (Nbk 30).

45 TuM 2/3 112 (Nbk 42).

46 TuM 2/3 75 (Nbk 15).

47 OECT 12 A 93 (Nbk 30), and TuM 2/3 127 (Nbk 35). Note that according to this last document he sold sheep to Lūṣi-ana-nūri-Marduk.

48 For more information on this individual, see Joannès 1989: 49–50.

49 Between TCL 12 56 (Nbk 30) and TuM 2/3 81 (Nbk 42).

50 TuM 2/3 128 (Nbk 37), TuM 2/3 77 (Nbk 38), TCL 12 55 (Nbk 38), L 4725 (Nbk 40), L 4731 (Nbk 41), and TuM 2/3 81 (Nbk 42).

51 TCL 12 56 (Nbk 30), OECT 12 A 180 (Nbk 40), TuM 2/3 155 (Nbk 40), and TuM 2/3 101 (Nbk 40).

52 See Joannès 1989: 50–56 for more information on this individual who was active in the reign of Nabonidus (ca. 555–539 BCE).

the texts written by Nabû-kāṣir (twelve),[53] Nabû-nādin-ahi (six),[54] and Nabû-mukīn-apli (four)[55] represent run-of-the-mill documents such as debt notes, receipts, and harvest estimates, which, however, required them to be on location in the countryside, they were all involved in more significant family events. Nabû-kāṣir, for example, wrote the marriage agreement between Nādin and his wife, ᶠKabtā//Ilī-bāni in Nbn 06 at which Nabû-mukīn-apli was present as a witness.[56] Nabû-nādin-ahi wrote the sales contract of a date grove sold by Nādin and his brother to a distant relative[57] as well as a proceeding of Nādin's business venture.[58]

The last of Nādin's contacts who should be mentioned here is Nabû-ēṭir-napšāti/Šumā/Ea-ilūtu-bani, possibly the brother of the temple-enterer Zēru-Bābili/Šumā (see above). In only a very short period of five years he is mentioned eight times as first witness in Nādin's business transactions. Like the three scribes, he is mainly found in documents related to agricultural management[59] with one important exception: he was present at the drafting of the same marriage contract as Nabû-kāṣir and Nabû-mukīn-apli. His presence in what might have been Nādin's most personal record distinguishes him as an intimate contact.

The final protagonist who deserves a closer examination is Ahušunu/Nabû-mušētiq-uddi (aka. Bazuzu)/Nannāhu.[60] The first individual who stands out as an influential associate is Nabû-ahhē-iddin/Nabû-zēru-ibni (aka Kalbā)/Nannāhu. His involvement, which spanned over fifteen years, is remarkable and can only stem from a particularly robust relationship. Firstly, he lent Ahušunu the sum of one mina of silver in Dar 13.[61] Secondly, in Dar 17 he stood

53 E.g., TuM 2/3 84 (Nbn 02), MLC 381 (Nbn 04), OECT 12 A 101 (Nbn 05), BM 96263 (Nbn 08) written in bīt-Apkallu, L 1637 (Nbn 09) written in Nuhšānitu, and OECT 12 A 178 (Nbn [x]).

54 E.g., TuM 2/3 158 (Nbn 09), NBC 8357 (Nbn 15), and NBC 8367 (Cam 01) written in Sūr-Amēlutu.

55 OECT 12 A 174 (Nbn 02), BRM 1 58 (Nbn 05), TuM 2/3 115 (Nbn 06), and BM 94885 (Nbn 08).

56 TuM 2/3 1.

57 NBC 8395 (Nbn 15).

58 TuM 2/3 86 (Nbn 08) documents the receipt of eleven *kur* of dates paid by Nādin//Ilī-bāni to Iddin-Nabû//Ēdu-ēṭir and Nabû-mukīn-zēri//Amēl-Ea. It then mentions another debt, said to be the debt note of the business venture (*u'iltu ša harrānu*) of two other individuals, who have to hand it over to Nādin.

59 This required him to accompany Nādin on at least three trips outside the city walls: TCL 12 85 (Nbn 05) written in Sūr-Amēlūtu; BM 96263 (Nbn 08) written in bīt-Apkallu; and L 1637 (Nbn 09) written in Nuhšānitu.

60 See Joannès 1989: 59–64 for this individual who can be traced in the documentation between circa 522 and 492 BCE.

61 OECT 12 A 123.

surety for a debt of two minas of silver drawn up against Ahušunu.[62] Thirdly, between Dar 17 and Dar 29 he repeatedly paid (*ina qātān*) taxes on behalf of (*ana muhhi*) Ahušunu.[63] Finally, Nabû-ahhē-iddin was present at both of Ahušunu's marriage contracts as a witness.[64] Few individuals in the Borsippa corpus are known to have maintained such a discernible relationship, but because the genealogy of the Nannāhus is still unknown this bond might have existed by virtue of being close relatives.

Before closing this section, there is one individual who remains to be mentioned. Even though he seems not to have been linked to one protagonist in particular, Nidinti-Bēl/Bēl-ahhē-iddin/Bēl-eṭēru is a good example of an individual who, although rarely mentioned, seems to have enjoyed a close relationship with the various branches of this family cluster. While he is first attested in Dar 18 as the scribe of an unremarkable debt note for Bēl-uballiṭ//Ilī-bāni,[65] some months later Nidinti-Bēl also recorded the inception of a *harrānu* business venture for him.[66] In the following years he seems to have remained in close touch with the family. The next time we meet him in Dar 26 he was married to ᶠAmat-Sutīti, daughter of Nādin//Ilī-bāni and cousin of Bēl-uballiṭ, who was formerly married to Mušēzib-Bēl//Ea-ilūtu-bani.[67] Two years later we find him as first witness at the marriage agreements of his stepdaughter, ᶠLurindu//Ea-ilūtu-bani and Ahušunu//Nannāhu, mentioned above.[68] The latter was, finally, also present as a witness at Nidinti-Bēl's second marriage in Dar 35.[69]

The majority of the contacts discussed above either belonged to the same clan (e.g. Ea-ilūtu-bani and Nannāhu) or to fellow temple-enterer families (e.g. Ahiya'ūtu). Relatives and members from the own professional group clearly assumed an important role in the relations of trust and intimacy among these families, a trend that also emerged strongly from other types of interaction. Even so, individuals from families that cannot be linked to the priestly circle of Borsippa can be found in the personal networks too (i.e. Gahal, Rē'anu, and Ur-Nanna). Even if this points to the fact that ties of friendship in Borsippa were not fully restricted by concerns of professional affiliation, it remains uncontested that individuals lacking family names are entirely absent. This holds for the following priests as well.

---

62 OECT 12 A 120.

63 TuM 2/3 169 (Dar 17), OECT 12 A 173 (Dar 18), L 4720 (Dar 25), and L 1651 (Dar 27).

64 NBC 8410 (Dar 18) and TuM 2/3 2, including part-duplicate BM 94577, (Dar 28),

65 TuM 2/3 96. For more information on Bēl-uballiṭ, see Joannès 1989: 56–58.

66 BM 94492.

67 BM 94608.

68 TuM 2/3 2 (Dar 18) and part-duplicate BM 94577.

69 L 1634.

2.2 *Ilia (A)*

Of the approximately 810 individuals mentioned with Marduk-šumu-ibni// Ilia (A), nearly four percent met him five times or more. Compared to other priests under investigation, Marduk-šumu-ibni had the largest number of close contacts. If we take a closer look at the identity of these ≥5-contacts it turns out that the great majority bore temple-based family names (approximately 81%). Equally important is the observation made earlier that more than half of these individuals (fifteen) were allied to the Ilias by marriage or blood and no less than eleven belonged to Marduk-šumu-ibni's immediate kin, i.e. brothers, cousins, nephews, father, wife, and son. Since this last set of ties are, so to speak, 'given' and not based on choice or voluntariness, I have excluded Marduk-šumu-ibni's close relatives from the following survey. An overview of the intimate contacts can be found in table 8.

The first individual who should be mentioned is Nabû-uṣuršu/ya-ahhē-iddin/Šēpê-ilia. He is attested twenty-seven times in the period between 516 and 493 BCE.[70] Notwithstanding his frequent occurrence, there are only two instances in which he assumed an active role. According to BM 109875 (Dar 10) and BM 94666 (Dar [x]), he is one of Marduk-šumu-ibni's partners in the production of beer for the cult of Nabû and perhaps for retail.[71] In general, his involvement in the affairs of Marduk-šumu-ibni was of a much more passive nature. He witnessed no less than twenty-five transactions (often as first witness), usually relating to agricultural[72] or prebendary management,[73] but he also witnessed at least one silver transaction,[74] a house rental,[75] and a family event.[76] Since this last transaction records the marriage negotiations of Marduk-šumu-ibni's daughter, ᶠAmat-Nanāya, his presence can be taken as a sign of intimacy between Nabû-uṣuršu and Marduk-šumu-ibni.[77] Finally, there are three more documents that should be mentioned here as they provide an extra

70 See BM 102336 (Dar 06) and BM 26500 (Dar 28) for his earliest and latest secured attestations, respectively.

71 It should be noted that in the domain of beer production the line between business partnerships (beer for the public market) and *ēpišānūtu* contracts (beer for cultic use) is not very clear and might well have gone hand in hand.

72 BM 95187 = AH XV no. 32 (Dar 15), BM 26751 (Dar 15), BM 95198 (Dar 17), BM 101999 (Dar 18), VS 5 86 (Dar 19), and VS 3 121 (Dar 16 or 19).

73 BM 94632 = AH XV no. 36 (ca. Dar 18), BM 17695 = AH XV no. 38 (Dar 22), BM 26758 = AH XV no. 39 (ca. Dar 23), and BM 26726 = AH XV no. 40 (Dar 25).

74 BM 26708 (Dar 10⁺).

75 BM 94731 ([-]).

76 BM 26483 (Dar 14).

77 Nabû-uṣuršu witnessed at least one transaction of the Ilia (A) archive at which Marduk-šumu-ibni was not personally present. BM 26629 (Dar [x]) is a cultivation contract of Marduk-šumu-ibni's daughter and was possibly written after the former's death.

dimension to the relationship between Nabû-uṣuršu and Marduk-šumu-ibni. Towards the end of his career Marduk-šumu-ibni functioned as a notary scribe in Borsippa and the archive holds a number of property deeds written (some also sealed) by him.[78] As far as we can see, these documents were composed for individuals with no obvious ties to the notary, presumably for the sake of neutrality, but it seems that the latter could bring his own confidants to the transaction. As it turns out, Nabû-uṣuršu accompanied Marduk-šumu-ibni in this capacity on at least three occasions.[79] Holding no stakes in these transactions, their co-occurrence can only be understood as the result of personal volition and trust.

Another partner of Marduk-šumu-ibni who seems to have enjoyed a more substantial relationship with the Ilias is Rēmūt-Nabû/Nabû-bāni-zēri/Bēliya'u. While he owed Marduk-šumu-ibni a small number of vats on two occasions,[80] presumably used for the production of beer for retail, he recorded eleven and witnessed four transactions well beyond this sphere between 546 and 522 BCE.[81] Most notably, he seems to have accompanied Marduk-šumu-ibni regularly on trips to the countryside for the purpose of harvest estimates and the management of rural property.[82] He also wrote an important property deed recording the transfer of prebends between Marduk-šumu-ibni and his close relatives and is found as witness in another.[83]

A final colleague of Marduk-šumu-ibni who deserves a closer look is Nabû-ēṭir-napšāti/Tabnēa/Kudurrānu. In addition to his single attestation as Marduk-šumu-ibni's cultic colleague and employer,[84] Nabû-ēṭir-napšāti acted

---

78 For an article on the function and the sealing practice of the Neo-Babylonian notary scribes, see Baker and Wunsch 2001. Tablets that have entered the Ilia (A) archive by virtue of his activity as notary include, among others, BM 26511 = AH XV no. 35 (Dar 16), BM 27746 (Dar 27), BM 26503 (Dar 27) BE 8 115 (Dar 27), and BM 26500 (Dar 28).

79 BM 87289 (Dar 19), BE 8 115 (Dar 27), and BM 26500 (Dar 28). See also Itti-Nabû-balāṭu/Nabû-tabni-uṣur/Kidin-Sîn who is attested six times in connection with Marduk-šumu-ibni between 514 and 494 BCE, including BM 26500, BM 27746, and BM 109363, texts related to Marduk-šumu-ibni's notary activities.

80 Ten vats of good beer in BM 27875 (Cam 01) and another ten in VS 6 111 (Cam 03).

81 BM 102311 (Nbn 10) and BM 26673 (Bar 01).

82 OECT 12 A 82 (Nbn 10+) and BM 94842 (Nbn 11) written in Bīt-ša-Nabû-damqā; BM 102267 (Cam [x]) and BM 82806 ([-]) written in Birit-aṣunê; and BM 21159 (Cam 00) and BM 26673 (Bar 01) written in Tīl-būri.

83 VS 5 37 (Cyr 02) and BM 26569 = AH XV no. 14 (Cyr 03).

84 BM 94699 = AH XV no. 43 ([-]). Unlike the previous two individuals who were employed by Marduk-šumu-ibni, perhaps we should see Nabû-ēṭir-napšāti as the superior party since he recruited Marduk-šumu-ibni to perform his cultic obligations.

as a scribe on eight occassions in the archive between 545 and 507 BCE.[85] Of particular interest is his involvement in the redistribution of property after Šulā's death.[86] That Nabû-ēṭir-napšāti enjoyed a durable and intimate relationship with Marduk-šumu-ibni is revealed most clearly by the fact that he also recorded the marriage negotiations of his daughter in Dar 14.[87]

The next individual to be examined is Nabû-bēlšunu/Mušēzib/Itinnu. He is attested twenty-four times in connection with Marduk-šumu-ibni in the period between 547 and 521 BCE[88] either as scribe (thirteen times) or witness (eleven times). In these capacities he was present at various transactions relating to agricultural management,[89] beer production,[90] prebendary administration,[91] taxation,[92] and a range of miscellaneous transactions.[93] More important was his repeated presence at family affairs after the death of Marduk-šumu-ibni's father during the reign of Nabonidus.[94] He was present at and wrote at least three documents dealing with the re-division of the patrimony between the four sons,[95] the management of outstanding debts,[96] and the transfer of property between relatives.[97] We can conclude that even if he assumed only limited roles in the archive of the Ilias, the fact that he made an appearance at most

85 His earliest and latest attestation in connection with Marduk-šumu-ibni are BM 17640 (Nbn 11) and BM 95187 = AH XV no. 32 (Dar 15), respectively. Note, however, that he is already mentioned earlier together with Šulā//Ilia BM 27879 (Nbn 05).

86 BM 26731 (Nbn 12), BM 17657 (Nbn 13), BM 26532 ([Nbn 13]), and BM 26569 = AH XV no. 14 (Cyr 03).

87 BM 26483.

88 Earliest and latest attestations: BM 27890 (Nbn 08) and VS 6 119 (Dar 01).

89 BM 102289 (Nbn 12), BM 94882 (Cyr 07), and BM 94729 ([-]).

90 BM 94744 (Cyr [x]).

91 BM 102313 = AH XV no. 15 (Cyr 06).

92 BM 17654 (Nbn [x]), BM 17717 (Cam 06), and VS 6 119 (Dar 01).

93 BM 87332 (Nbn 10) is a debt note for dates. BM 95007 (Nbn 11) is a receipt of pegs and dates. BM 26099 (Cyr 02) is a receipt of wages for the manufacture of a bronze kettle.

94 See Waerzeggers 2010: 378–381 for a brief overview of the family history.

95 BM 17657 (Nbn 13) and BM 26532 ([Nbn 13?]) are redivisions of a date grove between the four brothers. BM 94587 (Nbn 13) is a redivision of property (field and houses) in Tīl-būri between the three younger brothers.

96 BM 27890 (Nbn 08) is a debt note for silver between Marduk-šumu-ibni and his older brother. In BM 26731 (Nbn 12) he pays a sum of silver to his sister-in-law (presumably from her dowry), which his father still owed her. BM 27899 (Nbn 17) is a debt note for silver between Marduk-šumu-ibni and his cousin, perhaps related to the property exchanged in BM 25664, which was also written by Nabû-bēlšunu.

97 BM 25664 (Nbn 16) is an exchange of two date groves between Marduk-šumu-ibni and his cousin, written by Nabû-bēlšunu. VS 5 37 (Cyr 02) is a donation of a door-keeper's prebend to Marduk-šumu-ibni (and his nephew) by his cousin. BM 82695 = AH XV no. 19 (Cam [x]) is a transfer of a prebend to Marduk-šumu-ibni, written by Nabû-bēlšunu.

TABLE 8 Tie strength of Marduk-šumu-ibni//Ilia (A) (ca. 553–493 BCE)[a]

Individual	Attestation	Role	Duration in years
Nabû-uṣuršu/ Nabû-ahhē-iddin/Šēpê-ilia	27	witness/brewing partner	23
Nabû-bēlšunu/Mušēzib/ Itinnu	24	scribe/witness	26
Rēmūt-Nabû/ Nabû-bāni-zēri/Bēliya'u	17	scribe/witness/ brewing partner	24
Nabû-uṣuršu/ Bēl-ahhē-iddin/Ṣilli-ahi	14	tenant/witness	24
Nabû-ēṭir-napšāti/Tabnēa/ Kudurrānu	11	scribe/witness/ prebendary owner	38
Nabû-mukīn-zēri/ Taqīš-Gula/Siātu	10	witness	32
Nabû-zēru-iqīša/Kabtia/ Mušēzib	7	scribe/witness	26
Nabû-nādin-ahi/ Nabû-nā'id/Naggāru	7	witness	2
Itti-Nabû-balāṭu/ Nabû-tabni-uṣur/Kidin-Sîn	6	scribe/witness	20

a Table index: ++ = strong presence; + = normal presence; – = limited presence.
b His presence in this context is placed in brackets (+) because he is only attested in a property-deed that was written by Marduk-šumu-ibni in his capacity of notary scribe and does not pertain to his private property.
c It is not entirely clear whether his activity in the beer-brewing business of Marduk-šumu-ibni was situated in a prebendary or *harrānu* context. As one does not exclude the other, his presence in the temple context is placed in brackets (+).

of the family arrangements that took place in periods crucial for the development of the family, either as witness or as scribe, qualifies him as an intimate contact of Marduk-šumu-ibni and his family.

An individual who enjoyed a similar connection to the family is Nabû-mukīn-zēri/Taqīš-Gula/Siātu. Although with only ten attestations the frequency of encounter is relatively limited, the intimacy of his connection transpires, again, from the types of events he attended. Like Nabû-bēlšunu//Itinnu, he witnessed no less than five of the re-divisions of property between the Ilia

Temple	Agriculture	Family	Property sale	Silver	House	*Harrānu*	Tax
++	++	+	(+)[b]	+	–	+	
+	+	++	+	+	–	–	+
(+)[c]	+	+	+	+	+	+	+
	++				++		
+	–	+	+	+			
		++	++	–	–		–
	+						+
	+				+		
–	+		+				

brothers.[98] In addition, Nabû-mukīn-zēri was also present at Šulā's last will and testament in Nbn 02.[99] Nabû-mukīn-zēri along with Nabû-bēlšunu seem to have been the only individuals who enjoyed such an intimate relationship with the entire nuclear family. He is attested one final time in a receipt of silver of Marduk-šumu-ibni dated Dar 02, more than thirty years after his first appearance in the archive.[100]

Although the frequency of attestation has been a good indication of intimacy so far, there is at least one example that warns us that it is not always

98 BM 26731 (Nbn 12), BM 17657 (Nbn 13), BM 26532 ([Nbn 13?]) BM 94587 (Nbn 13), and BM 94617 ([-]).

99 BM 26498 = AH XV no. 7.

100 BM 102020.

the case. Between 529 and 505 BCE, Nabû-uṣuršu/Bēl-ahhē-iddin/Ṣilli-ahi is attested no less than fourteen times, making him one of the most frequently attested contacts in the archive.[101] However, he is only attested in two spheres of Marduk-šumu-ibni's business affairs: agriculture and housing. Nabû-uṣuršu was a tenant of Marduk-šumu-ibni during the reigns of Cambyses and Darius I, working his estates in the area of Tīl-būri.[102] Moreover, probably living in close vicinity to this village, he witnessed various documents related to the administration of property held by Marduk-šumu-ibni and his family in the countryside. Instead of identifying this relationship as an intimate one between equals, it can better be understood in terms of 'employer and employee' or 'patron and client'.[103]

In conclusion, even if Marduk-šumu-ibni's reliance on fellow temple brewers is limited – other than members of the Ilia clan there are only two individuals from the Allānu and Kudurrānu families, respectively – he found many of his closest contacts among local prebendary families (e.g. Bēliya'u, Šēpê-ilia). Still compared to the temple-enterers discussed above, there are more individuals from non-priestly families in Marduk-šumu-ibni's personal network (e.g. Itinnu, Siātu, Mušēzib), some of which seem to have been on intimate terms with his entire family. Again, entirely absent are individuals who lack family names or established pedigrees.

2.3 *Bēliya'u*

Of the 1,248 individuals mentioned in the archive of Šaddinnu//Bēliya'u, thirty individuals (2.5%) qualify as intimate contacts (≥5). Roughly two-thirds of these individuals bore local priestly family names, and at least half (fifteen) were prebendary bakers, i.e., Šaddinnu's immediate temple colleagues. This does not, however, apply to the most frequently attested contact, Bēl-ēṭir/Guzānu (aka. Nādin)/Šigûa. He appears over forty times in the period between circa 506 and 496 BCE.[104] His primary role in the archive of Šaddinnu was that of scribe (thirty-one times).[105] He wrote a great variety of texts and his services were clearly not restricted to one specific sphere of Šaddinnu's affairs. He

101 His earliest attestation is BM 25832 (Cam 00); his latest is BM 27992 (Dar 16).

102 BM 95194 (Cam/Cyr 01), Amherst x (Cam 02), BM 94659 (Cam [x]), and Berens 108 (Dar [x]).

103 This does however not rule out the existence of friendship according to the cross-cultural record. Anthropologists usually refer to these friendships between individuals of different (social) status as 'lop-sided friendships'. See Rezende 1999 and Hruschka 2010: 66.

104 His earliest attestation is BM 29416 (Dar 15?); his latest in BM 96234 (Dar 26).

105 E.g., BM 28981 (Dar 17), BM 96167 (Dar 18), BM 29447 (Dar 19), BM 29057 (Dar 20), BM 25653//25630 (Dar 20), BM 96190 (Dar 20), VS 3 128 (Dar 21), BM 96373 (Dar 22), BM 29092

composed documents related to agricultural administration such as harvest estimates (*imittu*) and cultivation contracts[106] that occasionally required him to be on location outside of the city walls[107] and he also wrote temple-related texts, usually recording the disbursement of prebendary income to Šaddinnu's cultic collaborators.[108] Bēl-ēṭir also authored documents of greater personal significance to the archive holder: property deeds,[109] protocol texts,[110] and the two documents settling the arrangement with Bēl-iddin//Kāṣir,[111] whose old-age maintenance Šaddinnu had assumed in return for property rights.[112] Last but not least, Bēl-ēṭir was also involved in *harrānu* business ventures. He wrote documents related to silver loaning and work contracts for the production of beer as well as the formal conclusion of a joint venture. However, his involvement in Šaddinu's business affairs was deeper than simply that of scribe. There is at least one instance when he was required to deliver 100 vats of beer, suggesting that he was responsible for running parts of this enterprise himself.[113] More evidence of his personal investment can be found in BM 25714 (Dar 20), which informs us that Bēl-ēṭir (and Nabû-uṣuršu//Bā'iru) owed Šaddinnu's son, Nabû-uballiṭ, the relatively high sum of 140 shekels of silver.[114] Even if the text does not specify the background of this debt, the amount of silver and the identity of the co-debtor suggest that we are dealing with the organisation

(Dar 23), BM 25644 (Dar 25), BM 96234 (Dar 26), BM 96193 (Dar [-]), and BM 96346 (Dar [-]).

106 For a cultivation contract, see BM 96190 (Dar 20). For *imittu*-texts, see BM 28983 (Dar 17), BM 29089 (Dar 21), and BM 96299 (Dar 22).

107 VS 3 128 (Dar 21) is composed in Ṭābānu and BM 96299 (Dar 22) in *tamirtu* Sippuli(?). For these toponyms, see Zadok 2006: 402 and 444.

108 For so-called *idū ša maššarti* documents, see BM 29514 (Dar 19), BM 29057 (Dar 20), and BM 29092 (Dar 23). In this context the various texts from the Apamû dossier should also be mentioned. See Waerzeggers 2010: 127–128 for a summary of this dossier. Note in particular BM 29447 (Dar 19), and BM 96167 (Dar 18?), published in Zadok 2003a, which record the leasing of rights to cultic leftovers by Šaddinnu.

109 Agricultural plots: BM 29666 (Dar [x]) and BM 96193 (Dar [x]). Slave: BM 21978 (Dar 24).

110 Both texts agree on the bailment of individuals that have to be brought before Šaddinnu on set date: BM 28981 (Dar 17) and BM 96205 (Dar 25).

111 Bēl-iddin might have been a retired baker. Note that he is only mentioned once before these transactions, as a witness in a document dealing with prebendary income. See BM 29512 (Dar 10).

112 BM 25653//25630 (Dar 20) and BM 21979 (Dar 20).

113 BM 28893 (Dar 21).

114 There is one further text that mentions Nabû-uballiṭ//Bēliya'u and Bēl-ēṭir//Šigûa and seems to be dealing with silver for *harrānu* purposes but unfortunately BM 28962 (Dar 24) is highly damaged.

of a business venture.[115] The house rented by Bēl-ēṭir from Šaddinnu in BM 29036 (Dar 25) may also feature in this context. There is at least one occasion on which he collected house rent presumably on behalf of Šaddinnu.[116]

To conclude, even if Bēl-ēṭir/Guzānu/Šigûa is only attested for a relatively short period of ten years, he can be identified as one of the most influential contacts of Šaddinnu during the second half of Darius I's reign. This is not only suggested by the high contiguity with Šaddinnu, but also by the active role he assumed on various occasions. As a scribe he wrote texts pertaining to a disparate range of social settings from run-of-the-mill receipts of silver and dates to important property-deeds and long-term arrangements. Besides his scribal activities, he is attested as a witness (usually as a first witness[117]), but more importantly he also acted as Šaddinnu's business partner in the production of beer and perhaps the renting of housing plots. Moreover, his association to Šaddinnu bridged generations as he was found running a business with Nabû-uballiṭ, the former's son. Nor was Bēl-ēṭir a stranger to Šaddinnu before his first appearance in the documentation. Their relationship can be traced back to at least 519 BCE (Dar 03) when Guzānu//Šigûa, the father of Bēl-ēṭir, acted as a witness to Šaddinnu's acquisition of a housing plot.[118] Far more momentous in this respect is the fact that only six months later Guzānu bought a house adjoining Šaddinnu's property,[119] making him and presumably his son the new next-door neighbours.[120] The relationship between Šaddinnu and Bēl-ēṭir can

---

115 For the co-debtor Nabû-uṣuršu/Rēmūt/Bā'iru, see Zadok 2008: 76+3. Apart from BM 25714, he is mentioned at least six more times in the Borsippa corpus. See BM 27813 (Dar 13), BM 25732 (Dar 21), BM 27870 (Dar 22), BM 25647 (Dar 22), BM 25686 (Dar 23), and BM 25655//BM 25648 (Dar 23). Even if Šaddinnu or his son are not mentioned in these texts they must have entered the Bēliya'u archive through his connection with Bēl-ēṭir//Šigûa and their joint *harrānu* enterprise with the family. In BM 25732 (Dar 21), for example, we find Nabû-uṣuršu concluding a joint venture with a certain Sîn-ibni/Kalbā. While no mention is made of the Bēliya'us the contract was drawn up by Bēl-ēṭir. It seems that Nabû-uṣuršu was also active in Babylon. Interestingly, two of the three texts written at the capital inform us that he coordinated building contracts for private houses. It is probably not a coincidence that both he and Šaddinnu were active in the housing sector and one might expect a link between their enterprises.

116 BM 25690 (Dar 21).

117 For texts in which he acts as witness to Šaddinnu's business affairs, see BM 29024 (Dar 18), BM 29408 (Dar [19]), BM 28966 (Dar 20), and BM 28899 (Dar 20).

118 BM 25589 (Dar 03).

119 VS 4 98 (Dar 03). Even though Šaddinnu's full filiation is not provided he can beyond doubt be identified as Šaddinnu//Bēliya'u.

120 Guzānu is further attested as a witness (four of six times as first witness) in house lease contract: VS 5 67 (Dar 05); receipt of rations for Carians: BM 29488 (Dar 06); cultivation contract: BM 29004 (Dar 10?); and receipt of a 'gift' in silver from Šaddinnu's wife to the

thus be characterised as frequent, diverse, protracted, and based on trust and intimacy, which are many of the aspects one might associate with friendship.

Another important individual in Šaddinnu's circle is Nabû-bullissu (aka. Nabû-balassu-iqbi)/Mār-bīti-iqbi/Kidin-Sîn. Attested some thirty times between 519 and 491 BCE,[121] he is by far the most frequently attested witness in the archive. While mainly found in documents written in the prebendary sphere[122] and in texts recording agricultural exploitation,[123] he accompanied Šaddinnu to a much wider range of settings. We find him in documents related to the running of *harrānu* ventures[124] and silver loaning,[125] but also in the contexts of house letting[126] and property acquisition.[127] Twice he was present at the settling of (legal) disputes,[128] which on one of the occasions required him to go to the capital of Babylon. While he is represented in almost as many different contexts as Bēl-ēṭir, his activities and roles were more restricted and passive. In fact, there is only one instance in which he acted in a capacity other than that of witness, namely, when Šaddinnu hired him to do some kind of work.[129] Although it is difficult to evaluate this relationship, based on frequency and multiplexity of context and role, it seems that Nabû-bullissu's association with Šaddinnu was of a less intimate kind compared to that of Bēl-ēṭir, even if it can be traced over a much longer period of time.

There are many more individuals who occur relatively often in the archive of Šaddinnu and who might for reasons of frequency be classified as important, intimate contacts. However, compared to the previous two, their involvement is usually restricted to a single, specific setting. This includes people

---

temple authorities: BM 28913 (Dar 25?). He once extended Šaddinnu a loan in dates: BM 29452//YBC 11289 (Dar 12).

121 See BM 96374 (Dar 03) and VS 3 151 (Dar 31) for the earliest and latest attestation, respectively.

122 BM 96320 (Dar 15), BM 29034 (Dar 16), BM 21962 (Dar 26), and BM 29460 = AH XV no. 97 (Dar 27).

123 BM 96374 (Dar 03), VS 3 111 (Dar 11), BM 96190 (Dar 20), and VS 3 151 (Dar 31).

124 BM 95861 (Dar 16) and BM 28927 (Dar 20).

125 BM 29716 (Dar 14^{+}), BM 22105 (Dar 16), and BM 96150 (Dar 21).

126 VS 4 137 (Dar 13).

127 VS 5 79 (Dar 15?).

128 BM 96218 (Dar 04?) and BM 25626 (Dar 25). The last document, written in Babylon, records a contestation of a plot of land more than ten years after the deed.

129 Unfortunately, the operative clause in BM 96388 (Dar 11) is illegible, making the identification of the requirement of this job difficult. However, the archive holds one text of Nabû-bullissu in which he advanced an amount of barley that was to be repaid in loaves of bread (BM 96328). Even if Šaddinnu was not presence at that transaction, I am tempted to link BM 96388 to the same line of work, presumably located in the (prebendary?) bread-making sector.

like Nabû-ahu-ittannu/Hašdāya/Ṣillāya, a distant relative of Šaddinnu's wife, ᶠNanāya-damqā//Ṣillāya, who acted eighteen times as a witness for Šaddinnu between 506 and 497 BCE.[130] With few exceptions,[131] his presence was restricted to proceedings in the prebendary and agricultural spheres.[132] His repeated attestation as first witness could indicate a more intimate connection to Šaddinnu. The fact that he is often found in texts with Bēl-ēṭir//Šigûa, most notably in BM 28962 (Dar 24) concerning a *harrānu* venture of Bēl-ēṭir and Šaddinnu's son, may also be of interest. Another kinsman of Šaddinnu's wife is Kidin-Marduk (aka. Kidinnu)/Nabû-uballiṭ (aka. Bibānu)/Ṣillāya. He is attested some eighteen times, usually as scribe in transactions related to prebendary matters,[133] but he also wrote at least one debt note for silver,[134] a receipt for house rent,[135] and a payment of wages.[136] By Dar 15, however, Kidin-Marduk seems to have accumulated considerable debts and we find Šaddinnu compensating his creditor and taking possession of the pledged property.[137] Whether this came to the relief of Kidin-Marduk is not clear, however, it turned out to be a complicated acquistion,[138] which his relatives later contested.[139]

Several temple colleagues appear frequently in the archive. For instance, Nabû-gāmil/Nabû-šumu-ukīn/Bēliya'u and his son, (Ina-)Qībi-Bēl were distant relatives of Šaddinnu who are both mentioned some fifteen times as cultic collaborators. At first Nabû-gāmil can be found alone (Dar 09–13)[140] after which he is supported by his son (Dar 17–20)[141] who eventually took over his father's responsibilities in full (Dar 29).[142] Both are very occasionally found in texts outside of the prebendary sphere.[143] Another example is Lâbâši/Rēmūt/

130 Earliest attestation: BM 29034 (Dar 16); latest attestation: BM 28962 (Dar 24).

131 A *harrānu*-related text: BM 95861 (Dar 16); a land sale: BM 29666 ([-]); a document related to the Bēl-iddin//Kāṣir arrangement: BM 25653//BM 25630 (Dar 20).

132 Prebendary: BM 29034 (Dar 16), BM 96253 (Dar 17), BM 29514 (Dar 19), BM 96288 = AH XV no. 91 (Dar 19), BM 29057 (Dar 20), and BM 28936 (Dar 20). Land exploitation: BM 96322 (Dar 18), BM 29473 (Dar 19), BM 96190 (Dar 20), and BM 96211 (Dar [x]).

133 BM 29532 (Dar 09), BM 29749 (Dar 09), BM 29512 (Dar 10), BM 29034 (Dar 16), and BM 96350 ([-]).

134 BM 29494 (Dar 09).

135 VS 5 80 (Dar 15).

136 BM 28996 (Dar 15).

137 BM 29420.

138 Apparently, some of the legal documents had gone missing. See BM 29404//BM 28914 (Dar 16).

139 BM 25626 (Dar 25).

140 BM 29749 (Dar 09), BM 29051 (Dar 12), and VS 5 124 (Dar 13).

141 BM 96253 (Dar 17), BM 29024 (Dar 18), and BM 29057 (Dar 20).

142 BM 82642 = AH XV no. 98 (Dar 29). Note that in this last text Šaddinnu is not mentioned.

143 BM 96374 (Dar 03), BM 96312 (Dar 07) BM 22105 (Dar 16), and BM 28966 (Dar 20).

Kidin-Sîn who performed (parts of) Šaddinnu's cultic service between 516 and 489 BCE.[144] Lâbâši's brother, Marduk-šumu-ibni//Kidin-Sîn (or perhaps Lâbâši under his full name?), set up a joint venture with Šaddinnu, according to BM 96246 (Cyr 06).[145]

Finally, we briefly need to consider the association of Šaddinnu with members of other baker clans, in particular the Kidin-Sîns and the Šēpê-ilias. In the previous chapter I argued that the relationship between these two families and the Bēliya'us and the Esagil-mansums could best be characterised in terms of discord and mutual exclusion. Šaddinnu, however, was in repeated contact with a number of members of the Kidin-Sîn family. While most of these contacts were restricted to only one or a few social settings, as was the case with Lâbâši//Kidin-Sîn,[146] his relationship with Nabû-bullissu//Kidin-Sîn was clearly more robust. Even if this seems to contradict the portrayal of the local bakers as in a state of conflict and disunity, it should be pointed out that members of the Šēpê-ilia clan are conspicuously absent from Šaddinnu's circle of trust and intimacy. Moreover, those members of the Kidin-Sîn family attested five or more times in Šaddinnu's network were absent from his more momentous and personally relevant transactions. Hence, no member of either the Kidin-Sîn or the Šēpê-ilia families was present at the donation and old-age arrangements of Bēl-iddin//Kāṣir.[147] The same is true for the marriage agreement of Šaddinnu's son, Nabû-uballiṭ, and ᶠAmat-Nanāya, daughter of Marduk-šumu-ibni//Ilia (A).[148] While a member of both the Šēpê-ilia and the Kidin-Sîn families can be found as witness in this transaction, the former was a well-known contact of Marduk-šumu-ibni[149] and the second is so far not attested in any other document known to us and could have been a particular contact of both or none of the parties.[150] Šaddinnu's network of intimate contacts is summarised in table 9.

144 For the earliest and latest attestation as Šaddinnu's cultic collaborator, see BM 96413 (Dar 06) and BM 28916 (Dar 33), respectively.

145 For this text, see Zadok 2003b.

146 Others include Nabû-tāriṣ/Marduk-ušallim/Kidin-Sîn (six times), Gimil-Nabû/Šāpik-zēri/Kidin-Sîn (six times), and Nabû-balassu-iqbi/Nabû-ahhē-iddin/Kidin-Sîn (five times).

147 BM 25653//25630 (Dar 20) and BM 21979 (Dar 20). Instead we find other intimate contacts such as Bēl-ēṭir//Šigûa (forty times), Nabû-ahu-ittannu//Ṣillāya (sixteen times), and Nabû-ittannu//Nappāhu (eleven times). See table 9.

148 BM 26483 (Dar 14).

149 Nabû-uṣuršu/Nabû-ahhē-iddin/Šēpê-ilia (see above).

150 Nabû-uṣuršu/Bēl-kēšir/Kidin-Sîn. He might be attested in a cultivation contract from the Bēliya'u archive, but the family name is broken off. See BM 29004 (Dar 10?).

TABLE 9 Tie strength of Šaddinnu//Bēliya'u (ca. 536–484 BCE)

Individual	Attestations	Role	Duration in Years
Bēl-ēṭir/Guzānu/Šigûa	40+	scribe/witness/ partner/agent	10
Nabû-bullissu/ Mār-bīti-iqbi/Kidin-Sîn	30	witness/employee	28
Kidin-Marduk/ Nabû-uballiṭ/Ṣillāya	18	scribe/debtor	10
Nabû-ahu-ittannu/ Hašdāya/Ṣillāya	16	witness	9
Ina-qībi-Bēl + Nabû-gāmil/ Nabû-šumu-ukīn/ Bēliya'u	15/14	*ēpišānūtu*/witness	13/23
Ina-qībi-Bēl/ Nabû-ēṭir-napšāti/ Kidin-Sîn	12	scribe/witness/ guarantor	9
Lâbâši/Rēmūt/Kidin-Sîn	14	*ēpišānūtu*/witness	27
Nabû-mukīn-zēri/ Kidin-Nabû/Kidin-Sîn	13	scribe/witness	34
Nabû-ušallim/ Nabû-šumu-ibni/ Esagil-mansum	12	scribe	16
Nabû-nādin-ipri/Šumā/ Bēliya'u	11	witness/seller	20
Nabû-ittannu/ Nabû-ēṭir-napšāti/Nappāhu	11	witness/debtor	27
Nabû-tabni-uṣur/Bēl-kāṣir/ Balāṭu	10	scribe/witness	10

a Presence placed in brackets (+) because it was probably his brother, Marduk-šumu-ibni, who set up a business with Šaddinnu, but the possibility remains that he should be equated with Lâbâši.

2.4 *Rē'i-alpi*

Of the approximately 1,315 individuals mentioned in the texts of Nabû-mukīn-zēri//Rē'i-alpi and his son, Rēmūt-Nabû, thirty-seven are attested five times or more (approximately 3.5% of the father's contacts and approximately 2% of the son's contacts).[151] The vast majority of these men (thirty-two) belonged

151 As one can see in the table below, some of these contacts were shared by both protagonists.

Temple	Agriculture	Family	Property sales	Silver	House	*Harrānu*	Tax
++	++	+	+	+	+	++	+
+	+		+	+	+	–	+
+	–		+	+			
+	+	–	–	–		–	
++	–		–	+			–
–			+	–	–	–	+
++						(+)[a]	
–			+	+	–	–	+
	++		–	–			
	–		+	–	–	–	+
+	+	+	+	–			
–	+		+	–			–

to temple-based families, while almost half (eighteen) were members of the Rē'i-alpi clan itself or of families affiliated by marriage. As one can see from table 10, many acted in a variety of roles and contexts. While this suggests that the family maintained overall stronger relationships in terms of tie strength compared to other archive holders, the answer should be sought elsewhere. Firstly, the multiplexity of roles usually applies to people from the Rē'i-alpi clan who in addition to their activity as witnesses or scribes acted as donors

TABLE 10 Tie strength of Nabû-mukīn-zēri//Rē'i-alpi (ca. 558–504 BCE) and Rēmūt-Nabû//Rē'i-alpi (ca. 528–492 BCE)

Individual	Attestations (NMZ/RN)	Role	Duration in Years
Nabû-mukīn-zēri/Zēru-Bābili/Nappāhu	21/5[a]	witness/scribe/proxy	24
Rēmūt-Nabû/Nabû-šumu-uṣur/Šarrahu	17/8	scribe/witness/creditor (close kin)	35
Nabû-erība/Nabû-mukīn-zēri/RA	7/12[b]	witness/scribe/seller/*ēpišānūtu*	37
Šamaš-iddin/Nabû-mušētiq-uddi/RA	14/8	scribe/witness/*ēpišānūtu*	23
Nabû-ahhē-šullim/Nabû-šumu-uṣur/RA	15/2	witness/donor preb./adoptive father/debtor	20
Iddin-Nabû/Nādin/RA	11/5	scribe/owner preb./witness	24
Nabû-ahhē-iddin/Nabû-zēru-ušebši/Ilia	11/3	witness/scribe (creditor?)	18
Rēmūt-Nabû/Nabû-ēṭir-napšāti/RA	11/1	donor preb./witness/scribe/guarantor	34
Marduk-šumu-uṣur/Mušēzib-Marduk/Ahiya'ūtu	9/1	witness/seller (land)/neighbour (land)	50
Nabû-ahhē-bulliṭ/Tabnēa/RA	8/4	scribe/proxy/exchange property/witness	37
Nabû-šumu-ukīn/Mušēzib-Marduk/RA	8/3	witness/donor preb./scribe/co-debtor (close kin)	between 15–23[c]
Dadia/Bunanu/Ibni-Adad	5/3	seller (land via proxy)/debtor/witness	12
Ašarēdu/Nabû-ēṭir/Iddin-Papsukkal	8/–	scribe	31

a He is found in three more documents acting on behalf of the archive holders, without them being present at the transactions.

b He is found in three more documents acting on behalf of the archive holders, without them being present at the transactions.

Temple	Agricultural	Family	Property Sales	Silver	Tax
+	+	++	++	++	++
–		++	++	++	++
++	+	–	+	+	
+	+	++	++	+	
+	–	+	+	+	
+		–	++	+	
+		+	+	+	+
++			+		
+	+	–	+	+	
+	–		+		
+		+	+	–	
	++		+		
	–		+	–	

c Note that the date on the property deed BM 26231 (Cyr [x]) is damaged. His first attestation in relation to Nabû-mukīn-zēri//Rē'i-alpi could thus date between 538 and 530 BCE.

(or sellers) of prebends and cultic partners. Since the ownership of the clan's prebendary patrimony was constantly changing hands in order to satisfy both demographic and cultic needs and because the family held a near monopoly on the oxherd prebend, the only individuals who could donate a prebend or act as cultic collaborator were obviously kinsmen. Secondly, the relatively high multiplexity of contexts is due, in part, to the fact that in the Rē'i-alpi archive transactions can often be interpreted as pertaining to a number of contexts simultaneously. For example, the sale of a prebend is a property sale belonging to a prebendary context, but in the case of the Rē'i-alpis it also represents a family matter.

Let us start with the most frequently attested contact in the archive, Nabû-mukīn-zēri/Zēru-Bābili/Nappāhu. He is found twenty-nine times in the period between 534 and 510 BCE.[152] His primary role in the archive is that of witness (eighteen times, often as first witness), followed by that of scribe (nine times). He is found in all domains of Nabû-mukīn-zēri's (and to a lesser extent, Rēmūt-Nabû's) business affairs: prebendary,[153] agriculture,[154] property acquisition,[155] moneylending,[156] and taxation.[157] Particularly noteworthy is his involvement in a highly sensitive family affair. In Dar 05 Nabû-mukīn-zēri//Rē'i-alpi arranged the transfer of a significant share of property to his daughter, grandchildren, and cousin. Nabû-mukīn-zēri//Nappāhu appears in four documents recording this transfer, twice as a witness and twice as the scribe.[158] Even though this

152 For the earliest and latest attestation, respectively, see BM 17670 (Cyr 05) and BM 102259 (Dar 12).

153 BE 8 106 = AH XV no. 180 (Dar 05) and BM 26552 = AH XV no. 188, (Dar [x]$^{+2}$).

154 Various debts of barley and dates include BM 26701 (Dar 02), BM 17663 (Dar 03), and BM 25834 (Dar 03^{+}). Note, however, that none of these documents clearly specify that the goods come from the harvest. Nabû-mukīn-zēri//Nappāhu is furthermore present at various acquisitions of landed estates.

155 BM 102276 = AH XV no. 166 (Cam 06), BM 82628 (Cam 06), BM 94546 (Dar 00), BM 94676 = AH XV no. 171 (Dar 01), BM 82619 (Dar 04), and BM 94662 (Dar 04).

156 BM 82644 (Dar 03), VS 4 100 (Dar 04), BM 102274 (Dar 04), and BM 94711 (Dar [x]).

157 BM 17670 (Cyr 05), BM 26657 = AH XV no. 167 (Cam 06), BM 82700 (Dar 07), BM 82634 (Dar 07), and BM 102259 (Dar 12). Note that the first three belong to the dossier dealing with the production of bricks for the temple by prebendary oxherds, which can be seen as belonging to the temple sphere as well. For more detail on the obligation of prebendary groups to manufacture bricks for Nabû, see Waerzeggers 2010: 337–345.

158 Nabû-mukīn-zēri//Nappāhu present as witness in EAH 213 (Dar 05) and BM 28872 = AH XV no. 179 (Dar 05). He is the scribe of BM 26514 (Dar 05) and BM 101980+ (Dar 05).

endowment meant that Rēmūt-Nabû was disinherited by his father,[159] it did not cause a major dent in the relationship of Nabû-mukīn-zēri//Nappāhu with Nabû-mukīn-zēri or, more importantly, with the latter's son. When Rēmūt-Nabû undid his father's action in Dar 06 and 07 by reclaiming full possession over his property, Nabû-mukīn-zēri//Nappāhu was called upon to act as a witness again.[160] Afterwards, Nabû-mukīn-zēri can still be found in Rēmūt-Nabû's documents, showing that his presence in the transactions of Dar 06 and 07 was not based on legal requirement alone.[161] Moreover, the fact that Nabû-mukīn-zēri's brother and sons also appear in documents of Rēmūt-Nabû further underlines the close relationship between these two households.[162] The strength of Nabû-mukīn-zēri's relationship with the Rē'i-alpis is reflected by its duration, cross-generational durability, and the variegated contexts in which he appears rather than by the multiplexity of roles he assumed in their affairs, either as witness or scribe. However, there are two important exceptions. Both Rēmūt-Nabû and his father relied on him to buy property in their names: in Cam 06 (BM 82628) he bought a slave for (*ana našê ṣibûtu*) Rēmūt-Nabû and in Dar 04 (BM 94662) he acquired a plot of land for (*ina našparti*) Nabû-mukīn-zēri. Even if a comprehensive study on such sales is outstanding and the exact rationale behind the use of a proxy still eludes us, these acts imply a degree of trust between the proxy and the actual purchaser.[163]

159 For a detailed account of this 'crisis between father and son', see Waerzeggers 2010: 561–562.

160 BM 26492//BE 8 108 (Dar 06) and BM 26494//BM 26496//BM 26485//BM 26512//BM 109861 = AH XV no. 183 (Dar 07).

161 BM 27795//BM 94645 (Dar 07) and BM 102259 (Dar 12).

162 Itti-Šamaš-balāṭu/Zēru-Bābili/Nappāhu is first witness in BM 82622 (Dar 15?). Two of Nabû-mukīn-zēri's sons, Nabû-uṣuršu and Arad-Bēl, are first and second witness in BM 26554 (Dar 17).

163 Most of the proxy sales from Borsippa are found in the Rē'i-alpi archive and include: BM 25627 (Nbn 00) with Nabû-ahhē-iddin//Arkāt-ilāni-damqā as proxy; BM 26499 (Nbn 01), via Nabû-ahhē-šullim//Nūr-Papsukkal; BM 94562 (Nbn 04) and BM 25712 (Nbn 04), with fṬabātu/Nabû-šumu-ukīn/fMaqartu as proxy or initial buyer (note that she is the cousin of Nabû-mukīn-zēri//Rē'i-alpi, who eventually bought this property); BM 94653 = AH XV no. 160 (Cam 01), with Nabû-ahhē-bulliṭ//Rē'i-alpi as proxy (he is a known scribe and witness in the archive); BM 94676 = AH XV no. 171 (Dar 01), with the same proxy; and BM 26623 and BM 82619 (Dar 04), via Bēl-uballiṭ//Atkuppu. Other proxy sales from Borsippa include from the Ibnāya archive: BM 29478 (Nbn 02), in which Nabû-mukīn-apli//Šikkûa, later known as the chief temple administrator (*šatammu*) of Ezida, acted as proxy. Ilia (A): BM 94567 = AH XV no. 33 (Dar 15), with Nabû-zēru-ušebši//Ardūtu as proxy. Unassigned: Amherst 242 (Dar 30?), with Nidinti-Bēl//Ēdu-ēṭir as proxy (he is known from the Rē'i-alpi and the Ilia (A) archives).

The next individual to be considered is Rēmūt-Nabû/Nabû-šumu-uṣur/Šarrahu who is attested over twenty times in the period between 539 and 504 BCE.[164] Married to Nabû-mukīn-zēri's daughter, ᶠInbā,[165] he is by far the most active in-law found in the archive.[166] Having written at least twelve documents pertaining to a variety of social contexts, his first and foremost role in the archive of the Rē'i-alpis was that of scribe.[167] In addition to his scribal activity, he is also attested as a witness six times. The most meaningful occasion was undoubtedly the marriage of Rēmūt-Nabû//Rē'i-alpi and ᶠAhatu//Arad-Ea at which Nabû-šumu-uṣur//Šarrahu, Rēmūt-Nabû's father, was present too.[168] Rēmūt-Nabû is also found in a more active role. Twice he collected debts on behalf of Nabû-mukīn-zēri[169] and once he extended a loan of forty-five shekels of silver to Rēmūt-Nabû//Rē'i-alpi.[170] It should be noted that the family crisis of Dar 05 and the (later cancelled) endowments to Rēmūt-Nabû//Šarrahu's children do not seem to have had a great impact on the relationship between the two brothers-in-law.

A final individual from a somewhat different background who deserves closer evaluation is Nabû-erība/Nabû-mukīn-zēri/Rē'i-alpi. Although he bears the same patronymic as Rēmūt-Nabû, C. Waerzeggers has argued that they were not brothers, but rather belonged to two different branches of the Rē'i-alpi clan.[171] Nabû-erība is attested twenty-two times in the period between 527

164 BM 26652 = AH XV no. 154 (Nbn 16) and KU 14 (Dar 18) are his earliest and latest attestations, respectively.

165 He is first attested as her husband in Dar 05 (BM 101980//BM 82607), but the marriage clearly preceded this date as they already had two children at this time.

166 In contrast, none of the in-laws of Rēmūt-Nabû's two marriages are mentioned in the archive.

167 While most of his texts were written for Nabû-mukīn-zēri (BM 26652 = AH XV no. 154 (Nbn 16), BM 94663 (Cyr 04), BM 94653 = AH XV no. 160 (Cam 01), BM 82767 (Cam 02), and BM 94682 (Dar 08)), he wrote at least three for Rēmūt-Nabû (BM 27795//BM 94645 (Dar 07), BM 26639 (Dar 08?), and BM 26572 = AH XV no. 187 (Dar 10)). It should also be noted that many texts were important property deeds.

168 BM 82609 (Dar 01) = Roth 1989 no. 22. Note that Nabû-šumu-uṣur//Šarrahu was also present at the dowry negotiations of Rēmūt-Nabû's first marriage to ᶠ[x]-Sutīti//Ardūtu in Cam 04 (BM 29375).

169 BM 94814 (Cam 05) and BM 82779 (Dar 05). Even though Nabû-mukīn-zēri was not present at either of these transactions, the idea that Rēmūt-Nabû was actually acting on his behalf transpires from the fact that in both cases the commodities were to be delivered in the 'measurement of Nabû-mukīn-zēri' (*mašīhu ša NMZ*).

170 BM 26678 (Dar 14). The background of this debt is not specified but it took place at a time when Rēmūt-Nabû seems to have been short of cash. See Chapter 3.4.

171 Waerzeggers 2010: 564.

and 490 BCE.[172] His primary role in the archive is that of cultic colleague of Rēmūt-Nabû. While he sold his rights to various days of the oxherd prebend to Rēmūt-Nabû early in the reign of Darius I, around 504 BCE he is found taking over the ritual obligations of a large share of the temple service again.[173] He remained in Rēmūt-Nabû's service until after the latter's death when we find him in the service of his sons.[174] In addition to his role in the cult, he wrote at least eight documents for Nabû-mukīn-zēri and Rēmūt-Nabû and witnessed a further five transactions, ranging from important property deeds to minor debt obligations and harvest estimates.[175] Although the nexus of Nabû-erība's and Rēmūt-Nabû's relationship is located in the cultic sphere, it was certainly not confined to prebendary matters alone.

2.5 *Atkuppu*

As we have said previously the Atkuppu archive is not particularly suited for the present investigation. The available information for this family is limited in size, coherence, and depth. In order to counter some of these drawbacks I have taken only the texts from the fourth and penultimate generation into consideration. Covering the period between roughly 534 and 494 BCE, it is represented by Nabû-šumu-uṣur/Marduk-šumu-ibni and his three younger brothers, Nabû-iddin, Murānu, and Iqīša. However, with just over eighty texts for a period of roughly forty years, there is still much left to be desired in terms of information density, especially since it lacks important family documents or property deeds. Nevertheless, close contacts can still be found in the records of the Atkuppu brothers.

Let us start with the most frequently attested individual, Gimil-Nabû/Mušēzib-Bēl/Šēpê-ilia. Mentioned seven times between 517 and 494 BCE, his primary role in the archive is that of scribe.[176] His most noteworthy contribution in this capacity was the recording of the dissolution of the *harrānu* enterprise between two of the Atkuppu brothers, Nabû-iddin and Murānu. Other than a promissory note for barley from the temple income (*maššarti*),[177] he

172 BM 26480 = AH XV no. 163 (Cam 05) and EAH 229 (Dar 32).

173 BM 26737 = AH XV no. 176 (Dar 02), BM 94579 = AH XV no. 182 (Dar 06); BM 26509//BM 94563//BM 94571 = AH XV no. 191 (ca. Dar 18).

174 BE 8 117 = AH XV no. 197 (Dar 32).

175 Property deeds written by Nabû-erība include: BM 94680 (Cam 05), BM 82686 = AH XV no. 162 ([Cam] 05), and BM 94712 = AH XV no. 172 (Dar 01). Harvest estimate: BM 94675 (Dar 18). He is found as witness in: BM 26671 (Dar 00), EAH 212 (Dar 02), BM 86290 (Dar 05), BM 17693 (Dar 06), and BM 82627 (Dar 07).

176 Earliest and latest attestation, respectively: BM 17680 (Dar 05) and VS 4 174 (Dar 28).

177 VS 3 84 (Dar 07).

mostly wrote debt notes for silver, some of which could have had a background in *harrānu* ventures.[178]

The next individual who needs examination is Iddin-Nabû/Nabû-šumu-ukīn/Rēš-ummāni. Attested between 517 and 496 BCE,[179] he assumed more diverse and active roles than Gimil-Nabû. Found for the first time as the scribe of a debt note for silver in Dar 05 (at which Gimil-Nabû was present as witness),[180] he repeatedly acted as creditor for the Atkuppu brothers (one loan amounting to one mina of silver and secured with a pledge).[181] In Dar 26 Iddin-Nabû took it upon himself to settle two accounts with the 'canal inspector' (*gugallu*) of Borsippa on behalf of the Atkuppu brothers.[182] Even though these last two transactions might infer a degree of trust, it is hard to determine whether Iddin-Nabû acted as an agent or a patron here. In the light of the various (secured) loans he extended to the Atkuppus, I prefer the latter option. Moreover, the brothers' joint venture was deployed in the agricultural sector (onions being part of their business assets) and the fact that at least one of Iddin-Nabû's loans was to be repaid from the surplus of their harvest suggests that he was in a formal business relationship with the brothers, presumably as the stronger, investing partner.[183]

Another individual who shows up in the inner circle of the Atkuppus is Nabû-uballiṭ/Nabû-ēṭir-napšāti/Gallābu. Mentioned five times between 517 and 496 BCE,[184] Nabû-uballiṭ's primary role was that of witness. He first appears in Dar 05 in a debt note in which Gimil-Nabû and Iddin-Nabû were present as well.[185] After taking out a loan of the Atkuppus in Dar 05[186] and witnessing a similar transaction one year later,[187] it is another twenty years before Nabû-uballiṭ reappears in the archive. In Dar 26 he witnessed the two transactions with the *gugallu* of Borsippa mentioned above. This shows that he was

178 BM 29678 (Dar 11), BM 26666 (Dar 19?), VS 4 156 (Dar 20), and VS 4 174 (Dar 28).

179 Earliest and latest attestation, respectively: BM 17680 (Dar 05) and BM 17707 (Dar 26).

180 BM 17680.

181 VS 4 156 (Dar 20). The other two debt obligations: VS 4 140 (Dar 14?) and BM 94733 (Dar 19).

182 Both were written on the same day in Dar 26: BM 17707 deals with the payment for two hirelings and BM 26702 with the tax obligation for 'work on the royal docks' (*dullu ša kāri ša šarri*).

183 Note also that Iddin-Nabû's brother, Mušēzib-Marduk, also acted as a creditor of the brothers. BM 26724 (Dar 26) records a loan of silver for which part of the patrimony was taken as pledge.

184 Earliest and latest attestation, respectively: BM 17680 (Dar 05) and BM 17707 (Dar 26).

185 BM 17680.

186 BM 17698 (Dar 05).

187 BM 26605 (Dar 06?).

not only connected to the Atkuppus, but also to their business partners or patrons. Another individual who should be mentioned in this regard is Nabû-bēl-zēri/Mušēzib-Marduk/Aškāpu. Although he is mentioned only three times between Dar 05 and Dar 06 (twice as debtor and once as scribe), he always appears in connection with the Atkuppus' intimate contacts. In BM 17680 (Dar 05) his debt was recorded by Iddin-Nabû and witnessed by Gimil-Nabû and Nabû-uballiṭ. In BM 17698 (Dar 05) he recorded a debt due from Nabû-uballiṭ. While BM 26605 (Dar 06?), another promissory note drawn up against him, was again witnessed by Nabû-uballiṭ. Although not much can be said about Nabû-bēl-zēri, his case does add evidence to the fact that the Atkuppu brothers and their close contacts formed a close clique. Even if the full extent of their relationship remains vague, it seems to have revolved around the running of business enterprises in the local countryside.[188]

Conclusion

In this chapter I tried to reconstruct the networks of intimate social relationships in the priestly community of Borsippa. In addition to psycho-emotional aspects most commonly associated with intimacy and friendship, it has been shown in the social sciences that intimate relationships can be identified and reconstructed based on structural features. This idea is captured most clearly by the concept of tie strength, which postulates that the intensity or robustness of a relationship can be determined using objective (interactional) criteria. The most basic and widely used yardstick in this respect is the amount of time two individuals spend together, i.e. frequency of contact. Other criteria, also incorporated in the present study, include duration of contact, multiplexity of roles and context, and intensity of encounters. Since intimate relationships such as friendship tend to be among the strongest ties in our lives they usually involve relatively high degrees of tie strength.

The first part of this chapter was devoted to a formal quantitative analysis of the data, based exclusively on the frequency of attestations. The underlying idea is that an individual's lifestyle and specific modes of behaviour vis-à-vis

188 There are at least two more individuals who may be relevant in this respect. First is Šamaš-iddin/Silim-Bēl/Sîn-imittī who is mentioned four times (three times as creditor, once as witness): VS 4 149 (Dar 18), BM 94733 (Dar 19), BM 26710 (Dar 19), and BM 26666 (Dar 19?). Second is Nabû-uballiṭ/Nabû-šumu-iddin/Ea-ibni who is only mentioned twice, but each time in significant contexts: in Dar 06 as first witness in the dissolution contract of the Atkuppu brothers' *harrānu* (BM 17683) and in Dar 10 as payer of taxes on behalf of Nabû-iddin//Atkuppu (BM 102330).

his or her social environment are reflected in his or her ego network, and vice versa. Hence, the aim of this initial investigation was to learn more about the structure of the personal networks in Borsippa and the interactional attitudes of local priests.

I started by assessing the contacts that occur only once. As expected, this was the case for the vast majority of individuals mentioned in our corpus. Percentages range from seventy percent in the archives that contain adequate, data-rich ego networks such as Ilia (A), Bēliya'u, and Rē'i-alpi to ninety percent in the more sparsely documented archives of the Ea-ilūtu-bani and the Atkuppu families. On the other side of the spectrum, only a very small number of individuals occur five or more times. These range between two and four percent in the single-generation archives to around one percent in the archives of the Atkuppus and the Ea-ilūtu-banis after close relatives and protagonists have been left out of the quantification.

The fact that the figures found in the latter two archives were consistently larger and smaller, respectively, seems to be related primarily to the paucity of information and should not be taken as a reflection of reality. The results gained from the single-generation archives with a much higher density of information and adequate ego networks are probably more representative. Unfortunately, the figures in these archives turned out to be too similar to make a meaningful comparison between them.

The question that imposed itself was whether diverging networks and distinct attitudes were to be expected in our analysis. All ego networks belong to priests and even if different comportments and business strategies have been observed in previous chapters, this quantitative procedure was probably not refined enough to detect these details.

Finally, while a comparison between the figures found in the Borsippa archives and the one found in Sippar by C. Waerzeggers is not particularly helpful for gaining more information about typical priestly behaviour or networks, it does warn us that evidence from one city cannot automatically be held as representative for other cities, even if the individuals involved are from a similar socio-economic background and own comparable archives. It should be clear that much more work is needed on Babylonian ego networks before we can fully grasp the meaning of the relationships found in the priestly archives of Borsippa. It is particularly helpful in the future to investigate exactly how and which factors influence the nature of these ancient networks.

In the second part I presented a more qualitative appreciation of the data. Narrowing in on the group of individuals attested five or more times, I assessed their relationship with the protagonists by introducing additional dimensions of tie strength: intensity, multiplexity, and duration. What did this analysis tell us about the circles of trust and intimacy and the formation of friendship in the priestly community of Borsippa? A general but important observation concerned the social background of the people involved. The great majority of the intimate relationships found in the archives of priests materialised with individuals from fellow priestly families. While this reconfirms my notion of the priesthood as maintaining a generally inward-looking attitude, it assumed even more rigid dimensions in the domain of friendship. The evidence suggests that in this priestly community relations of trust and intimacy occurred exclusively within the high social stratum marked by the use of family names. Moreover, the only possible exception I could find in the entire corpus seems to prove this rule. Between roughly 544 and 540 BCE[189] a certain Ana-bītīšu/Nūh-ilī is found four times as a witness in the archive of Nabû-zēru-ukīn//Gallābu: twice in a debt note of silver, once in a debt note of silver and vats, and once in a receipt of silver resulting from a property sale. It is very likely that the same Ana-bītīšu also received disbursements of flour in BM 85966 (not dated).[190] Admittedly, neither in terms of frequency, duration nor multiplexity does Ana-bītīšu seem to have been a particularly intimate contact of the protagonist. Yet, it is telling that the only instance in which a 'commoner' might have enjoyed such a relationship is found in a non-priestly archive. Although Nabû-zēru-ukīn// Gallābu descended from a family that traditionally performed the duties of the prebendary barber (*gallābūtu*), the archive does not place the protagonist in a prebendary context and references to the temple institution are entirely missing.[191] Even if individuals from lower strata are found in the archives of priests, no more than two such individuals are mentioned more than five times and neither of them represents intimate relationships.[192]

Even if factors like spatial proximity and legal convention might have contributed to the formation of this strict (segregational) pattern, I do not think it could have taken this clear-cut shape without the existence of a strong collective preference and conscious choice on behalf of the priests. Of course, to some extent, such a configuration was to be expected. Socio-anthropologists

189 See BM 85643 (Nbn 12) and BM 85610 (Nbn 16) for the earliest and latest attestation, respectively. Note however that the date of Smith Coll. no. 97 is damaged (Nbn 30-II-[x]) and BM 85966 is not dated at all.

190 See for a summary of this text, Zadok 2009: 28.

191 Jursa 2005: 82–83.

192 The first exception is [f]Tutubu-esu, a Caro-Egyptian mother who together with her son, received rations from Marduk-šumu-ibni//Ilia (A). See Waerzeggers 2006. The second is Liblut/Nabû-ušebši, a person in charge of the ration of the king (later the rations of Queen Apamû), who leased this income to Šaddinnu//Bēliya'u on several occasions. See Waerzeggers 2010: 127–129.

have long since noticed that friendships tend to be maintained among status or social equals.[193] Moreover, people can select friends only from among other people available to them and that pool is shrunken tremendously by the social contexts in which people participate. Still, the degree to which this trend manifests itself in the community under investigation is striking to say the least. It strongly suggests that the priests from Borsippa perceived of themselves as a discrete and socially exclusive unit and actively sought to maintain it. This observation is of great significance for the ultimate reconstruction of this community and we come back to this more extensively in the following chapters.

Let us now turn to the relations of trust and intimacy and take a closer look at their general features. What was the role of intimate contacts in the archives? In this study a person's status of intimacy depended on four dimensions of tie strength: frequency, duration, intensity, and multiplexity. While the first three could be applied fairly straightforwardly, the notion of multiplexity with its traditional emphasis on diversity of roles befitted our study much less. Individuals who scored high on the first three dimensions of tie strength did usually not fulfil a high diversity of roles or functions in the available documentation; they are predominantly found as scribe and witness. On a more general level, it seems that, apart from temple colleagues and tenants, individuals who entered in formal contract with priests do not frequently reappear in the archive. Parties tended to engage in business only once or a small handful of times. Rather than concentrate on the multiplicity of roles, I therefore focused my attention more on the range of social settings in which individuals appeared, i.e. the multiplexity of context. This allowed me to better assess the relationship of intimate contacts even if the range of functions they assumed was limited. But there are some notable exceptions. Take for instance Nabû-ahhē-iddin//Nannāhu, the best-known contact of Ahušunu//Nannāhu. Besides being present at both of Ahušunu's weddings, he also lent him money, stood surety for a heavily secured debt, and repeatedly paid taxes on his behalf. Another example can be found in the Bēliya'u archive: Bēl-ēṭir//Šigûa is attested over forty times in the documents of Šaddinnu//Bēliya'u. While he is most frequently attested as scribe and witness, he also acted as business partner and as agent, and presumably was Šaddinnu's next-door neighbour. Notwithstanding these and other examples, intimate contacts in this community are found predominantly in the passive roles of scribe and witness and only seldom assumed a more active role, let alone engaged as contracting parties. The adage not to do

193 Lazarsfeld and Merton 1964, Verbrugge 1977, McPherson *et al.* 2001, and Hruschka 2010: 65–66.

business with one's friends seems very much in evidence here. Or did friends simply not need to record their dealings in formal contracts?

This investigation also sheds more light on the presence of witnesses and scribes in the Neo-Babylonian documentation. Far from being selected at random, their presence can best be understood as a result of their association to one of the contract parties. While it has already been observed that individuals appear repeatedly as witnesses in Neo-Babylonian private archives,[194] this investigation made it clear that Babylonians or more specifically Babylonian priests relied on a small number of individuals to witness and record their transactions and accompany them on their day-to-day business in town and in the countryside. Among this retinue one finds the priests' most intimate contacts.

It is well known that being a witness (or a scribe for that matter) was not simply a passive function, but one that carried responsibilities. While specific individuals could be present at a transaction for a number of reasons (for example to provide consent), the presence of witnesses served in the first place to authenticate the transaction and the accompanying legal contract.[195] More important was the fact that they could be called upon to testify in case of litigation.[196] Needless to say, it was of prime importance that one was able to call on someone who could be summoned on short notice and trusted to provide unconditional support to one's claim, whether it was false or true. By bringing their most trusted and intimate contacts along to transactions, priests made sure they could always rely on the right support in case necessary.

Finally, while it should be clear that the presence of witnesses in legal contracts was often based on their connection to one of the parties, clear guidelines for their selection have eluded us so far, that is, if any existed. Yet, a glimpse of what might have been the customary, perhaps even ideal, set-up can be gleaned from BM 26483 (Dar 14), which was previously mentioned. This marriage agreement between the daughter of Marduk-šumu-ibni//Ilia (A) and the son of Šaddinnu//Bēliya'u is one of the few documents from Borsippa that involves protagonists of two known archives, offering us the unique opportunity to examine the list of witnesses from both sides. As expected, intimate contacts of both parties were present. Apart from the brother of the bride, two of Marduk-šumu-ibni's best-known contacts attended the transaction, Nabû-uṣuršu//Šēpê-ilia as witness and Nabû-ēṭir-napšāti//Kudurrānu as scribe.

194 Von Dassow 1999b: 6–7.
195 Von Dassow 1999b.
196 See Lambert 1996: 100–101 for an interesting passage on the charge (or rather the burden) to function as a witness in a Babylonian court.

While the entourage of the Ilias was slightly larger, presumably because the agreement was concluded at their place, the Bēliya'us did not come without support. On the side of the groom we find Nabû-ittannu//Nappāhu, a known witness from the archive of Šaddinnu. Apart from these trusted and familiar individuals there are three further witnesses who do not seem to have maintained a particularly strong relation with either of the parties. While this could simply be due to the accident of documentary recovery, they might have been invited to join the arrangements as neutral parties. This transpires also from Marduk-šumu-ibni's activities as notary scribe. There is so far no evidence that he was acquainted with any of the parties mentioned in the transactions that he recorded in this official capacity. This suggests that the involvement of a neutral party at important transactions, especially those involving the transfer of property, was desirable if not requisite.

In conclusion, the circles of trust and intimacy I reconstructed in this chapter emerged from the highly formalised contexts of the legal documents. As a result, the information gained from this analysis was obviously biased and fairly static in nature. In reality these relationships were likely more multifaceted, more complex, and steeped in a multitude of gradations and variations. Making more generalised statements about intimacy and friendship as it existed in this ancient community of priests would therefore be misleading. This brings us back to our initial question: is it valid to talk about friendship? While I have used terms such as circles of trust, intimacy, and friendship interchangeably throughout this chapter, the use of the last term is certainly open to discussion. Still, I believe that I was able to show that the relationships examined in this chapter were strong in terms of tie strength. Many of the people concerned knew each other and their families for many years, sometimes decades, kept close and repeated contact, and likely lived in close proximity. They witnessed and recorded each other's investments, weddings, and other family affairs, travelled together to the countryside and surrounding cities for business, and at times assumed significant responsibility by standing surety, setting up joint ventures, discharging cultic duties, and buying property on each other's behalf. While certainly not all of these relationships represented friendships, it stands to reason that such intimate bonds were formed, maintained, and terminated among this very set of relations.

The investigation offered here was obviously exploratory in nature and it should be clear that much more work still needs to be done on this topic. It should be possible and perhaps desirable to devise a simple algorithm allowing us to rank relations more absolutely in terms of tie strength. From a network analytic perspective it would be interesting to substantiate these claims by looking closer into the influence and the positions these individuals occupy in the overall networks. Finally, it would also be worthwhile for future research to investigate whether more dimensions of tie strength could be extracted from our sources such as reciprocity or other notions commonly associated with intimacy and friendship.

PART 2

Priests in Neo-Babylonian Society

CHAPTER 5

Homophily and Interaction

In Part 1 of this book I looked into the social interactions that structured the priestly community of Borsippa. This included the hypergamous marriage system (Chapter 1), the distribution and management of landholdings (Chapter 2), silver lending (Chapter 3), and the formation of friendship (Chapter 4). At least three important notions emerged. First, marriage functioned as a primary building block for this community, regulating interaction both inside and outside of the temple. Second, the purity-based hierarchy of the priesthood was mirrored in the social world of the priests, suggesting that social interaction was informed by the temple fabric. Third, priests interacted predominantly with individuals from fellow priestly families.

The interactional pattern of the priesthood of Ezida could be summarised as follows: the vast majority of their interaction took place within the circle of temple-based families. This showed especially in the more consequential and significant types of interaction such as marriage and friendship. Yet, a not insignificant minority took place with individuals from non-priestly elite families. While their involvement in the marriage system and the formation of friendship was limited, they appeared more often in the less symbolic or intimate transactions, especially related to the management of property or silver lending. Beyond the circle of traditional urban elite families, interaction was negligible. 'Outsiders', distinguishable by the non-usage of family names, are attested strikingly little, although they make up the vast majority of Neo-Babylonian society. They appear only on what might be called the fringes of the interactional landscape of Borsippa's priests (the occasional creditor, seller, tenant or witness) and do not participate in the more significant affairs of the priests. The same applies to ethnic minorities. Apart from the Caro-Egyptian mercenary families who were temporarily placed under care of the local priesthood,[1] individuals bearing West-Semitic or other non-Babylonian names are virtually absent from the documentation.

Figure 12 (below) is a schematic representation of this interactional pattern. It follows the viewpoint of the priests, which are located at the centre in black. The middle grey circle represents the larger elite stratum from Borsippa,

1 Waerzeggers 2006.

 | DOI:10.1163/9789004399969_007

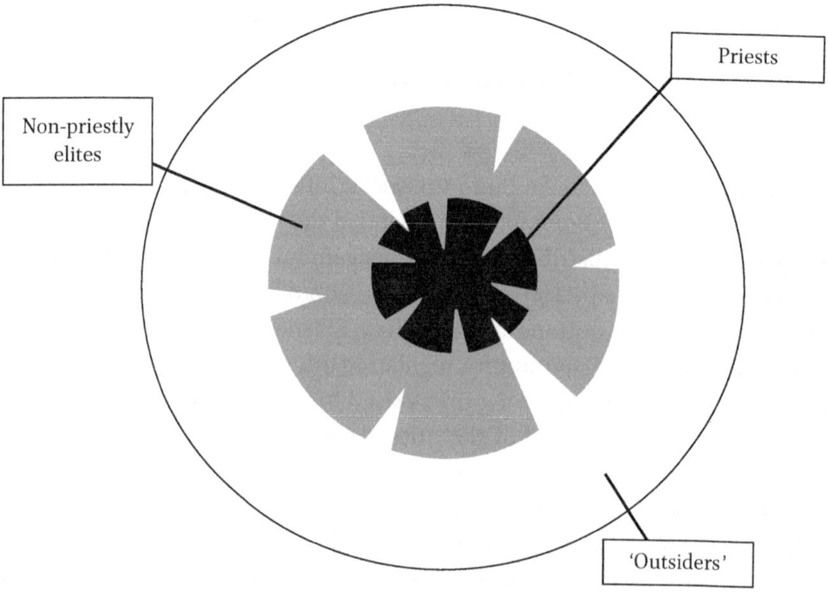

FIGURE 12 Abstract representation of the interactional pattern of priests

while the outermost white circle denotes the 'outsiders'. The latter basically represents the rest of Babylonian society and includes a very diverse range of individuals: poor and rich as well as native and foreign. The inward-pointing 'breaches' signify the interaction between these social segments, particularly how their encounters took shape in the social world of the priests in the middle.

In Part 2 I take a step back and approach the phenomenon from a higher perspective. Instead of further delineating the organisation between the various temple ranks and families within the priestly community, I attempt to situate this group as a distinct social segment within wider society. The question I would like to address in this part is how the emergence of the distinct pattern outlined above should be understood. Can we find possible causations behind the dynamics of interaction?

I start by providing two different explanations of figure 12, which correspond to two alternative understandings of the causation behind interaction. The first scenario of causation adopts a pragmatic and purely spatial rationale. For the second scenario I introduce the concept of homophily, which has been identified as a basic organising principle in human societies. Building further on the second scenario, I show that interaction can also be approached from a more structural perspective by introducing the concepts of rentier and entrepreneur. These two typologies have been applied recently to Neo-Babylonian society in order to characterise family archives and larger social segments on the basis of economic features. I argue that the interactional pattern of priests is in perfect congruence with the general economic mentality and objectives sustained by this social group as rentiers. Babylonian priests can thus be distinguished from other entrepreneurial elements in society based on more than economic features alone, namely, by a fundamentally different mode of interaction towards the social environment.

1 Spatial Distribution

The existence of the particular pattern of interaction represented in figure 12 could be explained simply by taking it as a natural outcome of the geographic or spatial situation of our priests and the demography of their most immediate social environment. The argumentation would run as follows: the priestly families from Borsippa clustered and lived together in the old quarters in the heart of the city immediately surrounding the temple precinct, similar to the residential patterns reconstructed for other Babylonian temple towns.[2] Working and living in close proximity to one another, it is only natural that most of their interactions took place within this socially- and geographically-restricted circle of temple families within which the most basic and everyday needs could be met. In this radius they found their creditors, sellers, witnesses, scribes, marriage partners, and friends.

Yet, priests were part of a much larger circle of urban families. Living in the better parts of town undoubtedly brought them in contact with individuals from other established elite families that did not enjoy a professional affiliation to the temple. I show in the following chapter that, on the whole, these families maintained a very similar socio-economic and cultural repertoire, and priests had ample opportunity to come into contact with them through, for example, joint neighbourhood networks, membership in legal bodies and administrative units, and attendance at public assemblies, among other mutual encounters.

Finally, individuals from outside this social stratum were much less present in the priests' most immediate social environment. It seems reasonable to assume that it was less likely for these people to live in the traditional (and certainly not inexpensive) parts of town surrounding the temple. Moreover, one has to realise that the majority of the individuals I subsumed under 'outsiders'

2 See Chapter 6.2.1.

belonged to the lower strata of society.[3] Their general inferior financial situation also meant that they were less likely to meet the standards of priests, whose needs, wants, and transactions were pursued on a higher social and financial level. Yet, contact between them was unavoidable. Other than appearing as the occasional witness or contract party, members of the lower strata were perhaps most visible in the management of landed estates in the countryside where they were hired as gardeners and lived as tenants. Without a professional connection to the temple, non-priestly elite families, in particular entrepreneurs, were likely to have engaged with these 'outsiders' on a larger scale.

In the first instance such a descriptive, down-to-earth approach seems very felicitous, not least because it resonates easily with our own present-day reality.[4] The downside of this interpretation, however, is that it cannot account for some important features of the pattern outlined above. Even if geographic space is an important (limiting) factor for interaction, this scenario of causation suggests that participation in society was determined solely by the spatial organisation of the social environment and its demographic configuration. It fails to explain adequately the more salient features of the interactional landscape in terms of the clearly defined hypergamous marriage circuit and the formation of friendship, especially in the latter domain where one can expect individual actors to have had a greater degree of self-determination and agency. In this arena it should have translated into a more representative reflection of society and, at the very least, shown a greater presence of individuals from non-priestly elite families. Rather than having emerged passively, I suggest in Chapter 6 that the distinct interactional pattern materialised at least as much through a conscious, collective attitude towards the social environment and a deliberate attempt to keep the 'us' apart from 'them'.

Drawing on a particular concept from the social sciences, called homophily, a more balanced position between these two perspectives can be obtained. I am able to include a higher degree of agency on behalf of the priests in the dynamics of their interaction without excluding limiting forces of existing structures such as space. This concept allows for an evaluation of causation in wholesale and theoretical term and results, I believe, in a more sophisticated account of figure 12.

---

3 But also included royal officials, Persian nobles, foreign merchants, and nouveau riches in general.

4 See McPherson *et al.* 2001: 429–430 for an overview of studies on community and interaction, which pays special attention to the role of geographic and spatial factors.

2 Homophily

While the concept of homophily, also known as the *like-me* hypothesis, has a long history in the social sciences, dating to the first half of the twentieth century, and the theoretical studies on interaction, the term was coined in the 1950s by P. Lazarfeld and R. Merton in their research on the formation of friendship.[5] It was thanks to their groundbreaking work that homophily was soon picked up and further developed by various scholars working on patterns of human association in general.[6] The concept has now been fully integrated in the fields of social capital studies and networks analysis and forms an essential principle for social scientists across the board.[7]

Homophily is the principle that 'contact between similar people occurs at a higher rate than among dissimilar people'[8] or, more precisely, that 'social interactions tend to take place among individuals with similar lifestyles and socioeconomic characteristics'.[9] The saying 'birds of a feather flock together' has often been used to encapsulate the empirical pattern of this principle. Found in the widest range of ties including marriage, friendship, professional affiliation, co-membership, advice, and information transfer and permeating through sociodemographic characteristics such as ethnicity, education, age, religion, gender, and class, homophily has been identified as one of the most basic and pervasive organising principles in society.

The concept of homophily is quite straightforward.[10] The point of departure is the idea of a positive reciprocal relationship between sentiment, similarity, and interaction.[11] In other words, the more people interact, the more likely it is that they share similar sentiments. Also, the more similar people are – be they famous movie stars, second graders, or members of an interest group – the more likely they are to have similar experiences, interests, and desires and the more likely it is that they interact. Hence, the basis for interaction is shared sentiment and vice versa. It is further implied that the more similar people are to each other the easier it is to interact, as fewer barriers need to be overcome.

5 Lazarfeld and Merton 1954.

6 See, for example, Laumann 1966, Verbrugge 1977, and Fischer 1982.

7 See, for example, Lin 2001 and McPherson *et al.* 2001, respectively.

8 McPherson *et al.* 2001: 416.

9 Lin 2001: 39. The realisation that similarity breeds connection, association and friendship did not escape the classical philosophers and can already be found in Aristotele's *Nichomachean Ethics*. See Irwin and Fine 1996: 274.

10 The following discussion is based on McPherson *et al.* 2001, Lin 2001 (especially Chapters 3–4), and Lin 2008: 59–62.

11 See especially the pioneering study of Homans 1950 on small primary groups.

Homophilous interaction is therefore seen as the normative and least demanding type of interaction in society. Moreover, patterns of homophily tend to become stronger as more types of relationship exist between two actors. In other words, the degree of homophily tends to be amplified in multiplex associations rather than in simplex ones, indicating that the principle has a cumulative effect.

In order to examine the relevance of homophily in a given context, scholars now often make a distinction between 'baseline homophily' and 'inbreeding homophily'.[12] The former is the degree of homophily that would be expected by chance, that is, based on the demography of the interactional pool of a given actor, which is limited by geographic space and other social structures. This ties in to the idea that the interactional pattern of the priests from Borsippa is a direct result of their geographic situation and the demography of their social environment. Inbreeding homophily is the degree of homophily measured over and above the baseline value. This is often induced by personal choice and is thus reminiscent of the idea that the interaction of priests was much more selective and done consciously within the boundaries of the social in-group.

Since census records or any other documents that can help us reconstruct the population size or demography of ancient Borsippa are lacking, it is beyond the bounds of possibility to quantify the measure of baseline versus inbreeding homophily. Even so, the interactional patterns, especially in terms of marriage and friendship, are indicative of a high degree of inbreeding homophily within the priestly community of Borsippa. In light of this basic organising principle, causation of interaction can now be re-evaluated and adjusted based on (socioeconomic) similarities without dismissing the factors of spatial distribution and demography. This leads to a somewhat different reading of figure 12.

As I show in extenso in Chapter 6, priests nurtured a distinct collective social identity. The most important of its markers was undoubtedly the ownership of cultic rights or, more loosely, a traditional affiliation to the temple.[13] In accordance with the principle of homophily as the normative and least effort-requiring type of interaction, the priests from Borsippa engaged predominantly with individuals with a similar lifestyle, i.e. individuals from temple-based families. Not only was interaction facilitated by professional and residential

12 McPherson *et al.* 2001: 419.

13 As is discussed in Chapter 6, their identity was further marked by the ownership of urban and landed property (Chapter 6.2) and an adherence to traditional Babylonian norms and values, most clearly expressed through a command of the cuneiform script (Chapter 6.3) and its native language (Chapter 6.4).

proximity, but in fact encouraged by similarities in social, cultural, and economic terms. However, with over eighty percent of marriages contracted between priestly families (and an even higher percentage of friendships), there was a clear tendency in this inner circle to engage in homophilous interaction over and above the baseline that could be expected by mere chance. Since an almost identical set of families reoccurs in other kinds of interaction, always at the expense of both non-priestly elites and 'outsiders', the hypergamous marriage circuit provides a clear outline of the 'social boundary' of this group.[14] Moreover, the multiplexity of associations and similarities by its members have only strengthened the degree of homophily within the social group and raised the probability of interaction. Hence, the outline of the black inner circle in figure 12 does not only represent the spatial distribution of priests in the heart of the city, but also the boundary of the priests as a distinct social group.

Non-priestly elite families, represented by the larger circle in grey, appear only rarely in significant types of interactions (e.g. they appear in less than twenty percent of marriages) while they are found much more often in dealings of secondary importance. These families were present in Borsippa in similar (if not much larger) numbers and differed from our priests primarily in the sense that they engaged in different economic activities and lacked an established affiliation with the temple. Yet, these socioeconomic differences were apparently significant enough to make interactions less common. Following the patterns of marriage and friendship, they were therefore largely excluded from the primary social circle maintained by the local priestly families. It presumably depended on specific circumstances whether or not they were drawn into the intimate in-group of the priests. All this supports the notion that interaction is determined by homophily (and a rigid social boundary as is discussed in Chapter 6).

Beyond this wider urban elite circle interaction became negligible as geographic and especially social distances increased dramatically. This refers to the large (white) circle of individuals belonging to other social strata of society, which made up the vast majority of Babylonia's population. These individuals were not only less likely to have lived in the city quarters surrounding the temple complex, but more importantly failed to associate with most of the socioeconomic characteristics of priests. They lacked illustrious ancestries and were excluded from the temple. While they may have spoken Babylonian Akkadian, they remained illiterate. Moreover, because they often belonged to a lower income class, these individuals owned very little, if any, real estate or

14 The existence of a so-called social boundary in the priestly community of Borsippa is discussed in Chapter 6.

any silver to dispense in lending. Hence, in accordance with the principle of homophily, these individuals appear only in the liminal regions of the social world of the priests both in terms of interaction (unimportant transactions and rarely as a contract party) and in actual geographic distance (as gardeners or tenants in the countryside).

Even if the principle of homophily does not provide the absolute key to understanding the causation of interaction, it does allow us to approach the matter from a socio-theoretic perspective. It tells us that the more similar one was to the priests the more likely he or she was to interact and be drawn into their social world.

3 Understanding Rentiers and Entrepreneurs

While the principle of homophily allowed us to evaluate the interactional patterns of the priestly community of Borsippa in light of similarities and dissimilarities in their social environment, the argument could be taken one step further and applied to another debated topic in Neo-Babylonian studies. More than just the notion that social interactions tend to take place among individuals with similar sentiments, the principle of homophily has recently been modified in social capital studies and might in fact help us understand much broader socioeconomic phenomena found in the Neo-Babylonian sources.

First, while the basic idea behind homophily is a positive relationship between sentiment and interaction, social capital expert N. Lin has recently expanded the concept to entail a triangular reciprocal relationship between 'sentiment – interaction – resources (/network position)' without insisting on a particular cause-and-effect sequence.[15] Here resources are understood in the broadest sense of the term and may involve material goods such as land, houses, money, and symbolic goods such as education, prestige, power, family name, and titles. This triangular relationship is based on the fact that lifestyle and socioeconomic characteristics are assumed to 'reflect resources embedded in individuals and their hierarchical positions in network locations'.[16] This idea correlates well with our perception of Babylonian priests who occupied very similar positions in society, had similar economic outlooks and property portfolios, and showed a distinct predisposition to interact with their social equals.

15 Lin 2001: 39–40.
16 Lin 2001: 39.

Second, N. Lin insists that there are two primary motives or behavioural consequences vis-à-vis (inter)action and resources: maintaining resources and gaining additional resources.[17] The first motive aims at protecting existing resources, which is best served through recognition of one's legitimacy in claiming these rights. Since it is only required that significant others share similar sentiments and acknowledge someone's legitimacy and do not demand any particular action on behalf of the interacting partners, it is said to involve 'expressive action'. This mode of (inter)action solicits support and is meant to promote sympathy. In contrast, the motive of gaining additional resources is best served by 'instrumental action'. In other words, more than obtaining (passive) recognition of one's existing rights, the aim of interaction here is to make a profit and gain additional resources. Hence, it requires action on behalf of the interacting partner who should make his or her resources available in order for the other to profit from them.

These two motives vis-à-vis resources correspond roughly with the two socio-economic profiles or behaviours labelled as 'rentier' and 'entrepreneur'. Formulated in the early twentieth century, most notably by V. Pareti and M. Weber, these typologies have recently been applied to Neo-Babylonian society by M. Jursa.[18] While these ideal types are based largely on economic criteria, I believe that they can be significantly deepened and strengthened from a social structural perspective by introducing the concept of homophily outlined above.

Rentiers can best be described based on what they own (property portfolio) rather than what they do (business activities) for their subsistence. In Neo-Babylonian society this economic behaviour is most clearly embodied by the priests.[19] As we see in more detail in the following chapter, the livelihood of this social stratum was largely based on two elements normally obtained through inheritance: prebend ownership and landownership. Most of their attention was centred on their cultic duties in the temple. Rather immobile and occupied predominantly with their duties in town, priests usually outsourced cultivation of their landholdings, and to some extent also the preparatory duties of their prebends, to third parties and thus relied on the labour of others to be able to enjoy their main income.[20] Apart from moneylending, their involvement in other business ventures and the (monetised) business economy

17 Lin 1982 and Lin 2001, especially Chapter 4.

18 Jursa 2004e: 121ff. See also Jursa *et al.* 2010: 282–294.

19 Note, however, that the same applies to non-priestly families that relied mainly on the management of their property and did not actively engage in the business economy for their subsistence.

20 Jursa *et al.* 2010: 283.

in general was limited.[21] Hence, rentier-priests relied predominantly on their inherited property, engaged in traditional activities, and pursued an altogether risk-free and conservative economic regime.[22] Their aim was foremost to manage and maintain the patrimony and maximise its security rather than to make large profits and add new resources.

Maximisation of profit and the acquisition of new resources are, however, characteristic for the entrepreneur's type of behaviour. Entrepreneurs can best be described by what they do, that is, based on the business activities they pursue for their subsistence. While they came from a much more diverse background compared to the Neo-Babylonian rentiers, these individuals did not usually belong to the traditional elite stratum that owned prebends and land.[23] In fact, the lack of tight links to the temple is one of the primary features that circumscribes this social group.[24] Rather than concern themselves with the preservation of (landed) patrimony and rely on its income for their livelihood, these individuals and families were actively engaged in the business economy in the form of agricultural contracting, tax farming, trade, and business companies.[25] It is assumed that the primary motivation behind these activities was a desire to maximise profit. Entrepreneurs were much more mobile compared to rentiers and pursued a much riskier but potentially profitable subsistence strategy in a highly competitive business environment.

Of course, the 'rentier' and the 'entrepreneur' represent ideal types that are first and foremost useful from a heuristic point of view. In fact, even if one type of behaviour usually dominates, most Babylonian family archives show elements of both. Yet, important for us here are the two primary motives underlying these economic mentalities, namely, the aim to maintain existing resources by rentiers and the aim to gain additional resources by entrepreneurs.

In theory, priests were thus primarily concerned with maintaining their existing resources, both material (wealth or property) and symbolic (social status, power or lifestyle), which was best served by the recognition and sympathy of significant others. It should be obvious by now that the homophilous interactional pattern of the priests is perfectly consistent with the motive of maintaining resources. In the words of N. Lin, '[d]efending one's resources requires the sentiment and support of those who are in the same social groups or

21 Jursa *et al.* 2010: 287f.

22 Jursa 2013.

23 Yet, profit could, of course, be invested in landed property as was the case with the Egibis. See Wunsch 2000.

24 Jursa *et al.* 2010: 288f.

25 Jursa *et al.* 2010: 289. For the typical activities of the Babylonian entrepreneur, see also Wunsch 2010: 247ff.

those who are in a similar position (e.g., class) in the hierarchical structure'.[26] This is exactly what priests did: they interacted predominantly with individuals from within their social in-group. Hence, the fundamentally conservative economic mentality of priests provides an additional structural explanation for the largely normative, least demanding homophilous mode of interaction one can observe for this social segment.

Finally, if maintaining resources is achieved through homophily, the motive of gaining additional ones requires a different mode of interaction. We have seen that interacting with similar others only gives access to similar resources already owned. Hence, in order to gain new ones the entrepreneur was obliged to interact with dissimilar individuals, i.e. engage in so-called heterophily. This form of interaction requires more effort since 'interacting partners, aware of the inequality in differential command over resources that can be brought to bear, need to assess each other's willingness to engage in exchange'.[27] In the Neo-Babylonian context these partners could include powerful institutions like the temple or palace with their large agricultural or tax farming contracts as well as, for example, merchants, tenants or labourers from the lower strata of society. Even if much more research is needed on the dynamics of interaction of those Neo-Babylonian families that qualify as entrepreneurs, it seems that heterophily was as fundamental to their interaction and economic behaviour as homophily was to rentiers. This can already be glimpsed from those priests who displayed a somewhat more entrepreneurial mentality compared to other members of their social group. Consider Šaddinnu//Bēliya'u who, unlike most of his fellow priests, engaged lower-stratum tenants on a large scale.[28] Another example is Marduk-rēmanni//Ṣāhit-ginê from Sippar. Besides owning various prebends, this man spent much of his time in the mercantile sector on the local quay where he engaged with foreign as well as lower stratum individuals on a large scale.[29]

The distinction between homophily and heterophily is obviously not always clear-cut just as it was not for rentiers and entrepreneurs in general. Yet, these concepts allow us to dissect Babylonian society from a particular social angle. Even if more research is needed in order to develop and apply these concepts to our sources, it should be clear that priests interacted on a fundamentally different basis with society than other more entrepreneurial elements. In other words, rentiers and entrepreneurs were not only dissimilar in

26 Lin 2001: 49.

27 Lin 2001: 47.

28 See Chapter 2.3.1 and Chapter 2.3.2.

29 Waerzeggers 2014.

terms of economic behaviour and subsistence strategy, but they can also be distinguished by two opposing modes of interaction. Moreover, this excursion tells us that phenomena like rentiers and entrepreneurs, more than just based on economic criteria, can be explained from a more fundamental or structural perspective, which at the same time allows us to refine our understanding about the functioning of this ancient society as a whole.

Conclusion

In this chapter we took a step back from the detailed examination of interactions within the priestly community of Borsippa and approached the interactional pattern as a whole. In order to better understand the position of priests as a distinct social segment in Neo-Babylonian society I started by examining possible causations behind their distinct interactional pattern. Priests engaged predominantly with members of fellow priestly families both in mundane transactions like silver loans and in highly symbolic affairs such as marriage. Individuals from non-priestly elite families are attested significantly less often, while 'outsiders', i.e. all those who did not belong to the established urban elite segment, are almost entirely missing. How can this be explained?

A satisfying and theoretically informed interpretation of interaction was reached by introducing the concept of homophily. This principle, which poses that social interaction tends to take place among individuals with similar lifestyles and socio-economic characteristics, has been identified as one of the most basic and pervasive organising principles in human society. Homophily represents the normative and least demanding mode of interaction. That homophily played a deciding role in Borsippa's priestly circle transpires from the fact that the significant types of interactions, marriage and friendship, materialised to a disproportionate degree within the social in-group, a feature that could not be explained with a spatial argumentation alone. While non-priestly elite families were occasionally welcomed into the hypergamous marriage system and the circles of friendship, they appear more often in less significant capacities and affairs. They seem to have been kept outside of the social boundary to a large extent. This applied a fortiori to individuals from other and predominantly lower strata of society, which were excluded from the social world of the priests almost in its entirety. The simple, although important, conclusion is that the more similar one was to priests the more likely he or she was to interact with and be drawn into their social world. How similarity and dissimilarity may have been assessed by priests and others in Neo-Babylonian society is discussed in the following chapter.

CHAPTER 6

Social Boundary and Collective Identity

In the previous chapter we looked into causations behind the interactional pattern of the priestly families in Borsippa. I demonstrated that the (economic) mentality sustained by this social group played an important role. As so-called rentiers, these families were first and foremost set on protecting their existing resources and preserving their traditional position in society. I argued that this motivation was best served through homophilous interaction, i.e. interaction with individuals with similar lifestyles, social positions, and resources. The analysis, however, remained theoretical and abstract and interaction was approached mainly from a structural perspective. How was similarity or homophily assessed and maintained in this community? What were the material and symbolic resources these families claimed? What exactly constituted a Babylonian priest and how did this specific social group correspond to and differ from other groups in society?

The points of departure are what I called the more salient features of the pattern of interaction, i.e., the areas that show the highest degree of inbreeding homophily: marriage and friendship. Leaving aside the rules of hypergamy, priests most often married daughters of fellow priests, but alliances with non-priestly clans were concluded to a limited extent as well. However, intermarriage with other (non-family-name-bearing) strata of society is thus far not attested and might for all we know have been considered undesirable. It is not surprising that priests adhered to a strict endogamous policy in the domain of marriage as it entailed deep ramifications on their social hierarchy and status and involved the transfer of women and property. Nevertheless, the fact that a very similar pattern is found in the domain of trust and intimacy is telling. To reiterate, friendship is understood as an informal social relationship based on choice, trust, and voluntariness. It seems likely that in this personal matter priests enjoyed much more freedom from social convention and regulation than in any of the interactions studied above. Yet, intimate connections were exclusive to members of temple-based families, while those with individuals from lower strata of society were entirely absent. In other words, the hypergamous marriage circuit as well as the circles of trust and intimacy of the priesthood of Borsippa comprised only individuals who boasted clan

 | DOI:10.1163/9789004399969_008

names, marking them as descendants of established ancestry and members of the urban elite. Hence, the fact that the priests' significant and most symbolic interactions took place exclusively within this restricted social group strongly suggests that they perceived of and maintained themselves as a discrete social unit.

I would like to argue that we are dealing with what is called a 'symbolic' or 'social boundary' in the social sciences.[1] According to M. Lamont and V. Molnár, symbolic boundaries are 'conceptual distinctions made by social actors to categorise objects, people, practice and even time and space', but can more practically also 'separate people into groups and generate feelings of similarity and group membership'.[2] Only after *symbolic* boundaries 'are widely agreed upon can they take on a constraining character and pattern social interaction in important ways' and become *social* boundaries, for example translating into patterns of social exclusion or racial segregation.[3] These outcomes serve as mere examples pertaining to specific historical contexts and cannot be applied to the community under investigation. Yet, the interactional patterns in our corpus are clear in their own right. Even if individuals from the lower strata are represented in the priestly archives and are at times found in more important roles as creditors, lessees, and landowners, they did not participate in the significant interactions of the priestly community. Not only did the strongest ties of marriage and friendship materialise inside a restricted circle, but interaction with these individuals in general was kept to an absolute minimum. It follows that priests upheld a collective attitude and agenda, which allowed them to keep control over their social environment and preserve the configuration of their community through a deliberate act of auto-segregation. I believe that the clear pattern of interaction of the priests of Borsippa justifies designating it as the more forceful type of boundary, the social boundary. This social boundary set the priests apart from the rest of society and segmented the 'us' from 'them'.

It is widely accepted among sociologists that before an objectified collective identity (the 'us') can emerge, individuals must first share a sense of togetherness and be able to differentiate themselves from others by drawing on a set

---

1 The idea of 'boundaries' has taken up a key position in scholarship across the social sciences since at least the mid-twentieth century and has become part of the standard conceptual toolkit. A good starting point into the various traditions, concepts, and applications of 'symbolic/social boundaries' are the review articles by Lamont 2001 and Lamont and Molnár 2002. Both articles include an extensive bibliography on the topic.

2 Lamont and Molnár 2002: 168.

3 Lamont and Molnár 2002: 168–169.

of common criteria.[4] Equally important is the fact that this process of identification should be recognised by outsiders.[5] It is in the encounter between the internal and the external that identification is to be found and negotiated, and that identities materialise. It is, in the words of F. Barth, the 'boundary that defines the group rather than the cultural stuff that it encloses'.[6] In this chapter I adopt the opposite approach to the topic. Having already detected a very clear boundary based on the interactional patterns of the priestly families under investigation, I now look for the markers along which this social boundary was drawn. To rephrase the question posed above, what exactly were the symbolic and material resources on which priests drew to create and maintain their social in-group? In other words, what were the attributes and criteria, the so-called 'cultural stuff', that defined their collective social identity and their closest circles? In the following I examine a range of these markers including the affiliation to the temple, ownership of property, scribal education, literacy, and language.

1 Affiliation to the Temple

1.1 *Prebend Ownership*

The first feature that comes to mind is the possession of priestly titles. Ownership of prebends and, if sanctioned, enrolment in the priesthood had prodigious effects on how individuals perceived themselves and organised their professional and private lives[7] and can be identified as the key feature unifying the social group under investigation. The right to enter the employment of the gods was reserved for a select number of families that scrupulously transferred this privilege from father to son. They legitimised their position by insisting on continuity with the past and the preservation of hallowed traditions. Hence, the prebendary brewers from the city of Nippur all claimed the person of Absummu as eponymous ancestor even if *de facto* they might not have shared consanguinity.[8] Other ritual specialists versed in the more arcane trades went

4 Barth 1969, Brubaker and Cooper 2000: 14–21, and Jenkins 2008, *passim*.
5 Jenkins 2008, especially Chapter 4, Eriksen 2002, especially Chapters 2–3, and Barth 1969.
6 Barth 1969: 15. In addition to social boundaries, Barth is especially interested in ethnic boundaries and identities in this article.
7 Waerzeggers 2010, especially Chapter 2. A more social-economic outlook is provided by Jursa *et al.* 2010, especially p. 155ff.
8 Joannès 1992: 90 and Beaulieu 1995: 88.

so far as to trace their roots back to the most remote, mythical past.[9] While no direct evidence of such an ideology is found in the documents of the priesthood of Borsippa, one can assume that they shared a 'deep-rooted concern for lineage and origins' very similar to their colleagues from other cultic centres.[10] The majority of the families from Borsippa managed to maintain their cultic positions during the entire long sixth century and some were there already long before while others persisted even thereafter.[11]

Prebends did not necessarily represent the most expensive asset in the property portfolio of priests,[12] but they were certainly among their most cherished ones. Even if prebendary titles could be bought and sold freely, there is plenty of evidence to suggest that priests strived to keep them firmly in the patrimony. They were hardly ever used as collateral on loans[13] and families usually avoided bequeathing prebends to female relatives.[14] Prebends were put up for

9 This idea is especially evident among ritual specialists like diviners, exorcists, and cultic singers. See Borger 1973: 172, Lambert 1998: 142, and Beaulieu 2007a. Note, for example, that a diviner (*barû*) had to be a descendant of Enmeduranki, the antediluvian king of Sippar, in order to be initiated in this trade. See Lambert 1998. Note that according to one tradition priests were instated by the chief god, Marduk, at the moment of creation. See Al-Rawi and George 1994: 135–139.

10 Waerzeggers 2010: 78. See her footnote 337 for possible evidence that the tradition about Absummu also circulated among the brewers of Ezida. Further interest in the past as a source of legitimation can be deduced from the fact that monumental inscriptions (*kudurrus*) commemorating the donation of land and/or prebends to individuals, usually by the king, were kept on display in the temple even centuries after the deed. See Slanski 2000: 96f. This is, for example, the case for VS 1 36, a *kudurru* from the mid-eight century BCE, which describes the inauguration of a temple-enterer of Nabû in Ezida. It was found in the ruins of the temple by H. Rassam. See Reade 1986. Interest in origins and history arises, moreover, from the composition of chronicles, a discipline that prospered in the Borsippean scribal circle. See Waerzeggers 2012.

11 All of the family names mentioned in the mid-eight century *kudurru* VS 1 36 are still found in the temple during the long sixth century. On the other side of the chronological spectrum, the Huṣābu family was still able to man brewers for the service of Nabû in the later Persian and Hellenistic periods. See the colophons and texts written by Nabû-kuṣuršu// Huṣābu in CT 12 and Hunger 1968: nos. 124–133.

12 BM 26576 = AH XV no. 192 from the Rēʾi-alpi archive illustrates this clearly. In this enormous sale of seventeen items of property prebends rank only third highest in terms of value in silver, well after the housing plot and agricultural land. For the relative value of types of private property, see Jursa *et al.* 2010, Chapter 3. Note, however, that the prices of prebends differed greatly. The prices roughly correlated with the relative status of the prebendary function in the temple hierarchy. See Pirngruber and Waerzeggers 2011. For a general comparison between the prices for houses, agricultural plots, and prebends, see Jursa *et al.* 2010: 176ff.

13 See Chapter 3.

14 Roth 1990: 2, 33f., and Waerzeggers 2010: 92–94.

sale only in the uttermost end of needs and even then these sales usually took place within the paternal family and among immediate colleagues.[15] Moreover, there are many examples of priests seeking to redeem previously alienated property, a context that saw the involvement of the so-called 'house of the father' (*bīt abi*). Recent studies by, for example, C. Waerzeggers and J.P. Nielsen have shown that the *bīt abi*, a flexible social institution that united several agnatic lines of descent headed by the 'big brother' (*ahu rabû*), i.e. the eldest son of the eldest son of the common ancestor, exercised a great measure of control over the property decisions of its members.[16] Most notably, it held the right to redeem alienated property, especially (albeit not exclusively) prebends. Besides a natural sense of solidarity or 'brotherhood',[17] members also shared an emotional attachment to their *bīt abi* and its patrimony.[18] This institution seems to have embodied a concrete locus[19] of togetherness and shared identity for close relatives within the wider kin groups. It represented a core feature of domestic and public life of the priesthood and indeed the urban upper stratum in general.

1.2 *Purity and Initiation*

The Babylonian priesthood was submitted to stringent requirements of purity well beyond the basic needs for hygiene and everyday cleanliness.[20] A priest needed to be pure in all aspects of his person, which meant pure of blood, mind, and body.[21] That is why before being admitted into the priesthood, cultic authorities would conduct extensive inquests into a candidate's health, past, and family in order to ensure his ritual fitness. Correct descent was of primary importance. Both ritual and practical texts inform us that only a biological

15 Waerzeggers 2010: 98–99.

16 Waerzeggers 2010: 81–90 and Nielsen 2011: 244–253.

17 Note that the use of the (fictive) kinship term 'brother' is found only in prebend related cases. Sales of houses and land were not dealt with in this framework, which shows that blood ties were especially important for the priestly identity. See Waerzeggers 2010: 87.

18 Van der Toorn 1996a: 20, Waerzeggers 2010: 90, and Nielsen 2011: 244ff.

19 Note that the *bīt-abi* could perhaps refer to a physical building or a home base in addition to the more symbolic concept of one's extended family unit. The reading of the relevant texts is, however, open to criticism. See Nielsen 2011: 56ff., 276–280.

20 See Sallaberger 2006 for an overview of the different concepts of purity and pollution in Babylonia.

21 The rules of admission in the Babylonian priesthood and the requirements of purity that existed in the Neo-Babylonian period have been discussed extensively in Waerzeggers and Jursa 2008. See also Waerzeggers 2010: 51–55. See Löhnert 2007 for the Neo-Assyrian evidence. See Borger 1973, Lambert 1998, and Löhnert 2010 for various ritual texts dealing with the initiation of Babylonian priests and ritual specialists.

son of an initiated priest could enter the service of the gods.[22] In practice, this could only be ascertained if the priest-to-be had been born in wedlock. Virginity of a bride upon marriage was apparently proof enough for uncontested paternal descent of her children,[23] while birth outside of matrimony led to a candidate's disqualification. Moral behaviour represented another aspect of purity.[24] Individuals convicted of homicide or thievery as well as those merely lacking proper devotion and humility were barred from entering the temple.[25] If in doubt, the temple authorities would summon witnesses and consult the candidate's past (criminal) record to make sure his integrity was beyond reproach. Only someone with an impeccable record, a truly virtuous person, was qualified for cultic service.

Once correct descent and conduct had been established and royal permission granted,[26] the candidate could be inducted into the priesthood. The initiation ritual is referred to literally as 'the shave' (*gullubu*) and occurred in the bathhouse the first time the successful candidate entered the sacred compounds of the temple.[27] Performed by the prebendary barber (*gallābu*) and a team of cultic experts, the primary purpose of this rite of passage was to check the candidate's physical purity and to shave his body and head. According to the ritual texts from Nippur edited by R. Borger, the *nešakku* and *pašīšu* priests were required to have bodies 'as pure as golden statues' (col. I 13–14) and be free from physical imperfections such as bad eyesight, kidney-stones, birthmarks (?), and an asymmetrical face.[28] A similar standard of bodily perfection was required from other ritual specialists. The diviner (*bārû*), for example, was considered unfit for service if he had squinting eyes, chipped teeth, a cut-off finger or suffered from a ruptured (?) testicle or leprosy.[29] Once the candidate

22 Waerzeggers and Jursa 2008: 10–13.

23 Virgin brides received pendants (*zību*) from their parents upon marriage. This pendant, thought to consist of a couch, which was a mark of female purity associated with the goddess Ninlil, functioned both as a symbol of virginity for the bride as well as proof of uncontested paternal descent for her future children. See Waerzeggers and Jursa 2008.

24 Waerzeggers and Jursa 2008: 13.

25 Waerzeggers 2010: 53.

26 Candidates had to be granted permission from the king or his local representative before being allowed to proceed with the consecration ceremony. See Waerzeggers and Jursa 2008: 18–19. The king was also actively involved in the recruitments of priests himself, at least in case of more senior cultic positions. Since these priests did not only enjoy proximity to the gods but also access to the persona of the king, careful selection was a matter of national security.

27 On the *gullubu* ceremony, see Scheyhing 1998, Sallaberger and Huber Vulliet 2005: 620–622, Löhnert 2007, Waerzeggers and Jursa 2008, and Löhnert 2010.

28 Borger 1973: 172.

29 Lambert 1998: 144.

had passed the physical examination in the bathhouse he could be cleansed and shaven, thereby ritually purified and separated from the profane.[30] The candidate had now become an initiated priest.

Even if it seems likely that all active priests had to go through some sort of rite of initiation, the act of shaving was reserved only for those priests who would operate in the sacred areas of the temple.[31] This included the temple-enterers who came into direct contact with the divine statues as well as purveyors such as brewers, bakers, oxherds, and fishermen who manipulated the sacrificial foodstuff and participated in the daily ceremony on the temple courtyard.[32] While the term *gullubu* only refers to the shaving ceremony at the threshold of office, it has been shown by C. Waerzeggers that these priests had to pay regular visits to the temple barber and were 'submitted to tests of cultic suitability in the course of their active careers'.[33] The demand for shaving provided a visual aspect to the temple's hierarchy, which was mirrored in the physical appearance of its personnel. It set the pure apart from the impure and the fit from the unfit. In addition, it also distinguished the priests from the rest of the population and served as a distinctive outward sign of priestly status and identity in society.[34]

While the removal of all bodily hairs was restricted to a select group, all Babylonian priests were required to wash their body with water before they

30 Scheyhing 1998: 73.

31 Waerzeggers and Jursa 2008: 14–17.

32 In the data sample used for the present study the reed-workers were probably the only priests who did not belong to the consecrated (i.e. shaved) part of the temple personnel of Ezida.

33 Waerzeggers and Jursa 2008: 20.

34 For other visible marks, which may have included specific garments and headgear, see Kessler 1999: 250ff., Sallaberger and Huber Vulliet 2005: 623, and Zawadzki 2006: 91, 94. Of special interest are the so-called *ṣibtu*-garment and the *mehēzu*-girdle, which, according to the Hellenistic Uruk text UVB 15, 40, were worn by various priests engaged in temple ritual. Some ritual specialists (e.g. the lamentation priest or *kalû*) even wore *lubāru*-garments, normally reserved for the gods. Since these articles of clothing are usually found in 'white work' (*dullu peṣû*) texts we can assume that the priests wore them in white too. See Zawadzki 2006 and Bongenaar 1999: 304ff. That the garments of the priests had to be in spotless condition follows from the fact that they paid regular fees to the temple washerman (*ašlāku*) who, besides cleaning the dirty cloths of the gods, was also responsible for washing the working cloths of his temple colleagues. See Waerzeggers 2010: 55. Note that priests can often be found on Neo-Babylonian seals. They are represented as bald, clean-shaven individuals wearing a girdle and a fringed robe that passes over the right shoulder. Their right hand is usually raised towards the mouth in reverence, while sometimes carrying cultic devices in their left hand. On the Neo-Babylonian cylinder seal and its iconography, see Collon 2001: 193–195.

were allowed access into the temple.[35] As a consequence, a priest who could no longer do the washing (*ramāka* a.meš) was immediately released from duty.[36] Hence, washing with water was an essential requirement for and, as a result, an inherent quality of a priest on duty.[37] This association is also found in a couple of literary and monumental texts that use the term *ramku* (pl. *ramkūtu*) to designate a 'priest' or the 'priesthood' in general.[38] A good example is found in the En-nigaldi-Nanna cylinder of Nabonidus (YOS 1 45) re-edited by H.-P. Schaudig.[39] This inscription, composed in honour of the restoration of the Egipar in Ur and the installation of Nabonidus' daughter as *entu*-priestess of Sîn, also records the exemption from taxation and corvée labour granted to the local temple personnel. The long list of priests who are accorded this privilege opens with the term, the 'bathed-ones' (*ramkūtu*).[40]

The priests' preoccupation with purity is also borne out by the particular diet they followed. On the one hand, they enjoyed the privilege to consume the remainders of the offerings.[41] Derived from the table of the gods, this food was meticulously sanctified and carefully distributed among the priesthood and the king.[42] On the other hand, priests observed dietary restrictions in order to maintain their ritual purity. Although the details largely escape us, a glimpse of this custom, relating to the priesthood of Ezida, can be found in the text SpTU III no. 58.[43] This polemic literary composition deals with the crimes and sacrileges committed by Nabû-šumu-iškun, a Chaldean king of the mid-eighth century BCE. In addition to appropriating temple property, introducing foreign

35 Waerzeggers 2010: 12–13, 55.

36 BM 26480 = AH XV: no 163.

37 Sallaberger and Huber Vuillet 2005: 612.

38 See CAD R: 126–127.

39 Schaudig 2001: 373–377.

40 Note that the list of priests is closed and summarized with *kiništu*, a term commonly translated as 'temple college/assembly', which may have functioned as a synonym of *ramkūtu*. That both terms were, at the least, closely related follows from TCL 9 143 (see below). Concerned with the cultic activities at the Eanna temple in Uruk, the letter writer tells the *kiništu* 'not to bring about any cultic interruption' and reminds them to 'wash themselves with water' (ll. 6–9). Nevertheless, *ramku* as a generic word for priests is rare and found mainly in literary contexts. We have to wait for the Hellenistic period to find it in administrative temple documents. See CAD R: 127. Here the term is clearly used as a classification to divide the consecrated from the non-consecrated temple personnel. BRM 1 99, for example, mentions rations of the '*sirāšû* [lú]tu$_5$.meš', or 'bathed brewers'.

41 Waerzeggers 2010, *passim*, especially Chapter 8.

42 McEwan 1983 and Corò 2004. See below for more information on the relationship between the king, the priesthood, and the gods.

43 See Cole 1994b and Glassner 2004: 300–312 for an edition of this text. This text belongs the late Achaemenid archive of the exorcist (*āšipu*) Anu-ikṣur//Šangû-Ninurta from Uruk.

gods, and flouting nearly every single ritual protocol, the king is said to have offered 'leek – a thing forbidden in Ezida – into the temple of Nabû' (col. ii 17–18) and made the temple-enterers eat it. The consumption of leek as well as other pungent foodstuff such as onion, garlic or fish were considered to turn a person temporarily impure, according to the Babylonian mind-set.[44] Forcing the priests to eat tabooed substances, Nabû-šumu-iškun was thus accused of having rendered the god's immediate servants unfit for service.[45]

The ideology of purity was obviously an important feature of the self-perception of Babylonian priests. Some of its aspects were transmitted from father to son, while others had to be nurtured and guarded carefully against profaning influences and miasma. Rules of purity not only regulated their activities inside the temple, but also demanded a very specific lifestyle from the priests.

1.3 *Sacrifices and Festivals*

Once initiated, prebendary titles gave their owners the right to perform a specific (ritual) task in the cult of the gods at a particular moment in the year. Priests did not, however, operate in isolation, but rather were grouped into larger professional units.[46] In the temple a priest thus came into contact with a large body of direct and indirect colleagues who were all part of the same system and ultimately served the same goal: the worship of the gods. As I have shown throughout this study, collaboration and association in the temple paved the ground for much of the social interaction of priests, most of which took place within this restricted group of temple colleagues and their relatives.

One can argue that the concept of priesthood materialised on a daily basis through joint action inside and outside of the temple walls. The cultic calendar of Ezida has been reconstructed by C. Waerzeggers.[47] She showed that the fundamental aspect of the cult of Ezida, like in any other Babylonian temple,

44 See, for example, van der Toorn 1985: 33ff. For injunctions against eating certain foodstuff in Babylonian hemerologies as well as medical and ritual texts, see Cole 1994b: 241 and Geller 2011.

45 The similarities between the Babylonian priests and the Brahmin on the Indian subcontinent are interesting on this point. Brahmans are known to follow a very strict diet in which leek, garlic, and onion have to be avoided according to the traditional Vedic scriptures. See Olivelle 2000: 53–55, 407–409. On the other end of their dietary spectrum, Brahmans officiating as priests in the temple hold the right to enjoy the remainders of the daily food offerings and, like their Babylonian counterparts, consume the sanctified food of the gods. See Fuller 1984: 14.

46 For the internal organisation of the priesthoods in Ezida, see Waerzeggers 2010: Chapter 4 on brewers, Chapter 5 on bakers, Chapter 6 on butchers, and Chapter 7 on oxherds.

47 Waerzeggers 2010: 111–152.

was the daily worship (*ginû*). It consisted of two identical ceremonies. one in the morning (*šēru*) and the other in the afternoon (*kīṣ umi*), during which the priests on duty presented two consecutive meals to the gods, the main meal (*rabû*) and the second meal (*tardennu*).[48] This quotidian ritual, staged within the intimate setting of the temple and concealed from the uninitiated eye, was considered the essential form of worship, the continuity of which was thought to correlate directly with the well-being of the land.[49]

If the 'daily care and feeding of the gods'[50] was the most crucial aspect in the self-perception of the individual priests, the group's public image took shape during the cultic activities beyond the temple precinct. As in any other Babylonian town,[51] in Borsippa too there existed a number of public (monthly/annual) festivals.[52] During many of these events the (images of the) gods left their cellae and were taken out on a procession through the city's streets and the countryside as they visited shrines and temples of divine relatives in Borsippa and neighbouring towns. Perhaps the most spectacular episode of the year took place during the New Year festival (*akītu*) held in Babylon in the beginning of the calendar year in the month of *Nisannu*.[53] As shown by both the ritual texts and administrative documents from Borsippa, on the fifth day of this month the god Nabû came forth from his cella in Ezida. After a procession through the streets of Borsippa Nabû took his sacred barge for the capital where he was welcomed by the Babylonian king at the Red Gate Quay and joined the public festivities of his divine father, Marduk, for the following days.[54] After numerous rituals, offerings, prayers, and processions through the capital and its countryside, Nabû was to return to Borsippa on the eleventh when he entered his cella following a reversed procession from the week before.[55]

48 Waerzeggers 2010: 113–118 including her exhaustive bibliographic references.

49 It is, therefore, not surprising that the Babylonian rulers took great pride in emphasising their role as protectors and providers of the cult. See Waerzeggers 2011.

50 This refers to the pioneering essay by A.L. Oppenheim on the Babylonian temple worship. See Oppenheim 1977: 183–198.

51 For cultic festivals in the cities of Babylon and Uruk, see Thureau-Dangin 1921, Çağirgan and Lambert 1991, and Linssen 2004.

52 Waerzeggers 2010: 119–141.

53 See Waerzeggers 2010: 119–121 including previous literature. Other public festivals in Borsippa reconstructed by C. Waerzeggers include, among others, the wedding ceremony between Nabû and his consort in month I, a celebration at the temple of Nanāya Euršaba at the end of month I, the procession of Nanāya Euršaba and other gods to Babylon and Kish, and a celebration held at least three times a year at the shrine of Šamaš in the countryside. See Waerzeggers 2010: 129ff.

54 Pongratz-Leisten 1994, Zgoll 2006, and Waerzeggers 2010: 119–121.

55 Waerzeggers 2010: 120–130.

Although our administrative documents, concerned above all with the bureaucratic control of the flow of commodities necessary for proper ritual, only tacitly inform us on the celebratory nature of festivals and the priests' public performances at such events, these aspects can to some extent be gained from the ritual (prescriptive) texts from first millennium Babylon and Uruk.[56] Paraded through the processional street on divine chariots or up and down the river on sacred barges, the statues of the gods, fully adorned with jewellery and dressed in magnificent garments, were the absolute centres of attention in the eyes of the spectators.[57] Though not nearly as richly decorated as the divine statues, the large priestly retinue that accompanied the gods on processions and assisted them at various other stages of these festivals must have been no less conspicuous. Besides their proximity to the gods, and at the New Year festival also to the king, the onlooker must have had no difficulty in identifying them as servants of the gods, which their immaculate priestly garments and their ritually shaved bodies clearly indicated. Hence, it was these public festivals that staged the dramatic interactions between the priesthood, the gods, the king, and the wider public, the intensity and sensation of which can perhaps best be understood in the light of similar festivals held on the Indian sub-continent today.[58]

At this point a few words should be said about the relation between the king and the priests who, after all, were closely tied together through their joint worship of the gods.[59] Rather than the ideal of the warrior-king promoted by the Assyrian predecessors, the most persistent theme of Neo-Babylonian kingship was that of the pious king as benefactor of the gods.[60] The renovation of temples, the provision of the regular sacrifice, and the supply of new cultic objects are heavily emphasised in royal inscriptions.[61] The epithets or short titles used most frequently by the Neo-Babylonian kings express a similar generosity towards the gods and their cults: 'the one who establishes the regular offerings' (*mukīn sattukkī*), 'the giver of wonderful gifts' (*mušarrih igisê*), and the most popular, 'the provider of Esangila and Ezida' (*zānin Esagila u Ezida*).[62]

56 Farber 1987, Çağirgan and Lambert 1991, and Linssen 2004.

57 Pongratz-Leisten 1994.

58 Younger 1980, Fuller 1984: 17–21, Fuller and Logan 1985, Good 1999, and Fuller 2004.

59 This relationship is the subject of an article by C. Waerzeggers in which most of the following information can be found in extenso. See Waerzeggers 2011.

60 Waerzeggers 2011: 726–730.

61 Waerzeggers 2011: 726–727.

62 Da Riva 2008: 94–107.

According to the royal ideology that was current in first millennium Babylonia, the gods directly appointed individual kings.[63] As the earthly representative of Marduk and the divine assembly, the king was thus invested with supreme religious authority. This meant that besides the allocation of resources necessary for cultic execution, the king had to keep a close check on the priesthood itself. Hence, it was a royal prerogative to endow temples with new cultic personnel as well as to remove incompetent priests from office or suspend their posts, even though this could not be done without good reason.[64] Despite being formally enrolled in the service of the gods, the privileged position of the priests rested, strictly speaking, upon the good grace of the king.

Even if the idiom of the royal ideology left little space for the mention of priests, their role was of crucial importance to the king. While he owned prebendary rights in the temple,[65] the Babylonian king did not have the authority to officiate as a cultic agent, not even to enter the presence of the divine statues unchecked.[66] As we have seen, it was the priests who looked after the care and feeding of the gods and performed the crucial daily temple ritual. Even if the king could offer a sacrifice to the gods, only the priest could operate it. Hence, the king had to rely on the interceding figure of the priest in order to interact with the gods.[67] Once more, this triadic relationship between the king, the priesthood, and the gods materialised most clearly during the New Year festival.

63 Dietrich and Dietrich 1998.

64 Waerzeggers 2011: 741–745.

65 Kleber 2008: 287–292.

66 Waerzeggers 2011: 733–737.

67 The similarities with the caste system of the Indian sub-continent are striking on this point. The king, traditionally a member of the so-called Kshatriya class, enjoyed supremacy in absolute political and military terms, yet he was deprived of any sacerdotal function, which was the right of the priestly or Brahmin caste alone. While the king claimed political power, and even retained some magico-religious aspects, the Hindu priests held spiritual authority. This gave rise to a very similar tripartite relationship between king, priest, and god observed in first-millennium Babylonia: the Brahmins relied on the king for his protection and patronage in order to conduct proper ritual, while the king in turn depended on the Brahmins in order to communicate with the gods and validate his kingship. As in Babylonia, this complicated relationship is reflected upon in various literary compositions in India too. For a brief survey of the traditional notion of kingship in India and the relation between the king and the priestly caste, see Fuller 1984: 104–106 and Dumont 1970: appendix C. For more thorough studies focusing on kingship and the role of the king in pre-colonial Indian society, see Dirks 1987 and Peabody 2003. For a collection of essays, dealing with the traditional or ideological position and authority of the Brahmin priests and the king, see Heesterman 1985.

Held in honour of Marduk's sovereignty over the universe, the New Year festival staged a crucial episode during which the king's legitimacy as the gods' representative on earth was ritually tested. Once all the gods were assembled in the Esagila temple on the fifth day, the king would enter the sacred compound of Marduk. There, well hidden from public gaze, he was met by the *ahu rabû*, literally, the 'big brother' of Esagila and the foremost among the priests who would strip the king of his royal insignia – sceptre, loop, mace, and the crown of kingship – which he would then carry off and place in front of Marduk.[68] Upon return, the high priest would slap the king across his face then pull him into the inner sanctuary by his ears and force him into submission before the statue of Marduk.[69] From this humiliating position, the king would avow that he had neither neglected the gods nor forsaken his responsibilities toward the city of Babylon, its people, and its main temple.[70] Once the king made his 'negative confession', the high priest would return the royal insignia and slap the king one final time to induce the following omen: 'if his (the king's) tears flow, Bēl (i.e. Marduk) is well disposed, if his tears do not flow, Bēl is angry'.[71] Manipulating the royal insignia and escorting the humiliated king, somewhat violently, in and out of the divine space, the high priest is absolutely indispensible in this ritual. Even if the kings derived their legitimacy from the gods, 'this relationship was negotiated through the temple and the priesthoods, who played a vital role in validating the power of the individual kings'.[72]

In addition to this dramatic annual confrontation, the relationship between god, king, and priest was also cultivated on a daily basis in the temples. Both king and priest were entitled to a portion of the divine meals and, as a result, it was customary that every temple sent sacrificial leftovers to the palace.[73] By sharing food the three parties were thus joined in an exclusive unit of commensality. This special bond was further underlined by the cult of the royal image.[74] Although the evidence pertaining to the long sixth century Babylonia is in short supply, the cult of the royal image is well known from earlier periods because it had been performed in Mesopotamian temples since at least the

68 Note that Sallaberger and Schmidt 2012 interpret this scene differently. They argue that this ritual did not involve the insignia of the king but the divine insignia of Marduk, which were presented before the king when he made his confession.

69 Pongratz-Leisten 1994.

70 Pongratz-Leisten 1997.

71 Linssen 2004: 232.

72 Waerzeggers 2011: 746.

73 McEwan 1983, Beaulieu 1990, and Kleber 2008: 292ff.

74 Cole and Machinist 1998: xiii.

third millennium BCE.[75] Statues of the kings were erected in temple courtyards and inner sanctuaries, which allowed the king to be in the presence of the divine and enabled a continuous transmission of worship to the gods. At the same time, these statues also received offerings, which made them into subjects of worship themselves.[76] The placement of royal images in the temple thus benefitted both sides: it allowed the kings a place in the sacred space, but also served 'to reinforce the privileges of the priest through his access to the sculpted images of both god *and* king'.[77] Their association to god and king was of great importance to the self-image of the priests and many of the literary works found in temple libraries and priestly archives focus exactly on this triangular relationship.[78]

While public festivals allowed priests to display their privileged status under the most dramatic and pompous circumstances, there must have been many more formal and informal occasions during which they broadcasted their ritual status and collective identity to the outside world. One example concerns temple-building projects. In addition to the (Assyrian and Babylonian) kings, the priests, too, are known to have been responsible for the renovation and construction of various parts of the temple area.[79] The best-known example is found in the archives of Borsippa's priests and pertains to construction work on Ezida's riverside wall during the reigns of Neriglissar and Nabonidus. This dossier tells us that the priestly divisions of Ezida contributed to the realisation of this project, specifically by manufacturing and supplying bricks.[80] Replicating the cultic organisation of the temple worship, various priestly divisions including the temple-enterers, butchers, and oxherds received a lump sum of silver from the temple treasury to produce bricks for the allotted section of the temple wall.[81] Although undoubtedly prestigious, participation in this and similar projects was not an entirely voluntary act on the side of the priests according

75 Kleber 2008: 269–271 on the Eanna in Uruk and Waerzeggers 2014c on the Ebabbar in Sippar.

76 Kleber 2008: 271–275 and Waerzeggers 2014c.

77 Waerzeggers 2011: 745.

78 Waerzeggers 2011, *passim*.

79 For references to royal construction works at the Ezida temple and Borsippa, see Langdon 1912: Nbk nos. 11, 15, and 44 for Nebuchadnezzar; Schaudig 1995, Schaudig 2001: 395–397 and VS 6 65 for Nabonidus; Kuhrt and Sherwin-White 1991 for Antiochus I.

80 These texts have been examined by Waerzeggers 2010: 337–345.

81 The clearest example pertains to the prebendary oxherds who knew a dual organisation: the top level based on the trimestral rotation of the oxherd's temple service (the *bēl-agurri* level) and the lower level based on length-units of fifty centimeters, the responsibility over which was assigned to individual priests or a group of oxherds belonging to these three rotas (the *bēl-ammati* level).

to C. Waerzeggers. The brick impost caused enormous financial setbacks for the concerned families, whom we find settling brick-related debts many years after the inception of the building project.[82] It is also dubious whether the priests engaged in the actual physical work themselves.[83] In spite of all this, it is hard to imagine that the priests would have missed the opportunity to broadcast their individual pious contributions and the beneficial role of their professional group to the outside world.[84]

1.4 *Representation*

An important platform for the priests to act as a collective within the community was the *kiništu,* commonly translated in the secondary literature as 'temple assembly'. This was a legal body composed of the principal prebendaries of a temple organisation.[85] While the term is hardly found in the private texts of Borsippa's priests,[86] it is more commonly attested in the institutional archives of the Ebabbar temple in Sippar and the Eanna temple in Uruk. In addition to the basic cultic responsibilities of the members of the *kiništu* themselves, the *kiništu* also functioned as an advisory board that assisted the higher temple authorities in legal matters, often related to (stolen) temple property,

82 Waerzeggers 2010: 344–345. The settlements of debts forced many priests to dispose of valuable (prebendary) property.

83 In fact, BM 26479 = AH XV no. 139: 4 mentions 'the workers of the house of the oxherds' (érin.meš *šá* é [lú]sipa.gud.meš), which might suggest that the priests hired a work gang to do the actual work.

84 Note that there is an interesting parallel in Nehemiah 3:1–32, reporting on the renovation of Jerusalem's damaged gates and walls. This passage gives a list of all the people who participated in the renovation work and assigns them very specific areas of construction. The result is that the entire fortification work of the city was divided in clearly identifiable units assigned to specific individuals, households, and/or professional groups. Priests figure prominently among this last set of contributors.

85 The most extensive treatment of the *kiništu* is still found in Bongenaar 1997: 150–153. It seems that the brewers, the bakers, and the butchers were particularly associated with *kiništu*, while the temple-enterers were traditionally set apart. However, other texts suggest that the term, *kiništu*, could mean 'prebendaries' more generally. The letter TCL 9 143, for example, states that the *kiništu* should not cause any interruptions in the regular service on days two, five, and fifteen and reminds them to cleanse themselves with water (*ramāku*). Note that in Uruk we sometimes find non-prebendary temple personnel subsumed under *kiništu*. YOS 6 77 and TCL 13 182 both mention the 'overseer of the herds' (*rab-būli*) who is a high official in the temple's sheep herding organisation.

86 Besides a reference in the eighth-century *kudurru* VS 1 36, the term is found on only three other occasions in the Borsippa corpus. BM 29400 = AH XV no. 78 (Dar 05?), BM 96231 = AH XV no. 83 (Dar 09), and BM 96226 = AH XV no. 79 (d.l.) belong to the Bēliya'u archive and mention the *kiništu* in relation to the preparation of corvée work in Elam.

correct cultic procedures, and taxation.[87] The *kiništu* also operated as an investigatory panel that collected information about (historic) conflicts, inquired about persons' backgrounds, interrogated offenders, dispatched messengers, and produced reports on behalf of the authorities. Finally, the *kiništu* was also invested with the power to represent the local temple (community) in imperial matters. As such, it was sent abroad to perform and/or supervise corvée work in Elam on behalf of the religious institution[88] and it stood in direct communication with the king.[89] In some instances the temple assembly might even have represented the city at large.[90] In conclusion, the *kiništu* allowed for the multifarious priesthoods of a temple to amalgamate into a single legal body representing the temple institution and exercising considerable juridical control in addition to or perhaps in tandem with other more inclusive civic constituencies in the community.[91] Much is still unknown about the exact composition and other roles of the *kiništu* and its development over the first millennium as an in-depth investigation is still outstanding.

1.5 *Priestly Families vs. the Individual Priest*

In the previous pages I have shown various examples of how the ownership of prebends and enrolment in the priesthood was crucial in shaping the identity of priests and their families. Yet, a note of caution should be voiced here once again. Belonging to a priestly family did not automatically turn an individual

87 For Uruk, see PTS 2097 (Nbn 01), YOS 6 77 (Nbn 04), AnOr 8 48 (Cyr 05), YOS 7 128 (Cam 02), TCL 13 182 (Dar 02). For Sippar, see CT 55 110 (Nbn 09) and BM 61344 (Nbn 14). For Akkad, see BM 61522 (Cyr 04+) and Smith Coll. 111 (Dar 04). For Babylon/Dilbat, see AO 2569 (Dar II 08).

88 BM 29400 = AH XV no. 78 (Dar 05?) BM 96231 = AH XV no. 83 (Dar 09), and BM 96226 = AH XV no. 79 (d.l.) from the Bēliya'u archive deal with the preparations and compensation of an individual who goes to Elam with the *kiništu* and performs or possibly supervises the corvée work on behalf of the prebendary bakers.

89 In YOS 6 71//YOS 6 72 (Nbn 09) the king asked the *kiništu* about a ritual garment. BM 113249 (Cam 03) narrates a royal demand to the *kiništu* to inform the royal messenger about royal stelae and inscriptions set up in the Eanna by previous kings. YOS 3 6 (d.l, probably Nbn) is a royal request to have an audience with ten or fifteen elders and/or members of the *kiništu* at the royal court in Babylon.

90 This is, for example, suggested by the Assyrian royal letter ND 2348. Here we find King Tiglath-pileser III (744–724 BCE) urging the 'temple-enterers, the *kiništu*, and the leaders of the [...] (and?) the citizens of Babylon' to take military action and seize the gates of the town of Hirdasu. See Luukko 2012: no. 1: ll. 2–5.

91 For other civic institutions in first-millennium Babylonia like the elders (*šībūtu*), the assembly (*puhru*), the foremost (*ašaredūtu*), and the citizens (*mār-banî*), and their potential juridical and prosopographical overlap with the temple assembly, see Barjamovic 2004.

into an initiated servant of the gods. In addition to the ownership of a prebend, a candidate needed to be declared ritually fit before being allowed into the priesthood. Not many were able to meet these stringent requirements. As a result, most individuals, indeed entire branches of families had to make a living in other sectors of society. Good examples of this are the Gallābus of Borsippa and the Egibis of Babylon.[92] Yet, there is evidence to suggest that some of the privileged (sacerdotal) status was also ascribed to and upheld by clan members who were not active priests themselves. The existence of the *bīt-abi* is a case in point. This flexible social institution incorporated several agnatic lines and united both male and female members into a social unit[93] that, besides maintaining a cooperative property policy, shared a sense of solidarity, emotional attachment, and collective identity, regardless of the fact whether one was enrolled in the priesthood or not. Once again, a cautious parallel could be drawn with the Brahmin of the Indian sub-continent. Although traditionally responsible for the religious rituals of the temple and thus required to officiate as cultic agents and meet the liturgical needs in society,[94] throughout history Brahmins have been known to have taken on many different professions. While this could and did have an effect on the prestige and social standing of the individual Brahmin, it never subverted his or her absolute status in the overall caste system because this was determined at birth.[95]

2 Ownership of Property

As we have seen in previous chapters, in addition to prebends, housing plots and agricultural land featured prominently in the property portfolios of priestly families. Although this has remained under-theorised and understudied for pre-industrial societies,[96] it is commonly accepted that ownership of real estate has played a crucial and pervasive factor in elite and class formation throughout history. This assumption can be backed by a large number of ancient and modern examples: from the senatorial rank in the Roman Republic

92 Jursa 2005: 65–66, 82–83.

93 For the role of women in the *bīt-abi*, see Van der Toorn 1996a: 20ff.

94 Dumont 1970: 66–72.

95 Béteille 2010: 112–113, Fuller 1984, *passim*, and Dumont 1970, *passim*.

96 The paucity is especially striking in anthropological scholarship where it applies to elite studies in general. Reasons that have been advanced for this gap range from practical obstacles and the historical conventions of the discipline itself to personal preferences of anthropologists who tend to sympathise with marginal and/or pre-modern equalitarian communities. See Gusterson 2001: 4417ff.

and the medieval nobility to the capitalist class of Marxist theory.[97] Not surprisingly, the ownership of urban and landed property played an equally important role for the priestly families under investigation and should be seen as a fundamental building block of their collective identity. J.P. Nielsen, following Levi-Strauss' theoretical model of the 'house society', settles on a particularly acute dependency of the family identity on the paternal estate (*bīt abi*), which consisted of real estate, among other things, and whose preservation was all-important.[98] He even points to some examples in which the ownership of a specific type of physical property seems to have prompted individuals to 'claim more permanent identities in the form of family names' (see more on this in Chapter 6.2.2).[99]

2.1 *Residential Property*

There is no doubt that the priestly families and their close contacts all had their main residences in Borsippa. This was their most important piece of property and could be of exceptional monetary value.[100] However, much more important than the (passive) economic value of urban property was the symbolic, social, and emotional significance that it conveyed upon the inhabitants. While already millennia-old by the time of the Neo-Babylonian period, the ideological dichotomy between sedentism and pastoralism, and between civilised town-dweller and barbaric nomad,[101] was still very much alive in the psyche of the urban upper stratum as it was being transmitted through the literary canon of the scribal education and its devastating consequences witnessed even in their recent past. According to chronicle ABC 24, a scholarly product of the Borsippean priesthood,[102] King Erība-Marduk (ca. 770s BCE) expelled the traditionally nomadic people of the Arameans 'who had taken by murder and insurrection the fields of the inhabitants of Babylon and Borsippa'.[103] Not only did life within city walls protect someone from such marauders, attacking armies or other unearthly forces, there can in fact be little doubt that

97 For a concise theoretical overview of various aristocratic groups, especially in pre-modern Europe, see Mączak 2001.

98 Nielsen 2011: 16–17, 276–280.

99 Nielsen 2011: 292.

100 For a good example in support of this, readers are referred to BM 26576 = AH XV no. 192 from the Rē'i-alpi archive. Among the many pieces of property that are being sold, the housing plot is by far the most expensive one, raising no less than 26 minas of silver. Cf. Jursa *et al.* 2010: 169–172, with some general considerations on the use and value of Babylonian houses.

101 Van de Mieroop 1997: 42–62.

102 Waerzeggers 2012.

103 Grayson 1975: 182–183; ABC 24, rev. 9–13.

for the urban Babylonians the only civilised mode of life was city life. It was not for nothing that the gods had chosen cities as their primary dwellings on earth.

Babylonian cities in the first millennium BCE were still to a large extent, if not always in terms of *Realpolitik*, then at least on an ideologically level, self-governed by a number of (overlapping) civic institutions that held the right to enforce a legal order upon its local population, even if the king remained the ultimate authority.[104] The sources make it abundantly clear that living in cities inspired a sense of communal affiliation that differed from the notion of kinship, the primary mode of identification, and prevailed over (ethnic, social, professional) diversity to unite the citizens, that is the city as a whole, on the basis of political identity and local belonging.[105] It stands to reason that living in town, if not actually owning a town house, must have facilitated admittance into this socio-political entity and enabled the residents to enjoy its communal rights and privileges.[106]

Our understanding of how residence relates to Babylonian family structure in the first millennium is limited, because a more general study that would integrate both the archaeological evidence and the material culture with the textual evidence is still outstanding.[107] There was apparently both great variation in the size of dwellings and a multiplicity of possible household or residence

104 For the various civic institutions in first-millennium Babylonia, see Barjamovic 2004. See for the local administration in the Babylonian towns and the centralising power of the monarchy, Jursa 2014b: 130–131.

105 Barjamovic 2004: 49ff. The high frequency of demonyms in the Assyrian state correspondence (i.e. *Barsipaya* = Borsippean(s), *Urukaya* = Urukean(s)) and the kinship terminology in this respect (i.e. citizens would term themselves 'son' (*māru*) of a city), shows that affiliation to a city was a defining marker in the way this urban population identified itself and was identified by outsiders.

106 Note, however, that this picture is somewhat complicated by the fact that people, while living in another town, could still uphold their traditional political/residential identity generations after migration. This was clearly the case in Neo-Babylonian Uruk, where one hears of two separate entities: the 'Babylonians' and 'Urukeans'. The group of the 'Babylonians' consisted indeed of families that migrated south from the capital to Uruk, and monopolised important posts in the religious institution until the early reign of Xerxes (Kessler 2004). Similar dynamics can be found in other Babylonian towns, cf. Jursa *et al.* 2010: 136–137, Waerzeggers 2014.

107 This and related issues is tackled in a forthcoming study of H.D. Baker [*forthcoming* (b)], on the urban landscape in first millennium Babylonia. For available studies on Neo-Babylonian housing readers are referred to other articles by this author, including Baker 2004: 47ff., Baker 2007, Baker 2010, Baker 2014, and Baker 2015. See Baker [*forthcoming* (a)] for the study of first millennium houses and urbanism from a theoretical point of view, and Miglus 1999: 307–314, for an archaeological catalogue.

scenarios.[108] Yet, there is no doubt that the household formed the fundamental unit of organisation in Babylonian society. Typically, an urban household consisted of a nuclear family of around five individuals,[109] that is, a married couple with a number of unmarried children, but it could be supplemented by the presence of a widowed parent or sister, slaves, and tenants. H.D. Baker has argued that instances of adult sons living with their fathers were not all that common in Neo-Babylonian society because they typically established their own households elsewhere upon marriage.[110] The same stands for brothers sharing the same house. At the death of the head of family, the oldest son would receive the principal or paternal home, sometimes referred to as *bītu rabû* or big house.

For the outside world these 'big' houses must have served as a clear indicator of wealth and status. However, for the owners and their families this property might actually have been much more important from a symbolic point of view. The archaeological record tells us that in the Neo-Babylonian period it was still common practice to bury relatives under the floor of the house.[111] While certainly not all inhabitants of a city could have been buried in this way, it stands to reason that this custom was practiced by the elites, like priests, who owned their own housing plots and held traditions in high regard. A proper burial was of paramount importance for the ghost of the deceased to enter the underworld. Failing to observe formal funerary rites, for whatever reason, could cause the ghost of king and slave alike to wander the face of the earth and torment the living.[112] An intramural burial was a good way to guarantee an undisturbed final resting place. This practice was, certainly in earlier times, closely linked to ancestral worship. Deceased ancestors received funerary offerings known as *kispu*.[113] This ritual, held at regular intervals by the head of the family, involved the offering of food and drinks, facilitated through pipes in the floor, which served to ease the lives of the dead in the netherworld. This domestic ritual represented the central moment of contact between the dead and the living and forged a direct link between past and present. Even though

108 See Baker 2014 for a concise overview of house size in the first millennium.

109 Baker 2014. However, a glimpse at the genealogical tables in Waerzeggers 2010:731–743 shows that some of the priestly families from Borsippa could be substantially larger. For example, both Marduk-šumu-ibni//Ilia (A) and Rēmūt-Nabû//Rē'i-alpi are known to have had at least five (grown) children.

110 Baker 2014: 14–15.

111 Potts 1997: 230–235, Van de Mieroop 1997: 83, Baker 1995: 218f., and Boehmer *et al.* 1995: 34ff.

112 Schwemer 2011: 430ff., Scurlock 2006, and Frahm 1999.

113 Tsukimoto 1985, van der Toorn 1996a: 42–65, and van der Toorn 1996b.

the textual evidence for the existence of the *kispu* or other forms of ancestor worship during the Neo-Babylonian period comes in very short supply,[114] it is hard to believe that priests who identified themselves through illustrious ancestral family names and showed a deep concern for lineage and origins otherwise would have failed to pay homage to their departed forefathers. Whether there existed a formal ritual or not, the fact remains that with the burying of relatives within the residence, the emotional value of the paternal house must have increased enormously among the family. It changed the house from an ordinary residential space into a locus of a collective identity that anchored the family's history into the very foundations of its structures.

In addition to the ancestral cult, the Babylonian house might also have accommodated an altar or shrine of a personal or family god. This form of domestic worship has been studied by K. van der Toorn who drew predominantly on second millennium evidence.[115] Indeed, house chapels and rooms with altars that have been identified as the loci of such worship in earlier periods[116] are entirely absent from the Neo-Babylonian archaeological record.[117] While

---

114 Tsukimoto 1985: 118–124 and Baker 2011: 547. Two texts are of particular interest here. The first piece of evidence comes in the form of a curse formula found in a fragmentary tablet from the city of Nippur dated to the second year of King Aššur-ētel-ilāni (ca. 629/28 BCE): 'Whoever breaks this agreement', the curse says, 'may Šamaš, the judge of heaven and earth, deprive him from a son who would libate water (*nāq mê*) for him and may his dead spirit (*eṭemmu*) in the [...] of the netherworld be robbed of *kispu*'. See BE 8 4: Rev. ll. 4–6 in San Nicolò 1951: no. 44. The reference to the *kispu* in this private administrative document indicates, at the very least, that ordinary citizens still honoured this tradition. The second text that mentions *kispu* is the ᶠAdad-guppi stele. See Schaudig 2001: 500–513. This inscription was found in the city of Harrān and purportedly written by ᶠAdad-guppi, mother of King Nabonidus and possible priestess of the god Sîn. In this (fictive) autobiography, ᶠAdad-guppi tells us that she was born during the reign of the Assyrian King Assurbanipal and lived for nearly a hundred years. Surviving all the eminent kings of the Neo-Babylonian dynasty and of an extremely pious disposition, ᶠAdad-guppi declares that it was left to her alone to carry out the offerings for the deceased monarchs in the following words: 'monthly, incessantly, in my good garments I brought them oxen, rams, bread, premium beer, wine, oil, honey and garden fruits of all sorts as *kispu*'. See Schaudig 2001: 507–508. Needless to say, this inscription cannot be taken at face value as it served a very specific political purpose, i.e. to bolster her son's right to rule as king of Babylon. It is doubtful whether ᶠAdad-guppi had actually carried out the *kispu* rituals, which were certainly not among the conventional duties required from a priestess. Yet, the message is clear. By performing the *kispu* rituals for the former kings, ᶠAdad-guppi assumed the responsibilities that conventionally fell to the first-born son, thus making, by extension, her son a suitable candidate, if not the rightful heir, to the Babylonian throne and, indeed, the Assyrian Empire. See Tsukimoto 1985: 122–123.

115 van der Toorn 1996a: 66–150.

116 Postgate 1992: 99–101.

117 Baker 2011: 547.

this might indicate changes in popular religion, there are some indications that suggest that domestic veneration still existed in the period under investigation. One example comes from Borsippa. BM 96331 (Dar 30) is an administrative document from the Bēliya'u archive dealing with the return of two items that were being held as collateral (*maškanu*) for a loan. The first item was a stand for vats (*šidattu,* note that this item was also used in the cult, cf. CAD Š/II: 402–403) and the second a *ṣibtu*-garment of the goddess Ninlil (^{túg}*ṣibtu ša* ^{d}*Ninlil*). While it is not inconceivable that a priest could have manipulated temple property for their own ends, it is perhaps more likely that the divine garment, and perhaps the *šidattu* too, belonged to the cultic paraphernalia of a domestic shrine of the debtor's family. However, this remains purely speculative. Still, whether or not specific rooms existed in the house that functioned as area of worship in the form of a chapel with altar, Babylonian houses hosted a variegated series of rituals that involved the nuclear and extended family. Even if these sacraments did not involve the veneration of a domestic god, they at least commemorated *rites de passage* like the birth of a child, the marriage of a daughter, and the death of a parent.

A final aspect I would like to mention with respect to the ownership of urban property concerns neighbourhoods. Beyond the mud-brick walls that accommodated domestic life stretched a network of streets, passages, and back alleys that linked neighbouring houses into larger residential units. Scholars have often classified these neighbourhoods as socially mixed units, hosting large as well as small houses of rich and poor alike.[118] While this seems to have applied to various periods of Mesopotamian history, H.D. Baker suggests that this was not always the case in the first millennium city since 'certain classes of society resided in separate districts'.[119] Drawing especially on evidence from Uruk and Babylon, she points to the fact that the residential areas surrounding the temples were inhabited mainly by (middle-ranking) temple personnel whose houses show a much greater degree of homogeneity in terms of size.[120] This trend seems to have persisted into the Hellenistic period.[121]

Baker's idea might find support in the evidence from Borsippa examined in previous chapters. Priests' circles of intimacy were composed exclusively of individuals from the urban upper stratum, the majority of whom belonged to priestly families. In light of the frequency at which such individuals occur in

---

118 See Stone 1987 for a study of two neighbourhoods in second-millennium Nippur. For a more concise survey, see Stone 2007 in which some comparisons are made to neighbourhoods dating to the Islamic era.

119 Baker 2011: 543–544.

120 This trend towards homogeneity of house size has also been noted in Miglus 1999: 206.

121 Baker 2011: 554. This issue is dealt with more extensively by Baker [*forthcoming* (b)].

the archives, especially as witnesses and scribes, one might suggest that there was at least some overlap between the circles of intimacy and the neighbourhood network since trust as well as physical proximity might have been factors determining someone's presence at a business recording.[122] Living in town, that is, owning a house, served the inhabitant in more ways than providing shelter, status, political affiliation, and family identity. Besides the prestige of living in a fancy part of town, it gave access to an extensive social network of neighbours, among whom confidants, business partners, spouses and friends could be found. There is no doubt that these neighbourhood connections inspired solidarity among its residents who, in addition to paying a communal tax (*dīku ša bābti* or 'levy of the city warden'[123]), must have shared many more responsibilities and concerns.

2.2 *Landed Property*

Landed property was a key attribute of priestly families, forming the traditional counterpart to their prebendary titles.[124] As opposed to houses,[125] landholdings represented the main income-producing asset. It allowed these families to live a (relatively) luxurious life and bought them the necessary time and money to enter the less lucrative service of the gods, or to invest in cultural capital through scribal education, and participate in local politics and decision-making.[126]

---

122 See Chapters 4.2 and 5.1. The clearest case comes from the Bēliya'u archive. The most frequently attested contact (more than forty times) is Bēl-ēṭir//Šigûa who, besides his recurring involvement as scribe, witness, and business partner, also lived or at least owned a house next to Šaddinnu//Bēliya'u. While there is plenty of evidence on housing in the Borsippa corpus, there are two obstacles that hinder the study of neighbourhood networks. First, the crucial information on neighbours is usually rendered in an abridged form, omitting full filiation since this was only of secondary importance to the contract and known to the parties anyway. Second, the available information usually deals with secondary houses that were rented out. As a consequence, we usually remain uninformed about the main residence of the archive owners.

123 For this tax, see Jursa and Waerzeggers 2009: 251–252.

124 This is borne out by some of the royal grants (*kudurrus*) from the early first millennium that show that the beneficiary received land in addition to the prebendary title. See van Driel 2002: 74–75.

125 Even if people did invest in houses, unless they owned several, they generally did not use them to generate wealth. See Jursa *et al.* 2010: 169–172. There are of course exceptions among priestly families. A case at hand is Šaddinnu//Bēliya'u who ran a housing business in town. See Jursa 2005: 81–82 and Jursa *et al.* 2010: 170f.

126 A recent analysis of household income in first-millennium Babylonia suggests that the yearly income of Borsippa's priestly families ranged from three to thirty times subsistence requirements. See Jursa *et al.* 2010: 296–305.

While this remains to be proven, in the light of other ancient and (pre-) modern agricultural societies landownership might well have been a necessary condition for elite membership and political participation in Babylonia.[127] Land surely invested the owner with status and (social) power, not in the least in terms of patron-client-relationships. Following a social-scientific understanding, the phenomenon commonly known as patronage or clientelism 'involves asymmetric but mutually beneficial, open-ended transactions based on the differential control by individuals or groups over the access and flow of resources in stratified societies'.[128] We have seen previously that all of Borsippa's priests owned at least one, but more often a couple of agricultural plots in the countryside. This allowed them to provide selective access to the landed resources they controlled. Because they were preoccupied with running their affairs in town, priests hired tenants who were often socially and economically weaker to cultivate and protect their gardens.[129] In other words, landownership allowed priestly (and other landed) families to employ individuals into their service: individuals who in return for a relatively modest remuneration, i.e. material security,[130] provided the landowner with their material and human resources. I have demonstrated earlier that these contractual relationships between landlord and tenant or, more appropriately, between patron and client could be very stable and sometimes lasted across generations.[131]

---

127 Barjamovic 2004: 68–69 and Jursa *et al.* 2010: 57–58. This could be the case for the social/legal group referred to as *mār-banê*. This term has often been translated as 'free man' or 'fully fledged citizen' (as opposed to, for example, unfree slaves) although some contexts indicate a more specific elevated status favouring a rendering as 'notable'. See Jursa 2005: 9–10, 15. In general, it seems that the term *mār-banê* refers to the politically active citizenry. See Barjamovic 2004: 77ff. It is noteworthy that in some contexts, landownership and *mār-banê* status are coupled. See BM 102319 (Dar 05), BM 96309 (Dar 09?), BM 29487 (Dar 12), BM 28954 (Dar [x]), BM 29020 (Xer 02), and VS 5 137 ([-]). All these texts are cultivation contracts stipulating that if the tenant neglects his work and does not cultivate the land under his responsibility, he must compensate the owner 'according to the yield of the neighbour', i.e. 'in accordance with two *mār-banês*' ('*akī itû šibšu akī ša 2 mār-banê … immidūšu*', in date cultivation contracts, or '*iṣṣid*' in barley cultivation contracts). Perhaps this should be understood as 'like two *mār-banês* (read: gentlemen) they impose (a penalty) upon him', that is, they come to a gentlemen's agreement.

128 See Roniger 2001 for a concise overview of the different ideas and traditions of patron-client-relationships in the social sciences.

129 While the evidence shows that our priests usually handed the management of their property over to individuals from within their social (family name bearing) stratum, it is likely that they in turn hired tenants from lower strata to do the actual physical work. See Chapter 2.3.

130 van Driel 1988: 132–133, van Driel 1990: 241ff., Jursa 1995: 126, and Jursa *et al.* 2010: 367, 431ff.

131 Similar dynamics of patron and client must have existed in the domain of house letting.

To what extent this clientele could be mobilised for political purposes or how it contributed to the patrons' prestige is an issue that awaits future investigation.

Landed property was economically and socially important and therefore highly valued by the priestly families under investigation. Individuals were clearly reluctant to sell their land as the goal was to pass it on to the next generation (see Chapter 2.1.5). In numerous cases it can be shown that sellers only disposed of their property as a result of economic hardship and indebtedness.[132] That this property was not only important to the individual owner, but contributed to the status and identity of his or her larger family follows from the various manifestations of the *bīt-abi* in matters of landownership.[133] As observed by J.P. Nielsen, there existed a correlation between the ownership of specific property and the desire among the upper-stratum families to claim more permanent identities.[134] A highly interesting case is preserved on the diorite stone tablet known as BBSt 28.[135] This commemorative inscription, dated in the ninth century BCE, records the grant of land by King Nabû-apla-iddin to a temple-enterer and namesake called Nabû-apla-iddin, son of Abunāya, descendant of Aqar-Nabû. This document is interesting for two reasons. First, there is the reference to the *bīt-abi.* Priest Nabû-apla-iddin claims that this land belonged to his paternal estate (*eqil bīt-ab*[*ia*...], l. 4). He appeals to the king, rather dramatically, to grant him this land so that his paternal house may not fall into oblivion (*šarru lirīmannima bīt-abia ana ṣīti la uṣṣi*, Rev. ll. 1–3). Second, there is Nabû-apla-iddin's filiation. In the long sixth century both Abunāya and Aqar-Nabû were known as family names, especially in the region of Borsippa. The question is whether this was already the case at the time of BBSt 28. Aqar-Nabû might already have functioned as a family name. Nabû-apla-iddin is primarily referred to as 'son (*māru*) of Abunāya', whereas the owner of a neighbouring plot was identified as Nabû-šaqû-ina-māti 'son (*māru*) of Aqar-Nabû'. It is thus possible to take Aqar-Nabû either as the family name or as the name of Nabû apla-iddin's actual grandfather (Nabû-šaqû-ina-māti then being his uncle), and Abunāya as the name of his father that happens to coincide with a (later known) family name. Yet, Nielsen raises the interesting question, whether the case at hand might not actually point to a segmentation of lineages and the (subsequent) emergence of the family name, Abunāya, based on the ownership of a concrete piece of property.[136] This

132 For an extensive list of such cases, see Wunsch 1999: 397–398^{+14}.

133 Wunsch 2003: no. 40, no. 42, and no. 44.

134 Nielsen 2011: 292.

135 King 1912: 104–106 and Paulus 2014: 644–646. The following discussion can be found more extensively in Nielsen 2011: 75–78.

136 Nielsen 2011: 78.

proceeds from the fact that, on the one hand, both Aqar-Nabû and Abunāya as family names are geographically restricted to Borsippa (and to a lesser extent Babylon and Sippar),[137] and, on the other hand, and, to my mind more compelling, that the property (re)claimed by Nabû-apla-iddin in BBSt 28 is referred to as *bīt Abunāya* (Rev. l. 15). The identity of this property as *bīt Abunāya* would have prompted heirs in subsequent generations to identify themselves as descendants of Abunāya in order to bolster their claim, thus resulting in the use of the patronymic Abunāya as a family name.

This nominal connection between family name and landed property was certainly not an alien concept to the Borsippeans of the long sixth century who used it specifically in relation to their *hanšû* lands. As I showed in Chapter 2.1, this land came into being through royal land allotment schemes in the early first millennium BCE. The principal beneficiaries of these grants were urban elite families whose loyalty the kings thereby wished to secure. Unlike other types of land usually identified on the basis of its geographic features alone, *hanšû* land in Borsippa was typically identified by the family name of the original beneficiary clan, i.e. *hanšû ša bīt Ea-ilūtu-bani* and *hanšû ša bīt Gallābu*, thus very much reminiscent of *bīt Abunāya* in BBSt 28.[138] This nominal connection between property and family was obviously very strong as the land retained its denomination even after it was lost to the original family. This accorded the families with a sense of permanence and antiquity and, more importantly, it projected their identity on specific properties that allowed them to lay claims to specific shares in the territory of their city, a territory that was carved-up between the temple, the crown, and the wider elite population.

Landed property was thus of great importance to the priestly families under investigation. It was the cornerstone of their subsistence strategy and it accorded them prestige as well as social and political power. Landownership also provided families with a platform to broadcast their collective identity, which was being anchored firmly in the landscape of their native country. The importance of this property and their rightful claim to it was not overlooked by the Borsippean elites who recorded it in their national history. I have already mentioned the passage from ABC 24 above. This chronicle, written within the 'academic' milieu of Borsippa, recalls the loss and subsequent restoration of land to the citizens of Babylon and Borsippa.[139] It is interesting to note that the

137 Wunsch 2014.

138 On the existence of a *hanšû ša bīt Abunāya* in the Babylon-Borsippa region, see Appendix 2.

139 See Chapter 2.1.2 and Grayson 1975: no. 24.

issue of landownership did make it explicitly into official history writing while, for example, prebends did not.[140]

In conclusion, it should be remembered that the ownership of houses as well as land was not a prerogative of the priestly families alone. There is ample evidence of other (both higher and lower strata) individuals owning real estate. In contrast, as a result of targeted royal interventions, ownership of *hanšû* land in Borsippa seems to have been reserved, at least traditionally, for the highest stratum of society. This domain held the concerns of the paternal houses of both priestly and non-priestly families who sought to strengthen their collective identity and claim continuity with their shared past by forging a durable nominal bond between families and their property.

3 Literacy and Scribal Education

The income that priestly families drew from their landholdings and to a lesser extent from their prebendary duties was not only invested in real estate and other (material) property. As part of the wealthier strata of Babylonian local society these rentier families accrued enough annual revenue to be able to also invest in cultural capital, namely, in the form of a scribal education. The Neo- (and Late-)Babylonian scribal education has been studied by P. Gesche based on the large corpus of 'school texts' now housed in the British Museum.[141] Following differences in text genre and tablet shape, she was able to distinguish different levels of scribal training.[142] The necessary first step for a student was to familiarise himself with the scribe's tool (stylus) and the writing medium (clay tablet)[143] before he could start his 'first grade' training and learn the fundaments of writing by copying extracts from lexical texts and other similar lists. While the student continued working on this genre during his 'second grade', the curriculum now also involved reproducing letters, contracts, colophons, proverbs, mathematical exercises, and literary compositions. The last category included such texts as the Epic of Gilgameš, the Epic of Creation (*Enūma Eliš*), and the Topographical Description of Babylon (*Tintir = Babylon*). These are of

140 Perhaps the walls of Borsippa and the Ezida simply did their work in defending the city from outside invasion, thus allowing the cult to continue without interruption since time immemorial, that is, without disturbances of a degree worth mentioning.

141 Gesche 2000. For the criteria used to identify a 'school text', see Gesche 2000: 55–57.

142 Gesche 2000: 44–52.

143 For the writing stylus and the methods used to make a proper clay tablet, see, most recently, Taylor 2011: 5ff. As it turns out, fashioning a decent tablet was not as easy as it sounds.

special importance as it was through these compositions that the fundamental values of Babylonian (high) culture were activated and transmitted most clearly among the literati.[144] At this stage the student had acquired a general working knowledge of the scribal art and its textual genres and could read and write cuneiform for his personal use.[145] However, this was not the end of Babylonian scribal education and some students continued with what Gesche calls the *Fachausbildungen*. In this final stage that was certainly not pursued by all, students received a more advanced and specialised training, instructing them in the arts of ritual specialists like that of the exorcists, astronomers or diviners or preparing them for a career in civic administration as a notary scribe or accountant.[146] The student, having spent most of his teen years perfecting his writing, was now a professional scribe, thoroughly skilled in the native Babylonian cuneiform lore.

Many school texts discussed by Gesche have been found inside temples. While this suggests that these religious institutions provided for the formal scribal training of presumably the young priests-to-be, the evidence can at least in part be interpreted differently. Some of these school texts bear colophons, perhaps better understood as votive inscriptions, stating that they were dedicated in a *rite-de-passage*-like act by the student to Nabû, the Babylonian god of writing and patron deity of scribes. The inscription on these specially manufactured tablets usually consisted of a prayer to the god, followed by wishes for the well-being of the student and his family.[147] Accordingly, one of the largest batches of school texts known from Neo-Babylonian times – almost all of them originally bore colophons – was dug up in the Nabû-ša-hare ('Nabû of accounts') temple in Babylon.[148]

Other evidence suggests that scribal education took place privately as well, that is, within the family from father to son. The clearest example comes from the archive of the Šangû-Šamaš (A) family from Sippar, dating between the sixth and early fifth centuries BCE, published by M. Jursa.[149] The Šangû-Šamaš was a prominent priestly family, which besides various shares in the service of the brewers, bakers, and butchers of Šamaš, also owned a prestigious

144 Gesche 2000: 149–152. For the figure of the Babylonian king and the dissemination of the royal ideology in the scribal curriculum, see Beaulieu 2007b: 140–148.

145 Gesche 2000: 61–169, 211f.

146 Gesche 2000: 213–218.

147 Gesche 2000: 153–166. For more on the contents of these dedicated school exercises and their social and religious context, see Veldhuis 2013 (with previous literature).

148 See Robson 2011: 560 and Cavigneaux 1981 for the publication of this collection, consisting of some 130 texts.

149 Jursa 1999. For a brief overview of this archive, see Jursa 2005: 127–128.

temple-enterer prebend. Together with the roughly two hundred private administrative tablets published by M. Jursa, some seventy magico-medical texts have been found, suggesting that members of the family also functioned as exorcists (*āšipu*) and healers (*asû*).[150] In both 'parts' of the archive, M. Jursa and I. Finkel independently found traces of on-going scribal training: this idea is based, among other things, on the high number of duplicates, unusual orthography, spelling mistakes, sloppy handwriting, and the unmistakable fact that some of the medical texts were purportedly written on dictation (*ana pî šaṭir*).[151] While this presents clear evidence for scribal training at home, these private texts do differ somewhat from the standardised school texts studied by P. Gesche in both contents and format, suggesting that we might be dealing with a different kind of education – for example, after school training – in this archive. A more systematic (museological) investigation of the presence of school texts in private archives is still outstanding.[152]

Be that as it may, this observation is significant for the topic currently under examination because it sheds light on a new dimension of family life and identity formation. If it is true that the scribal education in Neo-Babylonian times took place within the family, that is, transmitted from father to son, it follows that the concern of the paternal house did not only apply to real estate and prebendary titles. It was equally responsible for the transmission of scribal knowledge and for the preservation of the central concepts, symbols, and values of Babylonian culture, that is, cultural capital, from one generation to the next. The paternal house could thus be identified as the primary locus at which the new generation during its formative years was being submitted to and instilled with a very specific cultural identity that had been upheld among family members since time immemorial. In this light the colophon on the dedicated school text of young Bēl-erība is self-evident and his concerns easily understandable. He asks the god Nabû for 'the preservation of his offspring, the preservation of his house and the preservation of his paternal house (*bīt-abi*) – that the foundations of his house and that of his paternal house (*bīt-abi*) may remain firm'.[153]

But who exactly enjoyed a scribal education and how widespread was (cuneiform) literacy in these communities? Even if this is a conundrum in

150 Finkel 2000.

151 Jursa 1999: 12–31 and Finkel 2000.

152 Note, however, that the *āšipu* archives of Uruk (such as in the case of Iqīša) are usually explained as resulting from training as well as professional activities. See Clancier 2014 and Clancier 2009: 81–101.

153 Frahm 1995, ll. 11–12: gi nunuz-*šú* gi é-*šú* gi é [(lú)]ad-*šú* *kun-nu* suhuš-*šú* *kun-nu* suhuš é lúad-*šú*.

modern times still, M. Jursa postulated that literacy in first millennium temple communities was certainly not only reserved for high administrators, temple clerks, and ritual specialists such as temple-enterers, cultic singers, exorcists for whom reading and writing must have been a professional necessity, but also common among the lower 'purveying' priesthoods.[154] In fact, most of the evidence we have for literacy among priests concerns prebendary families from this last group. Based on a survey of the available priestly family archives, Jursa informs us that for twenty-four of the thirty-five (well-preserved) archives there is evidence that at least one of the chief protagonists is explicitly attested as scribe.[155] This implies that more than two-thirds of the priestly families were literate.[156] Moreover, the fact that it is uncommon for an archive to contain documents written by the archive holder himself suggests that this figure represents only a minimum. For a further number of archive holders, literacy can be assumed based on their occupation – for example, that of governor – or on the presence of literary ('library') texts found together with their administrative documents. We can be 'virtually certain', according to M. Jursa, 'that many, if not most of the first millennium priests could read and write'.[157]

Even if most of the documentation we have on first millennium Babylonian socio-economic history was produced by temple communities, which can be identified as the locus in which continuation, elaboration, and transmission of Babylonian religio-intellectual culture was guaranteed until the final stages of cuneiform writing in the first century CE,[158] priests did not have a monopoly on literacy. This transpires in the first place from cuneiform archives of non-priestly families who filed their business transactions and wrote their letters in cuneiform, the most extensive one being the Egibi family archive from Babylon whose *raison d'être* would be moot if not pointless were the archive holders unable to read and write. A similar picture of a more dispersed and less exclusive literacy can be deemed from taking a brief glimpse at the scribes attested in the Borsippa corpus itself. Of the approximately 4,600 individuals mentioned in the archive sample of the Ea-ilūtu-bani, Gallābu, Ilia, and Rēʾi-alpi families, some 700 individuals (approximately 15%) are attested as scribe. This number is obviously lower than the one argued above – no doubt a reflection of the

154 Jursa 2011: 191.

155 Ibid.

156 On the different levels of literacy during the third and second millennium BCE, see Veldhuis 2011. Private archives such as the Nappāhu and Sîn-ilī archives from Babylon reveal the activities of scribes who seem to have dropped out of scribal training on a relatively low level. See Baker 2004: 16–17.

157 Jursa 2011: 191.

158 Beaulieu 2006, Beaulieu 2007a, Clancier 2011, and Robson 2011.

fact that scribes commonly figure as one out of about six participants to a contract and a result of the practice by Babylonians to rely on a selected number of scribes (see Chapter 4.2). Nevertheless, the filiation of the scribes clearly shows that advanced literacy was achieved by priestly families as well as non-priestly families, even if the latter are fewer in quantitative terms. Besides a handful of scribes who did not bear tripartite filiation at all, the latter group includes families like the Bābāya, Barihi, Banê-ša-ilia, Hulamišu, Iddināya, Iššakku, ᶠMaqartu, Nikkāya, Nūr-Sîn, Pappāya, Purkullu, Pūṣu, Raksu, Ša-haṭṭu-ēreš, Ṣillāya, Šabrû, and Zērūtu. While we came across some of these families in earlier chapters, others have left next to no trace in the documentation at hand and it should be clear that their primary locus of activity was not the temple institution.

While writing was becoming more available to lower strata of society in first millennium Babylonia,[159] much of the day-to-day business in the suburbs and certainly in the countryside did not necessitate written cuneiform documentation. If documentation was needed, then many might have favoured the Aramaic script and language instead.[160] In Neo-Babylonian society one can therefore speak of a (highly) restricted spread of literacy. In addition, mastering the art of cuneiform was time-consuming and it can be taken as a given that this pursuit was largely reserved for those who commanded enough money and time. Cuneiform writing was very much a traditional urban affair at a time when Aramaic was becoming increasingly prevalent.[161] While Aramaic was becoming the dominant vernacular in Babylonia and the principal language of empire, especially under Persian rule,[162] it did not supplant the use of local languages. The cuneiform script continued to be favoured in Neo-Babylonian temples and their communities.[163] Owing to the use of perishable material like papyrus and leather, it must be said that the chances of recovering Aramaic administration are gravely diminished, but even so it is very likely that the families under investigation were no strangers to speaking, reading,

159 Jursa *et al.* 2010: 265–266.

160 Note, however, the use of cuneiform in the community of Neirabians in Dhorme 1928, and Tolini 2015, as well as in similar foreign communities like the Judeans from Āl-Yāhūdu in Pearce and Wunsch 2014. It is questionable whether these minorities could actually read the texts or whether they were simply kept by virtue of, for instance, their enduring legal importance. Evidence from Āl-Yāhūdu suggests that at least some individuals kept cuneiform records without actually being able to decipher them, according to personal communication with C. Wunsch. There are a few other archives that stem from a rural rather than city background. See Jursa 2005: 149–151.

161 Jursa 2014a, Beaulieu 2006.

162 Kuhrt 2014.

163 Jursa 2011.

and probably writing it. Still, so far the Borsippa corpus has not revealed any Aramaic endorsements, the absence of which could point to a deliberate preference for cuneiform if not a rejection of the Aramaic alphabetic script.[164]

In conclusion, it should be clear that the ability to read and write Babylonian cuneiform was not reserved for priests and their families alone. The wider urban elite shared the same cultural values and adhered to the same scribal traditions. Non-priestly families produced scribes and kept cuneiform archives like their priestly counterparts. This is not to say that everyone was equally literate. However, one can assume that the majority of elite families aspired to functional literacy, meaning that they had a rudimentary knowledge of cuneiform and were able to read a debt note and write their names. Even if there is no proof that literacy was a precondition to integrate and operate in Neo-Babylonian high society, being at least functionally literate not only meant that a person was much less at the mercy of middlemen in terms of business and communication, but it must also have opened doors to more prestigious civic functions and public roles. For well-to-do families it can only have been a wise and desirable investment to provide their heirs with at least a rudimentary knowledge of cuneiform. The transmission of scribal knowledge presumably within the paternal house should be seen as an important means for these Babylonian families to pass on their cultural and professional identity to the next generation. Moreover, participation in this cuneiform culture not only nurtured a distinct *esprit de corps* based on a set of common norms and values, but also represented a vehicle through which the urban elite families were able to reproduce and consolidate their dominant and privileged position in society for the better part of the first millennium BCE.

4 Language

Berossos, the Babylonian priest of Marduk who wrote a historical account of his native culture and its age-old traditions for the new Greek audience

164 These Aramaic dockets are short summary captions in Aramaic incised or inked on cuneiform tablets from first-millennium Assyria and Babylonia. The contents, geographical spread, and social implications of these dockets are the subject of a Leiden-based PhD manuscript by R. Sonnevelt. Note, however, that BM 25636 is a text rendering an alphabet in cuneiform script that, judging from its presence in the 98-2-16 collection, belongs to the Borsippa corpus. See Waerzeggers 2005: 349. Consequently, this text might indicate that local priests did engage with Aramaic, be it, perhaps, on a more intellectual level. For an edition of this text, see Geller 1997/2000.

in the beginning of the third century BCE, recounts that 'in Babylonia there was a large number of people of different ethnic origins who had settled Chaldea [i.e. Babylonia]'.[165] While he projects this situation back into primeval times we can take it as a reflection of the ethno-linguistic reality of the Late-Babylonian period. A very similar image is evoked in Genesis 11: 1–9 in which the blasphemous construction of the Tower of Babel led to the universal *confusio linguarum*. This episode in the Hebrew Bible was no doubt a reaction to the superabundance of different languages the Judeans encountered in first millennium Babylonia. Anyone entering the ancient capital of Babylon must have been welcomed with a veritable cacophony of languages including Babylonian, Aramaic, Egyptian, Arabic, and perhaps even some learned Sumerian mixed up with the tongues of various deportees from distant areas such as Judea, Phoenicia, Lydia, and Ionia, among many others.[166] This mixed linguistic bag can only have expanded with the conquest by Cyrus the Great in 539 and the establishment of the Persian Empire. In short, the linguistic landscape in Babylonian society of the first millennium can undoubtedly be described as highly diverse.

Yet, the variety in both population and language is not reflected faithfully in the existing documentation, which pertains largely to the urban upper strata of society. This has often led to a somewhat skewed representation of the Babylonian state as being governed by the interaction and negotiation between the monarchy and the old Babylonian towns, thereby leaving a highly influential third entity out of the equation: the Chaldean and Aramean groups.[167] During the late second and early first millennium Mesopotamia witnessed a massive influx of Arameans and Chaldeans from the West (Syria and beyond) who gradually infiltrated the region and colonised the rural areas, according to the communis opinio.[168] It is thought that the former settled mainly in the North and along the Tigris in the East, whereas the latter could be found along the Euphrates from Babylon down to the Persian Gulf, effectively taking control of the countryside of the Babylonian heartland.[169] Important for the present topic is that, according to the (traditional) onomastic evidence, both

165 Verbrugghe and Wickersham 1996: 44. For a recent re-evaluation of Berossos and his work known only through references of later historians, see the Groningen-based PhD manuscript by De Breucker 2012.

166 Beaulieu 2006: 193, Dandamaev 2004, and Zadok 2003c.

167 Jursa 2014a: 96ff., Beaulieu 2013a, Beaulieu 2006: 194–197, Barjamovic 2004, *passim*, and Frame 1992: 36–48.

168 Lipiński 2000: 409ff.

169 Lipiński 2000: 216ff., Beaulieu 2013a, and Beaulieu 2006: 194–197.

peoples were Aramaic speaking, thereby complicating the linguistic landscape of the region.[170]

Once settled, these groups could not easily be brushed aside. Between the ninth and seventh centuries BCE the Chaldean armies formed the spearhead of resistance to Assyrian rule, compromising repeated attempts to incorporate Babylonia firmly in the imperial framework.[171] Moreover, Chaldean leaders like Erība-Marduk and Merodach-Baladan II, who occupied the Babylonian throne during the eighth century, plainly demonstrated their successful bid for power. While we lose track of these entities almost completely with the collapse of the Assyrian Empire and the abandonment of its invaluable state archives, there are indications that they were still wielding significant political or, at least, military power in the subsequent Neo-Babylonian period.[172] The most striking testimony is the so-called *Hofkalender*.[173] This text, appended to a building inscription dated to the seventh year of Nebuchadnezzar II (598 BCE.), lists the chief dignitaries of the state who had contributed to the construction of the palace. The list can be divided into the court officials, governors of Babylonian cities and territories in the alluvium, and vassal rulers of subjugated provinces in the West.[174] As has been highlighted most recently by P.-A. Beaulieu, among the second group referred to as the 'territorial leaders of the land of Akkad [i.e. Babylonia]' (*rabûtu ša māt Akkadi*) one finds at least four (and probably more) leaders of Chaldean and Aramean groups, showing that these entities still played an important role in Babylonian state politics.[175] More than just a secondary factor of power, there is increasing evidence that the Neo-Babylonian kings themselves all had a Chaldean or Aramaic background – from Nabopolassar and his supposed connection with the Chaldean people of Dakūru and the usurper King Neriglissar, son of the leader of the Aramean Puqūdus, down to the last King Nabonidus who was not a native Babylonian but rather had his origins in the region of Harrān through his maternal line and was presumably of Aramean stock as well.[176]

This brief sketch of the Aramean and Chaldean presence in Mesopotamia is of importance for the present topic as it helps us understand the complex

170 Lipiński 2000: 216–224 and Beaulieu 2006: 194–197.

171 Brinkman 1968: 260ff. and Frame 1992: 36–48.

172 For occasional references in the late Babylonian sources, see Abraham 2004: no. 88 and Beaulieu 2013a.

173 For an edition of the text, see Unger 1931: 284–285, Beaulieu 2002: 99–101, Beaulieu 2013a: 34, and Da Riva 2013: 206–221. Cf. Jursa 2010b.

174 For this list of officials, see Jursa 2010b: 78–91 and Da Riva 2013: 201–205.

175 Beaulieu 2013: 33–35. See also Jursa 2014b: 127–130.

176 Jursa 2014a: 96–97, Jursa 2014b: 131–133, Jursa 2007b, and Beaulieu 2006: 200.

dynamics of the linguistic landscape of the long sixth century. It was as a result of the gradual infiltration of these people (besides massive deportations) that Assyria was starting to 'Aramaicise' since at least the ninth century BCE, leading to the adoption of Aramaic in the eight and seventh centuries BCE as the second administrative language in the Empire.[177] Styling itself as the natural successor of the Assyrian Empire, the Neo-Babylonian state administration was undoubtedly also bilingual, a practice that was not only facilitated by the high numbers of Arameans and Chaldeans in Babylonia and the 'ethnic' background of its kings, but was further encouraged by the continuous influx of Aramaic-speaking deportees from especially the Levantine corridor.[178] While it has been suggested that both the Assyrian and Babylonian states contributed much to the spread of a standardised form of Aramaic, dating between the seventh and third centuries BCE and known as Imperial or Official Aramaic, this process was accelerated by the establishment of the Persian Empire in 539 BCE.[179] Adopting Aramaic as *the* language of administration and imperial correspondence, the Persian rulers paved the way for Aramaic to disseminate at an unprecedented speed within Babylonia and beyond and to become the *lingua franca* from Bactria in the East to Egypt in the West.[180] It is generally assumed that Aramaic was now also becoming the dominant vernacular in Mesopotamia, if this had not already happened before.[181] However, because the Aramaic documentation from Babylonia was recorded on perishable materials, it has all but disappeared. The only traces left are a relatively small number of Aramaic endorsements on cuneiform tablets and the attestation of the so-called 'parchment-' or 'alphabetic-', that is 'Aramaic-scribe' (*sepīru*), in the documentation. It is thus practically impossible to evaluate the prevalence of Aramaic in this society and very difficult to trace its development and interaction vis-à-vis the local Babylonian language.

The vernacular language in Mesopotamia since at least the beginning of the second millennium BCE was Akkadian, an East-Semitic language that branched off into two main dialects, which are known as Assyrian and Babylonian according to their geographic distribution. After various stages of development in the course of the millennia, the Akkadian rendered in the cuneiform documents of Borsippa's priests from the long sixth century is commonly referred

177 Beaulieu 2006: 188, Nissinen 2014, and Radner 2014: 83–86.

178 Dandamaev 2004, Jursa 2014a, and Streck 2014.

179 Folmer 2011, Folmer 2012, and Kuhrt 2014.

180 Beaulieu 2006: 201–206 and Kuhrt 2014.

181 Beaulieu 2006.

to by Assyriologists as Neo- or Late-Babylonian.[182] In light of the linguistic diversity and especially the increasing spread of Aramaic portrayed above, Assyriologists traditionally relegated these language phases into the 'limbo of spät-und-schlecht'.[183] The frequent occurrence of complicated orthography, frozen forms, incorrect morphology, and corrupt syntax were taken as signs of the general decline of spoken Babylonian, which would gradually have been turning into a hybrid-language.[184] Indeed, some scholars even doubted whether (Late-)Babylonian was still a spoken language at all, recognising it merely as a '*Schrift- und Gelehrtensprache*' (much like Latin in medieval times) while the population spoke Aramaic.[185] In a recent reassessment of the evidence J. Hackl has challenged this idea and argued for a much longer existence of Babylonian as a living vernacular.[186] Concentrating primarily on the letter corpus from the eight until the first centuries BCE – a genre that allowed for more freedom from formulaic conventions of the legal documents and presumably written in a language that comes closest to the actual spoken vernacular – J. Hackl detects various complex linguistic innovations that can best be explained as having taken place in a spoken environment, and propelled by the influence of native speakers. Moreover, quite the opposite from being an Aramaeo-Babylonian *Mischprache*, recent scholarship has refuted much of the previously assumed influence of Aramaic on Babylonian, which displays a rather remarkable resilience to its contact language.[187] The question of when exactly Babylonian stopped being a spoken language and continued merely as a grapholect remains unresolved. Nevertheless, knowing the end result, one fact remains indisputable: Babylonian as a spoken language was on the wane, gradually losing ground to Aramaic, which seems to have become the vernacular of modern-day Iraq at the turn of the millennium.[188]

Be that as it may, Babylonian was undoubtedly still spoken by the priestly families under investigation and presumably represented their primary

182 Hackl [*forthcoming* (a)]. The term 'Neo-Babylonian' usually refers to the Babylonian dialects found in the documents from the Neo-Assyrian period (i.e. until ca. 626 BCE), whereas 'Late-Babylonian' is applied to the Akkadian found in the administrative documents dated in the Neo-Babylonian empire until the disappearance of cuneiform in the first century of our era (ca. 626 BCE–75 CE). However, this classification is based on historical events rather than linguistic development, which Hackl [*forthcoming* (a)] rightly criticises as 'largely arbitrary'.

183 Oppenheim 1967: 43.

184 Hackl [*forthcoming* (a)] and Beaulieu 2013b: 360–362.

185 Von Soden 1995: §2.

186 Hackl [*forthcoming* (a)]. See also Hackl 2007: 149–150.

187 Abraham and Sokoloff 2011, Beaulieu 2013b, and Hackl [*forthcoming* (a)].

188 Kutscher 2007: 352ff. and Healey 2014: 398f.

vernacular. What was the status of Babylonian during the increasingly bilingual long sixth century? What did the Babylonian language signify in the identity formation of the Neo-Babylonian priests and the urban elite in general? These questions, incredibly difficult to answer, are intimately linked to the use of cuneiform script discussed above and can in fact only be answered through the written word itself.

We have seen throughout this study that the priestly families from Borsippa recorded their business in cuneiform. The composition of these priestly archives, like the archives of non-priestly families, comprises a wide (if not the entire) range of legal administrative genres: from property deeds and intimate family documents like marriage agreements, adoptions, and inheritance divisions to more ephemeral records such as debt notes, receipts, administrative memoranda, and letters.[189] In my opinion, these documents are proof that the old-stock Babylonian families aimed for a wholesale adoption of cuneiform as well as Babylonian, the language they spoke at home and presumably within their immediate social milieu. This custom, expressed through a communal and very conservative naming practice, was intrinsically linked to the scribal education that was pursued by these traditional families as outlined above. In the course of their education students learned how to read and draw up documents and came into contact with the masterpieces of the Akkadian literature that proclaimed the central concepts, symbols, and values of Babylonian culture.[190] Moreover, some of the more advanced esoteric texts were classified as 'restricted' (*niṣirtu*) or 'secret' (*pirišti*) and were thought to have held a type of knowledge of which the dissemination should be restricted to the initiated only.[191] Possession of such documents and knowledge was undoubtedly a source of great pride but at the same time boosted the prestige of cuneiform culture and the Babylonian language that was not only ancient and very rich in literary traditions, but also offered the key to understanding cosmic truths and the fundamental mechanisms of the universe. Needless to say, Babylonian was also the language of the religious institutions. The large temple archives of the Ebabbar in Sippar and Eanna in Uruk bear witness to the fact that cuneiform formed the major backbone of temple management and was used for both internal administration as well as external communication.[192] It stands to

189 See Jursa 2005: 9–49 for the various text types and genres found in the administrative archives of first-millennium Babylonia.

190 While mostly written in Babylonian, education was intrinsically linked to Sumerian, a far older but no less of an indigenous language. For the use of Sumerian in the scribal education, see Gesche 2000, *passim*.

191 Beaulieu 1992 and Lenzi 2008, especially Chapter 1.

192 Jursa 2007 and Jursa 2011: 193–198.

reason that Babylonian was also the official language of the temple assembly (*kiništu*), a hallmark that must have set it apart from other more inclusive civic assemblies (*puhru*) where Aramaic might have been more admissible. Even if Aramaic was gaining a foothold in the temple as an (auxiliary) administrative language, a quick look at the ritual texts from first millennium Uruk and Babylon reveals that cult and festivals remained exclusively Babylonian.[193] As such, the public festivals can be identified as an important locus at which Babylonian was being promulgated as the language of religion and prestige. Most pompous of all was the New Year festival (*akītu*) held in Babylon. Staged in the streets of the capital and its countryside, the general public were afforded the opportunity to witness a series of spectacular processions, offerings, rituals, and prayers that were performed by the priests, the king, and the gods. Indeed, hearing the public recitation of the Epic of Creation, the Babylonian-speaking members of the audience could not have failed to notice that they, in fact, were speaking the very same language that Marduk used to shape and create their universe.[194]

I have already alluded to the fact that cuneiform and, by extension, Babylonian as a language was not only cultivated in the concealed domains of the temple, but also actively promoted on the official state level. The Neo-Babylonian kings adopted this medium for the communication of royal ideology, stressing their role as protectors and providers of the temples, teachers of native wisdom, and anointed champions of Babylonian civilisation.[195] This was done most effectively by commissioning (building) inscriptions, written in the contemporary as well as in a more archaising monumental cuneiform script, which were put up in the old Babylonian towns, but also in recently subdued regions in the West.[196] The rock reliefs at Wadi Brisa in Lebanon are one example. Hence, under the patronage of these ambitious royal houses, cuneiform and the native Babylonian languages were employed in the imperial ideology.[197] This ideological program is even more remarkable considering

193 Thureau-Dangin 1921, Çağirgan and Lambert 1991, and Linssen 2004. All prayers, recitation, salutations, and incantations found in these ritual prescriptive texts are either in Akkadian or in Sumerian.

194 See Edwards 2009: 103ff. for a sociological interpretation of similar sentiments found in early Jewish (Hebrew), Syriac (Aramaic), and Islamic (Arabic) traditions. He also includes more modern parallels from Israel, Ireland, and Scotland, among other nations.

195 See also footnote. 144, above.

196 Da Riva 2012. Note, however, that the self-representation of Nebuchadnezzar II in these twin-inscriptions, in contrast to the iconographic language of Neo-Babylonian kingship, harks to some extent back to Neo-Assyrian precedents. See Da Riva 2010a.

197 Aramaic was probably used as a practical administrative language in the royal administration, however. See Jursa 2014a.

the 'non-Babylonian' background of the Neo-Babylonian kings. Nevertheless, the notion that these rulers fully embraced Babylonian urban culture and its traditional religious constitution is reinforced by the fact that they all bore Babylonian names, usually commemorating Marduk or his son Nabû, the principal and most popular Babylonian gods.[198] One can perceive, in the words of P.-A. Beaulieu, 'a very clear political will to impose the old civilisation of Sumer and Akkad and traditional cuneiform learning as the sole official culture of Babylonia'.[199]

This also implies that participation in Babylonian high society required a degree of acculturation from the outsider's point of view and our sources seem to indicate that this is exactly what happened. The adoption of Babylonian customs by Aramaic-speaking groups can be observed most clearly in naming practices. The great majority of the official Aramaic scribes (*sepīrus*), which before the fall of the Babylonian Empire were typically members of the royal administration, bore Babylonian names.[200] The fact that we are not dealing with Babylonians who learned Aramaic, but rather with native Arameans who offered their services and know-how to the state might be drawn from YOS 3 19, an intriguing letter from the Eanna temple in Uruk discussed by M. Jursa.[201] In this emotional correspondence written in Babylonian by the royal commissioner (*bēl piqitti*) Nabû-ahu-iddin, he describes his nerve-racking circumstances to the chief temple administrator (*šatammu*) of Eanna inserting in the heat of the moment the Aramaic curse 'by the gods!' (*ba-'elāhīn*). Nabû-ahu-iddin is presumably switching to his native tongue in a moment of great perturbation.[202] While this is only one case of code-switching that, admittedly, does not deal with a *sepīru*-scribe, it is a clear example of an official of Aramaic (or at least bilingual) background who had assimilated fully into Babylonian culture. Working for the king of Babylon in a Babylonian religious institution, he bore a Babylonian name and wrote his letters (mostly) in Babylonian. It should also serve as a reminder, indeed a warning, that many more 'non-Babylonians' remain hidden behind conventional Babylonian names in the equally conventional cuneiform documentation. In fact, the Bible tells us as much in the Book of Daniel 1: 5–7. After having learned the local language[203] and studying its script for three years in order to serve in the royal court, Daniel

198 Da Riva 2010b.

199 Beaulieu 2006: 208.

200 Jursa 2012 and Beaulieu 2006: 194.

201 Jursa 2012: 380f.

202 Jursa 2012: 381.

203 Note, however, that the Bible speaks of the Chaldean language rather than the Babylonian language.

(and his companions) received new Babylonian names: Daniel became known as Belteshazzar or rather, Bēl-šarra-uṣur, in the cuneiform sources.[204] Although circumstantial, this evidence suggests that Babylonian culture was the dominant culture in the region and that 'ethnic' groups felt encouraged to adopt Babylonian names and even master the Babylonian language and traditional script in order to pursue a career in the civic or royal institution.[205]

For the old-stock urban families speaking Babylonian not only symbolised their affiliation to a specific and socially dominant language community, but it also nurtured a sense of continuity with the past as the language formed an important aspect of their ancestry. By the sixth century Babylonian boasted a long and esteemed history that dated back to at least the late third millennium BCE and the famed Sargonic kings. It had become the primary language of the temple and its native religion and gave rise to an extensive literary corpus. Certainly, no less significant was the large body of (astral and terrestrial) science[206] that would be among the most acclaimed intellectual traditions in later antiquity, especially known for its astronomical and astrological findings.[207] Babylonian was a language worthy of the gods and ambitiously adopted by their representatives on earth, the Babylonian kings. Even if Aramaic was gaining ground as an administrative and vernacular language, Babylonian retained much of its high status as a vehicle of native culture and traditions. All this can hardly have escaped the mind of the priests who, in fact, were the propagators of the Babylonian language and its written tradition and contributed to its survival (at least in written form) until the beginning of our era.

It is a long-established fact that the language we use forms an important part of our identity.[208] Moreover, language throughout history has functioned as an important marker of group membership.[209] Accordingly, for the priestly families under investigation Babylonian represented not only an instrumental

---

204 A similar naming practice is found among Judean (and other) deportees in Babylonia who often adopted Babylonian names as well. See Beaulieu 2011, Pearce 2015, and Tolini 2015.

205 The fact that the Chaldean and Aramean leaders also tried to approach Babylonian urban society on a socio-political level could be deduced from the marriage alliances between their daughters and prominent local priests. See Chapter 1.1.

206 Beaulieu 2005 and Robson 2011.

207 Gesche 2000: 32–35, Rochberg 2004: 21, 44–45, Rochberg 2010: 143–165, and Steele 2011.

208 Chambers 1995: 250ff. For an accessible introduction to the relationship between identity and language, incorporating a rich variety of modern as well as historical examples, and discussing both past approaches and future research prospects, see Edwards 2009, which includes a useful glossary of key terms and an extensive bibliography.

209 Chambers 1995: 251, Lamont and Molnár 2002: 185, Eriksen 2002, *passim*, and Edwards 2009, *passim*.

tool for private record keeping, but also fulfilled a symbolic function as an emblem of groupness.

Conclusion

In the previous pages I tried to reconstruct the social identity of the Babylonian priests and their intimate circles by pinpointing and contextualising various elements that might have played a defining role in shaping their collective image. Identity is a fluid concept that is situationally contingent, multi-layered, constantly negotiated, and (re)produced through contact with significant others.[210] Even if social anthropologists have shifted their analytical study away from the contents of identity to the boundaries of identity, I made an attempt to piece together the 'cultural stuff' that fostered a sense of collective identity among Babylonian priests and their families.

A fundamental element in the social organisation of the families under investigation was the *bīt-abi* or 'house of the father'. Besides being a social unit of brotherhood, the paternal house was intrinsically linked to specific property, which served as its basis of existence and over which it retained the right of redemption. As such, the *bīt-abi* inspired a sense of solidarity and emotional attachment among its members. It embodied a concrete locus of togetherness and shared identity and represented a core feature around which much of the priests' domestic and professional lives revolved.

At the same time, with regard to a collective identity shared by a larger social group, the *bīt-abi* assumes a somewhat ambiguous position. On the one hand, membership to specific paternal houses must have undermined rather than strengthened the basis for such a collective identity because it fostered an attitude of solidarity and togetherness on a much lower level, geared towards one's immediate relatives. Under the influence of *bīt-abi*s, corporate kin-groups were effectively divided into smaller, discrete units based on close kinship. On the other hand, the transmission and distribution of important pieces of property like houses, land, and prebends as well as scribal knowledge among the individual members of the *bīt-abi* ensured that they were all equipped with the necessary means to participate in the social discourse of the elite and to uphold a corresponding identity. Even if this was not its primary aim, one can conclude that the institution of *bīt-abi* or rather their collective efforts paved the way for a collective identity to materialise and be maintained in the community.

---

210 Jenkins 2008 and Schwartz *et al.* 2011.

There can be no doubt that the core of what might be called a priestly identity found expression through the prebendary system. Ownership of priestly titles was of key importance to the self-image of the families concerned since they gave ritually fit members access to the sanctified space of the temple. While most of their time and energy was put into perpetuating this daily worship in the sanctuary, and thereby effectively preserving the cosmic order, there were multiple occasions on which priests could broadcast their privileged position and collective identity to the outside world. Besides bodily markers of purity that were visible more or less permanently, priests distinguished themselves in the community by contributing to prestigious building projects and partaking in the temple assembly (*kiništu*). However, the most ostentatious display of a collective priestly identity materialised during public festivals. It was at these religious events that the priests emerged from the sacred enclosure to lead the liturgy into the open, while supervising and participating in spectacular processions alongside the gods. As the immediate servants of the gods, priests not only enjoyed physical proximity to the divine statues, but also were granted unique access to the person of the king. Together, god, king, and priest were bounded in a delicate relationship of worship and power.

While priestly families efficiently monopolised membership of the Babylonian priesthood, this was not the case for other aspects of their social identity like land ownership, urban residence, literacy, and language. These domains saw the participation of a much larger section of elite society and embodied a social, economic, and cultural repertoire in which priestly and non-priestly families had an equal stake. The traditional naming pattern of *hanšû* land, for example, clearly revealed that priestly as well as 'secular' families benefitted from the eighth-century BCE land schemes. The ownership of land provided beneficiary families with a solid basis of subsistence. Consequently, it is not surprising that it became an important landmark in the collective historical consciousness of later generations that was recorded in, for example, sixth-century BCE chronicle-writings.

Despite the fact that the distribution of land among upper stratum families across the board led to occasional frictions and rivalry in the community, I prefer to see it as a unifying factor. Owning land in the local countryside meant that these families shared very similar responsibilities and concerns that engendered cooperation at least as much as it created competition. Hence, rather than directly contracting lower-stratum tenants for the management of their landholdings, priestly families from Borsippa relied predominantly on individuals from within their own social stratum as lessors of their land. Landed property allowed elite families to lay claim to a very specific share in the local landscape and to participate in their collective history. This turned native urban elite families into a powerful interest group that shared similar concerns, values, and presumably political aspirations too.

The same stands for urban residential property. While it is likely that priestly families occupied large parts of the neighbourhoods surrounding the temple, they were not the only residents in Borsippa. One can be virtually certain that most, if not all, well-to-do families owned a house in the city. While the reason for this was certainly practical in nature – city walls offered protection against attackers from the outside – living in town also had significant ideological implications. It inspired a sense of communal affiliation, which united the citizens on the basis of political identity and local belonging. It stands to reason that living in town, if not the actual ownership of a town house, facilitated admittance into this socio-political entity and enabled individuals to enjoy its communal rights and privileges. Needless to say, not only priests, but also the urban upper stratum at large can be identified as the Babylonian citizens (*mār-banê* or *māru*). They wielded much of the local political power through neighbourhood connections, interlocking networks of patronage, participation in various civic assemblies, and, most conspicuously, by filling the highest legal-administrative posts like that of chief temple administrator (*šatammu*) and city governor (*šākin-tēmi*).

Besides comparable property portfolios, a shared sense of historical consciousness and local belonging, and similar political aspirations, priestly and non-priestly elite families were further linked through scribal education. While it stands to reason that compared to the rest of society, temple-based families strived for a more advanced level of literacy, they certainly did not hold a monopoly on education, which was open to a much wider non-priestly segment of society. Pupils of both priestly and non-priestly backgrounds were thus being familiarised and instilled with the fundamental concepts, symbols, and values of Babylonian (high) culture in the course of their scribal training. Even if there is no proof that literacy was a precondition to operate in high society, being at least functionally literate gave an individual more independence and might even have opened doors to more prestigious civic functions. Participation in the 'official' cuneiform culture nurtured an *esprit de corps* among the literati and represented a vehicle through which the native urban elites were able to reproduce and consolidate their dominant and privileged position in local society.

Along with the adoption of the cuneiform script, these old-stock Babylonian families also shared the same native Babylonian language. This transpires from the distinct and shared onomasticon and the fact that their archives include a wide range of genres. That it was actively spoken is supported by linguistic innovations found in the texts themselves. The use of Babylonian is an important feature of their collective identity for it clearly set these urban elite families apart from other segments of society in which Aramaic (and other non-native languages) was presumably more common or even standard. Since at least the beginning of the first millennium BCE, the region between the rivers Tigris and Euphrates witnessed a process of Aramaisation. This language would eventually become the predominant vernacular of modern-day Iraq at the turn of the millennium.

It is against this linguistic landscape that one should situate the use of cuneiform and the native Babylonian language by priestly and other urban elite families. It is likely that for them speaking Babylonian symbolised affiliation to a specific community. It nurtured a sense of continuity with the past since the language formed an important aspect of their ancestry. Even if Aramaic was gaining ground, Babylonian retained much of its status as a vehicle of native culture and traditions and as a language with legal authority. Perhaps even more significantly, the fact that groups other than the old-stock Babylonians adopted traditional Babylonian names and mastered the script in order to pursue a career in the civic or royal institution suggests that Babylonian and cuneiform writing still represented the dominant culture in the urban milieu of the long sixth century.

Once we integrate these findings with the concepts of homophily and social boundary, which formed our point of departure, the following picture could be drawn. For the social formation of the group that stands at the core of this study, the priestly families from Borsippa, membership to the priesthood, or, more generally, affiliation to the temple and the concerns of ritual purity that came with it was a major deciding factor. Given that the majority *and* the most significant types of interactions materialised within the circle of temple-related families, one can safely conclude that this represented their primary in-group. Needless to say, beyond their affiliation to this social circle and the temple institution, priests were an integral part of the much wider and more diverse urban community from which they should not be detached even if the one-sided documentation gives little evidence of interaction. A Babylonian priest was not only a devoted servant of the gods, but also a landholder, a town-dweller, and a literatus versed in the cuneiform lore. He also spoke Babylonian and had legal responsibilities and political aspirations on behalf of his family, his fellow citizens, and his community at large. This multiplex socio-economic repertoire with which Babylonian priests associated themselves, the so-called cultural stuff, was shared with a much wider, primarily elite section of society. Here we touch very much on the grey area of the social boundary: who was in and who was out? While impossible to answer with certainty, this question can best be approached from a practical point of view through a close investigation of the actual interactional pattern that is at the heart of this investigation. On a conceptual level, the principle of homophily poses that similarity leads to interaction. Hence, the more one's symbolic attributes and material resources corresponded to the social identity claimed by and assigned to Babylonian priests, the more likely it was to be drawn into their exclusive and carefully shielded social world.

Conclusion

In order to assess the findings of this study I start by summarising the major points raised in each chapter. The outcomes of this study are then be compared with the research questions outlined in the introduction in order to assess the degree to which these can be answered. Finally, the principal conclusions emerging from the book are discussed and their significance highlighted.

1 Summaries of Individual Chapters

Part one of this book (Chapters 1–4) focused on specific social events and interactions that took place within the priestly community of Borsippa.

Chapter 1: The Hypergamous Marriage System

Chapter 1 began this investigation by examining marriage alliances. With more than eighty percent of all attested marriages contracted among priestly families, the preferred marital practice can be described as 'sacerdotal endogamy'. However, by converting the marriage alliances into a directed graph, I was able to tease out a more complex underlying mechanism. As the resulting network followed a transitive and entirely acyclic organisation, the marriage system appeared to be hierarchised and non-reciprocal. Moreover, the fact that marriages in this community entailed a strict unidirectional flow of both women and property from the family of the bride (wife-giver) to the family of the groom (wife-taker) indicates that intermarriage involved a status difference in which wife-takers took precedence over their wife-givers.

A major discovery of this investigation was that the properties of this marriage network matched a specific alliance model called 'hypergamy'. In India, where we find the best-known examples of this model, marriage ideally follows the existing (caste) hierarchy independent of the alliance system. Among Borsippa's priests, the purity-based hierarchy of their priestly functions served as the framework for defining status in marriage.

By placing the alliance system in its historical context, I was also able to consider the practical shortcomings inherent to this hypergamous model. I argued that while in its initial phase the local alliance system followed the temple hierarchy neatly, the community must soon have faced the flaws of the system when participating families had problems finding suitable marriage partners. One of the resulting dynamics was a flattening of the social hierarchy in this community. This can be seen, for instance, in the inclusion of the brewers in the same rank as the temple-enterers who were more highly placed in the

 DOI:10.1163/9789004399969_009

temple hierarchy. Additionally, I was able to identify various compromising marriage strategies, one of which suggests that among the lower priesthoods outsiders were welcomed in the alliance system. I concluded that there existed essentially two different hierarchies in connection with marriage in Borsippa: the temple hierarchy, independent of marriage, and the wife-giver/wife-taker's hierarchy, dependent on marriage.

In the final part of this chapter I showed that priestly profession did not only influence the choice of marriage partner, but that marriage also influenced how priests interacted among each other in the cult. While collaboration in the cult was common between colleagues prior to intermarriage, once an alliance was forged between two families, cultic support was exclusively and without exception provided by the wife-giver. This shows that in Borsippa marriage did not only entail a movement of brides and property in the form of the dowry, but also of labour in the form of cultic support.

Chapter 2: Landholding

In this chapter I explored various aspects of landownership in Borsippa. This investigation was subdivided into three parts. In the first part, '*Hanšû* Estates and the Ancestral Family', I looked into historical aspects of landownership in Borsippa. Based on a combination of legal, administrative, and literary texts, I traced the origins of *hanšû* land, literally 'fifty'-land, in Borsippa back to the mid-eighth century BCE when these estates came into being as royal land grants. Two Chaldean kings in particular relied on the policy of land (re)distribution: Erība-Marduk (ca. 770 BCE) and Merodach-Baladan II (ca. 721–710 BCE). The former was also remembered in this role in the historiographical writings of the Borsippean priests themselves.

The *hanšû* estates in Borsippa are usually identified by the family name of the original beneficiaries. This practice allows for an examination into the range of families that had benefitted from these royal land allotments in the eighth century. Based on this information, I could show that in Borsippa the ownership of *hanšû* land was not a specifically priestly prerogative, but one enjoyed by a much larger section of the urban upper stratum including families with a royal or military background. This finding is important for reminding us that priests were not separate from urban society, as their near-exclusive endogamy could suggest, but that they participated in some of the same privileges as non-priestly elites.

In the conclusion of this section I considered which value the *hanšû* estates held for the descendants of the original beneficiaries during the long sixth century. The bond between the family and its eponymous land was very strong. Besides the fact that *hanšû* estates kept the names of the original families, their descendants usually still owned neighbouring plots and remained involved in matters concerning their land even if they had been forced to sell some parts. Moreover, there are examples of families who attempted to buy back their land and re-accumulate the patrimony even a long time after they had parted from it. The same impression transpired from examining the composition of dowries. While there are instances of *hanšû* being used as dowry property, this hardly ever involved the family's eponymous estate.

In the second part of this chapter, 'Land Sales and the Circulation of Property', I adopted a different approach to *hanšû* land and real estate in general. Delving deeper into the archives of Borsippa's priests, I took a closer look at the patterns of property sales, specifically by investigating the influence marriage and professional solidarity had on these transactions. As it turned out there was extremely little overlap between the ties of marriage and the ties of property sale. Families tended to acquire property from and sell it to families who did not belong to their direct or indirect marriage network. This suggests that in the priestly community of Borsippa marriage ties excluded property sales. The results from comparing property sales with professional affiliation were less clear. While most sales took place within the prebendary circle, which may point to an attitude of solidarity among priestly families, there is reason to believe that these figures result from the biased nature of our documentation and can therefore not be taken at face value.

In the third and final part of this chapter, 'Tenancy and Agricultural Collaboration', I investigated upon whom Borsippa's priests relied for the cultivation and management of their landed estates. Priests did not cultivate their land themselves but instead outsourced this work to others. Even if priests could draw from various sources of manpower, they relied to a large extent (75%) on individuals from within their social stratum. While some of their tenants or collaborators came from non-priestly families, the vast majority of these individuals belonged to local, temple-based clans.

The ensuing reconstruction of the pattern of tenancy showed that this followed the existing organisation of the community, as outlined first and foremost in the marriage system. Collaboration among the highest-ranking temple families (temple-enterers) was largely geared towards the prebendary in-group, while the lowest priestly families (reed-workers) recruited their tenants only from amongst kin or non-priestly 'outsider' families. Moreover, marriage ties seem to have played an important role in tenancy as priests often called upon individuals from direct and in-direct wife-giver families.

Chapter 3: Silver Lending

Silver lending represents one of the few businesses in which Babylonian priests invested their liquid capital. While occupation, family background, and individual circumstances generated a range of divergent lending profiles unique to each family or even individual, credit operations among members in the highest priestly group could again be characterised by a high presence of temple-based families, especially from within their professional group and/or kin. The lowest ranking reed-workers, on the other hand, represented the only priestly family that interacted more with non-priestly 'outsiders'.

The pattern of silver lending thus followed the same structure that I reconstructed for tenancy and marriage, but only partly so because this trend could not be confirmed among the middle-ranking prebendary groups. Part of the reason for this can be sought in the personal circumstances and background of the individuals used in the analysis, but also in the nature of the interaction itself. Loans seem to have often been contracted on an *ad hoc* basis. This notion finds support in the fact that many of the creditors and debtors resurfaced outside of these encounters, both with the protagonists and elsewhere in the corpus – something that could not be established to the same extent for actors in other spheres of interaction. This seems to indicate that lending partners were generally found in a limited geographic space and came from within the priests' immediate environment.

Finally, while it remained extremely difficult to qualify individual loans, one thing became clear once all documented loans were taken together: even if priests acted relatively often outside of the prebendary circles for the purpose of silver lending compared to other types of transactions, the majority of the loans (63%) were still contracted with members of fellow priestly families.

Chapter 4: Circles of Trust and Intimacy

While 'friendship' as a mutually confiding relationship with complex psycho-emotional qualities falls beyond the scope of our legal documentation, this chapter approached the phenomenon through a set of structural features delineated in the social sciences and known as tie strength in order to reconstruct the priests' most intimate social networks.

Frequency of interaction is the most basic indicator for the strength of a relationship and it therefore served as the starting point of my formal quantification of the data. In an attempt to understand to which degree priests preferred friends over strangers in their legal transactions, I set out to compare the number of individuals mentioned only once in their archives and the number of intimate contacts attested five times or more. The underlying idea is that an individual's lifestyle and specific mode of behaviour vis-à-vis the environment are reflected in his or her ego network and vice versa. Persons interacting more often with the same people may be expected to have a different outlook on life than those who interacted mostly with people they only met once.

Unfortunately, it proved difficult to interpret the figures obtained from this analysis. To a large extent, this is because the figures depend on the quality of the individual archives. It appeared that single- and multi-generation archives always yield results in the same general ranges, which indicates that structural features of the archive determine the results rather than the properties of the actual historical networks. Also, a comparison between the data from Borsippa and two archives from the city of Sippar, for which similar analyses are available, did little to better understand these results. Clearly, a more precise approach to the study of incomplete historical ego-networks is required in order for this kind of analysis to bear fruit.

In the second part of this chapter I adopted a more descriptive qualitative approach to the study of trust and intimacy. In particular, I attempted to establish more precisely the identities of the priests' most intimate contacts. Intimacy was defined on the basis of the following aspects of tie strength: multiplexity, duration, and frequency of interaction. While in social network analysis, multiplexity is commonly used as an indicator of the diversity of roles fulfilled by individuals, I adopted it in a slightly modified way as 'multiplexity of context', i.e. the range of different social contexts in which an individual appears (e.g. marriage, land management, rentals, etc.).

The first and major result of this investigation was that priests found the vast majority of their intimate contacts among the members of temple-based families. Only a few came from non-priestly families. Strikingly, not a single intimate contact came from the lower strata of society. It seemed unlikely that this trend could have manifested itself in such a rigid form without a conscious and collective attitude on the part of the priests. Second, based on the notion of intimacy adopted in this study, the priests' most intimate contacts were usually found among their scribes and witnesses, especially those who were present at significant personal events such as marriage agreements, inheritance divisions, and sales of property. It turned out that priests only very rarely engaged in formal business with these 'friends'.

In part two (Chapters 5–6) of this book I took a step back from the individual interactions and examined the interactional pattern of the Borsippean priests as a whole. This was approached from a more structural and theoretical perspective and linked with broader phenomena in Neo-Babylonian society. At the same time, the scope of the analysis was broadened from its original focus on the priests of Borsippa to the Babylonian priest in general in an attempt to situate this distinct social segment within wider society.

Chapter 5: Homophily and Interaction

Chapter 5 started by summarising the interactional pattern of the priestly community of Borsippa. As shown in Chapters 1–4, priests interacted predominantly within the circle of fellow temple-based families. While interaction with non-priestly families occurred not infrequently, these individuals were largely left out of more personal or significant events (marriage and friendship). Individuals from the lower strata of society were even *entirely* left out of significant forms of interaction.

I proposed two different explanations for this pattern of interaction. The first took a very pragmatic stance on the matter and interpreted it as a natural outcome of the geographic or spatial situation of our priests in the demography and topography of the Babylonian city. Even if geographic space is an important factor for interaction, it could not explain adequately the salient features of the interactional landscape. More precisely, it failed to account for the varying degrees of in-group interaction among priests, which differed markedly from one domain of their lives to the other. The second scenario adopted a more theoretically informed interpretation by using the concept of homophily, which postulates that contact between people with similar socio-economic characteristics occurs at a higher rate than among dissimilar people. Consequently, I argued that the interactional pattern of the priests did not depend so much on shared topographic space as on the degree of perceived similarity. That homophily represented an important principle for the interaction of the priests transpires from the fact that significant forms of interactions occurred to a disproportionate degree within their social in-group.

By building further on the concept of homophily, a more fundamental and structural underpinning was provided of two socio-economic typologies recently applied to Neo-Babylonian society. Social scientists have insisted that human society knows two primary motives vis-à-vis (inter)action and resources: the first aims at protecting existing resources, the second at gaining new resources. These also lie at the basis of two typological economic mentalities found in Neo-Babylonian sources: the rentier and the entrepreneur. In Babylonian society the former mentality is embodied most clearly by priests. While rentiers and entrepreneurs have thus far been distinguished from other groups based on economic criteria, this investigation pointed out that they are in fact characterised by a fundamentally different mode of interaction with their social environment.

Chapter 6: Social Boundary and Collective Identity

While the concept of homophily told us that the patterns of interaction found in the priestly archives from Borsippa can be understood in the light of the priests' perceived similarity and dissimilarity with other significant actors, this final chapter attempted to identify the markers of their collective social identity. I started my investigation by arguing that the dynamics of interaction in the priestly community of Borsippa point to the existence of a social boundary.

This implies a conceptual distinction made by social actors, one that allows them to separate themselves from other groups and generate feelings of similarity and cohesion. In our sources the outlines of this boundary emerge clearest from the ties of marriage and friendship. I argued that in order for priests to maintain such a tight control over their social environment, they must have been able to draw on a set of symbolic attributes and material resources, which besides fostering a strong cohesion among the in-group was also recognized by outsiders.

As it turns out, the Babylonian priests cannot only be characterised as cultic agents who enjoyed a professional affiliation with the temple, the gods, and the king, although this was arguably the strongest factor linking the in-group. The collective social identity I reconstructed was expressed by a multiplex social, cultural, and economic repertoire, which included aspects ranging from the ownership of property, a shared historical consciousness, and naming patterns to the adoption of a traditional set of concepts and values, citizenship, literacy, and language. The more an individual was able to identify with these symbolic attributes and material resources, the more likely he or she was to be drawn into the exclusive social world of the Babylonian priests.

2 Research Questions Revisited

This study attempted to reconstruct the social world of the Babylonian priest. For this purpose, the research aims were broken down into two principal points. The first was concerned with the impact of the temple fabric on the lives of priests. Since Babylonian priests were submitted to stringent rules of purity and organised according to a rigid hierarchy inside the temple, the first aim was to investigate to what extent these temple-based regulations influenced the priests' behaviour and affected their lives outside of their cultic activities. In order to fully assess this matter, the first four chapters of this study focused on particular spheres of interaction captured in the archives of Borsippa's priestly families. The specific patterns of interaction were systematically evaluated in light of the ideal temple regulations, but also dissected in their own rights. The second and related research aim was to examine whether priest can be identified as a distinct social group and whether it was possible to pinpoint the group more firmly in Babylonian society by closely investigating how they interacted with the in-group and the out-group. Building further on the findings from the first part of this book, this second matter was tackled in the final two chapters. Taken all together, I believe that the evidence presented over the course of my investigation has allowed for a more sophisticated understanding of the Neo-Babylonian priests, particularly in the ways they acted with their social environment and the basis on which they constructed their more or less exclusive group vis-à-vis outsiders. As a result, this book helps to elucidate some of the fundamental aspects of this ancient society.

3 Outcomes

3.1 *The Impact of Temple-Based Regulations*

The evidence presented throughout this study has shown that the temple left a great impression on the lives of priests. It informed their choices, affected their behaviour, and served as the ideal framework for their social organisation in society. The clearest example of this impact emerged from the study of marriages. While the preference by priests to take brides from fellow sacerdotal families already underlined the influence the temple fabric had on marital arrangements in this community, a methodical analysis of the data revealed that the marriage system was far more complex and the temple's influence went much deeper. The system reconstructed for the priestly community of Borsippa corresponded neatly with the marriage model known as hypergamy. This ideal model is characterised by the marriage of lower-status brides to higher-status grooms. In Borsippa more than seventy percent of documented marriages were arranged between daughters of lower-ranking families and sons of higher-ranking priestly families. The families adopted the purity-based temple hierarchy as the principal ideological framework for their local alliance system.

Marriage constituted a fundamental building block in this community. In addition to allowing families and individuals to forge deep-rooted alliances and turn colleagues, neighbours and acquaintances into kin, the arrangements of marriage resurfaced in various aspects of the priests' daily lives. Marriage patterned the sales of property, led to specific service arrangements in agricultural and cultic organisations, and engendered a general attitude of solidarity and collaboration that was at times strikingly lacking among clans that were not joined by marriage. These dynamics were in the first place based on ties of marriage. Because marriage, in turn, hinged strongly on the ideal temple regulations, it can be argued that the latter influenced the social dynamics in various domains.

The impact of the temple hierarchy also transpired from the particular ways in which the priesthood engaged with its social environment. It should be remembered that the priests of a Babylonian temple were ordered in a rigid hierarchy along an all-embracing axis of relative purity and physical proximity to the gods. Priests who worked in close contact with divine statues had to comply with more stringent purity rules than those working in more peripheral areas of the temple. This principle was also visible in the general pattern of interaction. Hence, the social interaction of high-ranking priests turned out to be structurally more inward-looking and geared towards close relatives and individuals with the same priestly status, while members of families located on the lower fringes of the temple hierarchy engaged with a much more diverse set of individuals, often relying less on fellow prebendaries and more on non-priestly outsiders. This emerged, for example, from the study of the local marriage system: temple-enterers, located at the very top of the temple hierarchy, intermarried primarily with families of the same (or similar) priestly rank as opposed to the lower-ranking oxherds and reed-workers who forged alliances with families that did not belong to the local prebendary circle. This trend also resurfaced in other spheres of interactions such as the formation of friendship, agricultural collaboration, and silver lending. Hence, temple-enterers relied predominantly on fellow temple-enterer families for the cultivation of their landholdings, while the reed-workers were the only priests who contracted more silver loans outside of the priestly circle than inside. It should be said, however, that this trend emerges most clearly from a comparison between the very highest and lowest edge-groups and cannot always be traced as clearly among the middle-ranking priesthoods.

These findings are important for our understanding of the social structure of the priestly community of Borsippa and its fundamental ordering principles. Firstly, we are left with little doubt that the purity-based hierarchy exerted a significant influence over the lives of priests outside of their cultic activities. However, it was shown that priests also actively tried to reproduce the temple's ideal order within their social environment. Secondly, this study led to a more nuanced appreciation of the figure of the Babylonian priest as such. Even if priests can be identified as a distinct social group when analysing Babylonian society as a whole, the evidence presented in this study revealed that the internal variance of this group could be great. Priests were embedded in the temple's sphere in greater or lesser degrees, which could, and sometimes obviously did, influence their attitudes and ways of interacting with fellow priests and other members of society in different ways. It is essential to acknowledge this fact when talking about Babylonian priests.

3.2 *Priests as a Distinct Social Group*

The evidence presented throughout this study demonstrates that priests can be identified as a distinct social group in Babylonian society. Despite the fact that each priest engaged in a unique way with his social environment, it was revealed that the interactional pattern of this social group as a whole followed a clear outline. It can be summarised in the following three points. Firstly, the majority of their interactions took place with fellow priests and members of priestly families. Secondly, while they regularly interacted with members of non-priestly families, this occurred on a much smaller scale. Finally, individuals from the lower strata of society including foreign minorities are almost entirely excluded from the day-to-day interactions and appear only on the fringes of the priests' social world. While this pattern emerged sharply from ties of marriage and friendship, it was less clearly defined in the sphere of silver lending or tenancy, which saw the participation of a more diverse group, including individuals from other strata of society.

Since it was demonstrated that many of the priests' contacts belonged to their immediate social environment, the interactional pattern could not simply be taken as a natural outcome of spatial and demographic factors. Much more helpful was to interpret it in the light of homophily, the principle postulating that interaction is most likely to occur among individuals that share similar lifestyles and socioeconomic characteristics. The engagement of priests in society could indeed be classified as largely homophilous, which matched the conservative economic mentality commonly ascribed to them as Babylonia's archetypical rentiers. However, of greater importance for our understanding of priests as a distinct group was the fact that the significant types of their interaction such as marriage and friendship occurred to a disproportionate (homophilous) degree within the social in-group to the near-exclusion of others. This indicates that the priests from Borsippa maintained a social boundary, which allowed them to consciously separate from other elements in society.

In order for this 'us' vs. 'them' dichotomy to take shape, priests called on a set of common criteria, which defined the group's collective social identity. These criteria included aspects ranging from their privileged affiliation to the temple and superior purity to landownership, residential profile, literacy, language, historical consciousness, and naming pattern. Even if many aspects of this multiplex social, cultural, and economic repertoire were shared by a larger, primarily elite section of society, the evidence indicates that Babylonian priests used the markers of their social identity both to delineate the group's social boundary and to establish guidelines for interaction. They provided priests with a very clear idea of what it meant to be a member of the in-group, which, while on the whole was very rigidly defined, could in certain circumstances shift its boundary to include a slightly more or slightly less diverse range of individuals into their social world.

These findings are crucial for our understanding of the Babylonian priests. The evidence presented in this book demonstrates that priests perceived of and maintained themselves as a discrete social unit. By adhering to a collective social identity and holding on to a shared practice of interaction, priests retained control over their social environment and preserved the configuration of their in-group. Even if it goes without saying that priests were an integral part of the much wider and more diverse urban community, the fact that the majority *and* the most significant types of interactions occurred among temple-related families indicates that this circle represented their primary in-group, which can now be pinpointed more securely in Babylonian society.

4 Outlook

The findings of this study demonstrate the benefits of taking social interaction as a basic object of analysis and investigating Babylonian society from below. By focusing our attention on the interactions of Borsippa's priests, it became possible to say more about how one specific group was structured internally and how it related to other segments in the community. Moreover, this empirical method gave us a good idea of what was the common, normative, and preferred way of conduct, and what was uncommon, largely avoided, and perhaps even considered undesirable in the priestly community of Borsippa.

This study has also shown that our findings can be extrapolated successfully to more general social phenomena in Babylonian society. Hence, the interactional patterns of Borsippa's priests could be described in light of the economic mentalities of the rentier and the entrepreneur and also help us gain a more fundamental understanding of these typologies. At the same time, caution is warranted. Facts established for the priestly community of Borsippa could not always be matched up adequately with those found in other units of observation such as, for example, the priestly community of Sippar. The apparent reason behind this is that these facts arose from a very specific setting defined by their own particular dynamics, factors, and parameters. Hence, the social structures reconstructed in Borsippa cannot be simply attributed wholesale to the burgeoning provincial town of Sippar, the capital of Babylon or the southern city of Uruk. Nor can they be expected to be found in the exact same shape elsewhere. While the findings of this study are thus of general relevance and transcend well beyond boundaries of the priestly community of Borsippa, only by recognising that they are embedded within a very specific context can they help us gain a more nuanced understanding of ancient Babylonian society.

The focus of this study was almost exclusively on Borsippa's priests, which could be studied in exceptional detail. However, I also showed that priests were part of a much larger and more diverse elite stratum of society. Unfortunately, the Borsippa corpus does not allow us to study this wider segment in detail as it remains largely outside the documentation. It would therefore be important, in order to fully assess the findings of this book, to expand the scope of future investigations by shifting the analysis to other social groups and other towns such as the entrepreneurial families of Babylon or the priesthood of Uruk.

Finally, I want to briefly address a general and, to my mind, important aspect of the evidence that has been left largely undiscussed. The findings presented throughout this book proved to be very static and fairly resistant to change over time, turning out to be diachronically flat. While this could be observed most visibly in the marriage network reconstructed at the beginning of this study, it actually applied to all spheres of interaction. It therefore represents an inherent feature of the interactional pattern in general. While this might be a result of the specific methodology adopted in this study or the nature of our textual corpus, I believe that it can be explained differently. This book has made it abundantly clear that the local priestly families acted as a self-contained, socially exclusive group. Even if they were part of a much wider and rapidly changing society that experienced wars, migrations, dynastic changes, and state reforms, the evidence suggests that these families were affected very little by the local and imperial politics of the time. On the contrary, by maintaining a rigid pattern of interaction and adhering to a conservative social system, the priestly families from Borsippa seem to have established a highly resilient and cohesive community that was effectively shielded from outside influence through a deliberate act of auto-segregation. It seems, therefore, that the absence of clear diachronic developments in the study serve as an ultimate testimony to the successful organisation of Borsippa's priests who were able to keep their close-knit community and its intricate dynamics remarkably stable for the better part of the first millennium only to see it all finally collapse in the abortive revolts of 484 BCE.

APPENDIX 1

Quantitative Analysis of Priestly Marriages in Borsippa

Introduction

The Borsippa corpus yields some 102 attestations in which marital unions are more or less explicitly expressed, i.e. 'Y wife of X' or 'Y mother of Z, son of X'. However, not all of them can be used. For two unions the family name of the husband is missing, while for nineteen others the family name of the wife has been lost or simply omitted. One can only speculate about the nature of these unions and they have therefore not been incorporated into the analysis. We can be virtually sure, however, that it does not concern individuals from the lower strata of society who lack ancestral family names altogether. These references only identify the husband or wife by personal name. They not only omit the family name, but also the father's name, suggesting that full filiation was simply not necessary and the individual was well known to the parties concerned. This leaves us with a dataset of eighty-one fully documented unions.

In this analysis I look into the marriage alliance of the individual priesthoods, taking special notice of the marriages arranged within the prebendary groups, those arranged with other prebendary groups, and those arranged with non-prebendary outsiders. The figures are summarised at the end of each section. I begin with the group that spawned the most marital unions, the temple-enterer families, followed by the brewers, the bakers, the butchers, and the oxherds. I end with the reed workers family for which there is only little information.

1 Temple-Enterers

The corpus informs us on the marriage of seventeen male and twenty-two female members belonging to the temple-enterer clans. It should be noted that information on this group is quite abundant, considering the fact that we have only one archive from a temple-enterer family, namely the Ea-ilūtu-bani archive. For other temple-enterer families from Borsippa, see Introduction 7.1 The marriages from this group are summarised in figures 13a–c.

1.1 *Intra-prebendary Unions*

With eight alliances arranged within the group of temple-enterers, almost half of the male and almost forty percent of the female members engaged in intra-prebendary

 | DOI:10.1163/9789004399969_010

marriages. These percentages are, however, somewhat misleading because they are largely based on two marriage-chains from a single archive cluster. The first cycle consists of three consecutive marriages within the Ilī-bāni clan. According to TCL 12 85 man 'Y' of the Ilī-bāni clan was married to woman 'X' of the same kin group.[1] This marriage was not blessed with longevity, given that only a few months later the husband married his late wife's sister. The last episode is described some fourteen years later when the Ilī-bānis called upon the brother of the recently deceased husband 'Y' to uphold the alliance and marry his sister-in-law.[2]

The second chain is represented by two documents and concerns the alliance between the Ea-ilūtu-bani and the Ilī-bāni families. The case presents itself in TCL 13 174 when woman 'X' from the Ilī-bāni clan divided her entire property.[3] She transferred the first half of the property to her son by man 'Y'; the second half was assigned to man 'Z', her husband. It has been demonstrated by F. Joannès that 'Y' and 'Z' were related, the former being the older brother of the latter, and that the wife was thus previously married to her second husband's older brother.[4] The last testimony suggests that the wife divided her property in anticipation of her death since only two months later, man 'Z' is married to a new woman, the paternal niece of his late wife 'X'.

1.2 *Inter-prebendary Unions*

Almost thirty percent, or five out of the seventeen unions, was arranged between male temple-enterers and women from other prebendary backgrounds. These marriages were usually arranged with prominent priestly groups that ranked just below the temple enterers: brewers (once),[5] butchers (once),[6] and bakers (twice).[7] The notability of these families is underlined when we look at the individuals in question. Šikkûa was a family of brewers that enjoyed a brief period of distinction when it provided two consecutive chief temple administrators (*šatammu*) of Ezida between 539 and 537 BCE.[8] Prosopographical evidence suggests that the woman marrying into the Ea-ilūtu-bani family was indeed the grand- and great-granddaughter of these *šatammus*.[9] The wife from the butcher family belonged to a branch of the Ibnāya clan that had supplied at

1 Joannès 1989: 52.
2 For more on this sororate and levirate chain of marriages, see Joannès 1987.
3 Joannès 1989: 41.
4 Ibid.
5 Ea-ilūtu-bani ∞ Šikkûa (BM 26264).
6 Kidin-Nanāya ∞ Ibnāya (BM 96151).
7 Kidin-Nanāya ∞ Kidin-Sîn (BM 25589); Ea-ilūtu-bani ∞ Kidin-Sîn (TuM 2/3 48).
8 See Waerzeggers 2010: 73 for references.
9 The woman in question is [f]Šaddinnātu/Nabû-šumu-iddin/Nabû-mukīn-zēri (*šatammu*)/Nabû-mukīn-apli (*šatammu*)/Šulā of the Šikkûa clan.

least one city governor (*šākin-ṭēmi*) of Borsippa.[10] The two alliances with prebendary bakers were both arranged with the prominent Kidin-Sîn family. Temple-enterers thus married the most illustrious members of lower-ranking clans. One apparent exception is the marriage between a temple-enterer and a daughter from the Rēʾi-alpi clan.[11]

Female members of temple-enterer families engaged far more often in this type of marriage. For them, forty-six percent, or ten out of twenty-two marriages, was arranged with lower prebendary families. Temple-enterer families tended to marry their daughters to families that occupied the rung just below themselves: brewers (six times),[12] butchers (once),[13] bakers (once).[14] Other marriages were arranged, respectively, between a man of the Nappāhus and a woman from the Atkuppu family,[15] and between a man of the Arad-Ea family and a wife from the Rēʾi-alpi clan.[16]

1.3 *Extra-prebendary Unions*

There are four marriages (24%) between temple-enterers and women from families that have no prebendary background or whose affiliation to the Ezida temple cannot presently be established: the Barihi, the Pahhāru, the Rab-banê, and the Siātu families. The Barihi family is a local Borsippean clan with only very few attestations in the corpus.[17] The three other clans occur repeatedly. Given that they were well connected, the Siātus may have played an important role in Borsippa's priestly community.[18] The same can be said about the Pahhāru clan.[19] The Rab-banê family provided a bride to the Naggārus.[20]

---

10 Her grandfather (and perhaps also her great-grandfather) functioned in this position. The daughter in question is ᶠGigītu/Nabû-šumu-ukīn/Nabû-nādin-šumi/Mušēzib-Marduk of the Ibnāya clan. See Waerzeggers 2010: 68 for references. For the Ibnāya (A) archive, see Jursa 2005: 83–84 and Waerzeggers 2010: 525ff.

11 Arkāt-ilāni-damqā ∞ Rēʾi-alpi (BM 96166).

12 Huṣābu ∞ Ea-ilūtu-bani (BM 82640 = AH XV no. 45); Huṣābu ∞ Ilī-bāni (NBC 8404 and L 1627), Ilia ∞ Arkāt-ilāni(-damqā) (BM 26473); Ilia ∞ Iddin-Papsukkal (BM 26473); Ilšu-abūšu ∞ Nūr-Papsukkal (Smith Coll. No. 92); and Mannu-gērûšu ∞ Ša-diš-luh (BM 87308).

13 Ilšu-abūšu ∞ Naggāru (BM 28863 = AH XV no. 115).

14 Esagil-mansum ∞ Iddin-Papsukkal (BM 29379 published in Zadok 2005).

15 OECT 12 A 158.

16 BM 82609 = Roth 1989 no. 22 and BM 26707.

17 The Barihis provided women to the Egibi family (*Camb* 315) and the temple-enterer family of the Nūr-Papsukkals (*Camb* 120, *Camb* 338).

18 The Siātu family gave brides to butcher and temple-enterer families, Ibnāya (BM 96151; VS 5 25) and Iddin-Papsukkal (BM 94691; VS 4 70), respectively. The family itself received a wife from a prominent butcher branch of the Ilšu-abūšu family (BM 28865 = AH XV no. 116; VS 5 28).

19 It received a wife from Esagil-mansum (BM 29067; BM 28861) and provided a bride to Arkāt-ilāni-damqā (Wunsch 2000 no. 116).

20 BM 94504.

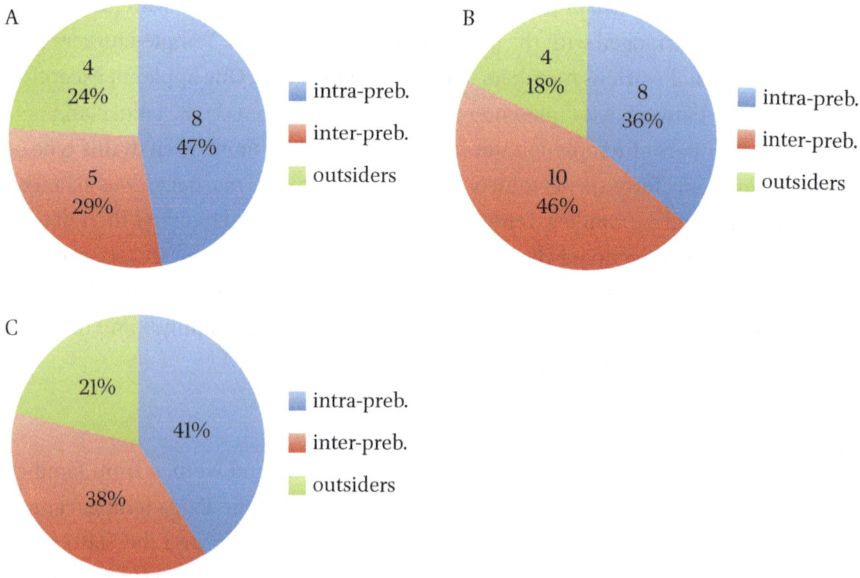

FIGURE 13 (a) Marriages of temple-enterers (♂); (b) Marriages of temple-enterers (♀); (c) Total marriages of temple-enterers (♂ + ♀)

The alliances arranged for female members of the temple-enterer clans provide a similar picture. Less than twenty percent, or four out of twenty-two women, was married into clans who did not belong to the prebendary circle of Borsippa: Bēl-eṭēru (twice),[21] Rē'i-sisê (once),[22] and an obscure family whose name ends on '[x]-zēri' (once).[23] So far no member of the Bēl-eṭēru family is attested as priest of Ezida, but the family did occupy high positions in sanctuaries of other Babylonian towns.[24]

2 Brewers

With nine archives, the brewers of Borsippa are the best-attested group in the corpus (see Introduction 7.2). Moreover, the archives appear to be a representative sample, informing us on both prominent and peripheral brewer clans. This analysis includes

21 Bēl-eṭēru ∞ Ilī-bāni (BM 94548); Bēl-eṭēru ∞ Nappāhu (BM 94696).

22 Rē'i-sisê ∞ Nūr-Papsukkal (BM 27858).

23 [x]-zēri ∞ Iddin-Papsukkal (OECT 12 A 129 = Roth 1989 no. 21).

24 Sippar: the temple-enterer's prebend (cultic singer) of the sanctuary of Šarrat-Sippar seems to have been completely in their hands (Bongenaar 1997: 242ff., 289). Babylon: the family is attested selling an *ērib-bītis*/*nârūtu* prebend (Baker 2004 nos. 54, 55, 56 and 57). Dilbat: Bēl-eṭērus functioned as measurers (*mādīdu*) of Uraš in Eimbianu (VS 5 105 and VS 5 75). That they also took part in higher temple functions is clear from, for example, VS 5 108, an exchange of a piece of land against an *ērib-bīti* prebend in Dilbat involving the temple authorities.

the marriage of thirty-three brewers: nineteen male and fourteen female members. Note, however, that more than one-third of these unions is attested in the Ilia archives. The marriages from this group are summarised in figures 14a–c.

2.1 *Intra-prebendary Unions*

The most striking feature of the marriage pattern of the brewers is the high number of unions within the professional group. Our data indicates that more than sixty percent of all their marriages was arranged within the professional group. Especially noteworthy is the bond between the Ilia (A) and the Ilšu-abūšu families who seem to have pursued a conscious alliance policy.[25] In short, the Ilia family was made up of three branches, headed by the three sons of the first attested member, Ṣillā. In the third generation all three branches arranged a marriage with a daughter from the Ilšu-abūšu clan,[26] thus joining the entire Ilia (A) family to the Ilšu-abūšu clan. While the Ilia family widened its horizon to other brewer families during subsequent generations,[27] the alliance with the Ilšu-abūšus was solidified with another marriage in the fifth generation.[28]

Another interesting notion is that the marriages among brewers were concluded between families of similar status. For example, Lā-kuppuru, a clan that was only marginally involved in the domain of Ezida's brewers, was married to a family whose role in this profession was equally marginal, the Allānus.[29] On the other hand, prominent families like the Ilia gave and received wives from important clans such as Kudurrānu[30] and Ša-nāšīšu.[31]

2.2 *Inter-prebendary Unions*

Eight male and four female members of brewer clans were married to families of other prebendary groups (42% and 29%, respectively). With six out of seven arranged in this way, there was a clear tendency among the brewers to take their wives from the higher-ranking temple-enterers. Two further unions were arranged with bakers[32] and

25 Waerzeggers 2010: 95.

26 The founder of the Ilia (A) branch, Ṣillā, had three sons: Šulā, (Itti-Nabû-)Balāṭu, and Šāpik-zēri. Each had a son who married a woman from the Ilšu-abūšu family: Nabû-ēṭir-napšāti/Šulā/ilia ∞ ᶠAmtia//Ilšu-abūšu (VS 5 126), Nabû-ušallim/Balāṭu/Ilia ∞ ᶠTuqpītu//Ilšu-abūšu (BM 102308 = AH XV no. 18), and Marduk-nādin-ahi/Šāpik-zēri ∞ ᶠQudāšu//Ilšu-abūšu (BM 87267).

27 Marduk-šumu-ibni, the main protagonist of the Ilia (A) archive, married his daughter to the Kudurrānu family (BM 87265).

28 BM 102261.

29 Lā-kuppuru ∞ Allānu (BM 29385). The same document mentions a union within the Lā-kuppuru clan.

30 BM 87265.

31 See, for example, LB 874. The remaining unions are Kudurrānu ∞ Ahiya'ūtu (OECT 12 A 120, Joannès 1989: 62, 281) and Ilia ∞ Ilia (BM 26544).

32 Ilia ∞ Esagil-mansum (BM 26731).

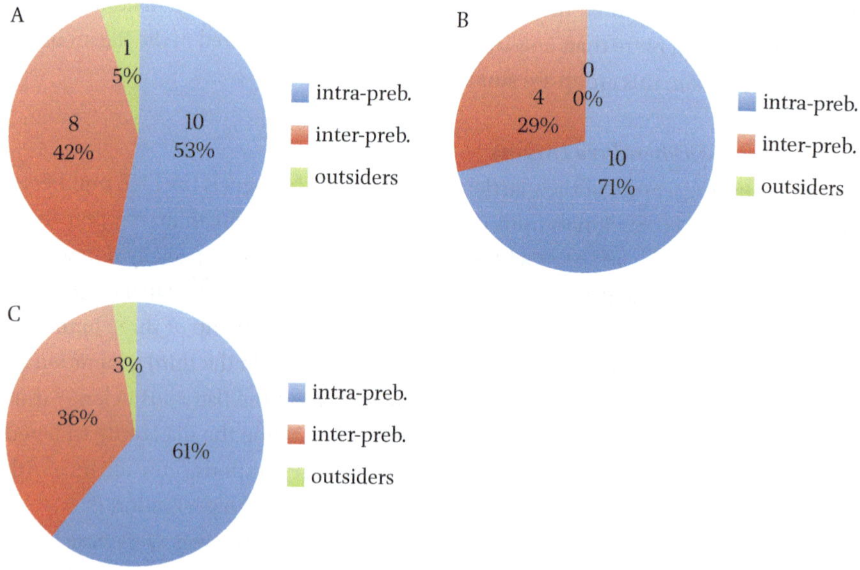

FIGURE 14: (a) Marriages of brewers (♂); (b) Marriages of brewers (♀); (c) Total marriages of brewers (♂ + ♀)

oxherds.[33] Turning to the opposite sex, our data seems to suggest that brewer families often gave their daughters in marriage to more junior prebendary families.[34]

2.3 *Extra-prebendary Unions*

There is only one marriage between a brewer and non-prebendary outsider family. A son of the minor brewer clan of Lā-kuppuru married the daughter of the Rišāya family.[35] Note, however, that the latter seems to have originated from the nearby city of Dilbat where its members are attested as prebendary bakers and occur in various prebend-related texts.[36]

3 Bakers

The corpus bears evidence to the marriages of ten male and eight female members of prebendary bakers. For an overview of the local families of bakers and our main source

33 Kudurrānu ∞ Rē'i-alpi (BM 96259).

34 One time into a higher prebendary group: [ērib-bīti] Ea-ilūtu-bani ∞ Šikkûa (BM 26264). Three times into a lower prebendary group: [baker] Bēliya'u ∞ Ilia (BM 26483), [barber] Gallābu ∞ Ilia (BM 85570 = Zadok IOS 18 no. 1), and [oxherd] Rē'i-alpi ∞ Ardūtu (BM 29375).

35 BM 103458.

36 BM 77508+, VS 5 21, VS 5 83, and VS 5 161.

on this group, see Introduction 7.3. It is interesting to find a confirmation of the Kidin-Sîn's central position among the prebendary bakers in the fact that they figure most prominent in our sample of marriages even though their family archive has not been recovered. The marriages from this group are summarised in figures 15a–c.

3.1 *Intra-prebendary Unions*

Except for the Nabû-mukīn-apli clan, all baker families are known to have engaged in intra-prebendary marriages. The Kidin-Sîn clan figures most prominently in this respect. Two marriages were arranged within the clan[37] and one with the Šēpê-ilias.[38] Another alliance within the prebendary group was forged between the Bēliya'u and the Esagil-mansum clans.[39] Due to the small quantity of this sample, these four marriages account for forty percent of this group's male marraiges and fifty percent of this group's female marriages, respectively.

3.2 *Inter-prebendary Unions*

There are, in total, six individuals, three men and three women, who married individuals from outside their own professional group. One baker married a woman from the prebendary barber or Gallābu clan.[40] Others married individuals from brewer (twice)[41] and temple-enterer families (three times).[42]

3.3 *Extra-prebendary Unions*

Three men and one woman married individuals whose family background remains unknown. The three men received their wives from the Kāṣir,[43] Nabûnnāya,[44] and Ṣillāya families, respectively.[45] A baker's daughter was married to the Pahhāru family.[46]

---

37 The first marriage is attested in BM 94697 and BM 82654 and the second in BM 29021.

38 BM 82608.

39 Bēliya'u ∞ Esagil-mansum (VS 5 26 and BM 96102).

40 Kidin-Sîn ∞ Gallābu (BM 85447). For the prebendary involvement of the Gallābu clan, see Waerzeggers 2010: 79[+352].

41 Male bakers: Bēliya'u ∞ Ilia (BM 26483). Female bakers: Ilia ∞ Esagil-mansum (BM 26731).

42 Male bakers: Esagil-mansum ∞ Iddin-Papsukkal (BM 29379, cf. Zadok 2005). Female bakers: Ea-ilūtu-bani ∞ Kidin-Sîn (TuM 2/3 48, Joannès 1989: 33.); Kidin-Nanāya ∞ Kidin-Sîn (BM 25589).

43 Nabû-mukīn-apli ∞ Kāṣir (BM 25588). Note that the Kāṣir family might have had some links to the service of the prebendary baker too. Bēl-iddin//Kāṣir, whose daughter was married to the Nabû-mukīn-aplis, is attested on one earlier occasion in a document dealing with the prebendary income of Šaddinnu//Bēliya'u (BM 29512).

44 Kidin-Sîn ∞ Nabûnnāya (BM 25589).

45 Bēliya'u ∞ Ṣillāya (BM 96313 and BM 21976).

46 Pahhāru ∞ Esagil-mansum (BM 29067; BM 28861). Note that the woman from the Esagil-mansum clan was previously married to Balassu//Bēliya'u. It thus represents her second marriage.

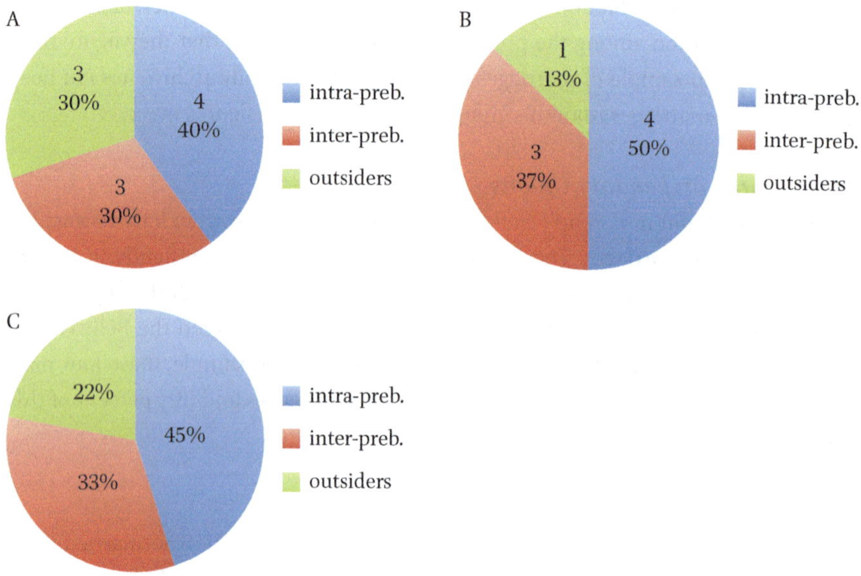

FIGURE 15 (a) Marriages of bakers (♂); (b) Marriages of bakers (♀); (c) Total marriages of bakers (♂ + ♀)

4 Butchers

Four families have so far been identified as butchers of Ezida: Eppēš-ilī, Eṭēru, Ibnāya, and Ilšu-abūšu.[47] While we have several smaller archives from the Ibnāya clan,[48] there is only little information on marriage alliances. We know of the marriage of three male and four female members. The marriages from this group are summarised in figures 16a–c.

4.1 *Intra-prebendary Unions*

The union between two members of the Ibnāya clan is so far the only known marriage arranged within this professional group.[49]

47 Waerzeggers 2010: 79. The Eppēš-ilī and Eṭēru families seem to have owned butcher prebends in Ezida passively, performing the temple service through agents only. See Waerzeggers 2010: 79[+349]. They probably had stronger ties to the temples in Babylon. Note that the Ilšu-abūšu is a family that had strong ties to the priesthood of the brewers too.

48 Jursa 2005: 83–84 and Waerzeggers 2010: 19 and 525ff.

49 Ibnāya ∞ Ibnāya (VS 4 176).

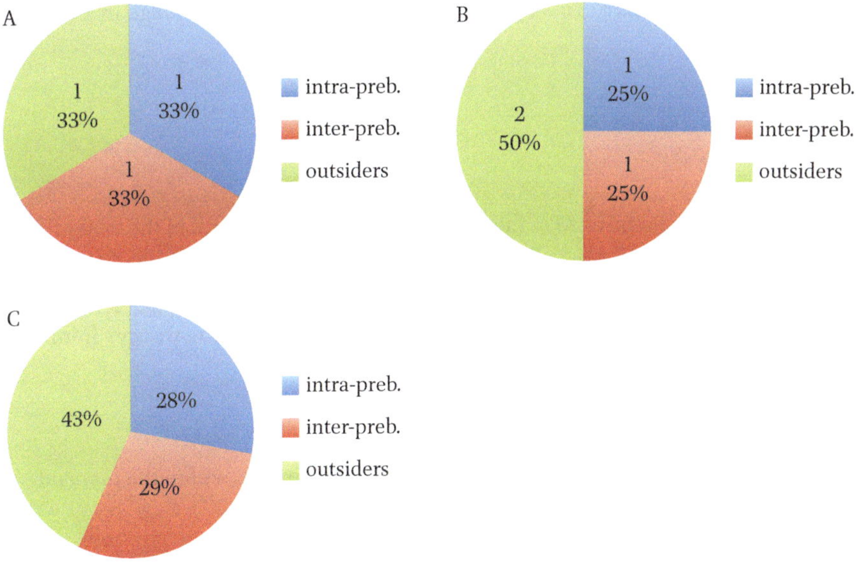

FIGURE 16 (a) Marriages of butchers (♂); (b) Marriages of butchers (♀); (c) Total marriages of butchers (♂ + ♀)

4.2 *Inter-prebendary Unions*

Two unions were arranged with other prebendary groups. In one instance, a woman was received from the Naggāru family in marriage.[50] In the other instance, a woman from the Ibnāya family, the granddaughter of a city governor (*šākin-ṭēmi*) of Borsippa, was married to the temple-enterer family of the Kidin-Nanāyas.[51]

4.3 *Extra-prebendary Unions*

It seems surprising that most marriages of this group were arranged with families that can be classified as non-prebendary (three times). The governor's son of the Ibnāya clan married a woman from the Siātu family.[52] The latter also received a bride from the Ilšu-abūšus, another family of butchers.[53] This must have been an important alliance since the bride was the daughter of the overseer (*šāpiru*) of the butchers of the Ezida temple.[54] A final marriage involved a woman from the Ibnāya and a man

50 Ilšu-abūšu ∞ Naggāru (BM 28863 = AH XV no. 115.)
51 Kidin-Nanāya ∞ Ibnāya (BM 96151).
52 Ibnāya ∞ Siātu (VS 5 25 and BM 96151).
53 Siātu ∞ Ilšu-abūšu (BM 28865 = AH XV no. 116; VS 5 28).
54 ^{f}Ilāt was the daughter of Ezida-šumu-ukīn//Ilšu-abūšu who occupied the function of overseer (*šāpiru*) of the butchers (ca. 583 BCE), see Waerzeggers 2010: 254^{+900}.

from the Ṣāhit-ginê clans. This family is thus far only attested as judge in Borsippa (VS 4 32).[55]

5 Oxherds

It has already been mentioned in the introduction that the prebend of the oxherd (*rē'i-alpūtu*) was entirely dominated by the Rē'i-alpi clan (see Introduction 7.4). This means that the marriages we take into consideration here belong to one clan only. There are in total ten marriages involving members of the Rē'i-alpis. The marriages from this group are summarised in figures 17a–c.

5.1 *Intra-prebendary Unions*

There is no evidence that the Rē'i-alpi clan arranged marriages within the prebendary group or, in this case, among members of the same family.

5.2 *Inter-prebendary Unions*

There are five marriages (50%) with other prebendary families. The oxherds received brides from both the brewers[56] and the temple-enterers.[57] The first woman came from the Ardūtu clan, a minor brewer clan that is attested only a couple of times in relation to this trade.[58] The second woman came from the Arad-Ea family. While this clan appears as early as the Kassite period[59] and occupied high positions in Borsippa during the eighth century BCE,[60] it seemed to have lost its prominence in the local religious sphere by the time of this union.[61] Families that obtained women from the Rē'i-alpis are the Arkāti-ilāni-damqā,[62] Kudurrānu,[63] and Gallābu[64] families. These were prominent families belonging to the ranks of temple-enterers, brewers, and barbers, respectively.

55 Ṣāhit-ginê ∞ Ibnāya. See Waerzeggers 2010: 127.

56 Rē'i-alpi ∞ Ardūtu (BM 29375).

57 Rē'i-alpi ∞ Arad-Ea. See BM 82609 = Roth 1989 no 22 and BM 26707.

58 Waerzeggers 2010: 84. Note that in the three attestations the Ardūtu family works in close tandem with the Mannu-gērûšu clan, another rather peripheral family.

59 Nielsen 2011: 73.

60 VS 1 36.

61 The Arad-Ea family might have been more successful in the royal administration. In Borsippa members worked in tandem with the local 'canal inspector' (VS 6 160, Dar 33). In Babylon they occupied the position of royal resident (*qīpu*) of the Esagil temple (VS 6 155, Dar 29). See Nielsen 2011: 73f.

62 Arkāt-ilāni-damqā ∞ Rē'i-alpi (BM 94606 = AH XV no. 143).

63 Kudurrānu ∞ Rē'i-alpi (BM 96259).

64 Gallābu ∞ Rē'i-alpi (BM 94696).

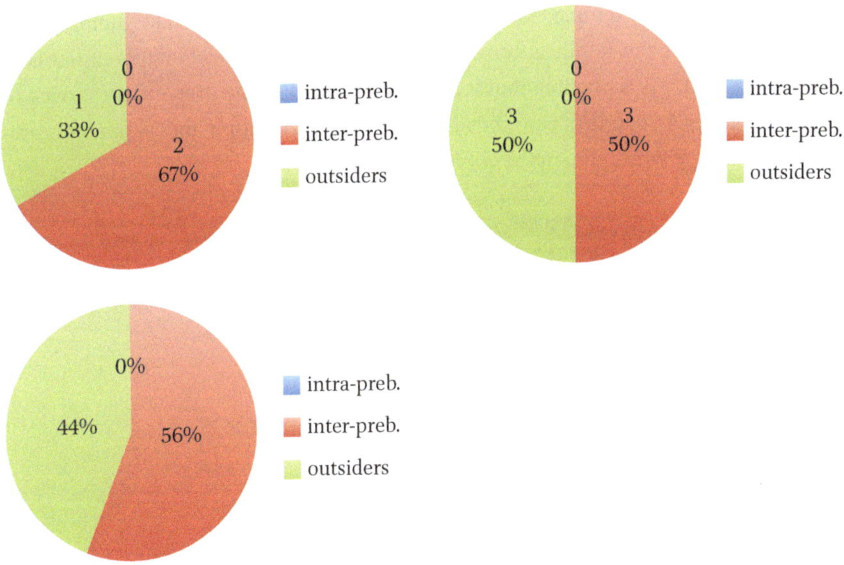

FIGURE 17 (a) Marriages of oxherds (♂); (b) Marriages of oxherds (♀); (c) Total marriages of oxherds (♂ + ♀)

5.3 *Extra-prebendary Unions*

The Rēʾi-alpi family arranged many marriages with families outside of the prebendary circle. The family received one bride from the Mubannû clan.[65] While it is not impossible that the latter was involved in the homonymous 'arranger-of-the-sacrificial-table' (*mubannūtu*) prebend, this is not substantiated in the corpus. Families that obtained daughters from the Oxherd family were the ^{f}Maqartus,[66] Rišāyas,[67] and Šarrahus.[68]

6 Reed-Workers

The information on this prebendary group is provided by the Atkuppu family archive (see Introduction 7.5). Unfortunately, there is very little known about the marriage alliances for this clan. The archive informs us only of the marriage of two male members. On the one hand, the reed-workers received a bride from the Adad-nāṣirs, a family with

65 Rēʾi-alpi ∞ Mubannû (BM 94698).
66 ^{f}Maqartu ∞ Rēʾi-alpi (BM 26487).
67 Rišāya ∞ Rēʾi-alpi (EAH 203).
68 Šarrahu ∞ Rēʾi-alpi (EAH 213 and BM 101980//BM 82607).

no apparent ties to the temple.[69] On the other hand, they received a daughter from the Nappāhus.[70] While this family is known to have provided two local temple-enterers of Ninlil in the past,[71] it is possible that it also was involved in the prebendary service of the smith (*nappāhu*). In that case the alliance between Atkuppu and Nappāhu represented a marriage within the ranks of temple craftsmen.

69 Atkuppu ∞ Adad-nāṣir (BM 82629 = Roth 1990 no. 13).
70 OECT 12 A 158.
71 Waerzeggers 2010: 76.

APPENDIX 2

Annotated List of *Hanšû* Land in Borsippa

hanšû ša…[1]

1) ***bīt*** **Abunāya** (or, **Adnāya**): one hears of this estate in the famous case of high treason committed against King Nebuchadnezzar II in his eleventh regnal year.[2] The Abunāya family seems to have lost this land already before the reign of Nebuchadnezzar II. The history recounted in this text tells us that this *hanšû* was taken from the traitor of the Rēš-ummāni family and returned to the Ezida temple to which it had previously belonged. It was then given to an individual of the Šigûa clan.

1b) **Nabû-remēni//Abunāya** (or, **Adnāya**): an individual of the Ša-ṭābtišu clan (and his uncle) sold a part of this *hanšû* estate to the Kidin-Sîn clan in the early Neo-Babylonian period (VS 5 140; date lost).

2) ***bīt*** **Apkallu**: this property is recorded between the reigns of Šamaš-šumu-ukīn and Nabonidus (ca. 664–548 BCE). The first attestation of this *hanšû* dates to Ššu 04 at the occasion of an inheritance division in the Aqar-Nabû family (OECT 12 A 83). This text probably entered the archive of the Ea-ilūtu-bani family retroactively when a member acquired the land. It is found in their possession between circa Nbk 21+ (YBC 9194) and Nbk 40 (YBC 9189). At one point a share of this *hanšû* was held by the Ilī-bānis (a clan related to the Ea-ilūtu-bani through marriage) as can be seen from text BM 96263 (Nbn 08). Note that most documents dealing with this property do not use the term *hanšû* (e.g. TuM 2/3 151, TCL 12 56, OECT 12 A 180).

3) ***bīt*** **Ašgandu** (or, **Šukandu**): this property occurs for the first time in an inheritance division of the Ilia family in the reign of Nabonidus (BM 94587, Nbn 13, note that here the term *hanšû* is not used). Various texts record the subsequent management of this land by the family (e.g. BM 95042, HSM 1904.4.23).[3] The Ilias acquired an additional share from the Nappāhu family in Dar 06 (BM 95042).

4) ***bīt*** **Atkuppu**: this *hanšû* is mentioned once in Nbk 11 (TCL 12 30). The text records the sale of three larger plots in this *hanšû* unit by the Nannāhus to a clan whose name is unfortunately not preserved. Members of the Atkuppu family feature as neighbours of two of the sold plots.

1 The list of *hanšû* land is in alphabetic order, following the family or professional name when units are identified by PN//FN. The references to most of these *hanšû* units can be found in Zadok 2006.

2 Weidner 1956: 1–5.

3 Zadok 2006: 440.

 DOI:10.1163/9789004399969_011

5) ***bīt*** **Bābāya:** this *hanšû* estate is only mentioned once in a cultivation contract from the Gallābu family archive (BM 96291, Nbn 12). Note that the scribe comes from the Babāya clan, suggesting that this clan kept an interest in their eponymous land.

6) ***bīt mār*** **Bā'iru:** land in this unit is bought by the Rē'i-alpis from an individual without family name in Dar 12 (BM 26510). The completion of payment was still due a year and a half later (BM 94540, Dar 14). The land might have been sold together with various other pieces of property to an unknown buyer in Dar 20 (BM 26576 = AH XV no. 192).

7) ***bīt*** **Banê-ša-ilia:** in BM 93001 (Kan 07) two plots of land in this *hanšû* are exchanged between relatives of the Banê-ša-ilia clan.

7b) **Šumā//Banê-ša-ilia:** this estate is mentioned once in a cultivation contract arranged within the Banê-ša-ilia family (BM 27854, Kan 19).

8) **Nabû-šumu-iškun//Bārû:** a share in this *hanšû* was bought by the Adad-nāṣirs from the Barû clan sometimes before Nbk 14 (BM 26392). This field probably came into the possession of the Atkuppu family upon marrying a daughter of the Adad-nāṣir family.[4]

9) ***bīt*** **Basia:** in Nbn 09 a woman from the Basia family donated her dowry field in this *hanšû* to her son who was a descendant of the same clan (BM 21975). At least one of the gardens in this *hanšû* was used as dowry property for a woman of the Ṣillāya family who was married to Šaddinnu//Bēliya'u. The Basia family, however, still owned certain rights to the land, and members occasionally appear as co-owners or creditors in *imittu* texts. While the Bēliya'us seem to have had their own interest in this area (BM 28912, Dar 20), various texts bear witness to the fact that the dowry field of the Ṣillāyas came under management of the Bēliya'u family after marriage (e.g. BM 28961, Cam 07; BM 28952, Dar 10$^?$; and BM 96337, Dar 27). Ownership of this *hanšû* unit was obviously complex with as many as three clans holding rights to it simultaneously: Basia, Bēliya'u, and Ṣillāya (e.g. BM 96389, date lost).

10) ***bīt*** **Bēlāya:** a garden in this *hanšû* was held as a pledge for a debt of silver by the Gallābu family in Nbn 10 (BM 96239). Unfortunately, the family name of the debtor is lost. The Kudurrānu family might also have owned a piece of land in this unit as early as Nbn 13 (BM 22064, term *hanšû* not used), if indeed it concerns the same plot mentioned in BM 22012 (Nbk IV 01, term *hanšû* used).

11) ***bīt*** **Bēliya'u:** this estate is mentioned in BM 28904, dated Nbk 33. It is thought to mark the arrival of the Bēliya'u family in the Borsippa milieu.[5] The text records how the Bēliya'u clan receives lands in the *hanšû* [PN] *ša Kidin-Sîn* from a fellow baker clan. While the designation of *hanšû* is not (yet) attached to this newly created property, called only *bīt Bēliya'u*, the text does seem to refer to it as 'this *hanšû*' (ll. 1–2: 11 ha.la.

4 See Abraham [*forthcoming*].

5 Waerzeggers 2010: 207–208.

meš *šá* é ^{m}en-*ia*-[*ú*...] *ina* 50-a_4). Incidentally, the fact that the Bēliya'u clan, a newcomer in town and the latest addition to the prebendary bakers of Nabû, receives land in or next to estates held by other baker clans like the Kidin-Sîn and Esagil-mansum, suggests a link between *hanšû* property and professional identity. One wonders whether the allocation of *hanšû* land was not related to or conditional on the performance of certain services, at least in its original stage. This could also be inferred from the use of 'son' or perhaps 'member' (*māru* and *aplu*) in the designation of *hanšû* units attached to various professional (family) names: *hanšû ša mār Bā'iru* (fisherman), *hanšû ša mār Lāsimu* (express messenger/scout), and *hanšû ša apil Nappāhu* (smith).

12) ***bīt*** **Bibbê**: this unit is mentioned in TuM 2/3 137 (Camb 02). The owner is from the Ilī-bāni family. The family name Bibbê is only attested three times in the corpus and is found more often as a personal name of Chaldean individuals like for example the royal magnate called Bibêa, son of Dakūru, in the *Hofkalender* of King Nebuchadnezzar II.[6]

13) ***bīt*** **Bitahhi**: BM 26504//BM 26481 (Cam [x]) documents the exchange of fields between two relatives of the Rē'i-alpi clan. A plot in the *hanšû ša Rē'i-sisê* and some additional silver were exchanged against a larger plot in the *hanšû ša bīt Bitahhi*. While the family name Bitahhi is only attested twice in the Borsippa corpus, there is prosopographical evidence suggesting that it was an alternative spelling for the somewhat better-known family name of Barihi.

14) **Kāṣir//Ēdu-ēṭir**: a plot in this unit was reclaimed by a member of the homonymous clan through the exchange of a field with the Išpāru family in BM 17599 (Npl 09). Note that the Ēdu-ēṭir clan still held neighbouring plots.

15) ***bīt*** **Esagil**: in Nbk 39 a plot in this *hanšû* was owned by the Bābāyas (VS 3 24). This text records the payment of an amount of dates for the services to the 'canal inspector' (*gugallu*) of Borsippa. The fact that this document belongs to the Atkuppu archive suggests that this family had a stake in this land as well. That this *hanšû* refers to the Esagil temple and not to a family is suggested by the absence of a Personenkeil.

16) ***bīt*** **Esagil-mansum**: this unit is found in two documents recording a transfer of property within the homonymous family. In BM 29379 (Cam 07) a woman donates a garden in *bīt Esagil-mansum* to her son. In BM 28902 (Dar 01) two individuals from the same family exchange date palm gardens (parts of the ancestral patrimony, *bīt abišu*). A share of this estate came into the possession of the Ea-ilūtu-bani family, in whose archive it is found in Nbk III 00 (YOS 17 8).[7] Between Dar 09 and Dar 26, a plot in this *hanšû* (probably as part of the dowry of the Ṣillāya family, see *hanšû bīt* Basia above) was held by the Basia, Bēliya'u, and Ṣillāya families (e.g. VS 3 104, 09; BM 28984, Dar 14; BM 29432, Dar 21; BM 28989, Dar 26; and BM 96186, Dar x).

6 Beaulieu 2013a: 34.

7 Joannès 1989: 326.

17) ***bīt* Gallābu:** parts of this estate were already lost to the ancestral family during or even before the reign of King Nebuchadnezzar II when it was controlled by the Ea-ilūtu-banis (YBC 9158). After being divided and partly sold to the Iddin-Papsukkal family, a member of the Gallābu clan was able to reclaim some of his ancestral land during the reign of Nabonidus (BM 96351). This land was subsequently sold off to the Mannu-gērûšus (BM 29401). According to R. Zadok, the Ilia family also owned a share of land in this *hanšû* unit.[8]

18) ***tamirtu* humamātu:** land in this *hanšû* was sold by a member of the Gallābu family to the Mudammiq-Marduk family. However, in BM 96267 (Nbn 06) this transaction was successfully contested and reclaimed by a brother of the seller.

19) **Ahu-ēreš//Huršanāya:** this estate is mentioned in BM 87239 (Nbk 11). In this text a member of the Nabû-šemê family sells two *kur* of land stretching over this *hanšû* and the *hanšû šaNabû-ēṭir//Purattāya* for the staggering amount of seventy-two minas of silver to the Pahhāru family. The Huršanāya family is attested only once in the corpus (BM 28826).

20) ***bīt* Huṣābu:** in the earliest documentation of this unit the land is (temporarily) held by Banê-ša-ilia as collateral for a debt of silver due from a member of the Huṣābu family (TuM 2/3 106, Nbk 15). Another dossier documents the acquisition of a garden in this *hanšû* by the Rē'i-alpis. The first text shows that a member of the Adad-ibni clan bought part of this land from the Mubannû clan, which had previously bought it from the Asalluhi-mansums (before Cam 06, VS 5 48). This share was then sold to a member of the Atkuppu family (BM 85239 and BM 26623, Dar 03). In a document dated one year later it is, however, revealed that the Atkuppu acted only as a proxy for the actual buyer from the Rē'i-alpi family (BM 82619). Documentation for this land continues until Dar 18 (e.g. BM 82713, BM 94716, and BM 102022).

21) **Iddin-Amurru:** the earliest secured attestation of this *hanšû* comes from BM 26487 (Nbk 22). Rēmūt-Gula//Rē'i-alpi requests his son-in-law from the ᶠMaqartu family to assign property to his wife. He assigns to her the ownership of a house and a garden on the *nār-Mihir* in the *hanšû ša* Iddin-ᵈx. While the reading of the name is unsure, this is one of the few *hanšû*s in Borsippa named after an individual without a family name. Contrary to, for example, Uruk where Iddin-Amurru can denote an ancestral name, in Borsippa it is only attested as a personal name. That it should be interpreted as such in this case also is suggested by the lack of the term 'house' or 'family' (*bīt*). Moreover, in Dar 00 Nabû-mukīn-zēri//Rē'i-alpi showed further interest in this (*hanšû*) area and exchanged three slaves with the Allānu family for a garden in the vicinity of the *nār-Mihir* in the Iddin-Amurru area (BM 94546, *hanšû* not mentioned).

22) ***bīt* Iddin-Papsukkal:** according to OECT 12 AB 241 (Cyr 06), a man from the Aqar-Nabû family and his wife from the Huṣābu family sold four plots in this *hanšû* to the

8 Zadok 2006: 431.

Ahiya'ūtus. The text further specifies that the property was held undivided with the Nūr-Papsukkal and the Išparu families. Moreover, the Iddin-Papsukkal still owned neighbouring plots. Another neighbour is Nabû-mukīn-zēri//Rē'i-alpi who would later buy this land from the Ahiya'ūtu family (BM 82764 Dar 02).

22b) Saggillu//Iddin-Papsukkal: this *hanšû* is attested in BM 26493 (ca. Nbk 08). The Raksu family sold the land to an individual of the Adad-nāṣir clan. The buyer already owned a neighbouring plot. This text probably belongs to the Atkuppu archive and it is likely that this field entered into their possession through the marriage alliance with the Adad-nāṣir family.

23) *bīt* (Ea-)ilūtu-bani: this *hanšû* is mentioned in two cultivation related contracts (NBC 8362, AmM 02 and BM 94780, Nbn 13) involving Zēru-Bābili//Ea-ilūtu-bani and his son, respectively. Some parts of this *hanšû* were presumably lost to the ancestral family at an earlier phase because in Nbk 18 the Ilī-bāni family (linked to the Ea-ilūtu-banis by marriage) bought a plot in this *hanšû* from the Damēqu family (TuM 2/3 15).

23b) Illûa//(Ea-)ilūtu-bani: this estate was kept largely within the Ea-ilūtu-bani family from the reign of Šamaš-šumu-ukīn until at least the reign of Cyrus. The first period of documentation is characterised by a series of sales of smaller shares between relatives (e.g. YBC 11426, Ššu 12; and OECT 12 A 131, Ššu 12). The land was kept by Puhhuru//Ea-ilūtu-bani until the reign of King Nabopolassar.[9] In Npl 16 Puhhuru divided this property among his sons (TuM 2/3 5) who successfully passed it down to his grandson and great-grandson (e.g. TuM 2/3 195, Nbk 01; TuM 2/3 135, Ner 03; 94780, Nbn 13; and BM 94692, Cyr 06). This dossier has been discussed extensively in the past.[10]

23c) Nādin-ahi//(Ea-)ilūtu-bani: evidence on this *hanšû* came into existence when the Ea-ilūtu-bani family sold various plots to the Iddin-Papsukkal family around the 660s BCE (TuM 2/3 17, TCL 12 9, and TuM 2/3 11). It was sold to an individual member of the Nappāhu clan only a short time later (TuM 2/3 12, Ššu 10). The land eventually ended up in the possession of the Gallābus. It was only sometime during the reign of King Nebuchadnezzar II, some fifty years later, that the Ea-ilūtu-bani family regained this property (OECT 12 A 163).

23d) Suppê-Bēl//(Ea-)ilūtu-bani: in Ššu 12 Puhhuru//Ea-ilūtu-bani exchanged parts of this *hanšû* for a plot in the *hanšû ša bīt Pahhāru* owned by the *šāpiru* of the brewers from the Ilia family (TuM 2/3 23//MAH 16232).[11] Puhhuru already owned a neighbouring field and it has been stressed previously that this transaction was part

9 Note that in most texts the term *hanšû* is not used. See, for example, TuM 2/3 133, Kan 04 and TuM 2/3 134, Npl 07.

10 Joannès 1989: 65f. and Nielsen 2011: 91f.

11 See Joannès 1989: 174 for an edition of this text. Corrections can be found in Nielsen 2011: 92[+310].

of a coherent strategy to assemble a bloc of several pieces of land.[12] That the ancestral family remained in control of most of the *hanšû Suppê-Bēl//(Ea-)ilūtu-bani*, however, is clear from a later transaction. In TCL 12 16 (Kan 06) Puhhuru sold a plot in this unit to a relative; both owned neighbouring plots.

24) ***bīt* Iššakku**: a garden in this *hanšû* was kept as pledge by the Kudurrānu family for a debt of silver against the Iššakkus in Dar 27 (BM 29007). The land was at that time held by members of the Iššakku and the Purkullu families.

25) ***bīt* Kidin-Sîn**: an orchard located here was part of the property transferred by Nabû-mukīn-zēri//Rē'i-alpi to his grandson and subsequently claimed by his own son, Rēmūt-Nabû (e.g. BM 26514, Dar 05 and BM 26492//BE 8 108, Dar 06). The land was held undivided with a member of the Kidin-Sîn clan.

25b) **Nabû-šumu-līšir (or, -ukīn)//Kidin-Sîn**: this *hanšû* is mentioned first in a complicated division of dowry property in Cam 07 (BM 94697). In this document Nabû-šumu-uṣur//Kidin-Sîn grants a garden in this unit to his daughter and her husband (Gimillu//Kidin-Sîn) as a dowry. It is not exactly clear why, but a member of the Bēliya'u also receives a share in this *hanšû*. One year later, Gimillu sells part of his land to Nabû-mukīn-zēri//Rē'i-alpi (BM 82656). The presence of a royal scribe (*ṭupšar šarri*) suggests that this sale was not completely voluntary. The transaction dragged on for another year when a re-confirmation of the sale was written (BM 82654). It seems, however, that Gimillu still owned some land in this *hanšû* (this time not belonging to his wife's dowry), which he later sold to the same buyer in Dar 02 (EAH 212).

25c) **[PN]//Kidin-Sîn**: this is the estate where members of the Bēliya'u family received land from the Kidin-Sîns in Nbk 33, see *hanšû ša bīt Bēliya'u* (above). It might be identical to the *hanšû* discussed before (25b).

26) ***bīt* Kudurru *u bīt* ᶠLe'itu**: the dossier from the Ilia (A) family dealing with these units has been discussed elsewhere.[13] The four sons of Šulā//Ilia inherited land in this area in the reign of Nabonidus. The eldest brother sold part of this property to his siblings who initially kept it undivided (e.g. BM 102289, Nbn 12; BM 26532, Nbn 13; and BM 17657, Nbn 13). The rest of the documentation concerns the management of this land by especially one of the three brothers, Marduk-šumu-ibni (e.g. BM 17641//VS 3, 196, Cam 02; BM 25718, Dar 02; BM 102012, Dar 08; and BM 102307, Dar 15). It is interesting to note that this unit is only explicitly called a *hanšû* once (BM 25718). The land is usually said to be located in the *eblu* (meaning unsure) *ša bīt Kudurru u bīt* ᶠ*Le'itu*.

27) ***bīt* Kurgarrê**: based on parallel attestation this *hanšû* name has been restored previously by R. Zadok.[14] The first attestation of this estate comes from the marriage

12 Joannès 1989: 66–67.
13 Jursa *et al.* 2010: 368–371.
14 Zadok 2006: 442.

contract between the Arad-Ea and the Rē'i-alpi families dated Dar 01.[15] This land is later said to be located on the canal (*harru*) of the *bīt Kurgarrê* and probably sold by the Rē'i-alpi family to an unknown buyer in Dar 20 (BM 26576 = AH XV no. 192).

28) ***bīt* Lahāšu:** this *hanšû* is mentioned only once in Nbk 11 (TCL 12 30) as a neighbouring estate of the *hanšû ša bīt Atkuppu* (see above).

29) ***bīt mār* Lāsimu:** a garden here is sold by the Lāsimu clan to Šaddinnu//Bēliya'u in Dar 10 (BM 96289). While the term *hanšû* is not used in this text, it can be restored from the *imittu* text BM 96299 (Dar 22). Šaddinnu only completed his payment in Dar 20 when the remainder was given to the Lāsimu family (BM 29113). There are thus far only two individuals attested with the family name Lāsimu in the Borsippa corpus.

30) ***bīt* Mubannû:** a field belonging to the dowry of fNanāya-bulliṭiš//Mubannû, wife of Nabû-mukīn-zēri//Rē'i-alpi, was located in this *hanšû*. It is only attested in a short period between Dar 05 and Dar 09. In Dar 05 the couple assigned this plot first to their daughter fInbā (BM 101980//BM 82607) and then to their grandson Lâbâši-Marduk (BM 26514). This transaction was later cancelled to the benefit of their son Rēmūt-Nabû (BM 26492//BE 8 108 Dar 06). This land is mentioned once more when Rēmūt-Nabû used it as a pledge for 5/6 minas of silver in Dar 09 (BM 82728).

31) **Nabû-mutakkil**(?): this unit is mentioned in a very fragmented text in Cyr 06 (VS 5 36). It probably belonged to the Ilia (A) family.

32) ***bīt* Naggāru:** land in this *hanšû* was held as a pledge by the Gallābu family for a debt of barley, dates, and silver drawn against a member of the Maṣṣār-abulli family in Nbn 15 (BM 85641). According to the *imittu* text BM 96315 (Dar 18) Šaddinnu//Bēliya'u owned a garden here as well. He also obtained ownership of another field here in return for the old-age care of a member of the Kāṣir clan (BM 25630//BM 25653, Dar 20).

32b) **Nummuru//Naggāru:** three members of the Naggāru family sold this unit, apparently in its entirety, to the Ilia family in Links Ššu 04 (*RA* 10 no. 46) for only 5 shekels of silver. It should be noted, however, that no dimensions are given.

33) ***bīt apil* Nappāhu:** land in this unit was used as dowry property of fAhattu//Arad-Ea who married into the Rē'i-alpi clan in Dar 01 (BM 82609 = Roth 1989 no. 22). The management of this plot (still held with some other members of the Arad-Ea family, according to BM 26707 and BM 26561//BM 94879) is recorded until Dar 29 (BM 26335). This property was, however, temporarily pledged to the Ea-imbi family in Babylon around Dar 19 (BM 26624//BM 102002 and BM 94685).

34) ***bīt* Nikkāya:** this *hanšû* is mentioned as neighbouring estates of the *hanšû ša bīt Atkuppu* in Nbk 11 (TCL 12 30) (see above).

15 BM 82609 = Roth 1989 no. 22.

35) *bīt* **Pahhāru:** land in this unit was originally bought from the Damēqu family by the *šāpiru* of brewers of the Ilia family. The latter then exchanged it in Ššu 12 against a plot in *hanšû* Suppê-Bēl//(Ea-)ilūtu-bani (see above).

36) ***mār* Pa-ni-a-su-šu-du**(?): this land was part of the dowry of ᶠAhattu//Arad-Ea who married into the Rē'i-alpi clan around Dar 01 (BM 82609 = Roth 1989 no. 22). The reading of this name is unsure.

37) **Nabû-ēṭir//Purattāya:** see *hanšû ša* Ahu-ēreš//Huršanāya above.

38) **Rabî:** this *hanšû* is mentioned once in an *imittu* text from the Ilī-bāni archive.[16]

39) *bīt* **Rē'i-alpi:** this *hanšû* is documented through numerous transfers of property within the Rē'i-alpi family between Nbn 00 and Dar 29. It is first attested in Nbn 00 when an individual from the Arkāt-ilāni-damqā family bought land from ᶠAmat-Ningal//Rē'i-alpi as proxy for Nabû-mukīn-zēri//Rē'i-alpi (BM 25627). A year later Nabû-mukīn-zēri made use of another proxy to buy a different plot of land here from his relatives (BM 26636 and BM 109871). The presence of a royal scribe at the latter transaction suggests an involuntary sale, perhaps as a result of indebtedness. A final transaction is found in BM 26571 (= AH XV no. 147, Nbn 08), which records the exchange of two days of the oxherd's prebend against a field in this *hanšû*. This *hanšû* seems to have been kept firmly in the family until Dar 29 (BM 86442).

39b) **Nabû-zēru-ibni/Nabû-aplu-iddin/Rē'i-alpi:** an orchard in this unit was sold in Nbn 04 by Nabû-ušebši//Rē'i-alpi (perhaps the grandson of the individual who gave his name to this *hanšû*) to ᶠṬabātu//ᶠMaqartu (Rē'i-alpi from her mother's side) in order to pay off a long-standing debt to the Ezida temple (BE 8 44//BM 94562). The fact that it was written in the presence of the royal scribe suggests that there was pressure from higher-up. According to the quittance text BM 26687//BM 26656, ᶠṬabātu paid the full price to Nabû-ušebši in Nbn 05. However, a few years later disagreement arose over the exact boundaries of the field. Unfortunately, from the document that records its settlement it is not entirely clear who the real owner was in Nbn 10 (BM 26648). It only tells us that the land was jointly bought by Nabû-mukīn-zēri//Rē'i-alpi and ᶠṬabātu.

40) *bīt* **Rē'i-sisê:** a plot in this *hanšû* was exchanged by a member of the Ēdu-ēṭir family against land in the *hanšû ša Kāṣir//Ēdu-ēṭir* owned by the Išparus in Npl 09 (BM 17599). During the reign of King Nabonidus the Šagimmu family sold a share to the Huṣābus (BE 8 43). This transaction was later cancelled and the land was bought by another individual whose name is lost (BM 26474). During the reign of King Cambyses shares in this *hanšû* came under control of the Rē'i-alpi family. BM 26504//BM 26481 (Cam [x]) records the exchange of two fields within the Rē'i-alpi clan: a field in the *hanšû ša Rē'i-sisê* was exchanged for one in the *hanšû ša bīt Bitahhi*. The land was later sold to the Šarrahus, a family related to the Rē'i-alpi family by marriage.

16 See Joannès 1989: 87 and 269.

41) *bīt* Rīšāya: this *hanšû* is attested as a dowry field in BM 29375 ([Ach?] 04), a document that records the division of dowry gifts among three generations of the Ardūtu family. Given that one of the daughters married into the Rē'i-alpi family, it is likely that this land followed her into the new conjugal household.

42) *bīt* Ṣillāya: land in this *hanšû* is attested in the Bēliya'u archive between Dar 09 (BM 96309) and Dar 18 (VS 3 119). It is very likely that the Ṣillāya clan held this land until it married one of its daughters to the Šaddinnu//Bēliya'u, sometime during the reign of King Cambyses, and used it as dowry property.

43) Ša-Nabû-šū: a field in this *hanšû* was bought by the Egibis from Babylon in Nbn 08, perhaps from the Arad-Ea family.[17]

44) *bīt* Ṭābihu: Šaddinnu//Bēliya'u bought a date grove in this estate in Dar 20 from the Ibnāya family (VS 5 92). It is interesting to see that members of the Ibnāya family, who traditionally performed the function of the prebendary butcher of Nabû, also held land in the *hanšû* of the butcher (*ṭābihu*).

17 Wunsch 2000: no. 116.

APPENDIX 3

Property Sales in the Borsippa Corpus

Sales of *Hanšû* Land

Museum No.	Date	Seller	Buyer	Profession seller	Profession buyer
A 163 (OECT 12)	[≥Nbk]	Gallābu	Ea-ilūtu-bani	barber	ērib-bīti
AB 241 (OECT 12)	Cyr 06	Huṣābu ∞ Aqar- Nabû	Ahiya'ūtu	brewer ∞ ērib-bīti	brewer/ ērib-bīti
BE 8 43	Nbn 03	Šagimmu	Huṣābu		brewer
BM 25627	[Nbn] 00	Arkāt-ilāni-d. (proxy)	Rē'i-alpi	ērib-bīti	oxherd
BM 26474	Nbn 03	Šagimmu	[...]		
BM 26493	Nbk [08]	Raksu	Adad-nāṣir		
BM 26499	Nbn 01	Rē'i-alpi	Nūr-Papsukkal	oxherd	ērib-bīti
BM 26510	Dar 12	(no family)	Rē'i-alpi		oxherd
BM 26567	Dar 05	Nappāhu	Ilia (A)	ērib-bīti/ craftsman	brewer
BM 29401	Cam 02	Gallābu	Mannu-gērûšu	barber	brewer
BM 82656	Dar [00]	Kidin-Sîn	Rē'i-alpi	baker	oxherd
BM 82764	Dar 02	Ahiya'ūtu	Rē'i-alpi	brewer/ērib-bīti	oxherd
BM 85239	Dar 03	Adad-ibni (proxy)	Rē'i-alpi		oxherd
BM 87239	Nbk 11	Nabû-šemê	Pahhāru		
BM 94552	[Cam/Dar]	Rē'i-alpi	Šarrahu	oxherd	
BM 94562//BE 8 44	Nbn 04	Rē'i-alpi	Mubannû	oxherd	(mubannû?)
BM 94662	Dar 04	Nabû-mukīn-apli (proxy)	Rē'i-alpi	baker	oxherd
BM 96218	> Dar 04	Kidin-Sîn	Bēliya'u	baker	baker
BM 96267	Nbn 06	Gallābu	Mudammiq-Marduk	barber	
BM 96289	Dar 10	Lāsimu	Bēliya'u		baker
BM 96351	Nbn 14	Ea-ilūtu-bani	Gallābu	ērib-bīti	barber
RA 10 no. 46	Ššu 04	Naggāru	Ilia	ērib-bīti/ craftsman	brewer
TCL 12 9	Ššu 07	Ea-ilūtu-bani	Iddin-Papsukkal	ērib-bīti	ērib-bīti
TuM 2/3 12	Ššu 10	Iddin-Papsukkal	Nappāhu	ērib-bīti	ērib-bīti/ craftsman
TuM 2/3 15	Nbk 18	Damēqu	Ilī-bāni		ērib-bīti

 | DOI:10.1163/9789004399969_012

Museum No.	Date	Seller	Buyer	Profession seller	Profession buyer
VS 5 48	> Camb 04	Asaluhhi-mansum	Mubannû		(mubannû?)
VS 5 48	Camb 04	Mubannû	Adad-ibni	(mubannû?)	
VS 5 92	Dar 20	Ibnāya	Bēliya'u	butcher	baker
VS 5 140	[Npl/Nbk]	Ša-ṭābtišu	Kidin-Sîn		baker
YBC 9189	Nbk 19	Gallābu	Ilī-bāni	barber	ērib-bīti

Sales of Non-*hanšû* Land

Museum No.	Date	Seller	Buyer	Profession Seller	Profession Buyer
Amherst 256	Dar 05	[...]	Pahhāru		
BM 25588	Dar 21	Arad-Nergal	Kāṣir		
BM 26520	Dar 18	Rē'i-alpi	Marduku	oxherd	
BM 26623	Dar 03	Adad-ibni	Atkuppu		reed-worker
BM 26656//BM 26687	Nbn 05	Rē'i-alpi	fMaqartu	oxherd	
BM 29090	Cyr 06	Gallābu	Pahhāru	barber	
BM 29117	Dar 11	Babūtu	Bēliya'u		baker
BM 29478	> Nbn 02	Mubannû	Šikkûa	(mubannû?)	brewer
BM 29478	Nbn 02	Šikkûa (proxy)	Ibnāya	brewer	butcher
BM 29666	Dar [x]	Bēl-ušumgal	Bēliya'u		baker
BM 82608	≥Dar 20	Kidin-Sin ∞ Šēpê-ilia	lúRi?-i[...] (+ Kidin-Sîn)	baker ∞ baker	(baker)
BM 82612	Nbn 04	[...]	[...]		
BM 82619	Dar 14	Atkuppu (proxy)	Rē'i-alpi	reed-worker	oxherd
BM 85542	Nbn 16	Ea-ilūtu-bani	Gallābu	ērib-bīti	barber
BM 85643	Nbn 12	Ša-nāšišu	Gallābu	(brewer?)	barber
BM 87274	[late Dar]	Bā'iru (woman)	Nappāhu		ērib-bīti/ craftsman
BM 87289	Dar 19	Kinia	Lā-kuppuru		brewer
BM 94677	Dar 13	Dannēa	Rē'i-alpi		oxherd
BM 94739	Dar 14	Ilia (D)	Iddin-Papsukkal	brewer	ērib-bīti
BM 95003	Nbn 10+	Ilia (A)	Rē'i-alpi	brewer	oxherd

Museum No.	Date	Seller	Buyer	Profession Seller	Profession Buyer
BM 96113	Dar 14	Ṣillāya	Iddināya		
BM 96371	Nbn 09	[...]-Nabû	Gallābu		barber
BM 101981	Dar 17	Rē'i-alpi	Siātu	oxherd	
VS 4 176	Dar 29	Ibnāya	Lā-kuppuru	butcher	brewer
VS 5 91	Dar 19	Lā-kuppuru	Lā-kuppuru	brewer	brewer
VS 6 105	Cyr 08	Rē'i-alpi	Pahhāru	oxherd	

Sales of Housing Plots

Museum No.	Date	Seller	Buyer	Profession Seller	Profession Buyer
BE 8 115	Dar 27	Sippê ∞ Itinnu	Siātu		
BM 21938	Dar 15	Eppēš-ilī	Bēliya'u	butcher	baker
BM 25100	Dar 09	Bēliya'u	Bēliya'u	baker	baker
BM 25589	Dar 03	Kidin-Sîn	Bēliya'u	baker	baker
BM 25712//BM 82790	Nbn 04	Rē'i-alpi	ᶠMaqartu	oxherd	
BM 26231	Cyr [x]	Ur-Nannā	Rē'i-alpi		oxherd
BM 26500	Dar 28	Kudurrānu	[...]	brewer	
BM 26503	Dar 27	Ilšu-abūšu	[...]	brewer	
BM 26528	Nši 10	Nabû-ēṭir	Miṣirāya		
BM 27746 + BM 109363	Dar 27	Naggāru	Basia	ērib-bīti/ craftsman	
BM 27785	Cam [x]	Nappāhu	Bēliya'u	ērib-bīti/ craftsman	baker
BM 28963	Dar 03	[...]	Bēliya'u		baker
BM 29019	Dar 06	Imbu-īnia (?)	Bēliya'u		baker
BM 29185	Nbk 40	Etel-pî	Kudurrānu		brewer
BM 82632	Dar 01	Rē'i-alpi	Rē'i-alpi	oxherd	oxherd
BM 82679	Nbn 05^{+}	Gallābu	Ilia	barber	brewer
BM 85312	Ner 01	(no family)	Atkuppu		reed-worker
BM 87358	Nbn 11	Nūr-Papsukkal	Ilia (D)	ērib-bīti	brewer
BM 94557	[< Nbn]	Arad-Ea	Ilia	ērib-bīti	brewer

Museum No.	Date	Seller	Buyer	Profession Seller	Profession Buyer
BM 94593	[late Nbk]	Kutimmu (?)	Itinnu (?)		
BM 94633	[> Nbn]	Arkāt-ilāni-d. ∞ Iddin-Pap.	Ilī-bāni	ērib-bīti ∞ ērib-bīti	ērib-bīti
BM 96143	Dar 20	Sāmu	Bēliya'u		baker
BM 96255	[Dar] (?)	Suqāya	Bēliya'u		baker
BM 96294	Dar 14	Šangû-Nanāya	Bēliya'u		baker
Camb 233	Cam 04	Ša-haṭṭu-ēreš (woman)	[...]		
Dar 367	Dar 13	Pahhāru	Egibi (Babylon)		
Iraq 59 no. 55	[early Dar]	[...]	Bēliya'u		baker
LB 886	[Dar]	Pahhāru (woman)	Iddin-Papsukkal		ērib-bīti
VS 4 98	Dar 03	Rē'i-sisê	Šigûa		
VS 5 6	Nbk 13	Ninurta-ušallim	Kidin-Nanāya		ērib-bīti
VS 5 96	Dar 25	(no family)	Iddin-Pap. (woman)		ērib-bīti
BM 82740	[Nbn 04/ Cam]	Ea-ilūtu-bani	Ilia (D)	ērib-bīti	brewer
BM 85364	Ner 03	Arkāt-ilāni-d.	(no family)	ērib-bīti	royal merchant

Bibliography

Abraham, K. 1992, The Dowry Clause in Marriage Documents from the First Millennium B.C.E., in: D. Charpin and F. Joannès (eds), *La circulation des biens, des personnes et des idées dans le Proche-Orient ancient*, CRRAI 37, Paris: 311–320.

Abraham, K. 2004, *Business and Politics under the Persian Empire: The Financial Dealings of Marduk-nāṣir-apli of the House of Egibi (521–487 B.C.E.)*, Bethesda.

Abraham, K. 2005/2006, West Semitic and Judean Brides in Cuneiform Sources from the Sixth Century BCE, *AfO* 51: 198–219.

Abraham, K. [forthcoming], *The Atkuppu Family Archive from Borsippa (608–486 BCE): Typology, Content and Text Editions.*

Abraham, K. and Sokoloff, M. 2011, Aramaic Loanwords in Akkadian: a Reassessment of the Proposals, *AfO* 52: 22–76.

Al-Rawi, F.N.H. and George, A.R. 1994, Tablets from the Sippar Library, III: two royal counterfeits, *Iraq* 56: 135–148.

Alster, B. 1997, *Proverbs of Ancient Sumer: The World's Earliest Proverb Collection* (2 vols.), Bethesda.

Baker, H.D. 1995, Neo-Babylonian Burials Revisited, in: S. Campbell and A. Green (eds), *The Archaeology of Death in the Ancient Near East*, Oxford: 209–220.

Baker, H.D. 2004, *The Archive of the Nappāhu Family* (*AfO* Beih. 30), Vienna.

Baker, H.D. 2007, Urban form in the first millennium BC, in: G. Leick (ed.), *The Babylonian World*, London: 66–77.

Baker, H.D. 2008, Babylon in 484 BC: the Excavated Archival Tablets as a Source for Urban History, *ZA* 98: 100–116.

Baker, H.D. 2010, The Social Dimensions of Babylonian Domestic Architecture in the Neo-Babylonian and Achaemenid Periods, in: J. Curtis and S. Simpson (eds), *The World of Achaemenid Persia. History, Art and Society in Iran and the Ancient Near East*, London: 179–194.

Baker, H.D. 2011, From Street Altar to Palace: Reading the Built Environment of Urban Babylonia, in: K. Radner and E. Robson (eds), *The Oxford Handbook of Cuneiform Culture*, Oxford: 533–552.

Baker, H.D. 2014, House Size and Household Structure: Quantitative Data in the Study of Babylonian Urban Living Conditions, in: H.D. Baker and M. Jursa (eds), *Documentary Sources in Ancient Near Eastern and Greco-Roman History: Methodology and Practice*, Oxford: 7–23.

Baker, H.D. 2015, Family Structure, Household Cycle, and the Social Use of Domestic Space in Urban Babylonia, in: M. Müller (ed.), *Household Studies in Complex Societies. (Micro) Archaeological and Textual Approaches*, Chicago: 371–407.

Baker, H.D. [forthcoming (a)], The Babylonian Cities: Investigating Urban Morphology Using Texts and Archaeology, in: N. May and U. Steinert (eds), *The Fabric of Cities: Aspects of Urbanism, Urban Topography and Society in Mesopotamia, Greece and Rome*, Leiden.

Baker, H.D. [forthcoming (b)], *The Urban Landscape in First Millennium B.C. Babylonia.*

Baker, H.D. and Wunsch, C. 2001, Neo-Babylonian notaries and their use of seals, in: W.W. Hallo and I.J. Winter (eds), *Proceedings of the XLV*[e] *Rencontre Assyriologique Internationale. Part II. Yale University. Seals and Seal Impressions*, Bethesda: 197–213.

Barjamovic, G. 2004, Civic Institutions and Self-Government in Southern Mesopotamia in the mid-first Millennium BC, in: J.G. Dercksen (ed.), *Assyria and Beyond. Studies Presented to Mogens Trolle Larsen*, Leiden: 47–98.

Barth, F. 1969, *Ethnic Groups and Boundaries: The Social Organization of Culture Difference*, Oslo.

Barth, F. 2005, *Britain and the Commonwealth*, in: F. Barth *et al.* (eds), *One Discipline, Four Ways: British, German, French, and American Anthropology* (*The Halle Lectures*), Chicago: 1–57.

Beaulieu, P.-A. 1989, *The Reign of Nabonidus, King of Babylon (556–539 B.C.)*, New Haven.

Beaulieu, P.-A. 1990, Cuts of Meat of King Nebuchadnezzar, *NABU* 1990/93.

Beaulieu, P.-A. 1991, Neo-Babylonian Larsa: A Preliminary Study, *Or* 60: 58–81.

Beaulieu, P.-A. 1993, Prébendiers d'Uruk à Larsa, *RA* 87: 137–152.

Beaulieu, P.-A. 1998, Review of *Uruk: Spätbabylonische Texte aus dem Planquadrat U18. AUWE 12*, by E. von Weiher, *JNES* 57: 313–316.

Beaulieu, P.-A. 2000, A Finger in Every Pie: The Institutional Connections of a Family of Entrepreneurs in Neo-Babylonian Larsa, in: A.C.V.M. Bongenaar (ed.), *Interdependency of Institutions and Private Entrepreneurs* (MOSS 2 = PIHANS 87), Istanbul: 25–41.

Beaulieu, P.-A. 2002, Ea-dayān, Governor of the Sealand, and Other Dignitaries of the Neo-Babylonian Empire, *JCS* 54: 99–123.

Beaulieu, P.-A. 2003, *The Pantheon of Uruk during the Neo-Babylonian Period* (CM 23), Groningen.

Beaulieu, P.-A. 2006, Official and Vernacular Languages: the Shifting Sands of Imperial and Cultural Identities in First-Millennium B.C. Mesopotamia, in: S.L. Sanders (ed.), *Margins of Writing, Origins of Culture*, Chicago: 187–216.

Beaulieu, P.-A. 2007a, Late Babylonian Intellectual Life, in: G. Leick (ed.), *The Babylonian World*, New York: 473–484.

Beaulieu, P.-A. 2007b, Nabonidus the Mad King: A Reconsideration of His Steles from Harran and Babylon, in: M. Heinz and M.H. Feldman (eds), *Representations of*

Political Power. Case Histories from Times of Change and Dissolving Order in the Ancient Near East, Winona Lake: 137–166.

Beaulieu, P.-A. 2011, Yahwistic Names in Light of Late Babylonian Onomastics, in: O. Lipschits *et al.* (eds), *Judah and the Judeans in the Achaemenid Period. Negotiating Identity in an International Context*, Winona Lake: 245–266.

Beaulieu, P.-A. 2013a, Arameans, Chaldeans and Arabs in Late Babylonian Sources, in: A. Berlejung and M.P. Streck (eds), *Aramaeans, Chaldaeans, and Arabs in Babylonia and Palestine in the First Millennium B.C.*, Wiesbaden: 31–55.

Beaulieu, P.-A. 2013b, Aspects of Aramaic and Babylonian Linguistic Interaction in First Millennium BC Iraq, *Journal of Language Contact* 6: 358–378.

Beer, B. 2001, Friendship, Anthropology of, in: N.J. Smelser and P.B. Baltes (eds), *International Encyclopedia of Social & Behavioral Sciences*, Oxford: 5805–5808.

Béteille, A. 2010, Caste, in: A. Barnard and J. Spencer (eds), *The Routledge Encyclopedia of Social and Cultural Anthropology* (2nd edition), London: 112–113.

Black, L.T. 1972, Relative Status of Wife Givers and Wife Takers in Gilyak Society, *American Anthropologist n.s.* 74: 1244–1248.

Boehmer, R.M., Pedde, F., and Salje, B., 1995, *Uruk: Die Gräber* (AUWE 10), Mainz.

Bongenaar, A.C.V.M. 1997, *The Neo-Babylonian Ebabbar Temple at Sippar: its Administration and its Prosopography* (PIHANS 80), Istanbul.

Bongenaar, A.C.V.M. 1999, Money in the Neo-Babylonian Institutions, in: J.-G. Dercksen (ed.) *Trade and Finance in Ancient Mesopotamia* (PIHANS 84), Istanbul: 159–174.

Borger, R. 1973, Die Weihe eines Enlil-Priesters, *BiOr* 30: 163–176.

Bourdieu, P. 1977, *Outline of a Theory of Practice*, Cambridge.

Brinkman, J.A. 1964, Merodach-Baladan II, in: R.D. Biggs and J.A. Brinkman (eds), *Studies Presented to A. Leo Oppenheim*, Chicago: 6–53.

Brinkman, J.A. 1968, *A Political History of Post-Kassite Babylonia: 1158–722 B.C.* (*AnOr* 43), Rome.

Brinkman, J.A. 1984, *Prelude to Empire: Babylonian Society and Politics, 746–626 BC* (Occasional Publications of the Babylonian Fund 7), Philadelphia.

Brinkman, J.A. 1995, Reflection on the Geography of Babylonia, in: M. Liverani (ed.), *Neo-Assyrian Geography*, Rome: 19–29.

Brinkman, J.A. 2006, The use of Occupational Names as Patronyms in the Kassite Period: A Forerunner of the Neo-Babylonian Ancestral Names?, in: A.K. Guinan *et al.* (eds), *If a Man Builds a Joyful House: Assyriological Studies in Honor of Erle Verdun Leichty* (CM 31), Leiden.

Brinkman, J.A. and Kennedy, D.A. 1983, Documentary Evidence for the Economic Base of Early Neo-Babylonian Society: A Survey of Dated Babylonian Economic Texts, 721–626 BC, *JCS* 35: 1–90.

Broekman, G.P.F. 2010, The Leading Theban Priests of Amun and their Families under Libyan Rule, *The Journal of Egyptian Archaeology* 96: 125–148.

Brubaker, R. and Cooper, F. 2000, Beyond "identity", *Theory and Society* 29: 1–47.

Çağirgan, G. and Lambert, W.G. 1991, The Late Babylonian Kislīmu Ritual for Esagil, *JCS* 43/45: 89–106.

Carpenter, C. 1994, Gentry and Community in Medieval England, *Journal of English Studies* 33: 340–380.

Cavigneaux, A. 1981. *Textes scolaires du temple de Nabû ša harê*, Texts from Babylon, 1. Baghdad: Ministry of Culture and Information, State Organization of Antiquities and Heritage.

Chambers, J.K. 1995, *Sociolinguistic Theory: Linguistic Variation and its Social Significance*, Oxford.

Clancier, P. 2009, *Les bibliothèques en Babylonie dans la deuxième moitié du Ier millénaire av. J.-C.* (AOAT 363), Münster.

Clancier, P. 2011, Cuneiform Culture's Last Guardians: the Old Urban Notability of Hellenistic Uruk, in: K. Radner and E. Robson (eds), *The Oxford Handbook of Cuneiform Culture*, Oxford: 752–773.

Clancier, P. 2014, Teaching and Learning Medicine and Exorcism at Uruk during the Hellenistic Period, in: A. Bernard and C. Proust (eds), *Scientific Sources and Teaching Contexts Throughout History: Problems and Perspectives*, Dordrecht: 41–66.

Cocquerillat, D. 1955, Les prébendes patrimoniales dans les temples à l'époque de la Ire dynastie de Babylone, *Revue Internationale des Droits de l'Antiquité* 3.2: 39–106.

Cocquerillat, D. 1968, *Palmeraies et cultures de l'Eanna d'Uruk (559–520)* (ADFU 8), Berlin.

Cocquerillat, D. 1984, Compléments Aux "Palmeraies et Cultures de l'Eanna d'Uruk" (II), *RA* 78: 49–70.

Coelho de Souza, M. 2009, The Future of the Structural Theory of Kinship, in: B. Wiseman (ed.), *The Cambridge Companion to Lévi-Strauss*, Cambridge: 80–100.

Cole, S.W. 1994a, Marsh Formation in the Borsippa Region and the Course of the Lower Euphrates, *JNES* 53: 81–109.

Cole, S.W. 1994b, The Crimes and Sacrileges of Nabû-šuma-iškun, *ZA* 84: 220–252.

Cole, S.W. and Gasche, H. 1998, Second- and First-Millennium BC Rivers in Northern Babylonia, in: H. Gasche and M. Tanret (eds), *Changing Watercourses in Babylonia. Towards a Reconstruction of the Ancient Environment in Lower Mesopotamia, Vol. 1*, Ghent: 1–64.

Cole, S.W. and Machinist, P. 1998, *Letters from Priests to the Kings Esarhaddon and Assurbanipal* (SAA 13), Helsinki.

Cooper, J, 1980, Aristotle on Friendship, in: A. Rorty (ed.), *Essays on Aristotle's Ethics*, Berkeley: 301–340.

Corò, P. 2004, Meat, Prebends and Rank: A Short Note on the Distribution of Sacrificial Meat in Seleucid Uruk, in: C. Grottanelli and L. Milano (eds), *Food and Identity in the Ancient World* (HANE Monographs 9), Padova: 257–67.

Corò, P. 2005, *Prebende Templari in Età Seleucide* (HANE Monographs 8), Padova.

Dandamaev, M.A. 1984, *Slavery in Babylonia from Nabopolassar to Alexander the Great (626–331 B C)*, DeKalb.

Dandamaev, M.A. 1996, An Age of Privatization in Ancient Mesopotamia, in: M. Hudson and B.A. Levine (eds), *Privatization in the Ancient Near East and Classical World*, Cambridge (MA): 197–217.

Dandamaev, M.A. 2004, Twin Towns and Ethnic Minorities in First-Millennium Babylonia, in: R. Rollinger and C. Ulf (eds), *Melammu Symposia 5: Commerce and Monetary Systems in the Ancient World. Means of Transmission and Cultural Interaction. Proceedings of the Fifth Annual Symposium of the Assyrian and Babylonian Intellectual Heritage Project. Held in Innsbruck, Austria, October 3rd–8th, 2002*, Stuttgart: 137–151.

Da Riva, R. 2002, *Der Ebabbar-Tempel von Sippar in frühneubabylonischer Zeit (640–580 v. Chr)* (AOAT 291), Münster.

Da Riva, R. 2008, *The Neo-Babylonian Royal Inscriptions: An Introduction* (GMTR 4), Münster.

Da Riva, R. 2010a, A Lion in the Cedar Forest: International Politics and Pictorial Self-Representations of Nebuchadnezzar II (605–562 BC), in: J. Vidal (ed.), *Studies on War in the Ancient Near East: Collected Essays on Military History*, Münster: 165–185.

Da Riva, R. 2010b, Dynastic Gods and Favourite Gods in the Neo-Babylonian Period, in: G.B. Lanfranchi and R. Rollinger (eds), *Concepts of Kingship in Antiquity*, Padua: 45–61.

Da Riva, R. 2012, *The Twin Inscriptions of Nebuchadnezzar at Brisa (Wadi esh-Sharbin, Lebanon): A Historical and Philological Study* (*AfO* Beiheft 32), Vienna.

Da Riva, R. 2013, Nebuchadnezzar II's Prism (EŞ 7834): A New Edition, *ZA* 103(2): 169–229.

De Breucker, G.E.E. 2012, *De Babyloniaca van Berossos van Babylon: Inleiding, Editie en Commentaar*. PhD Dissertation, Groningen University.

Dhorme, P. 1928, Les Tablettes Babyloniennes de Neirab, *RA* 25: 53–82.

Dietrich, M. 2003, *The Babylonian Correspondence of Sargon and Sennacherib* (SAA 17), Helsinki.

Dietrich, M. and Dietrich, W. 1998, Zwischen Gott und Volk: Einführung des Königtums und Auswahl des Königs nach mesopotamischer und israelitischer Anschauung, in: M. Dietrich, and I. Kottsieper (eds), *'Und Mose schrieb dieses Lied auf': Studien zum Alten Testament und zum Alten Orient: Festschrift für Oswald Loretz zur Vollendung seines 70. Lebensjahres mit Beiträgen von Freunden, Schülern und Kollegen*, (AOAT 250), Münster: 215–264.

Dirks, N.B. 1987, *The Hollow Crown: Ethnohistory of an Indian Kingdom*, Cambridge.

Dirks, N.B. 2001, *Castes of Mind: Colonialism and the Making of Modern India*, Princeton.

Dumont, L. 1964, Marriage in India, the present state of the question II: marriage and status; Nayar and Newar, *Contribution to Indian Sociology* 7: 80–98.

Dumont, L. 1970, *Homo Hierarchicus: The Caste System and its Implications* (complete revised English edition, 1980), London.

Dumont, L. 1971, *Groupes de Filiation et Alliance de Mariage: Introduction à deux theories d'anthropologie social*, Paris.

Dumont, L. 1983, *Affinity as Value: Marriage Alliance in south India, with comparative essays on Australia.* Chicago.

Edwards, J. 2009, *Language and Identity*, Cambridge.

Eriksen, T.H. 2002, *Ethnicity and Nationalism: Anthropological Perspectives,* (2nd edition, first published 1993), London.

Evans-Pritchard, E.E. 1951, *Kinship and Marriage among the Nuer*, Oxford.

Farber, W. 1987, Rituale und Beschwörungen in Akkadischer Sprache, in: O. Kaiser (ed.), *Texte aus der Umwelt des Alten Testaments* (vol. 2.2), Gütersloh: 212–281.

Finkel, I.L. 2000, On Late Babylonian Medical Training, in: A. George and I.L. Finkel (eds), *Wisdom, Gods and Literature: Studies in Assyriology in Honour of W.G. Lambert*, Winona Lake: 137–223.

Fischer, C.S. 1982, *To Dwell Among Friends: Personal Networks in Town and City*, New York.

Fischer, C.S., Jackson, R.M., Stueve, C.A., Gerson, K., and Jones, L.M., with Baldasare, M. 1977, *Networks and Places: Social Relations in the Urban Setting*, New York.

Flood, G. 1996, *An Introduction to Hinduism*, Cambridge.

Folmer, M.L. 2011, Imperial Aramaic as an Administrative Language of the Achaemenid Period, in: S. Weninger (ed.), *The Semitic Languages. An International Handbook*, Berlin: 578–589.

Folmer, M.L. 2012, Old and Imperial Aramaic, in: H. Gzella (ed.), *Languages from the World of the Bible*, Boston: 128–159.

Frahm, E. 1992, *Babylonia 689–627 BC: A Political History* (PIHANS 69), Istanbul.

Frahm, E. 1995, Ton vom Ton des Heiligen Hügels, *NABU* 1995/9.

Frahm, E. 1997, *Einleitung in die Sanherib-Inschriften* (*AfO* Beih. 26). Vienna.

Frahm, E. 1999. Nabû-zuqup-kēnu, das Gilgameš-Epos und der Tod Sargons II., *JCS* 51: 73–90.

Frahm, E. 2002, Zwischen Tradition und Neuerung: Babylonische Priestergelehrte im achämenidenzeitlichen Uruk, in: R.G. Kratz (ed.), *Religion und Religionskontakte im Zeitalter der Achameniden*, Gütersloh: 74–108.

Frahm, E. 2013, *The Archive of Mušēzib-Marduk Son of Kiribtu and Descendant of Sîn-nāṣir: A Landowner and Property Developer at Uruk in the Seventh Century BC* (Babylonische Archive 5), Dresden.

Frame, G. 1984, The 'First Families' of Borsippa During the Early Neo-Babylonian Period, *JCS* 36: 67–80.

Fuchs, A. and Parpola, S. 2001, *The Correspondence of Sargon II, Part III: Letters from Babylonia and the Eastern Provinces* (SAA 15), Helsinki.

Fuller, C.J. 1976, *The Nayars Today*, Cambridge.

Fuller, C.J. 1984, *The Servants of the Goddess: The Priests of a South Indian Temple*, Cambridge.

Fuller, C.J. 2004, The Renovation Ritual in a South Indian Temple: The 1995 Kumbhābhiṣeka in the Mīnākṣī Temple, Madurai, *Bulletin of the School of Oriental and African Studies* 67: 40–63.

Fuller, C.J. and Logan, P. 1985, The Navarātri Festival in Madurai, *Bulletin of the School of Oriental and African Studies* 48: 79–105.

Geller, M. 1997/2000, The Aramaic Incantation in Cuneiform Script, *JEOL* 35–36: 127–147.

Geller, M. 2011, Speiseverbote (food prohibition/taboo). A. In Mesopotamien, *RLA* 12: 640–642.

George, A.R. 2000, Four Temple Rituals from Babylon, in: A. George and I.L. Finkel (eds), *Wisdom, Gods and Literature: Studies in Assyriology in Honour of W.G. Lambert*, Winona Lake: 259–299.

George, A.R. 2003, *The Babylonian Gilgamesh Epic: Introduction, Critical Edition and Cuneiform Texts*, Oxford.

Gesche, P.D. 2000, *Schulunterricht in Babylonien im ersten Jahrtausend v. Chr.* (AOAT 275), Münster.

Gilbert, E. and Karahalios, K. 2009, Predicting Tie Strength with Social Media, in: D.R. Olsen Jr. *et al.* (eds), *Proceedings of the 27th International Conference on Human Factors in Computing Systems, CHI 2009, Boston, MA, USA, April 4–9, 2009*, New York: 211–220.

Glassner, J.-J. 2004, *Mesopotamian Chronicles*, Atlanta.

Goetze, A. 1947, Texts and fragments (5), *JCS* 1: 352.

Good, A. 1999, The Burning Question. Sacred and Profane Space In a South Indian Temple Town, *Anthropos* 94: 69–84.

Goody, J. 1990, *The Oriental, the Ancient and the Primitive: Systems of Marriage and the Family in the Pre-Industrial Societies of Eurasia*, Cambridge.

Goody, J. and Tambiah, S.J. 1973, *Bridewealth and Dowry*, Cambridge.

Gough, K. 1961, Nayar: Central Kerala, in: D.M. Schneider and K. Gough (eds), *Matrilineal Kinship*, Berkeley.

Granovetter, M.S. 1973, The Strength of Weak Ties, *The American Journal of Sociology* 78 (vol. 6), 1360–1380.

Granovetter, M.S. 1982, The Strength of Weak Ties: A Network Theory Revisited, in: P.V. Marsden and N. Lin (eds), *Social Structure and Network Analysis*, Beverly Hills: 105–130.

Grayson, A.K. 1975, *Assyrian and Babylonian Chronicles*, Locust Valley.

Grayson, A.K. and Novotny, J. 2012, *The Royal Inscriptions of Sennacherib, King of Assyria (704–681 BC), Part 1*, Winona Lake.

Gusterson, H. 2001, Elites, Anthropology of, in: N.J. Smelser and P.B. Baltes (eds), *International Encyclopedia of Social & Behavioral Sciences*, Oxford: 4417–4420.

Hackl, J. 2007, *Der subordinierte Satz in den spätbabylonischen Briefen* (AOAT 341), Münster.

Hackl, J. [forthcoming (a)], Language death and dying reconsidered: the rôle of Late Babylonian as a vernacular language, to be published in: C. Wunsch (ed.), *Proceedings of the 53rd Rencontre Assyriologique Internationale (Moskau/Petersburg), Late Babylonian Workshop. Babel und Bibel.* Pre-paper available on: http://iowp.univie.ac.at.

Hackl, J. [forthcoming (b)], *Materialien zur Urkundenlehre und Archivkunde der spätzeitlichen Texte aus Nordbabylonien*. PhD Dissertation, Vienna University.

Hage, P. and Harary, F. 1983, *Structural Models in Anthropology*, Cambridge.

Hage, P. and Harary, F. 1996, The Logical Structure of Asymmetric Marriage Systems, *L'Homme, 36e Année* 139: 109–124.

Healey, J.F. 2014, Aramaean Heritage, in: H. Niehr (ed.), *The Aramaeans in Ancient Syria*, Leiden: 391–402.

Heesterman, J.C. 1985, *The Inner Conflict of Tradition: Essays in Indian Ritual, Kingship, and Society*, Chicago.

Henkelman, W.F.M., Kuhrt, A., Rollinger, R., and Wiesehöfer, J. 2011, Herodotus and Babylon Reconsidered, in: R. Rollinger *et al.* (eds), *Herodot und das Persische Reich. Herodotus and the Persian Empire*, Wiesbaden: 449–470.

Homans, G.C. 1950, *The Human Group*, London.

Hruschka, D.J. 2010, *Friendship: Development, Ecology, and Evolution of a Relationship*, Berkeley.

Hunger, H. 1968, *Babylonische und assyrische Kolophone* (AOAT 2), Neukirchen–Vluyn.

Inden, R.B. 1990, *Imagining India*, Oxford.

Irwin, T. and Fine, G. 1996, *Aristotle: Introductory Readings: Translated with Introduction, Notes and Glossary*, Indianapolis.

Jakob-Rost, L. 1985, Mischbier für Nabû, *Or* 54: 73–76.

Janković, B. 2004, *Vogelzucht und Vogelfang in Sippar im 1. Jahrtausend v. Chr.* (AOAT 315), Münster.

Janković, B. 2007, Von gugallus, Überschwemmungen und Kronland, *WZKM* 97: 219–242.

Janković, B. 2013, *Aspects of Urukean Agriculture in the First Millennium BC*. PhD Dissertation, University of Vienna.

Jenkins, R. 2008, *Social Identity (Key Ideas)*, London.

Joannès, F. 1980, Textes néo-babyloniens de Strasbourg, *RA* 74: 145–169.

Joannès, F. 1984, Contracts de marriage d'époque récente, *RA* 78: 71–81.

Joannès, F. 1987, Un Cas de Remariage d'Époque Néo-Babylonienne, in: J.-M. Durand (ed.), *La Femme dans le Proche-Orient antique, XXXIIe Rencontre Assyriologique Internationale, Paris 7–10 juillet 1986*, Paris: 91–96.

Joannès, F. 1989, *Archives de Borsippa: La famille Ea-ilûta-bani: Étude d'un lot d'archives familiales en Babylonie du VIIIe au Ve siècle av. J.-C.*, Genève.

Joannès, F. 1990a, Pouvoirs locaux et organisations du territoire en Babylonie achéménide, *Transeuphratènes* 3: 173–189.

Joannès, F. 1990b, *Les tablettes néo-babyloniennes de la Bodleian Library conservées à l'Ashmolean Museum* (OECT 12), Oxford.

Joannès, F. 1990c, Textes babyloniens de Suse d'époque achéménide, in: F. Vallat (ed.), *Contribution à l'histoire de l'Iran. Mélanges offerts à Jean Perrot*, Paris: 173–180.

Joannès, F. 1992, Les archives de Ninurta-ahhê-bulliṭ, in: M. deJong Ellis (ed.), *Nippur at the Centennial: Papers read at the 35e Rencontre Assyriologique Internationale*, Philadelphia: 87–100.

Joannès, F. 1995, Private Commerce and Banking in Achaemenid Babylonia, in: J. Sasson (ed.), *Civilizations of the Ancient Near East, Vol. 3*, New York: 1475–1485.

Jursa, M. 1995, *Die Landwirtschaft in Sippar in neubabylonischer Zeit* (AfO Beih. 25), Wien.

Jursa, M. 1999, *Das Archiv des Bēl-rēmanni* (PIHANS 86), Leiden.

Jursa, M. 2002, Debts and Indebtedness in the Neo-Babylonian Period: Evidence from the Institutional Archives, in: M. Hudson and M. Van de Mieroop (eds), *Debt and Economic Renewal in the Ancient Near East*, Bethesda: 197–220.

Jursa, M. 2004a, Pacht. C. Neubabylonische Bodenpacht, *RLA* 10: 172–183.

Jursa, M. 2004b, Pallukkat-Kanal, *RLA* 10: 282–283.

Jursa, M. 2004c, Auftragsmord, Veruntreuung und Falschaussagen: Neues von Gimillu, *WZKM* 94: 111–134.

Jursa, M. 2004d, Pfand. G. Neu- und Spätbabylonisch, *RLA* 10: 451–454.

Jursa, M. 2004e, Grundzüge der Wirtschaftsformen Babyloniens im ersten Jahrtausend v. Chr., in: R. Rollinger and C. Ulf (eds), *Commerce and Monetary Systems in the Ancient World: Means of Transmission and Cultural Interaction*, Wiesbaden: 115–136.

Jursa, M. 2005, *Neo-Babylonian Legal and Administrative Documents: Typology, Contents and Archives* (GMTR 1), Münster.

Jursa, M. 2005b, Das Archiv von Bēl-eṭēri-Šamaš, in: H.D. Baker and M. Jursa (eds), *Approaching the Babylonian Economy: Proceedings of the START & Project Symposium Held in Vienna, 1 & 3 July 2004*, Münster: 197–268.

Jursa, M. 2007, The Transition of Babylonia from the Neo-Babylonian Empire to Achaemenid Rule, in: H. Crawford (ed.), *Regime and Change in the Ancient Near East and Egypt: From Sargon of Akkad to Saddam Hussein* (PBS 136): 73–94.

Jursa, M. 2007b, Die Söhne Kudurrus und die Herkunft der neubabylonischen Dynastie, *RA* 101: 125–136.

Jursa, M. 2010, *Aspects of the Economic History of Babylonia in the First Millennium BC: Economic Geography, Economic Mentalities, Agriculture, the Use of Money and the Problem of Economic Growth* (AOAT 377), Münster. With contributions by: J. Hackl, B. Jankovic, K. Kleber, E.E. Payne, C. Waerzeggers and M. Weszeli.

Jursa, M. 2010b, Der neubabylonische Hof, in: B. Jacobs and R. Rollinger (eds), *Der Achämenidenhof/The Achaemenid Court*, Wiesbaden: 67–106.

Jursa, M. 2011, Cuneiform Writing in Neo-Babylonian Temple Communities, in: K. Radner and E. Robson (eds), *The Oxford Handbook of Cuneiform Culture*, Oxford: 184–204.

Jursa, M. 2013, Die babylonische Priesterschaft im ersten Jahrtausend v. Chr., in: K. Kainut *et al.* (eds), *Tempel im Alten Orient* (Colloquien der Deutschen Orient-Gesellschaft 7), Wiesbaden: 151–165.

Jursa, M. 2014a, The Lost State Correspondence of the Babylonian Empire as Reflected in Contemporary Administrative Letters, in: K. Radner (ed.), *State Correspondence in the Ancient World: From New Kingdom Egypt to the Roman Empire*, Oxford: 94–111.

Jursa, M. 2014b, The Neo-Babylonian Empire, in: M. Gehler and R. Rollinger (eds), *Imperien und Reiche in der Weltgeschichte. Epochenübergreifende und globalhistorische Vergleiche*, Wiesbaden: 121–148.

Jursa, M. and Waerzeggers, C. 2009, On Aspects of Taxation in Achaemenid Babylonia: New Evidence from Borsippa, in: P. Briant and M. Chauveau (eds), *Organisation des pouvoirs et contacts culturels dans les pays de l'empire achéménide* (Persika 14), Paris: 237–269.

Kämmerer, T.R. and Metzler, K. 2012, *Das babylonische Weltschöpfungsepos Enūma elîš* (AOAT 375), Münster.

Kessler, K. 1991, *Uruk: Urkunden aus Privathäusern: die Wohnhäuser westlich des Eanna-Tempelbereichs, vol. 1* (AUWE 8), Mainz.

Kessler, K. 1999, Ein Einbruch in ein *Bīt Šutummu* eines Tempelbäckers, in: B. Böck *et al.* (eds), *Munuscula Mesopotamica: Festschrift für Johannes Renger* (AOAT 267), Münster: 245–257.

Kessler, K. 2004, Urukäische Familien versus babylonische Familien: Die Namengebung in Uruk, die Degradierung der Kulte von Eanna und der Aufstieg des Gottes Anu, *AoF* 31: 237–262.

Kessler, K. 2006, Provinz. B. Babylonien im 1. Jahrtausend, *RLA* 11: 38–42.

King, L.W. 1912, *Babylonian Boundary-Stones and Memorial-Tablets*, London.

Kleber, K. 2008, *Tempel und Palast: Die Beziehungen zwischen dem König und dem Eanna-Tempel im spätbabylonischen Uruk* (AOAT 358), Münster.

Kleber, K. 2011, Neither Slave nor Truly Free: The Status of the Dependents of Babylonian Temple Households, in: L. Culbertson (ed.), *Slaves and Households in the Near East, Papers from the oriental Institute seminar slaves and Households in the near east Held at the oriental Institute of the university of Chicago 5–6 March 2010*, Chicago: 101–112.

Korošec, V. 1938, Ehe, *RLA* 2: 281–299.

Kozuh, M. 2014, *The Sacrificial Economy: Assessors, Contractors, and Thieves in the Management of Sacrificial Sheep at the Eanna Temple of Uruk (ca. 625–520 B.C.)*, Winona Lake.

Kuhrt, A. 1990, Nabonidus and the Babylonian Priesthood, in: M. Beard and J. North (eds), *Pagan Priests: Religion and Power in the Ancient World*, Ithaca: 119–155.

Kuhrt, A. 2010, Xerxes and the Babylonian Temples: A Restatement of the Case, in: J. Curtis and S.J. Simpson (eds), *The World of Achaemenid Persia*, London: 491–494.

Kuhrt, A. 2014, State Communications in the Persian Empire, in: K. Radner (ed.), *State Correspondence in the Ancient World: From New Kingdom Egypt to the Roman Empire*, Oxford: 112–140.

Kuhrt, A. and Sherwin-White, S. 1987, Xerxes' destruction of Babylonian Temples, in: H. Sancisi-Weerdenburg and A. Kuhrt (eds), *Achaemenid History 2: The Greek Sources*, Leiden: 69–78.

Kuhrt, A. and Sherwin-White, S. 1991, Aspects of Seleucid Royal Ideology: The Cylinder of Antiochus I from Borsippa, *JHS* 111: 71–86.

Kümmel, H.M. 1979, *Familie, Beruf und Amt im spätbabylonischen Uruk: Prosopographische Untersuchungen zu Berufsgruppen des 6. Jahrhunderts v. Chr. in Uruk* (Abhandlungen der Deutschen Orient-Gesellschaft 20), Berlin.

Kuntner, W. and Heinsch, S. 2013, Die babylonischen Tempel in der Zeit nach den Chaldäern, in: K. Kaniuth (ed.), *Tempel im Alten Orient*, Wiesbaden: 219–262.

Kuntner, W., Heinsch, S. and Allinger-Csollich, W. 2011, Nebuchadnezzar II., Xerxes, Alexander der Große und der Stufenturm von Babylon, in: M. Fahlenbock *et al.* (eds), *Inszenierung des Sieges – Sieg der Inszenierung*, Innsbruck: 263–268.

Kuper, A. 1982, *Wives for Cattle: Bridewealth and Marriage in Southern Africa*, London.

Kutscher, E.Y. 2007, Aramaic, in: M. Berenbaum and F. Skolnik (eds), *Encyclopaedia Judaica*, Detroit: 342–359.

Lambert, W.G. 1957, Ancestors, Authors, and Canonicity, *JCS* 11: 1–14, 112.

Lambert, W.G. 1962, A Catalogue of Texts and Authors, *JCS* 16: 59–77.

Lambert, W.G. 1996, *Babylonian Wisdom Literature*, Oxford.

Lambert, W.G. 1998, The Qualifications of Babylonian Diviners, in: S.M. Maul (ed.), *Festschrift für Rykle Borger zu seinem 65. Geburtstag am 24. Mai 1994* (CM 10), Groningen: 141–158.

Lambert, W.G. 2013, *Babylonian Creation Myths*, Winona Lake.

Lamont, M. 2001, Symbolic Boundaries: Overview, in: N.J. Smelser and P.B. Baltes (eds), *International Encyclopedia of Social & Behavioral Sciences*, Oxford: 15341–15347.

Lamont, M. and Molnár, V. 2002, The Study of Boundaries in the Social Sciences, *Annual Review of Sociology* 28: 167–195.

Landsberger, B. 1967, The Date Palm and its By-Products According to the Cuneiform Sources (*AfO* Beih. 17), Vienna.

Langdon, S. 1912, *Die neubabylonischen Königsinschriften* (VAB 4), Leipzig.

Laumann, E.O. 1966, *Prestige and Association in an Urban Community*: An Analysis of an Urban Stratification System, Indianapolis.

Lazarsfeld, P.F. and Merton, R.K. 1954, Friendship as a Social Process: A Substantive and Methodological Analysis, in: M. Berger *et al.* (eds), *Freedom and Control in Modern Society*, New York: 18–66.

Leach, E.R. 1954, *A Political Systems of Highland Burma: A Study of Kachin Social Structure*, London.

Leach, E.R. 1961, *Rethinking Anthropology*, London.

Leemans, W.F. 1945, Marduk-apla-iddina II: zijn tijd en zijn geslacht, *JEOL* 10: 432–455.

Lemos, T.M. 2010, *Marriage Gifts and Social Change in Ancient Palestine: 1200 BCE to 200 CE*, Cambridge.

Lenzi, A. 2008, *Secrecy and the Gods: Secret Knowledge in Ancient Mesopotamia and Biblical Israel* (SAAS 19), Helsinki.

Levavi, Y. 2017, Betting on the Right Horse: Loyalty in the Early Years of the Neo-Babylonian Empire, in: O. Drewnowska and M. Sandowicz (eds), *Fortune and Misfortune in the Ancient Near East: Proceedings of the 60th Rencontre Assyriologique Internationale at Warsaw 21–25 July 2014*, Winona Lake: 177–190.

Levavi, Y. 2018, *Administrative Epistolography in the Formative Phase of the Neo-Babylonian Empire* (Spätbabylonische Briefe, published by Michael Jursa. Band 2, Dubsar 3), Münster.

Levi, G. 1985, *L'eredita immateriale. Carriere di un esorcista nel Piemonte del seicento*, Torino.

Lévi-Strauss, C. 1949, *Les structures Élémentaire de la Parenté*. Paris (in translation 1969: *The elementary Structures of Kinship*, London).

Lin, N. 1982, Social Resources and Instrumental Action, in: P.V. Marsden and N. Lin (eds), *Social Structure and Network Analysis*. Beverly Hills: 131–145.

Lin, N. 2001, *Social Capital: A Theory of Structure and Action*, London.

Lin, N. 2008, A Network Theory of Social Capital, in: D. Castiglione *et al.* (eds), *The Handbook of Social Capital*, Oxford: 50–69.

Linssen, M.J.H. 2004, *The Cults of Uruk and Babylon: The Temple Ritual Texts as Evidence for Hellenistic Cult Practices* (CM 25), Leiden.

Lipiński, E. 2000, *The Aramaeans: Their Ancient History, Culture, Religion* (OLA 100), Leuven.

Löhnert, A. 2007, The Installation of Priests According to Neo-Assyrian Documents, *SAAB* 16: 273–286.

Löhnert, A. 2010, Reconsidering the Consecration of Priests in Ancient Mesopotamia, in: H.D. Baker *et al.* (eds), *Your Praise is Sweet: A Memorial Volume for Jeremy Black from Students, Colleagues and Friends*, London: 183–191.

Luukko, M. 2012, *The Correspondence of Tiglath-Pileser III and Sargon II from Calah/Nimrud* (SAA 19), Helsinki.

MacGinnis, J. 1991, Neo-Babylonian Prebend-texts from the British Museum, *AfO* 38/39: 74–100.

MacGinnis, J. 1995, *Letter Orders from Sippar and the Administration of the Ebabbara in the Late- Babylonian Period*, Poznań.

MacGinnis, J. 1999, Additional Prebend Texts from the British Museum, *AoF* 26: 3–12.

Mączak, A. 2001, A History of Aristocracy/Nobility/Gentry, in: N.J. Smelser and P.B. Baltes (eds), *International Encyclopedia of Social & Behavioral Sciences*, Oxford: 737–742.

Madan, T.N. 1975, Structural Implications of Marriage in North India: Wife-givers and Wife-takers among Pandits of Kashmir, *Contributions to Indian Sociology n.s.* 9: 217–243.

Marsden, P.V. and Campbell, K.E. 1984, Measuring Tie Strength, *Social Forces* 63: 482–501.

Maul, S.M. 1992, *Kurgarrû* und *assinnu* und ihr Stand in der babylonischen Gesellschaft, in: V. Haas (ed.), *Außenseiter und Randgruppen* (Xenia 32), Konstanz: 159–171.

McEwan, G.J.P. 1981, *Priest and Temple in Hellenistic Babylonia* (Freiburger Altorientalische Studien 4), Wiesbaden.

McEwan, G.J.P. 1983, Distribution of Meat in Eanna, *Iraq* 45: 187–198.

McPherson, M., Smith-Loving, L., and Cook, J.M. 2001, Birds of a Feather: Homophily in Social Networks, *Annual Review of Sociology*, 27: 415–444.

Van de Mieroop, M. 1997, *The Ancient Mesopotamian City*, Oxford.

Miglus, P.A. 1999. *Städtische Wohnarchitektur in Babylonien und Assyrien*, (Baghdader Forschung 22), Mainz am Rhein.

Mullet, M. 1997, *Theophylact of Ochrid: Reading the Letters of a Byzantine Archbishop*. Aldershot.

Needham, R. 1962, *Structure and Sentiment: a Test Case in Social Anthropology*, Chicago.

Needham, R. 1987, *Mamboru: History and Structure in a Domain of Northwestern Sumba*, Oxford.

Nielsen, J.P. 2010, Three Early Neo-Babylonian Tablets Belonging to Bēl-ēṭir of the Miṣirāya Kin Group, *JCS* 62: 95–104.

Nielsen, J.P. 2011, *Sons and Descendants. A Social History if Kin Groups and Family Names in the Early Neo-Babylonian Period, 747–626 BC* (CHANE 46), Leiden.

Nielsen, J.P. 2015, Taking Refuge at Borsippa: The Archive of Lâbâši Son of Nādinu, *AfO* 53: 93–109.

Nielsen, J.P. and Waerzeggers, C. 2016, Interactions Between Temple, King and Local Elites: The *Hanšû* Land Schemes in Babylonia (8th–6th centuries BC), in: J.C. Moreno García (ed.), *Dynamics of Production in the Ancient Near East, 1300–500 BC.*, Oxford – Philadelphia: 331–344.

Nissinen, M. 2014, Assyria, in: H. Niehr (ed.), *The Aramaeans in Ancient Syria*, Leiden: 273–296.

Oelsner, J. 1995, Review of *Uruk: Spätbabylonische Texte aus dem Planquadrat U18. AUWE 12*, by E. von Weiher, *OLZ* 90: 381–391.

Oelsner, J. 2001, The Neo-Babylonian Period, in: R. Westbrook and R. Jasnow (eds), *Security for Debt in Ancient Near Eastern Law*, Leiden: 289–305.

Oelsner, J. 2007, Das zweite Regierungsjahr des Xerxes (484/3 v. Chr.) in Babylonien, *WZKM* 97: 289–303.

Oelsner, J., Wells, B. and Wunsch, C. 2003, Neo-Babylonian Period, in: R. Westbrook (ed.), *A History of Ancient Near Eastern Law* (HdO 1.72), Leiden – Boston: 911–974.

Olivelle, P. 2000, *Dharmasūtras: The Law Codes of Āpastamba, Gautama, Baudhāyana, and Vasiṣṭha*, Delhi.

Oppenheim, A.L. 1967, *Letters from Mesopotamia: Official Business and Private Letters on Clay Tablets from Two Millennia*, Chicago.

Oppenheim, A.L. 1977, *Ancient Mesopotamia: Portrait of a Dead Civilization, Revised Edition Completed by Erica Reiner*, Chicago.

Padgett, J.F. and Ansell, C.K. 1993, Robust Action and the rise of the Medici, 1400–1434, *American Journal of Sociology* 98: 1259–1319.

Parker, R.A. and Dubberstein, W.H. 1956, *Babylonian Chronology 626 BC–AD 75*, Providence.

Parkin, R. 1990, Ladders and Circles: Affinal Alliance and the Problem of Hierarchy, *Man n.s.* 25: 472–488.

Parkin, R. 2005, *The French Speaking Countries*, in: F. Barth *et al.* (eds), One Discipline, Four Ways: British, German, French, and American Anthropology, Chicago: 155–254.

Parpola, S. 1993, *Letters from Assyrian and Babylonian Scholars* (SAA 10), Helsinki.

Parry, J.P. 1979, *Caste and Kinship in Kangra*, London.

Paulus, S. 2014, *Die babylonischen Kudurru-Inschriften von der kassitischen bis zur früh-neubabylonischen Zeit: Untersucht unter besonderer Berücksichtigung gesellschafts- und rechtshistorischer Fragestellungen* (AOAT 51), Münster.

Peabody, N. 2003, *Hindu Kingship and Polity in Precolonial India*, Cambridge.

Pearce, L.E. 2015, Identifying Judeans and Judean Identity in the Babylonian Evidence, in: J. Stökl and C. Waerzeggers (eds), *Exile and Return: the Babylonian Context* (BZAW 478), Berlin: 7–32.

Pearce, L.E. and Wunsch, C. 2014, *Documents of Judean Exiles and West Semites in Babylonia in the Collection of David Sofer* (CUSAS 28), Bethesda.

Peat, J.A. 1983, *Hanšû* Land and the *rab hanšî*, *Iraq* 45: 124–127.

Peled, I. 2014, *Assinnu* and *Kurgarrû* Revisited, *JNES* 73: 283–297.

Petschow, H.P.H. 1956, *Neubabylonisches Pfandrecht*, Berlin.

Petschow, H.P.H. 1976/80, Inzest, *RLA* 5: 144–150.

Pirngruber, R [*forthcoming*], Land and Power in a Northian Perspective: State Building and its Reflection in Private Archives from 1st millennium BC Babylonia. Pre-paper available on: http://iowp.univie.ac.at/node/340.

Pirngruber, R. and Waerzeggers, C. 2011, Prebend Prices in First Millennium BC Babylonia, *JCS* 63: 111–144.

Pocock, D.F. 1954, The Hypergamy of the Patidars, in: K.M. Kapadia (ed.), *Professor Ghurye Felicitation Volume,* Bombay: 195–204.

Pocock, D.F. 1972, *Kanbi and Patidar*, Oxford.

Pomponio, F. 1978, *Nabû: Il culto e la figura di un dio del Pantheon babilonese ed assiro,* Rome.

Pomponio, F. 2001, Nabû, A. Philologisch, *RLA* 9: 16–24.

Pongratz-Leisten, B. 1994, *Ina šulmi īrub: Die kulttopographische und ideologische Programmatik der akītu-Prozession in Babylonien und Assyrien im I. Jahrtausend v.Chr.* (BaF 16), Mainz.

Pongratz-Leisten, B. 1997, Das 'negative Sündenbekenntnis' des Königs anläßlich des babylonischen Neujahrsfestes und die *kiddinūtu* von Babylon, in: A. Assmann and T. Sundermeier (eds), *Schuld, Gewissen und Person: Studien zur Geschichte des inneren Menschen* (Studien zum Verstehen fremder Religionen 9), Gütersloh: 83–101.

Postgate, J.N. 1992. *Early Mesopotamia: Society and Economy at the Dawn of History,* London.

Powell, M.A. 1972, Der neubabylonische Familienname Ašgandu und die Urkundengruppe Nbn 314, TCL XII 122, Nbn 668, *ArOr* 40: 124–129.

Powell, M.A. 1999, *Wir müssen alle unsere Nische nutzen*: Monies, Motives, and Methods in Babylonian Economics, in: J.-G. Dercksen (ed.) *Trade and Finance in Ancient Mesopotamia* (PIHANS 84), Istanbul: 5–23.

Prell, C. 2012, *Social Network Analysis: History, Theory and Methodology*, London.

Quigley, D. 1993, *The interpretation of Caste*, Oxford.

Radner, K. 1999, *The Prosopography of the Neo-Assyrian Empire*, Volume 1/II: B-G, Helsinki.

Radner, K. 2014, An Imperial Communication Network: the State Correspondence of the Neo-Assyrian Empire, in: K. Radner (ed.), *State Correspondence in the Ancient World: From New Kingdom Egypt to the Roman Empire*, Oxford: 64–93.

Reade, J. 1986, Rassam's Excavations at Borsippa and Kutha, 1879–82, *Iraq* 48: 105–116.

Regan, A. 2007, *The Neo-Babylonian Širku: A Social History*. PhD Dissertation, Harvard University.

Reynolds, F.S. 2003, *The Babylonian Correspondence of Esarhaddon and Letters to Assurbanipal and Sin-šarru-iškun from Northern and Central Babylonia* (SAA 18), Helsinki.

Rezende, C. 1999, Building affinity through friendship, in: S. Bell and S. Coleman (eds), *The Anthropology of Friendship: Enduring Themes and Future Possibilities*, Oxford: 79–97.

Ries, G. 1976, *Die neubabylonischen Bodenpachtformulare*, Berlin.

Robson, E. 2011, The Production and Dissemination of Scholarly Knowledge, in: K. Radner and E. Robson (eds), *The Oxford Handbook of Cuneiform Culture*, Oxford: 557–576.

Rochberg, F. 2004, *The Heavenly Writing: Divination, Horoscopy, and Astronomy in Mesopotamian Culture*, Cambridge.

Rochberg, F. 2010, *In the Path of the Moon: Babylonian Celestial Divination and Its Legacy*, Leiden.

Rollinger, R. 1998, Überlegungen zu Herodot, Xerxes und dessen angeblicher Zerstörung Babylons, *AoF* 25: 339–373.

Rollinger, R. 2000, Herodotus and the Intellectual Heritage of the Ancient Near East, in: S. Aro and R.M. Whiting (eds), *The Heirs of Assyria* (Melammu Symposia 1), Helsinki: 65–83.

Roniger, L. 2001, Patron–Client Relationships, Anthropology of, in: N.J. Smelser and P.B. Baltes (eds), *International Encyclopedia of Social & Behavioral Sciences*, Oxford: 11118–111120.

Rosenthal, N., Fingrutd, M., Ethier, M., Karant, R. and McDonald, D. 1985, Social Movement and Network Analysis: A Case Study of Nineteenth-century Women's Reform in New York State, *American Journal of Sociology* 90: 1022–1054.

Roth, M.T. 1987, Age at Marriage and the Household: A study of Neo-Babylonian and Neo-Assyrian Forms, *Comparative Studies in Society and History* 29: 715–747.

Roth, M.T. 1989, *Babylonian Marriage Agreements 7th – 3rd Centuries BC* (AOAT 222), Neukirchen–Vluyn.

Roth, M.T. 1989b, Marriage and Matrimonial Property in the First Millennium B.C., in: B.S. Lesko (ed.), *Women's Earliest Records from Ancient Egypt and Western Asia* (Brown Judaic Studies 166), Atlanta: 245–260.

Roth, M.T. 1990, The Material Composition of the Neo-Babylonian Dowry, *AfO* 36/37: 1–55.

Roth, M.T. 1991, The Dowries of the Women of the Itti-Marduk-balatu Family, *Journal of the American Oriental Society* 111: 19–37.

Roth, M.T. 1995, *Law Collections from Mesopotamia and Asia Minor*, Atlanta.

Ruffini, G. 2008, *Social Networks in Byzantine Egypt.* Cambridge.

Sallaberger, W. 2006, Reinheit. A. Mesopotamien, *RLA* 11: 295–299.

Sallaberger, W. 2008, *Das Gilgamesch-Epos: Mythos, Werk und Tradition*, München.

Sallaberger, W. and Huber Vulliet, F. 2005, Priester I.A. Mesopotamien, *RLA* 10: 617–640.

Sallaberger, W. and Schmidt, K. 2012, Insignien des Königs oder Insignien des Gotter? Ein neuer Blick auf die kultische Königskrönung beim babylonischen Neujahrsfest, in: H.D. Baker *et al.* (eds), *Stories of Long Ago: Festschrift für Michael D. Roaf* (AOAT 397), Münster: 566–594.

Sandowicz, M. 2012, *Oaths and Curses: A Study in Neo- and Late-Babylonian Legal Formulary* (AOAT 398), Münster.

San Nicolò, M. 1947, Due atti matrimoniali neobabilonesi, *Aegyptus* 27: 118–143.

San Nicolò, M. 1951, *Babylonische Rechts Urkunden des ausgehenden 8. und des 7. Jahrhunderts v. Chr.*, München.

San Nicolò, M. and Ungnad, A. 1929, *Neubabylonische Rechts- und Verwaltungsurkunden,* Leipzig.

Schaudig, H. 1995, Ein Zylinder Nabonids im Vorderasiatischen Museum zu Berlin, *AoF* 22: 247–264.

Schaudig, H. 2001, *Die Inschriften Nabonids von Babylon und Kyros' des Großen samt den in ihrem Umfeld entstandenen Tendenzschrifte: Textausgabe und Grammatik* (AOAT 256), Münster.

Scheyhing, H. 1998, Das Haar in Ritualen des alten Mesopotamien: Der Umgang mit Haar im Bereich von Religion und Kult, *WdO* 29: 58–79.

Schloen, J.D. 2001, *The House of the Father as Fact and Symbol: Patrimonialism in Ugarit and the Ancient Near East* (Studies in the Archaeology and History of the Levant 2), Winona Lake.

Schwartz, S.J., Luyckx, K. and Vignoles, V.L. (eds) 2011, *Handbook of Identity Theory and Research*, New York.

Schwemer, D. 2011, Magic Rituals: Conceptualization and Performance, in: K. Radner and E. Robson (eds), *The Oxford Handbook of Cuneiform Culture*, Oxford: 418–442.

Scott, S. 1991, *Social Network Analysis. A Handbook*, London.

Scurlock, J. 2006, *Magico-medical Means of Treating Ghost-induced Illnesses in Ancient Mesopotamia* (Ancient Magic and Divination 3), Leiden.

Slanski, K.E. 2000, Classification, Historiography and Monumental Authority: The Babylonian Entitlement "narûs (kudurrus)", *JCS* 52: 95–114.

Slanski, K.E. 2003, Middle Babylonian Period, in: R. Westbrook (ed.), *A History of Ancient Near Eastern Law* (HdO 1.72), Leiden – Boston: 485–520.

Sprenger, G. 2010, From Power to Value: Ranked Titles in an Egalitarian Society, Laos, *The Journal of Asian Studies* 69: 403–425.

Steele, J. 2011, Visual Aspects of the Transmission of Babylonian Astronomy and its Reception into Greek Astronomy, *Annals of Science* 68: 453–465.

Stolper, M.W. 1985, *Entrepreneurs and Empire. The Murašû Archive, the Murašû Firm, and Persian Rule in Babylonia* (PIHANS 54), Istanbul.

Stolper, M.W. 1990, The Kasr Archive, in: H. Sancisi-Weerdenburg and A. Khurt (eds), *Achaemenid History Workshop IV: Centre and Periphery*, Leiden: 195–205.

Stone, E.C. 1987, *Nippur Neighborhoods* (Studies in Ancient Oriental Civilization 44), Chicago.

Stone, E.C. 2007, Mesopotamian Cities and Countryside, in: D.C. Snell (ed.), *A Companion to the Ancient Near East*, Oxford: 157–70.

Streck, M.P. 2010, Grosses Fach Altorientalistik: Der Umfang des keilschriftlichen Textkorpus, *MDOG* 142: 35–58.

Streck, M.P. 2014, Babylonia, in: H. Niehr (ed.), *The Aramaeans in Ancient Syria*, Leiden: 297–318.

Thureau-Dangin, F. 1919, Une acte de donation de Marduk-zâkir-šumu, *RA* 16: 117–156.

Thureau-Dangin, F. 1921, *Rituels Accadiens*, Paris.

Tolini, G. 2015, From Syria to Babylon and Back: The Neirab Archive, in: J. Stökl and C. Waerzeggers (eds), *Exile and Return: the Babylonian Context* (BZAW 478), Berlin: 58–93.

Tsukimoto, A. 1985, *Untersuchungen zur Totenpflege* (kispu) *im alten Mesopotamien*, Neukirchen–Vluyn.

Uberoi, P. 1994, *Family, Kinship and Marriage in India*, Delhi.

Unger, E. 1931, *Babylon, die Heilige Stadt nach der Beschreibung der Babylonier*, Berlin.

Unger, E. 1932, Barsippa, *RLA* 1: 402–429.

Van der Toorn, K. 1985, *Sin and Sanction in Israel and Mesopotamia*, Assen.

Van der Toorn, K. 1996a, *Family Religion in Babylonia, Syria, and Israel: Continuity and Change in the Forms of Religious Life* (CHANE 7), Leiden.

Van der Toorn, K. 1996b, Domestic religion in ancient Mesopotamia, in: K.R. Veenhof (ed.), *Houses and Households in Ancient Mesopotamia: Papers Read at the 40e Rencontre Assyriologique Internationale. Leiden, July 5–8, 1993*, Istanbul: 69–78.

Van Driel, G. 1988, Neo-Babylonian Agriculture, *BSA* 4: 121–159.

Van Driel, G. 1989, The British Museum Sippar Collection: Babylonia 1882–1893, *ZA* 79: 102–117.

Van Driel, G. 1990, Neo-Babylonian Agriculture III. Cultivation, *BSA* 5: 219–266.

Van Driel, G. 1992, Neo-Babylonian Texts from Borsippa, *BiOr* 49: 28–50.

Van Driel, G. 2002, *Elusive Silver: In search of a role for a market in an agrarian environment: Aspects of Mesopotamia's society* (PIHANS 95), Leiden.

Van Driel, G. 2005, Pfründe (Prebends), *RLA* 10: 518–524.

Vargyas, P. 2000, Silver and Money in Achaemenid and Hellenistic Babylonia, in: J. Marzahn and H. Neumann (eds), *Assyriologica et Semitica. Festschrift für Joachim Oelsner* (AOAT 252), Münster: 513–21.

Veldhuis, N.C. 2011, Levels of Literacy, in: K. Radner and E. Robson (eds), *The Oxford Handbook of Cuneiform Culture*, Oxford: 68–89.

Veldhuis, N.C. 2013, Purity and Access: A Catalog of Lexical Texts Dedicated to Nabû, *JCS* 65: 169–180.

Verbrugge, L.M. 1977, The Structure of Adult Friendship Choices, *Social Forces* 56: 576–597.

Verbrugge, L.M. 1979, Multiplexity in Adult Friendships, *Social Forces* 57: 1287–1309.

Verbrugghe, G.P. and Wickersham, J.M. 1996. *Berossos and Manetho, Introduced and Translated: Native Traditions in ancient Mesopotamia and Egypt*, Ann Arbor.

von Dassow, E. 1994, Archival Documents of Borsippa Families, *AulaOr* 12: 105–20.

von Dassow, E. 1999a, On writing the history of southern Mesopotamia, *ZA* 89: 227–246.

von Dassow, E. 1999b, Introducing the Witnesses in Neo-Babylonian Documents, in: R. Chazan, W.W. Hallo and L.H. Schiffman (eds), *Ki Baruch Hu: Ancient Near Eastern, Biblical, and Judaic Studies in Honor of Baruch A. Levine*, Winona Lake: 3–22.

von Soden, W. 1995, *Grundriss der akkadischen Grammatik*, (3rd edition, AnOr 33), Rome.

Waerzeggers, C. 2000/2001 *Het archief van Marduk-rēmanni. Studie van de familie Ṣāhit-ginê in Nieuwbabylonisch Sippar* (548–484 *v. Chr.*), PhD manuscript, University of Ghent.

Waerzeggers, C. 2001, A note on the Marriage Gift *biblu* in the Neo-Babylonian Period, *Akkadica* 122: 65–70.

Waerzeggers, C. 2002, Endogamy in Mesopotamia in the Neo-Babylonian Period, in: C. Wunsch (ed.), *Mining the Archives: Festschrift for Christopher Walker on the Occasion of His 60th Birthday*, Dresden: 319–342.

Waerzeggers, C. 2004, The Babylonian Revolts Against Xerxes and the 'End of Archives', *AfO* 50: 150–173.

Waerzeggers, C. 2005, The Dispersal History of the Borsippa Archives, in: H.D. Baker and M. Jursa (eds), *Approaching the Babylonian Economy: Proceedings of the START Project Symposium Held in Vienna, 1–3 July 2004* (AOAT 330), Münster: 343–363.

Waerzeggers, C. 2010, *The Ezida Temple of Borsippa. Priesthood, Cult, Archives.* (AH XV), Leiden.

Waerzeggers, C. 2011, The Pious King: Royal Patronage of Temples, in: K. Radner and E. Robson (eds), *The Oxford Handbook of Cuneiform Culture*, Oxford: 725–751.

Waerzeggers, C. 2012, The Babylonian Chronicles: Classification and Provenance, *JNES* 71: 285–298.

Waerzeggers, C. 2014, *Marduk-rēmanni: Local Networks and Imperial Politics in Achaemenid Babylonia* (OLA 233), Ghent.

Waerzeggers, C. 2014b, Social Network Analysis of Cuneiform Archives. A New Approach, in: H.D. Baker and M. Jursa (eds), *Documentary Sources in Ancient Near Eastern and Greco-Roman Economic History: Methodology and Practice*, Oxford: 205–233.

Waerzeggers, C. 2014c, A Statue of Darius in the Temple of Sippar, in: M. Kozuh *et al.* (eds), *Extraction & Control: Studies in Honor of Matthew W. Stolper*, Chicago: 323–329.

Waerzeggers, C. [forthcoming], The rise of the Ša-nāšišu family in Babylonia under Darius I: Aspects of provincial administration and elite policy in the Persian Empire, in: C. Wunsch (ed.), *Proceedings of the Workshop in Honor of M.A. Dandamaev Held in St- Petersburg 2007*.

Waerzeggers, C. and Jursa, M. 2008, On the Initiation of Babylonian Priests, *ZAR* 14: 1–23.

Wagner, A., Levavi, Y., Kedar, S., Abraham, K., Cohen, Y., and Zadok, R. 2013, Quantitative Social Network Analysis (SNA) and the Study of Cuneiform Archives: A Test-Case based on the Murašû Archive, *Akkadica* 134: 117–134.

Wasserman, S. and Faust, K. 1994, *Social Network Analysis: Methods and Applications*, New York.

Weidner, E.F. 1952, Keilschrifttexte nach Kopien von T.G. Pinches: 1. Babylonische Privaturkunden aus den 7. Jahrhundert v. Chr., *AfO* 16: 35–46.

Weidner, E.F. 1956, Hochverrat gegen Nebukadnezar II: Ein Grosswürdenträger vor dem Königsgericht, *AfO* 17: 1–5.

Westbrook, R. 1988, *Old Babylonian Marriage Law*, Horn.

Wunsch, C. 1993, *Die Urkunden des babylonischen Geschäftsmannes Iddin-Marduk: Zum Handel mit Naturalien im 6. Jahrhundert v. Chr* (CM 3), Groningen.

Wunsch, C. 1995/1996, Die Frauen der Familie Egibi, *AfO* 42/43: 33–36.

Wunsch, C. 1997/1998, Und die Richter berieten…: Streitfälle in Babylon aus der Zeit Neriglissars und Nabonids, *AfO* 44/45: 59–100.

Wunsch, C. 1999, The Egibi Family's Real Estate in Babylon (6th Century BC), in: M. Hudson and B.A. Levine (eds), *Urbanization and Land Ownership in the Ancient Near East*, Cambridge: 391–419.

Wunsch, C. 2000, *Das Egibi Archiv*, vol. 1: *Die Felder und Gärten* (CM 20), Groningen.

Wunsch, C. 2002, Debt, Interest, Pledge and Forfeiture in the Neo-Babylonian and Early Achaemenid Period: The Evidence from Private Archives, in: M. Hudson and M. Van de Mieroop (eds), *Debt and Economic Renewal in the Ancient Near East*, Bethesda: 221–255.

Wunsch, C. 2003, *Urkunden zum Ehe-, Vermögens- und Erbrecht aus verschiedenen neubabylonischen Archiven* (Babylonische Archive 2), Dresden.

Wunsch, C. 2003/2004, Findelkinder und Adoption nach neubabylonischen Quellen, *AfO* 50: 174–244.

Wunsch, C. 2005, Das Šangû-Ninurta-Archiv, in: H.D. Baker and M. Jursa (eds), *Approaching the Babylonian Economy: Proceedings of the START Project Symposium Held in Vienna, 1–3 July 2004* (AOAT 330), Münster: 356–379.

Wunsch, C. 2010, The Neo-Babylonian Entrepreneur, in: D. Landes *et al.* (eds), *The Invention of Enterprise: Entrepreneurship from Ancient Mesopotamia to Modern Times*, Princeton: 40–61.

Wunsch, C. 2014, Babylonische Familiennamen, in: M. Krebernik and H. Neumann (eds), *Babylonien und seine Nachbarn in neu- und spätbabylonischer Zeit. Wissenschaftliches Kolloquim aus Anlass des 75. Geburtstags von Joachim Oelsner, Jena, 2. Und 3. März 2007*, Münster: 289–314.

Younger, P. 1980, A Temple Festival of Māriyammaṉ, *Journal of the American Academy of Religion* 48: 493–517.

Zadok, R. 1985, *Geographical Names According to New- and Late-Babylonian Texts* (RGTC 8), Wiesbaden.

Zadok, R. 1998, Notes on Borsippean Documentation of the Eighth–Fifth Centuries B.C., *IOS* 18: 249–296.

Zadok, R. 2003a, Updating the Apammu Dossier, *NABU* 2003/33.

Zadok, R. 2003b, Two Deeds from the Shaddinnu Archive, *NABU* 2003/51.

Zadok, R. 2003c, The Representation of Foreigners in Neo- and Late-Babylonian Legal Documents (Eight through Second Centuries B.C.E.), in: O. Lipschits and J. Blenkinsopp (eds), *Judah and the Judeans in the Neo-Babylonian Period*, Winona Lake: 471–589.

Zadok, R. 2005a, Contributions to Neo/Late-Babylonian Documentation, in: Y. Sefati *et al.* (eds), *"An experienced scribe who neglects nothing". Ancient Near Eastern Studies in Honor of Jacob Klein*, Bethesda: 624–669.

Zadok, R. 2005b, On the Esaggil-mansum Clan, *NABU* 2005/25.

Zadok, R. 2006, The Geography of the Borsippa Region, in: Y. Amit *et al.* (eds), *Essays on Ancient Israel in Its Near Eastern Context: A Tribute to Nadav Na'aman*, Winona Lake: 389–453.

Zadok, R. 2008, The Quarters of Borsippa, in: S. Bar (ed.), *In the Hill-Country, and in the Shephelah, and in the Arabah (Joshua 12, 8): Studies and Researches Presented to Adam Zertal in the Thirtieth Anniversary of the Manasseh Hill-Country Survey*, Jerusalem: 75*–98*.

Zadok, R. 2009, *Catalogue of Documents from Borsippa or Related to Borsippa in the British Museum, vol. 1* (Nisaba 21), Messina.

Zadok, R. 2012, Occupations and Status Categories (Classes) in Borsippa, in: Y. Shahar *et al.* (eds), *Te'uda XXV: Israel and the Diaspora in the Time of the Second Temple and the Mishnah: Aryeh Kasher Memorial Volume*, Tel Aviv: xxxi–lxiii.

Zawadzki, S. 2006, *Garments of the Gods: Studies on the Textile Industry and the Pantheon of Sippar according to the Texts from the Ebabbar Archive* (OBO 218), Fribourg.

Zawadzki, S. 2013, *Neo-Babylonian Documents from Sippar Pertaining to the Cult*, Poznań.

Index of Sources

1. Sources

Index of Names

2.1 Personal Names lists individuals in the following manner: either own name (PN), or own name/father's name (PN/PN), or own name/father's name/family name (PN/PN/FN), or own name//family name (PN//FN). In 2.2 Persons by Family Names the same persons are sorted according to their family names. References to families in general can be found in 3. Families.

2.1 Personal Names

2.2 Persons by Family Name

3. Families

Index of Akkadian Terms

4. Akkadian Terms

Printed in the United States
By Bookmasters